IGNCA

कान्था - वस्त्र पर कढ़ा काव्य

KANTHA

Poetry embroidered on cloth

Kantha Collection of IGNCA: A Catalogue

KANTHA
Poetry embroidered on cloth

Text: Krishna Lal
Design: Neeraj Sahai, Pallavi Sahai - Picture Street

First Published in 2014 by:
Indira Gandhi National Centre for the Arts
Central Vista Mess, Janpath, New Delhi - 110 001 (India)

Printed by: D. K. Printworld (P) Ltd., New Delhi

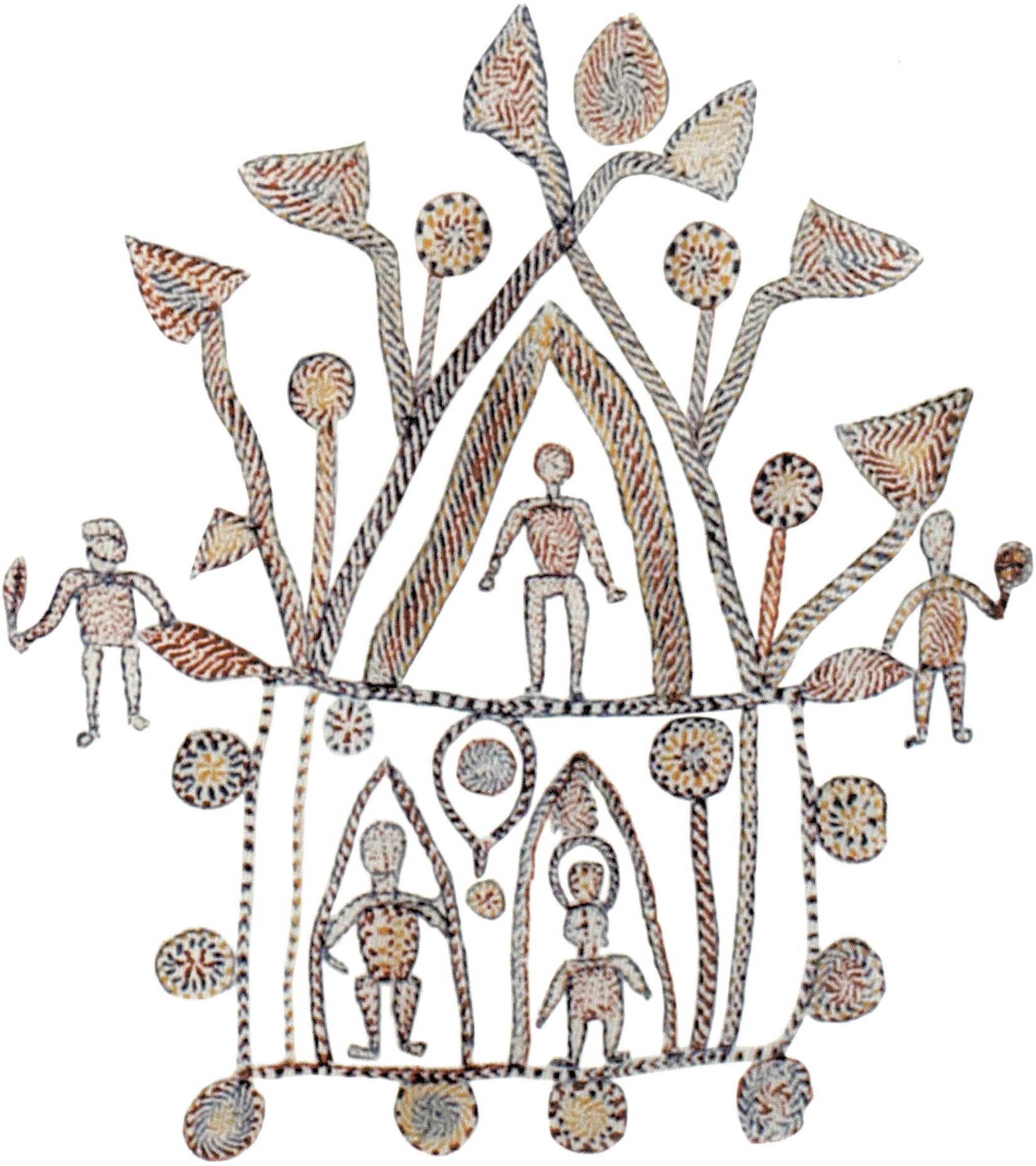

IGNCA

कान्था - वस्त्र पर कढ़ा काव्य

KANTHA

Poetry embroidered on cloth

Kantha Collection of IGNCA: A Catalogue

Krishna Lal

CONTENTS

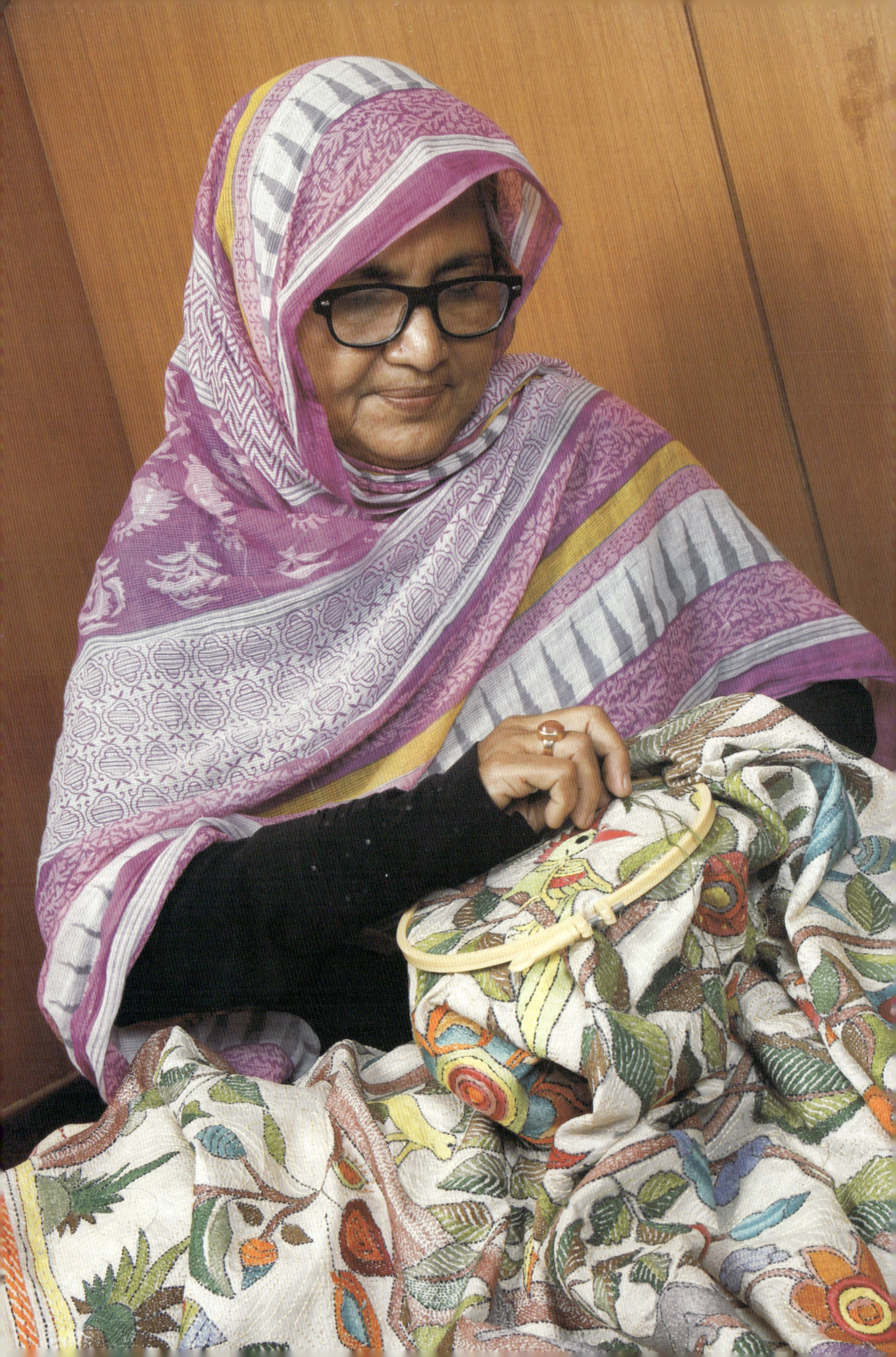

INTRODUCTION

The Indira Gandhi National Centre for the Arts (IGNCA), was established in the memory of Late Smt. Indira Gandhi and is visualized as a centre encompassing the study and experience of all the arts, each form with its own integrity yet within a dimension of mutual interdependence, interrelated with nature, social structure and cosmology.

The Janapada Sampada Division of the IGNCA undertakes research of the Indian cultural phenomenon in its totality and builds core collection of material and documentation on folk and tribal arts through multi disciplinary approach. One of the major programmes of the Division is Ethnographic Collection under which creativity at different levels is explored, researched and documented. A core collection has been built that includes textiles, masks, puppets, ritual objects from all over the country. Kantha embroidery pieces are one of the constituent of this collection.

Kantha – the embroidered poetry on cloth ~ speaks volumes about the imagination of Bengali women and the aspirations that her craftwork reflects. It is a well-conceived art work, which has always attracted people from all walks of life. She creates the most amazing *Kanthas* with great love and affection for her dear ones. Her creativity stands unmatched when she breathes life into a discarded saree, worn out from constant use and laundering. She transforms this simple five metres of old cloth into a most admirable, attractive and unparalleled utilitarian artefact. Initially, light coverlets or quilts - to withstand the mild winters and cool monsoon nights of Bengal - were made using the *Kantha* embroideries, which was limited to simple stitches and a few colours. Some *Kanthas* were used as swaddling clothes for babies; expectant mothers spent their last stages of pregnancy in making a *Kantha* for the new born, with the belief that this piece of cloth would bring good fortune for the family and protect the baby from diseases. Every home in a Bengali village housed a number of *Kanthas* that were more for personal use than commercial gain.

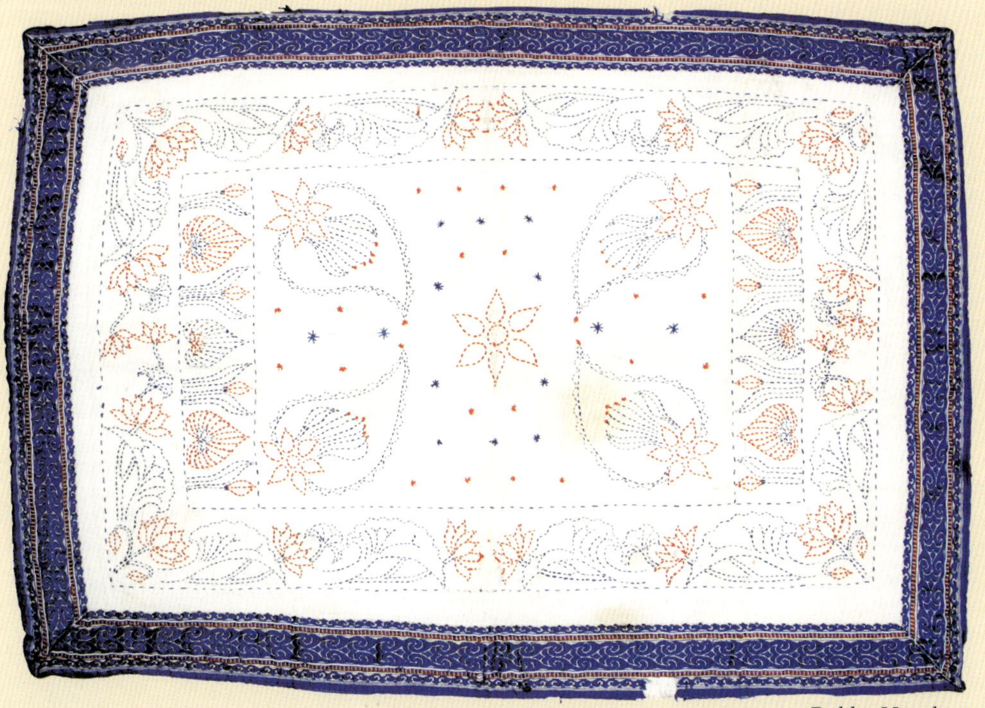

Babby Kanthas

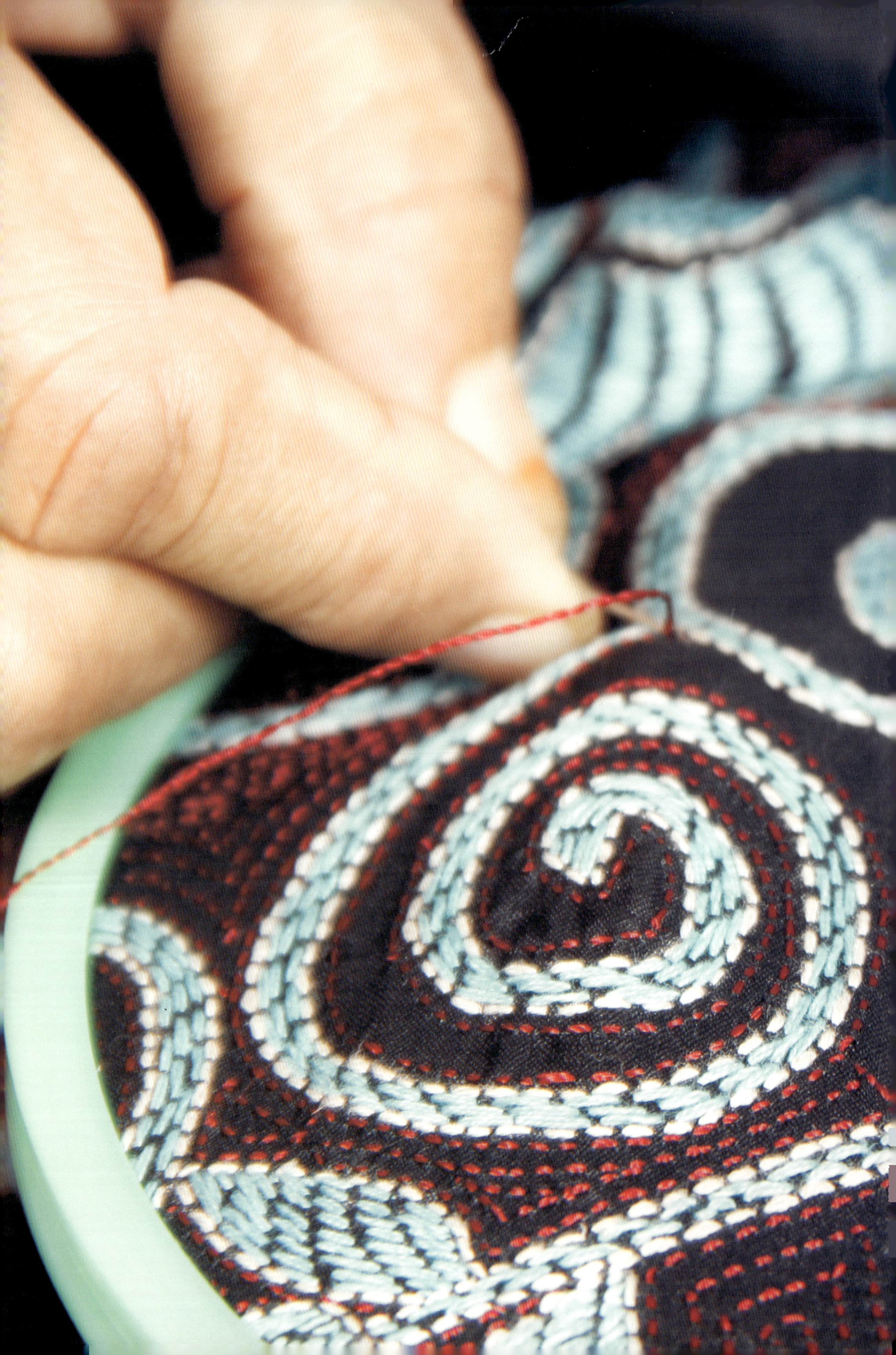

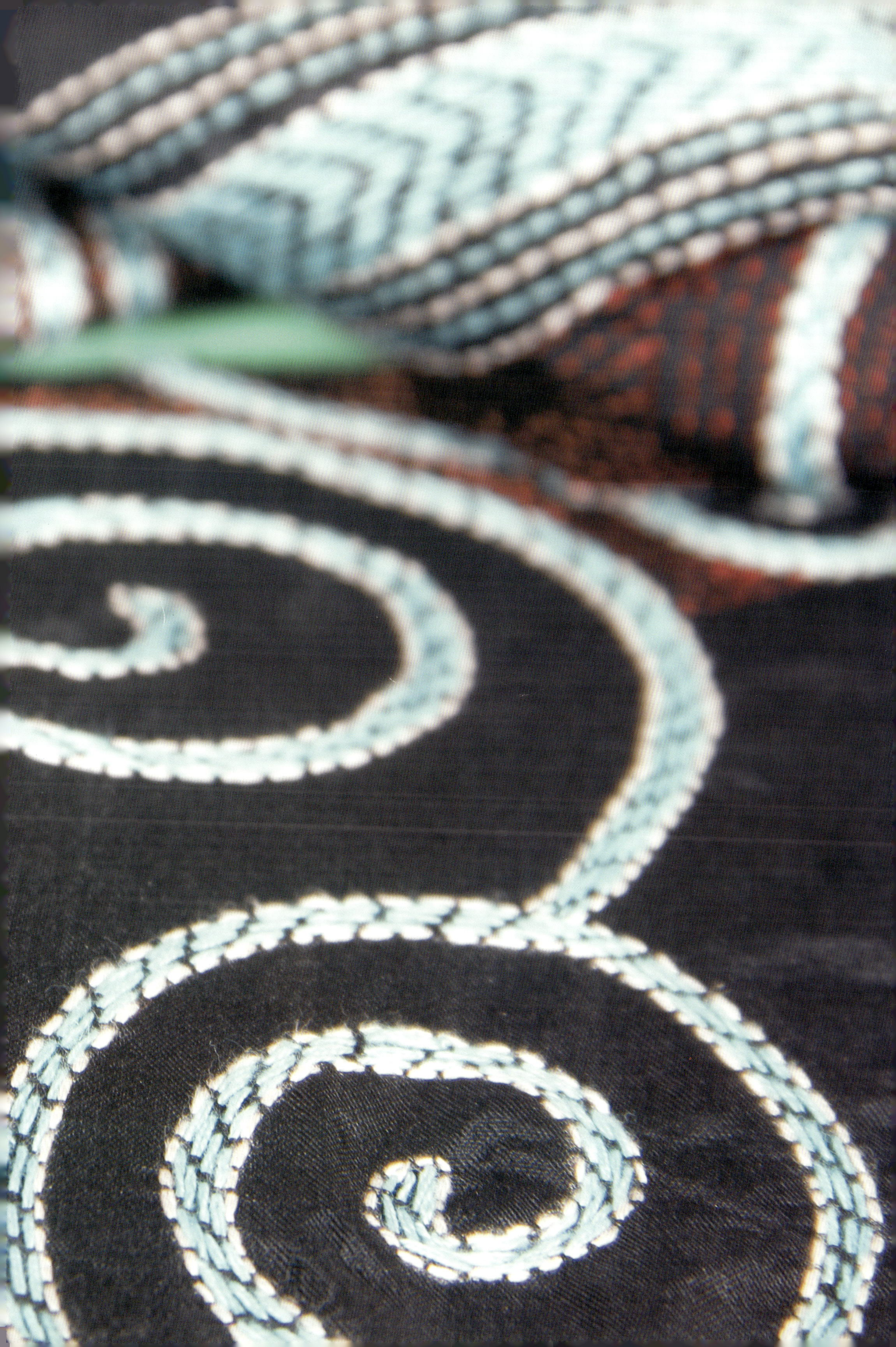

This folk art emerged from a combination of materialistic circumstances and daily needs, climate, geography and economic factors. The motifs embroidered were influenced by religious beliefs and superstitions, and of course what the women saw around them. These rural women gave a free rein to their imagination while capturing on their old and used pieces of cloth the colours and designs of the flowers they saw or the pond they bathed in or even the conch shell they blew before praying. This ordinary piece of cloth, embroidered in the simplest of running stitches, speaks of folk beliefs and practices, religious ideas, themes and characters from mythology and epics, flora, fauna, man and nature; they also reflect the social and personal life of people in their own way.

Defining *Kantha* art, Gurusaday Dutt, who pioneered the resuscitation of the folk art of Bengal, correctly noticed that "the name '*Kantha*' signifies a poor man's wrap consisting of old used up cloth patched up and sewn into a single garment. It seems probable that patch works *Kantha* constituted the original form of *Kanthas* and that *Kanthas* of a decorative 'appliqué' type were evolved from this" **(Chakarbarti, 2007, p21)**

Kantha since then has had a long history and seen many ups and downs. It has travelled many miles, from a poor Bengali home to the markets of Bengal, then almost disappearing from the scene; it has seen a rebirth or revival and has been finally reinvented as per the need of the times into its present form that is more colourful, with more dynamic designs and more uses. Today, the *Kantha* is just not limited to a Bengali home but has carved a special niche for itself and sees itself in great demand not only domestically but also in the export market. What must have begun as the aesthetic use of an old cloth due to lack of money is today a most respected craft universally. Many hundreds of years back, when a Bengali woman created her used cloth into a quilt, not once would it have crossed her mind that, in the years to come, her basic needlework would become a work of art. Never would she have dreamt that her household item, fashioned from rags to cover her family's modesty, would one day find new materials, uses, functions, and stitching.

The Bengal *Kantha* is very different from other quilting skills of the world in the sense of the material used and even in the stitching method. There is no denying the fact that Bengal cotton and silk had long made its mark and were in great demand even during Pericles' time. Bengal silk, 'muslin', 'mulmul' were its various names, which were crafted into beautiful saris and other embroidered cloths. Bengali women preserved these beautiful sari borders and soft male dhotis. Thus, the first recycling art began when these dhotis were placed layer upon layer and stitched together, enclosed by these sari borders. The stitching patterns used in the Bengal *Kanthas* are very simple but its simplicity cannot be perceived in the intricate designs that finally emerge.

Renowned for its bewitching and eye catching colours and designs, this craft which had such a humble beginning is now the crown jewel of embroideries around the world. Queen Elizabeth-II, ex- President Bush, Pope Johannes Paulus, Robert McNamara and late President Mitterrand - all have a piece of *Kantha* among their possessions.

MEANING OF THE WORD '*KANTHA*'

The word '*Kantha*' (in Sanskrit), or 'kathari', 'kath' and 'gadari' (in Hindi), refers to a patched garment, a bag or a hold-all, traditionally worn or carried by ascetics. Most Sanskrit dictionaries such as Gode's Sanskrit-English Dictionary (1957) or Apte's Sanskrit-Hindi Kosh (1966:529), and the Hindi-English Dictionary by Chaturvedi (2004:110) all house this word. It has also been used by European scholars like Monier-Williams (1966:244) (**Pathak**, 2012, p-172). Many dictionaries have mentioned that Kanthas were patched garments; however, when we look at the Kantha collections in various museums, galleries or in private collections, usually the Kantha coverlet Kantha is found.

HISTORY OF EMBROIDERY

The art of designing pieces of cloth with a needle and thread is as old as the history of mankind, from the time man learned to cover himself. As soon as ancient man started to live in a settlement and learnt to build a home, he also learnt to beautify his surroundings. The Bhimbhetka caves are a perfect example of this, justifying the point that using aesthetics to titivate his surroundings is an ancient art. Perhaps he might have been encouraged to arrange leaves and flowers to make patterns on the wall and floor, and then followed the wisdom of using the same to cover himself. The different hues of Nature, the brightly coloured birds and animals must been an inspiration for man to become a designer and inventor of the needle.

The famous Indus valley site, Mohenjo-daro, has revealed the use of cotton cloth. An inscription at Babylon says cotton reached there from the Indus valley. Finds of bone and metal needles of different lengths from Harappa, Mohenjo-daro (now in Pakistan), Dhaulavira (Gujarat), Rakhigarhi (Haryana) indicate its various uses; for stitching and probably for embroidery.

India enjoys a long and glorious tradition of needle work and weaving. The figures excavated at Harappa and Mohenjo-daro provide evidence of the beautifully woven and embroidered clothes that used to be worn in those early days (**Basak, 2007, p-23-24**).

The art of weaving can be traced back to the time of the Rig Veda. The earliest mention of *Kantha* is found in the Rig Veda, Upanishads and in Panini's text (**Vatsyayan, 2010, p-77**). There is evidence which point at Portuguese traders buying *Kantha* in bulk in the sixteenth century and selling them abroad.

During the New Stone Age civilisation around 3000 to 1500 BC, Bihar, Orissa and Assam existed as Bangla. Bengal extended from the foot of the Himalayas to the Bay of Bengal and from the Chotanagpur plateau to the boundaries of Assam and the frontier region of Burma. But in the early 20th century, with the partition of Bengal, it was divided into two new provinces comprising Western Bengal (as well as the provinces of Bihar and Orissa) and East Bengal and Assam with Dacca (Dhaka).

Before partition, the art of *Kantha* had evolved over the centuries. These simple coverings continue to be made even today with the same sentiment and belief and are a part of our living tradition. *(http://www.britannica.com/EBchecked/topic/60754/partition-of-Bengal).*

The onslaught of time, repeated invasions, the British Raj and the terrible Bengal famine did not affect this traditional craft and it has triumphed in upholding its originality, novelty, uniqueness and innate imagery. In fact, some of the symbols used in this craft have been traced back to the Harappan civilization.

REFERENCES TO KANTHA IN ART AND LITERATURE

This traditional and ancient craft finds mention in the Sanskrit grammar written by Panini around the 6th century B.C. Two centuries later, Valmiki had mentioned in his epic 'Ramayana' about Sita's skills and her being an expert in Chandrabati's *Kantha* stitching. The earliest reference of the making of the 'patched garment' is found in the Buddhist text Vinaya Pitaka. Here it has been mentioned that it was used by *bhikkus* and also that Lord Buddha wore a patched robe (*sanghati*), which can be perceived in some of the relics of the Mathura School of circa 2nd century A.D. (Pathak, 2012,pp-172-73). Sculptures of Kanishka, Huvishka and Wimokadphises have also been found clad in embroidered patched clothes, whose motifs resemble that of *Kanthas*.

Early literature mentions that saints from Hindu, Buddhist, Jain, and Islamic cultures use to cover themselves in *Kantha* wrappings to keep themselves warm in winters. Later on, it was considered a symbol of simple living. Perhaps inspired by the Buddhist tradition, later artists also began depicting Sufi saints and other Hindu gods and goddesses wearing patched garments.

Ananda K. Coomaraswamy (1889-1947), the renowned Indic scholar, posited that the folk arts that have survived in Bengal are directly descended from the pre-Harappan–Indus-Saraswati civilization, which is at least 5000 years old.

The earliest reference to the Bengal *Kantha* is found in Krishnadas Kaviraj's 'Sri Sri Chaitanya Charitamrita', authored some 500 years ago. The poet writes that Sachi, the mother of Chaitanya sent a homemade *Kantha* to her son at Puri through some pilgrims. (Mohanty, cited in Zaman 2006:99). Benoy Kumar Sarkar in his famous book, "The Folk Element in Hindu Culture," clearly states that Lord Chaitanya, the Krishna-cult prophet, reformist, missionary and visionary, used to be draped in a *Kantha* when he went into devotional ecstasies (Chakarbarti, 2007, p26). The author further observes in the same volume that Aula Chand, a contemporary spiritual leader (1616-1691 A.D.) "assumed the koupina and went out with a *Kantha* on his person."

The next reference is in Zaman's book about the famous artist Abanindranath Tagore, who seemed to have encountered a woman in a village in a district of Srihatta in Bangladesh, who recorded her life story in her *Kantha*, spanning a period starting from her marriage till old age. Many words with the *Kantha* as prefix and suffix have been found in scriptures like Maharshi Harit's 'Samhita' etc. "While renouncing the world, do not take with yourself any article of comfort except the loins, a *Kantha* for protection against cold and a pair of wooden slippers" was cited from this scripture **(Chakarbarti, 2007, p25).**

Among the Muslims too, Sufi saints and dorbaish (dervishes), including the *Baul* singer Lalan Fakir - so revered in undivided Bengal - were known to use layered and quilted *Kanthas* as an attire. The Baul singer referred to *Kanthas* in their mystical music as a metaphor for their spiritual wanderings, free from material ties. In one of his Baul 'gaan' or songs, Lalan Fakir says, "Lalan *saier Chhera Kantha, Gaye dile ki sit mane"* (Can Lalan 's tattered *Kantha* keep this cold away?) **(Sethi, 2012).**

Other early references in folk songs and verses indicate that the *Kantha*'s reworking of old fabrics into new objects was viewed as rebirth and revival (Rahman 1988: 23).

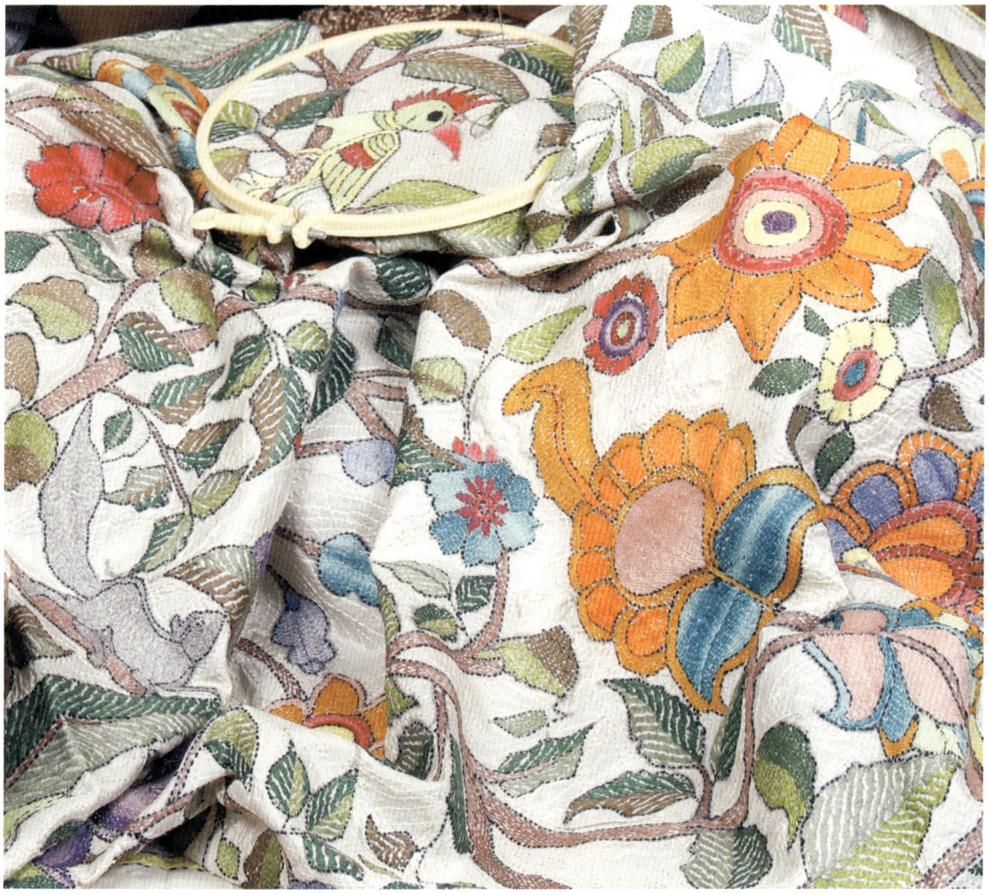

The *Kantha* was naturally seen as a symbol of an ascetic's surrender of material ties:

"Sanaih Kantha

Sanaih Kantha

Sanaih Parvata langhanam"

Slowly one stitches rags

Slowly one traverses the path

And slowly one climbs to the top of the mountain.

In the Sikh school (of the Punjab region), miniature paintings dating back to the last quarter of the 19th century depict Guru Nanak **(Goswamy, 2000)** wearing patched clothes or the chaddar as a wrap.

In another painting, which has been dated to the second quarter of the 18th century, Guru Nanak is depicted more like a fakir. He is shown wearing a knee-length cloak and a skull cap and sitting on a white floor rug (ibid.: 122, pl. 3.3). Both the garments and the floor rug are decorated with *Kantha*-style stitches (ibid.:130, pl. 3.7).

Over time, the patched garment described in Buddhist and Hindu literature, depicted in sculptures, murals and other paintings, and associated with ascetics and holy men, came to be adopted more commonly **(Pathak, 2012, P180)**.

The designers of North India created magic with their needles and threads of gold and silver on silk, as did the folk art of *Kantha* stitching and designing in Bengal. Similar to the *Kantha* stitch, the Satgaon quilts also came into existence. Satgaon was the old mercantile capital of Bengal, located on the Saraswati tributary of the river Hooghly which used to be the main centre for commerce in Bengal till the mid- 16th century. In 1537, its trade was gradually diverted to the port of Hooghly which was founded by the Portuguese.

Wonderful embroidery on quilts and bedcovers were taken to Europe by the Portuguese and gained immense popularity there. John Irwin and Margaret Hall have spoken of the *Kanthas* of Satgaon and Hooghly which they called, "satgaon quilts". It can be hypothesised that the satgaon embroidery tradition both enriched and influenced the *Kantha* and led to the making of the elaborately figurative Nakshi *Kantha* **(Basak, 2007, p24-29).**

Perhaps the first person to recognize the significance of the *Kantha* and its association with the lives of the women of rural Bengal was Jasimuddin, the poet of the Bengal countryside. In his Nakshi *Kantha* Maath or The Field of the Embroidered Quilt, he immortalized the *Kantha*. The poem is a story of the love between a village girl and boy who are separated. The girl, in wait of her lover, embroiders a quilt of *Kantha*:

Spreading the embroidered quilt

She works the livelong night,

As if the quilt her poet were

Of her bereaved plight.

Many a joy and many a sorrow

Is written on its breast.

In the early 20th century, societies were developing and the folk arts started diminishing. Then, Rabindranath Tagore initiated a search into the indigenous roots of Bengali culture, with its revitalisation of various traditional skills. In 1919 he established Kala Bhavana, the house of art, where the *Kantha*, alpana, mat-making, dyeing, printing, and batik were introduced under the guidance of Tagore's daughter-in-law Pratima Devi **(Sethi, 2012, p41).** She and her students put this folk needlecraft to contemporary urban usage, which was aimed at the revival of this so-called dying folk-craft.

It can be clearly noticed that the use of the *Kantha* prevailed in the past and in fact, does so even today.

MAKING OF A *KANTHA*

Kantha - re-cycling of old and used cloth, fashioned into functional quilts to exquisite embroidered heirlooms - speaks volumes of the grandeur of the Indian artistic textile heritage. *Kantha* quilts produced by rural Bengali women folk are indicative of their superior proficiency and imaginative elegance. The joy of the *Kantha* is in the simplicity of the design and the stitch. The fabric is covered in running stitches, with threads from coloured sari borders, and the lyrical, flowing and artistic embroidery that thus emerged takes the form of a picture from everyday life. The path this running stitch crosses through the hand of its designer and the shape that finally emerges are quite extraordinary and mind blowing.

Traditionally and technically, the village women used layers of old, soft, discarded dhotis and saris held together or stitched with running stitches along the edges, using a thread usually drawn out of the faded borders of the saris. Earlier, thorns of date palm trees were used to fasten the ends of the layers, but have now been replaced by pins. Borders were often torn from the sari and kept aside, especially for this purpose. If the *Kantha* was meant to be a quilt, then five or six or sometimes even seven layers of fine cloth were stitched together. If it was for some other purpose, then three or four layers were used. The top and bottom layers were customarily of white or of a very light colour, so that the embroidery was visible. The sides were stitched all around so that the cloths became a single piece, and then the thorns or pins were removed. The village women of the olden days did not have mangles at their disposal, so they depended on heavy metal vessels with flat bottoms to smoothen the top of the stitched clothes. The vessels would be warmed and then pressed along the surface so that no part would remain wrinkled.

The creator gave free rein to her imagination and with a free hand drew the motif or central design and the borders onto the cloth. To trace out her imagination onto the cloth, she used charcoal or colour made from the barks of various trees. However, with the arrival of the pencil on the scene, marking the outlines became quite convenient.

The thread pulled out from the coloured borders were wound around a wooden reel or the woman's own fingers. Thereafter, using that thread and a needle, the designer would embroider poetry onto the cloth, allowing her deft fingers to go wherever her thoughts took them. She would breathe life into those precise designs, creating a breathtakingly gorgeous piece of art. In the final result, the whiteness of the uppermost layer would be fully covered by the use of many colours and elaborate patterns and would have an overall rippled effect.

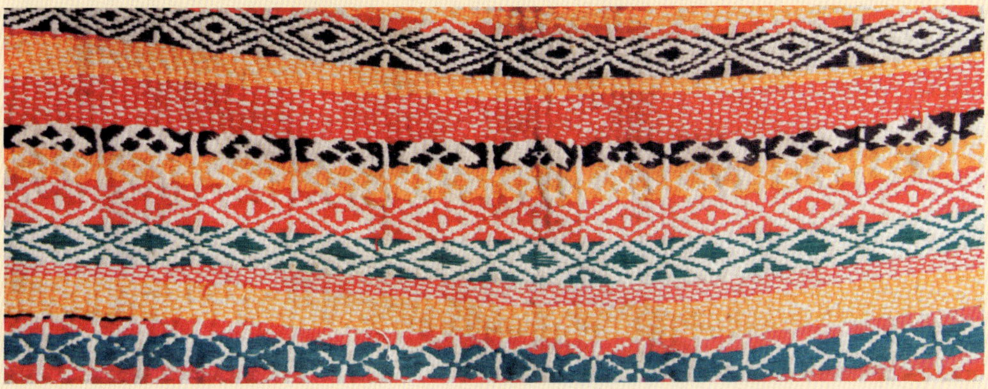

Types of Stitches

The most important part of the *Kantha* is the stitch itself; not only do they have to be firm enough to hold together the various layers, but good enough to make the designs look attractive and eye catching. The *Kanthas* show the ingenious use of the running stitch for working motifs and border patterns. The predominant form of this stitch should be called the *Kantha phor* or *Kantha stitch*.

There are many other stitches also that are used in the *Kantha*. Some of the commonly as well as rarely used stitches are:

1. Herringbone stitch
2. Double running stitch
3. Leak stitch
4. Darning stitch
5. Dorokha stitch
6. Button hole stitch
7. Bending stitch
8. Chatai stitch
9. Stem stitch
10. Back stitch
11. Cross stitch
12. Chain stitch
13. Arrowhead stitch and
14. Satin stitch

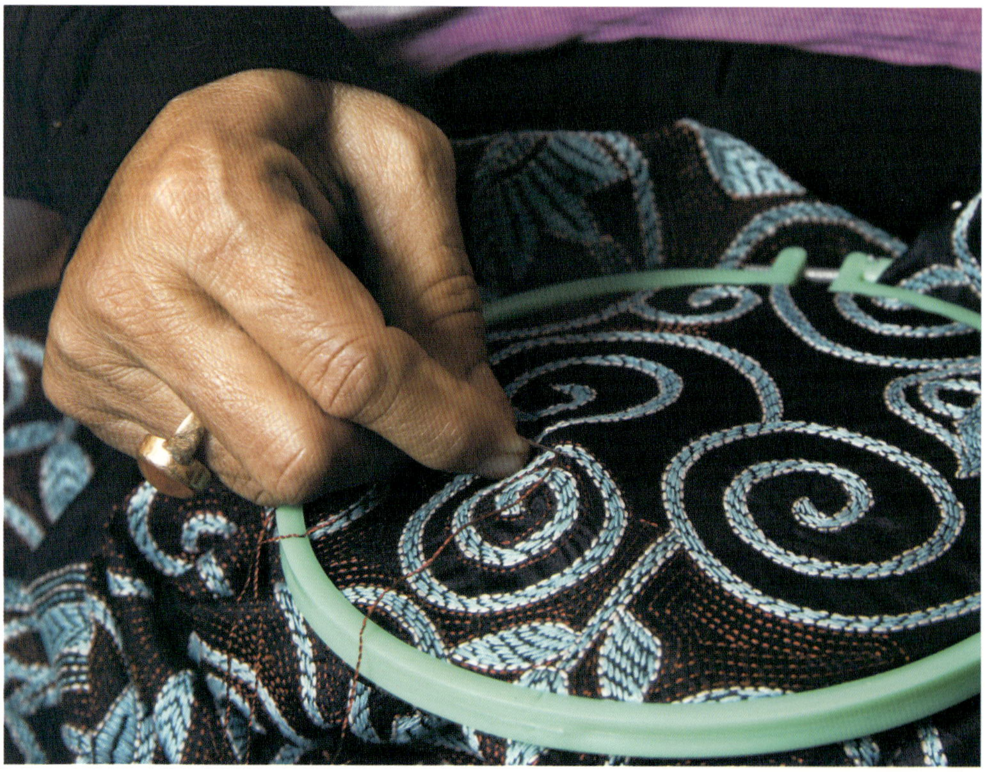

The Chatai Nakshi *Kantha* stitches are found in some places in Jessore, Kushtia, Pabna, Rajshahi, Rangpur and Mymensingh. Other types of *Kanthas* include the pad tola *Kantha*, which is embroidered entirely with sari border patterns. In the lohori *Kantha*, thick yarn is used for close pattern darning. In the most intricate of pad tola *Kanthas*, there is no space between the concentric border patterns, so the entire *Kantha* apparently seems to be a piece of woven cloth. (Independent, March 28, 2008).

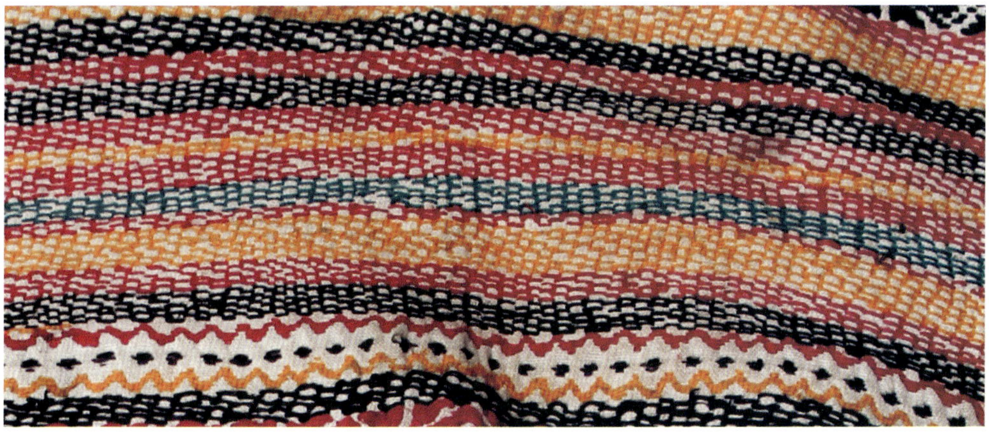

1. Running Stitch- This may be long and short, alternating with those in the preceding and succeeding rows, or bending slightly forward. When *Kantha* stitches are taken around motifs there is still a tendency to have parallel rows, but each row curves with the motif at its centre. This manner of working around a motif often creates an almost sculptured effect. The square effect can be worked from the outside edge inwards. As the worker proceeds round and round the square, each row of stitches that is taken is parallel to the outer edge. When one **square** is finished another is worked next to it in the same manner. **[Zaman, 2004, p 46]**

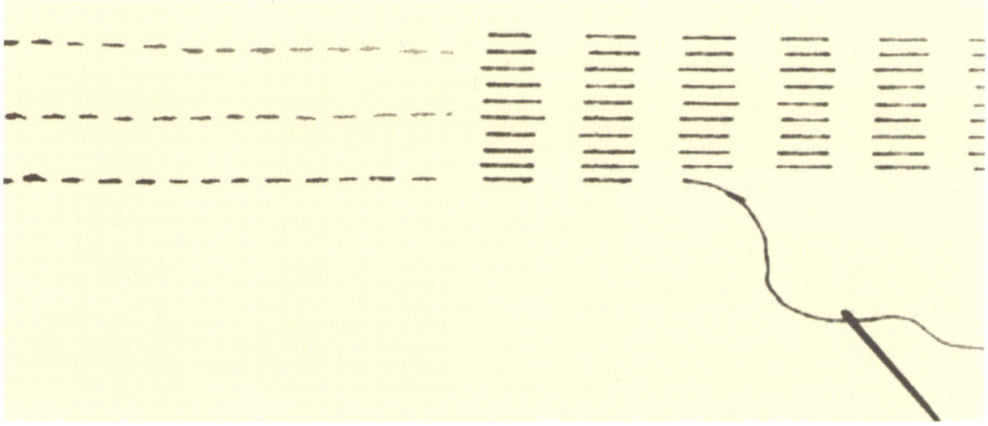

2. Chatai or Pattern Darning -This stitch is also referred to as the *pati phor*. In this form, the stitches are placed closely parallel to each other. The effect of such embroidery often resembles that of the satin stitch. In the *chatai*, the worker makes closely parallel rows of running stitches, the rows and stitches both being parallel to each other. The areas covered with embroidery on the surface of the *Kantha* are bare on the reverse. There is only minimum thread wasted, but the works proceeds at a faster rate than in the satin stitch. Some characteristic motifs are embroidered using the *chatai, for e.g., leaves, flowers, the chakra or wheel, the kalka, the betel leaf.* **[Zaman, 2004, p 47-49]**

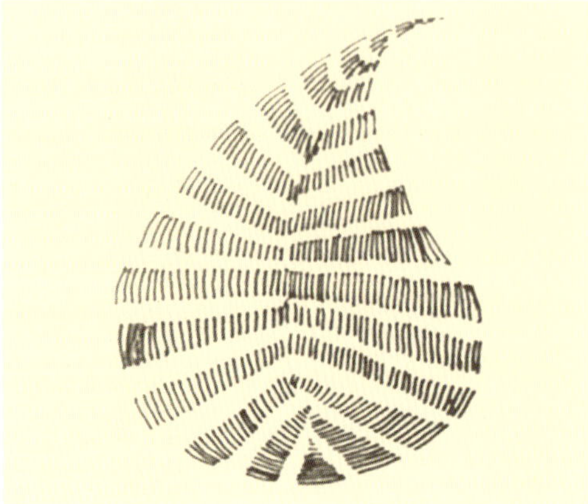

Kalka, Chatai

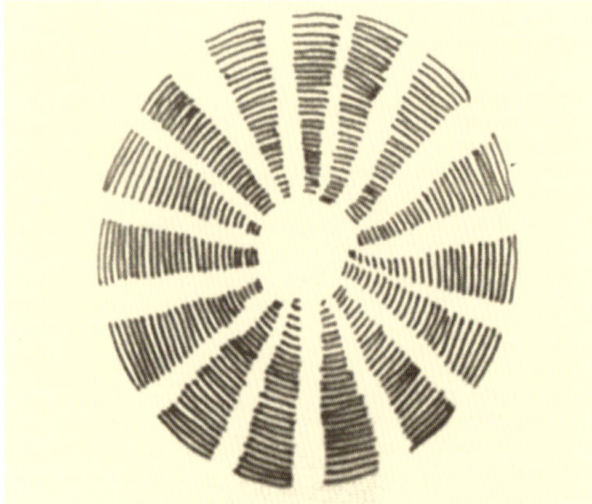

Chakra, Chatai

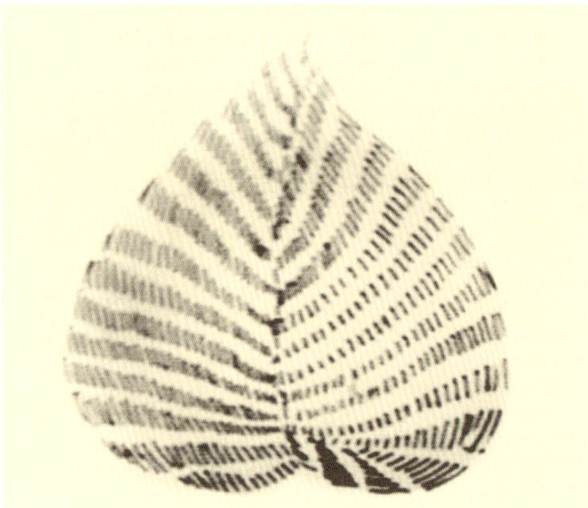

Kalka, Chatai

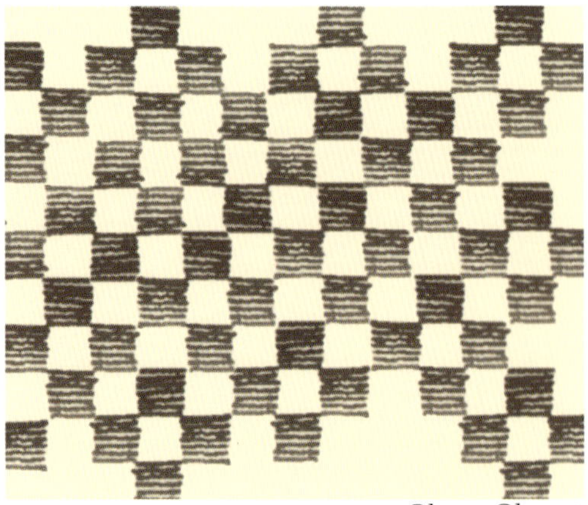

Chati, Chatai

3. The Kaitya, or Bending Stitch - In this form of the running stitch, the stitches are taken in closely parallel rows. Each stitch, however, moves slightly forward. The whole line seems to bend, the name of the stitch being derived from this effect. In the same way, motifs can also be worked in a short space of time using this variation of the running stitch. Examples are *shostir chino or swastika, kalka motif*. The motif seems to move before our eyes, giving rise to the feeling that it represents a moving wheel. **[Zaman, 2004, p 49-50]**

Many motifs can be embroidered using either the *chatai* or the *kaitya*. The different forms of the running stitch used will create different effects. *Chatai* work is thicker and bolder, whereas *kaitya* work produces a more delicate effect and is used for background stitching.

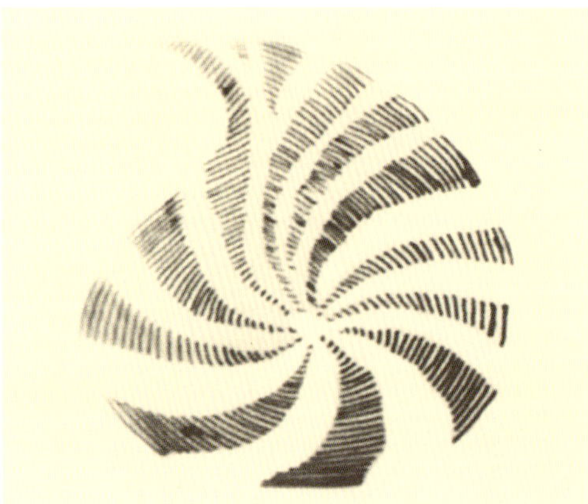

Kalka, **Kaitya**

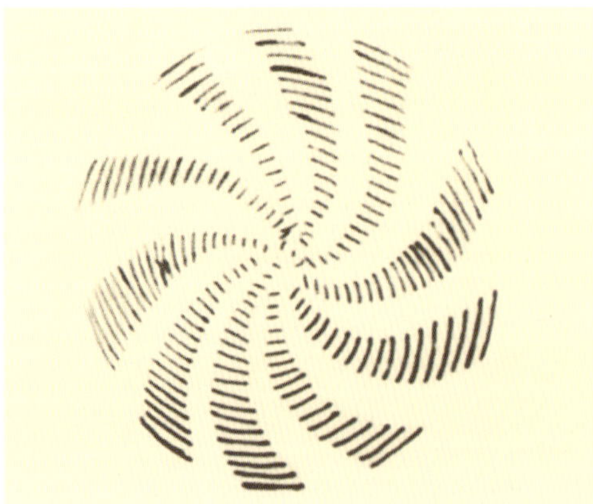

Chino , **Kaitya**

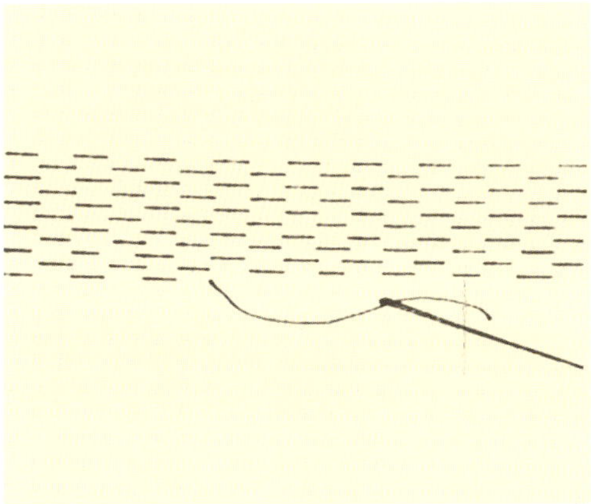

Double running stitch

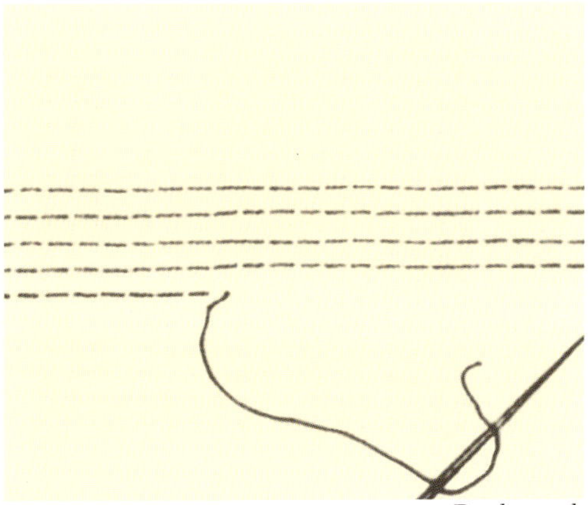

Back stitch

4. Darning Stitch - It is used for filling the gaps between the running ones. After the outlines of a motif are drawn, the darning stitch helps to cover the enclosed space. **[Zaman, 2004, p 51]**

5. Stem Stitch or dal phor - Double rows of running stitches are often used to outline motifs, and the stem or *dal phor* is occasionally used to do so, especially in the newer *Kanthas*. The stem is also sometimes used to fill a motif, producing an effect of solid colour. **[Zaman, 2004, p 57]**

6. Arrowhead Stitch - This is composed of two straight stitches meeting at an angle, and is used in various ways. It is a quick way to fill motifs which are then neither heavily embroidered nor left without embroidery. It is also used to produce a variety of border patterns. **[Zaman, 2004, p 57]**

7. Back Stitch or *bahkya* – In this stitch, the needle is brought out of the cloth a stitch length ahead of the stitch worked. The needle is then taken back along the line and again brought out of the fabric a stitch length ahead. It is used for outline motifs. **[Zaman, 2004, p 58]**

8. Cross Stitch – The stitching is done at two diagonally opposite ends, the lines crossing at the centre. The stitch is generally not used for *Kantha* except in Rajshahi, where it is called *carpet* design.

9. Buttonhole Stitch- It is not popular with the *Kantha* makers, and is generally used for borders or particular motifs.

10. Chain Stitch- One of the oldest forms of stitching, it is found in silk garments of China dating back to the pre-Christian era. The stitch resembles a chain stitch and is used in *Kanthas* for motifs of flowers and leaves.

Illustrations of some other stitches can be seen on the following pages

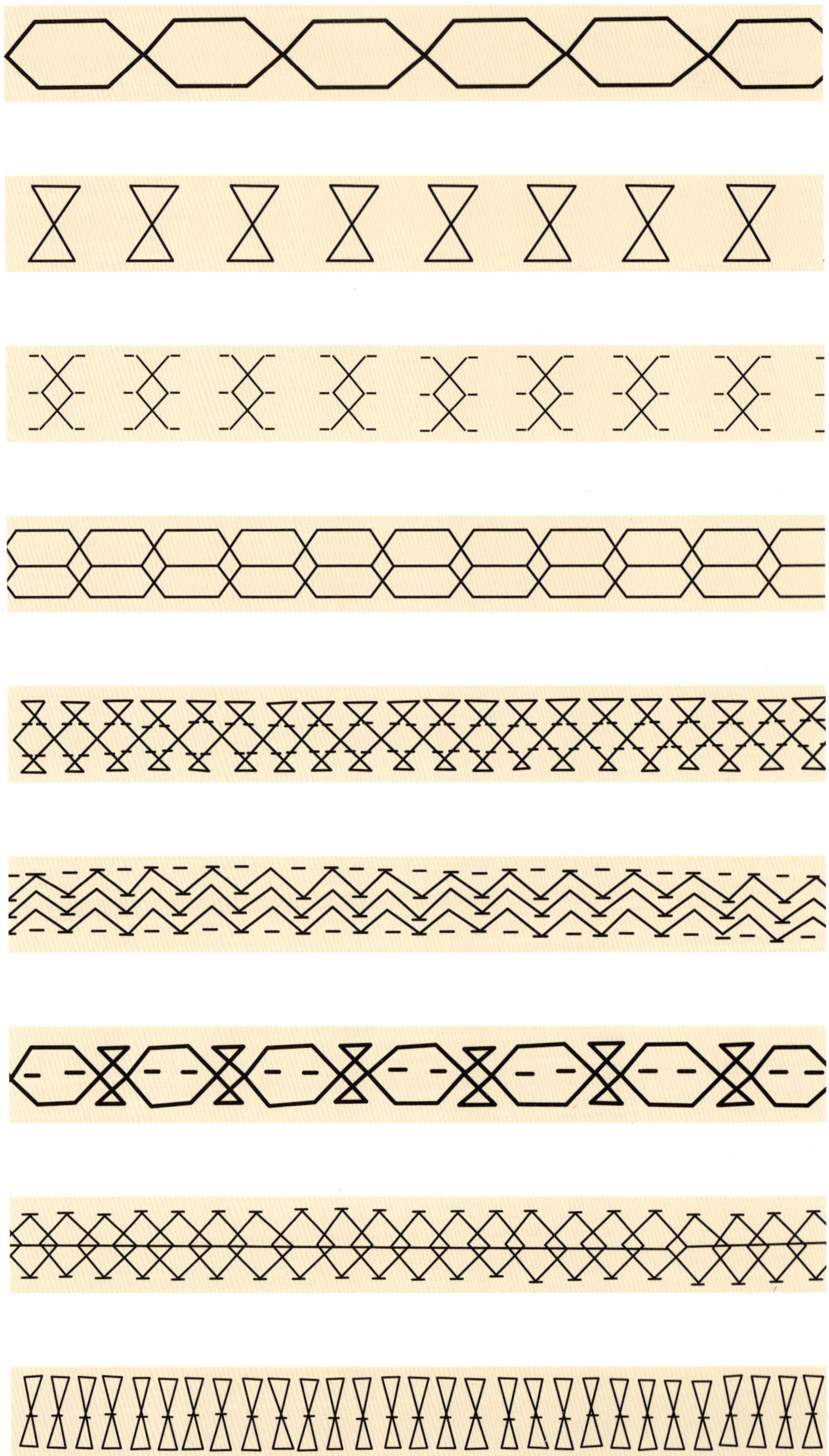

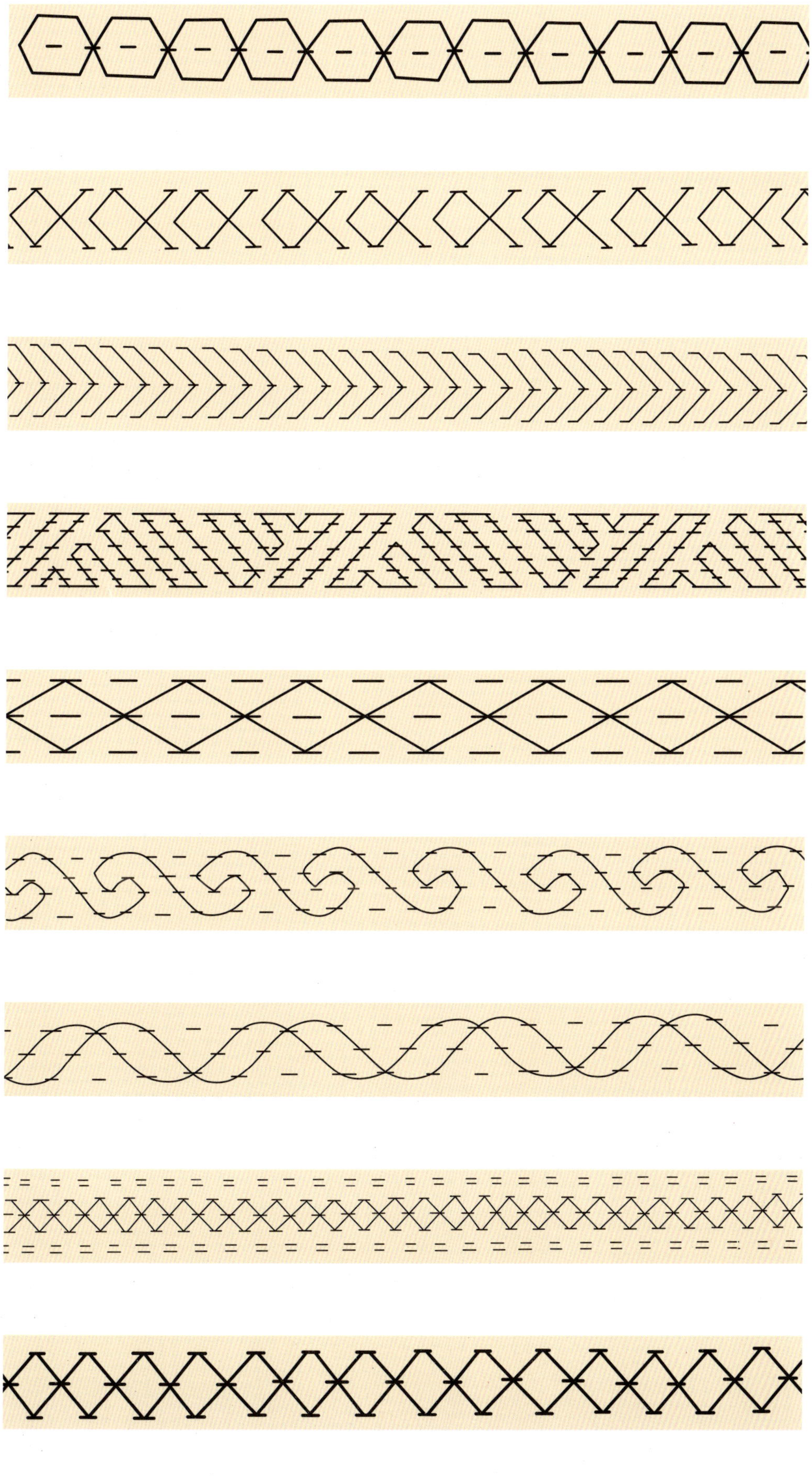

Types / Variations of Kanthas

Kanthas were embroidered by the village womenfolk of Bengal after being free of their household chores. They tried to complete their work before the rainy season or before the winter invaded these villages encompassing the Ganges Delta, primarily to be used as pallets and light wraps. Small *Kanthas* were used as swaddling clothes for babies.

Depending on their size and use, *Kanthas* range from lep *Kanthas* (winter quilts) and sujni *Kanthas* (spreads and coverlets) to one-foot square rumal (handkerchief) *Kanthas*. Others include the asan (a spread for sitting), the bastani or gatri (a wrapper for clothes and other valuables), the arshilata (a wrap for mirrors or toilet articles), the dastarkhan (a spread for placing food and plates for dining), the gilaf (an envelope-shaped *Kantha* to cover the Quran), and jainamaz (prayer rug).

Broadly on the basis of their utility, *Kanthas* have been categorized into two types i.e. personal and religious. Traditionally, personal *Kanthas* are meant to be used for personal use – as a light wrap or covering, or swaddling clothes. They were not meant to be gifts, but used inside the four walls of the creator's home. In the background of different political scenarios and with the *Kantha* finding a modern arena and a commercial market, it has found more uses and is now being created as hangings, coverlets, box mirrors, saris, kurtis, to name a few. The traditional way of the *Kantha* has been replaced by new types of cloth and more commercial designs and uses.

The traditional *Kantha* quilts were of the following types:

1. Sujni Kantha

Spread on the bed for guests to sit or lie upon, this *Kantha* is generally six feet long and four and half feet wide. It has a lotus motif at the centre, the borders designed with different types of flowers and plants. A special characteristic of this *Kantha* is that the designs are printed with the help of wooden blocks.

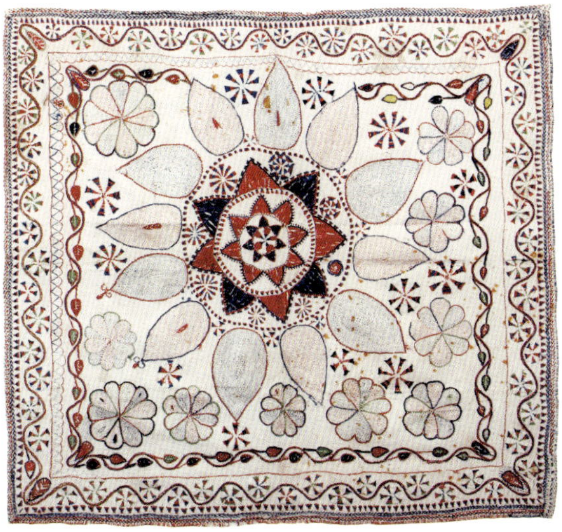

2. Lep Kantha

These are bigger in size as they are used as quilts during the winter months. At places where the winter is more severe, the *Kantha* can be of seven layers. The lotus is again the central motif with the other designs sewn in small stitches to give the surface a wavy look, also called lahari, meaning waves. It has geometric patterns as designs, though motifs of trees and plants can be seen.

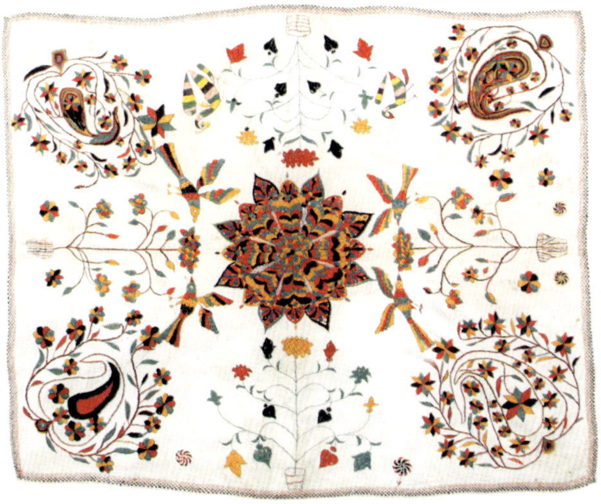

3. Betan Kanth

These are smaller pieces, which are square in shape and measuring around three feet in length and breadth, and used to wrap books and valuables. Such *Kanthas* depict animal and human figures and the floral designs add charm to the Betan *Kantha*.

4. Baby Kantha

These act as a towel for babies and are designed as the others. It is customary in many families to present such *Kantha*s when a child is born. These are small in size, as are the ones used as pillow covers.

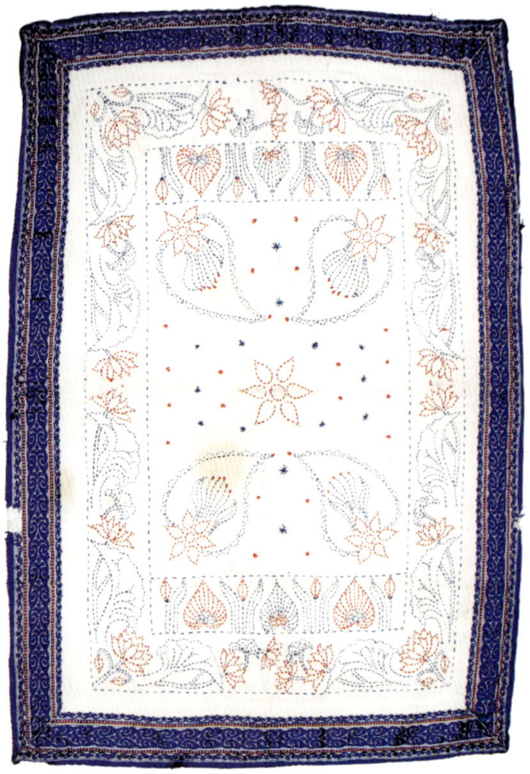

5. Bartan Kantha

Bartan means 'utensil' and this *Kantha* is used to cover plates containing food and are designed with motifs of flowers and plants.

6. Dastarkhan

About ten feet long and one and half feet wide, this is spread between two rows of guests as they sit down to meals and the plates containing food are placed on its circular designs. This *Kantha* is restricted to Muslim homes only.

7. Durjani, Batua or Nakshi Tholi

Ten inches long and six inches wide, it is also used as a carry bag. Three ends are folded at the centre, the top fold a little shorter than the other two. It can be used as a purse or to carry small items like betel leaf or nuts. Motifs are geometric shapes and plants.

8. Arshilata

Arshi means 'mirror' and the *Kantha* is used to keep small mirrors, combs and toiletry. It is made of a thin strip of cloth between one and two feet long and six inches wide. Motifs are peacocks, the kadam tree, moon, stars etc.

9. Rumal Kantha

Made up of four square pieces of cloth and measuring a foot both ways, it is used as a handkerchief or to keep crockeries covered. It is a thin *Kantha* and is often gifted to dear ones; the artists write their names at one corner and the name of the person to whom it is being gifted. Motifs are butterflies, birds, lotus, rose and various varieties of flowers and creepers.

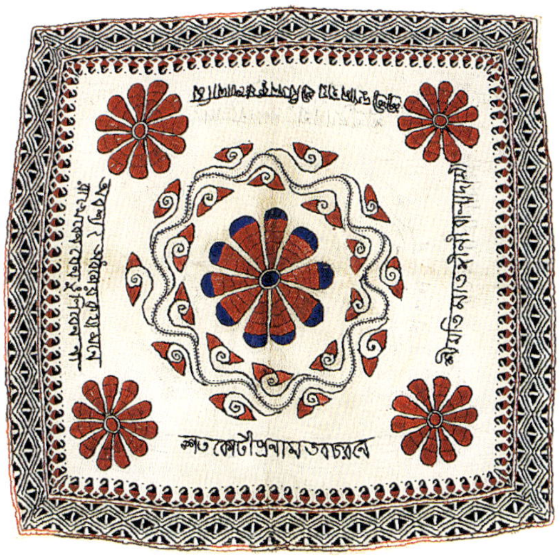

10. Joth or Jot

A long thin *Kantha*, it is used to keep things wrapped up in the house. Geometric patterns can be seen on it as also inter-twined motifs.

11. Hanging Kantha

A decorative piece, it can be of various sizes. Its beautiful designs are a testimony to the needlework of village women.

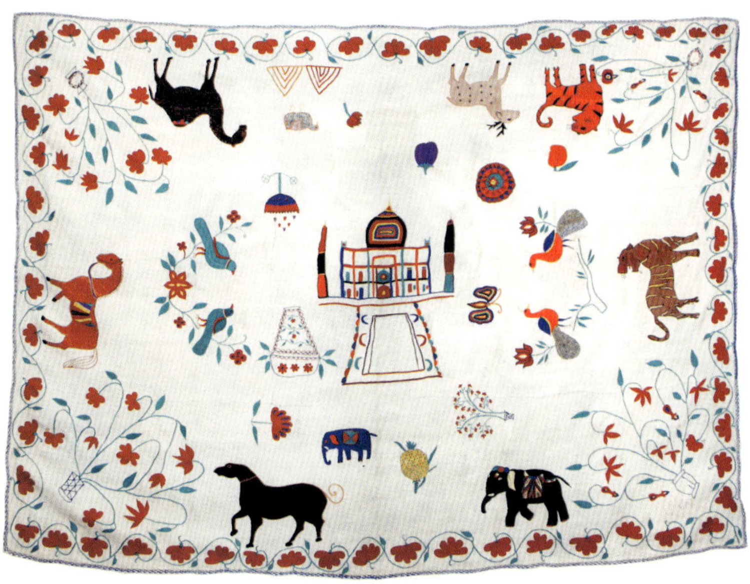

12. Bastani or Bochka Kantha

This is square in shape and as the two names suggest, it is used as a sack to carry things , the two ends tied together with a piece of thread . It may have the lotus as a single central motif or may be designed all over with various patterns.

13. Dhakni Kantha

Dhaka means to cover and this *Kantha* is used to cover furniture in the house to protect them from dust. Geometric and other patterns form the motif.

14. Gelap, Chadar or Shawl Kantha

Used to wrap around the body, it is six feet long and two feet wide and has two layers of cloth. It is dotted with designs of flowers and plants at the centre.

15. Parda Kantha

Parda means curtain and this *Kantha* is used in palanquins, boats and bullock carts to keep the interior hidden from view. The motifs include butterflies and flowers.

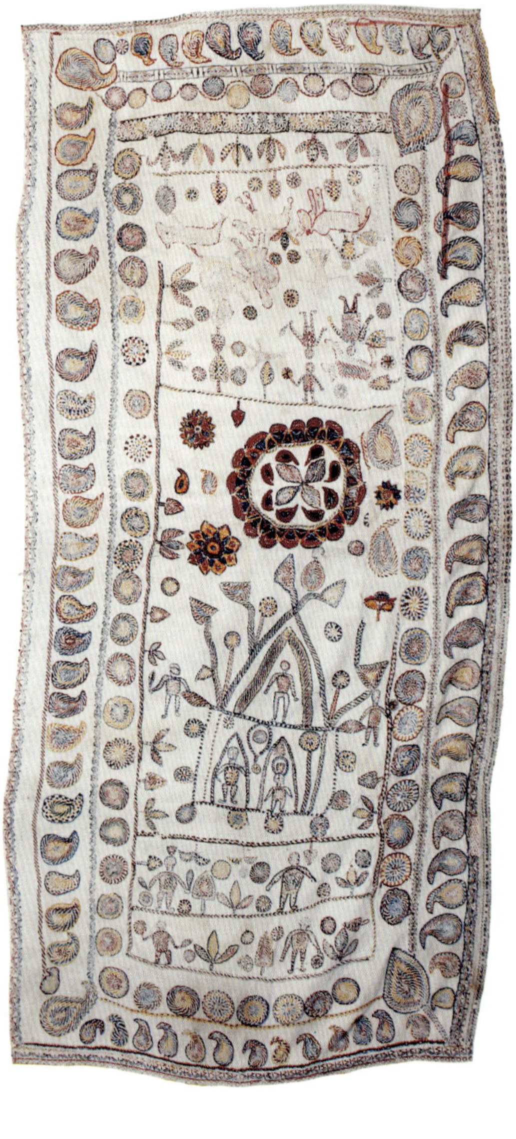

16. Sarinda or Abarani Kantha

To keep the sarinda and other such string instruments. They act as a cover, and hence its other name is *abarani.*

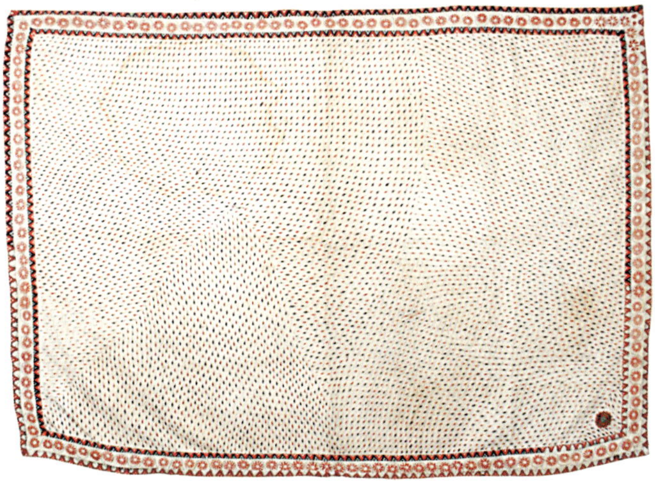

17. Paan Panchan

Like the nakshi tholi, it is used to keep paan and rolled betel nuts, hence panchani. Designs are of betel-leaves and various creepers. Its size is about 16 inches long and 8 inches wide.

18. Religious Kanthas

They are used as covers for religious books like the holy book cover [gilaf], jainamaz, and asan for the purpose of some religious ritual functions.

1.Gilaf

It is used to keep religious books like the Holy Koran. Geometric patterns dominate, though plant life can also be seen.

2. Jainamaz

It is about five feet long and two feet wide, used by Muslims at the time of *namaz*. Motifs mainly are scenes of Mecca and Medina.

[Basak, 2007, p 39, 64, 85]

KANTHA DESIGNS

The *Kantha* reflects the life, aspirations, and culture of the women of rural Bengal. The motifs used are the symbols which have given the *Kantha* a special place in the folk art tradition. *Kanthas* emerge as multi-religious products and also as multi-racial expressions.

Free of all inhibitions in symmetry, colour, form, composition, and methodology of design, the craft is guided by the free, inexhaustible spirit of the human mind alone. This makes the craft and its makers unusually liberal and truly post-modern.

It is really a matter of little or no consequence for the *Kantha* artist if an elephant and a rat or a peacock depicted on a piece are proportionally sized or not, whether the human forms look real or whether the right and left, top and bottom of their canvases are symmetrical.

An artist is free to choose from her environment: creepers, vines, leaves, flowers, dogs, cats, peacocks, frogs, insects, elephants, horses, birds, tigers, bulls, crocodiles, men, women, sepoys, Durga, Ravana, Krishna, moon, stars, umbrellas, knives, combs, pots, lamps, nut cutters, mirrors or whatever it is that may have caught her imagination. Moreover, she could place all or any of these anywhere on her canvas.

Both Hindu and Muslim women are adept at making *Kantha* textiles. Once the centres of **Hindu culture,** post 12th century this region came under the influence of **Vaishnavism** and **Sufism,** resulting in rapid changes in all folk art expressions. Bengal *Kantha* makers reflect their traditions in choosing their designs. The Hindu *Kantha* makers would tend to choose from religious motifs, like gods and goddesses, the "*alpanas*" representing the lotus flower, Hindu festivals, folk festivals, marriage ceremonies, the lotus, Lord Buddha's footprint, fishes, snakes, boats, horses, carts, flowers, elephants, umbrellas, Rathajatra (Procession of Chariots), Jhulanjatra (Swing festival of Krishna and Radha), Swastika (symbolizing the early Indus valley civilization), trees, wheels, conch shells, various birds and beasts like peacocks, parrots, elephants, lions, tigers etc. On the other hand, the Muslim women were usually restricted to geometrical designs and floral motifs, the crescent, stars, domes, minarets, verses of the holy Quran and the like. Within that restriction, they are able to create wonderful artefacts in jainamaz *Kantha*,dastarkhan, or *gilaf* embroidery.

Composition

A casual glance at a *Kantha* reveals a plethora of images of flowers and leaves, of birds and fishes, of human figures and huge animal forms, of kitchen utensils and toilet articles. But as we look longer and closer, these sift into some sort of order. A finely embroidered *Kantha* will always have a focal point, despite the multitude of motifs and pictorial representations and the appearance of being unplanned. At the centre of most *Kanthas* is a lotus. Around the lotus, there are undulating vines or floral motifs or sari border patterns. Occasionally, the outer- most border around the lotus is not circular but square. In the corners of this square, floral motifs or *kalkas* are embroidered, pointing towards the central lotus. The four corners of the *Kantha* also usually have tree-of-life motifs or *kalkas*. There is also an outer border. Often, a number of different par patterns are embroidered to create a broad border. The empty space between the central motif and the corner motifs is filled up with motifs ranging from vegetal, animal, human motifs to agricultural implements and common domestic objects. Symbolic motifs juxtapose scenes from myths or from contemporary life. The *Kantha* maker does not try to be representational. Every available space between the lotus and the corner motifs is filled with motifs, symbols, and scenes, with size and colour being guided by the imagination of the artist. Themes from legends juxtapose scenes of contemporary life, and both are often permeated with symbolic meanings.

Centre Pattern: In principle, *Kanthas* have a central circle occupied by a multi-petalled *padma* (lotus) signifying the universe. *Astadal* (eight petalled) and *shatadal* (hundred petalled) lotuses are encompassed by a mandala represented by a bordered square.

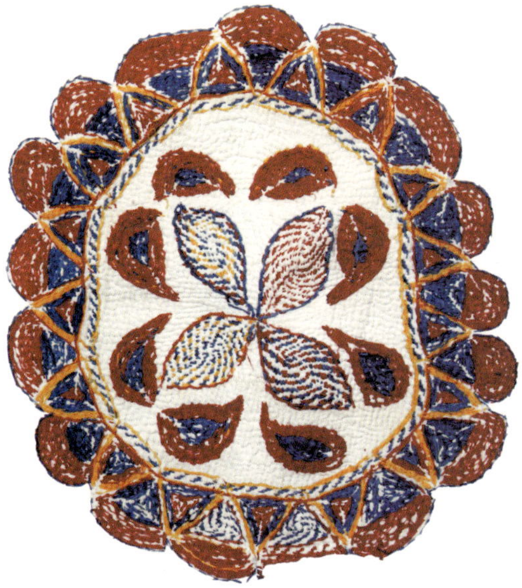

Corners: On the four corners are usually the four *kalkas* (paisleys) or *jibanbriksha* (tree-of-life). The four trees are symbols of the four directions; their meaning stems from Mesopotamia.

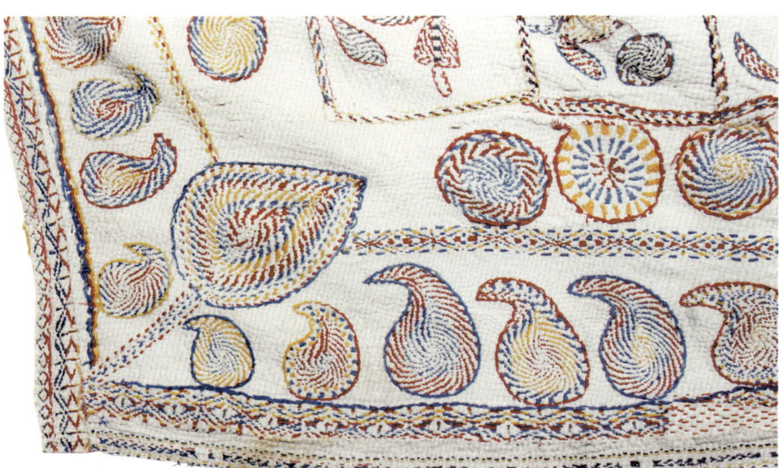

Borders: In *Kanthas, padmas, kalkas,* leaves, and flowers are enclosed in linear and floral borders. Exquisite borders are embroidered where the needle imitates the shuttle to recreate superb sari borders. Occasionally, an especially fine sari border is itself used as a *Kantha* border, creating an unusual combination of weaving and embroidery.

Many of the patterns are traditional and have definite names, but occasionally traditional names are used for innovations as well. Several of the names come from agriculture or from folk beliefs and superstitions. While most come from nature, a few - because of the receptive mind of the *Kantha* artist - come from the machines that are increasingly becoming a part of life everywhere.

From agriculture come the names *dhaner shish* and *khejur chhori, motor dana, phul par, jhop taga, anaj taga.* From superstitions and folk beliefs come the names *ta'abiz par and chok par.* From water symbolism comes the *beki* or the wave-patterned border. From nature we have *maach taga.* From the world of machines come the names *wrench taga* and *grafi taga.*

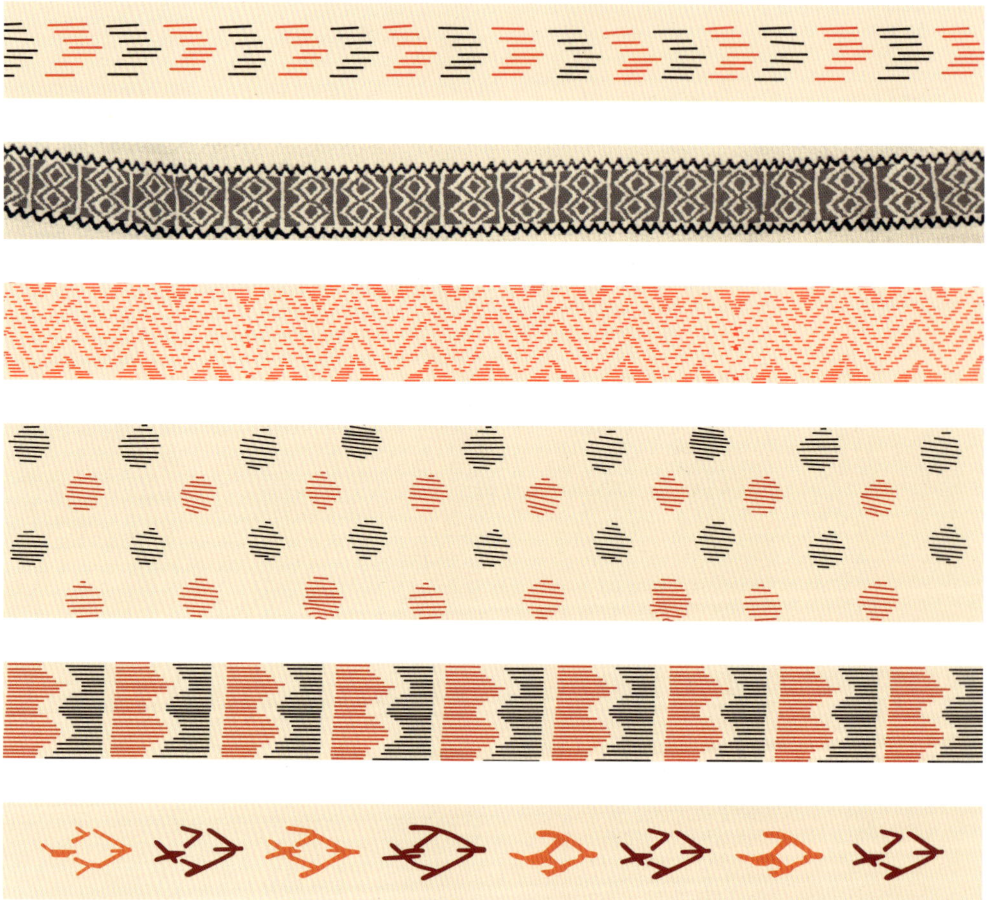

Field: The entire expanse of the quilted cloth between the lotus and the directional trees is filled with figures, objects, symbolic devices, and scenes whose shapes and combinations are dictated by the imagination of the artist.

The space is filled with ritualistic motifs, luxuriant vegetation, animals, and birds. Also toiletry articles, ornaments, kitchen utensils and harvest implements are embroidered alongside quaint vehicles, from palanquins to trains and airplanes.

MOTIFS USED IN *KANTHA*

There is a sense of unity and harmony in the *Kantha* which can also be seen in the blending of motifs belonging to many cultures and many waves of influence. There are traditional Indian motifs handed down from the early civilization of the Indus Valley; there are also motifs ranging from the farthest western fringes of the Asiatic continent to its farthest eastern ones. Indigenous motifs blend with foreign ones and traditional motifs with contemporary pictorial representations.

Thus, the central lotus motif is reminiscent of the ritualistic *alpana*. At the same time, the irradiating petals of the *satadal padma*, or hundred-petalled lotus, also resemble the central motifs on the domed ceilings of Persian mosques. At the corners of the *Kantha* are trees-of-life similar to the trees-of-life motif in Persian carpets. *Kalkas*, or paisleys, are reminiscent of Kashmiri shawls, but they might also be drawn from the Chinese symbol of Yin and Yang, the symbol of man and woman.

Kramrisch notes how some motifs in the *Kantha* may be found in other traditions. "The symbols stored in the *Kantha* belong to the primeval images in which man beholds the universe." The solar motif, the lotus motif, the water motif and the earth motif are common to different races and different times. The lotus motif is a ubiquitous one: it ranges from China to Iran and is very much at home in India. The tree-of-life motif is as common in Iran as it is in the *Kanthas* of Bengal.

Water plays a symbolic role in almost all religions; we may note here the baptismal rites of Christianity, *Ganga-snan* or bathing in the Ganges in Hinduism, *wuzu* or ablutions in Islam. It is not surprising, then, that the water motif should be found in the *Kantha*, in the ripples of the surface of the Jessore *Kanthas*, in the fish motif, in the *lohori* design of the Rajshahi *Kantha*, in the *beki* or wave designs of the Jessore border. The sun, too, plays a part in religion: in the fire symbolism of the Zoroastrians, in the early morning prayer of Hinduism. The lotus symbol combines in itself both the sun and the water symbols.

There are also, in the *Kantha*, several motifs that we do not find elsewhere, created as they were from the environment and culture of Bengal. When the *Kantha* maker needed motifs, she looked around her and embroidered whatever she saw. But she also embroidered what she desired, not only for herself but also for the loved ones for whom she was embroidering the *Kantha*. She embroidered the *kula* or the *beri* not only because they were objects familiar to her, but because they were associated with harvests and brimming pots. She embroidered leaves and fish, not only because she lived in a green land crisscrossed with many rivers, but also because she had seen them carved on temple reliefs.

The kitchen utensils, harvesting implements, natural forms, both animal and vegetal, which find their place in the *Kantha* reflect not only the life of a people but also their hopes and aspirations.

While *Kanthas* employ motifs common to other cultures, and to all Indian art, there are some motifs that are unique only to the *Kantha* (and to the other arts which are wholly women's art). This is so because *Kanthas* are the work of women, unlike the traditional paintings or sculptures and even embroideries done all over India by men. This element may be termed the female element in the *Kantha*. Among the numerous recurrent images, for example, are also articles of daily feminine use: mirrors, combs, betel-cutters, earrings, fish cutter, a *kajal lata*, a *kula*, etc.

The toilet articles and the ear-rings are objects used by a married woman and are thus associated with the married state. From being actual articles of daily use, they become symbols of the married state, prayers for happiness in marriage. In the same way, the palanquin, a common mode of travel in the past, becomes associated with marriage. The mother embroidering a quilt for her daughter would embroider a palanquin, symbolic of the marriage palanquin that would at some juncture take her daughter to her husband's home. In one *Kantha*, it is interesting to note that there are two palanquins. A close observation will reveal that one contains a female figure, the other a male; the unknown *Kantha* artist has portrayed a marriage procession.

The *dheki* or the husking machine and the winnowing fan are not only articles used in the kitchen or the homestead; they become symbols of material and agricultural prosperity. They become prayers for plenty, for the fertility of the fields. Apart from these agricultural implements, there are motifs drawn from nature: the tree motif, creepers, and birds of different types, horses and elephants. These too are linked to the prayers for prosperity. The fish becomes a symbol of fertility. Most of these are common motifs in *Kanthas*, but sometimes a woman will portray something desired by her for herself or her husband. An example of this may be seen in a *Kantha* where there are pictures of a bicycle, an umbrella, and a hurricane lamp.

While most of these symbols are naturalistic in form - though not in colour, as colour is quite indiscriminately used, blue leaves, green fish, etc. - there are some symbols which are abstract in form. Lakshmi's footprints, for instance, while originally a detailed footprint as may still be seen in *alpana* designs, is an abstract symbol which is often used in *Kanthas*. In the same way the swastika, or *shostir chinho,* is an abstract symbol quite popular in *Kanthas*. Geometric motifs are popular in the traditional Rajshahi *Kanthas*. Most *Kanthas* have some initial pattern; none of the finest *Kanthas* proceed exactly according to a set pattern. Traditional motifs are repeated no doubt, but in an array of endless stitches, colours and shapes, and with the creator's own touch; in each piece its distinctive individuality is revealed. Perhaps that is why no two *Kanthas* are the same. Some motifs are recurrent, and a brief note on the more common ones is perhaps useful.

The Lotus Motif:- The lotus has been a popular motif from time immemorial, used by artisans and craftsmen over vast areas ranging from China in the east to Persia in the west. It is to be found in the stone columns of Asoka. It is the seat of the gods and goddesses of Hindu mythology, as well as the seat of the Buddha.

The lotus motif is associated with Hindu iconography and thus is also popular in the *Kantha*. Generally speaking, it is the divine seat, but it is also symbolic of cosmic harmony and essential womanhood.

The lotus represents the life giving powers of water but is also associated with the sun, at whose rising it expands and opens its petals, at whose setting it contracts and closes them. The lotus is a symbol of eternal order, of cosmic harmony, of the union of earth, water and sky.

The lotus is associated with purity and the goddess Lakshmi. The lotus goddess is also the goddess of good fortune. She is the presiding goddess of *dhanya* (paddy) which is wealth in India. She is the goddess of abundance. She is the goddess of the earth.

Lakshmi is embodied in the lotus, but the lotus is more than these qualities; it is also the symbol of the essential woman.

There are many forms that the lotus takes, ranging from the eight-petalled *astadal padma* to the *satadal* or hundred-petalled lotus. In the older *Kanthas* the central motif is almost always a fully bloomed lotus seen from above.

The Solar Motif:- The solar motif is intimately associated with the sun. Often the lotus and the solar motifs may be seen together in the centre of a *Kantha*. The solar motif symbolizes the life giving powers of the sun. "The sun indeed is life," says the *Arthavaveda*. The sun has been one of the first deities worshipped by the earliest peoples, and some remnants of this are still to be found in most religions. With the sun is associated fire, and not the Zoroastrians alone gave a symbolic meaning to fire. Fire plays a prominent part in Hindu rites, religious and matrimonial. For Christians Easter is a spring festival, replacing a pagan solar festival. The importance of fire and light has not completely faded. A Muslim housewife will light a fire or switch on a light as soon as it is dark.

It must, of course, be pointed out here that the solar motif, like the lotus, may have lost its religious overtones but continues to be embroidered in all *Kanthas* regardless of the religion professed by the *Kantha* maker. This is not the case with the moon motif.

The Moon Motif:- The moon motif has religious overtones which make it popular in Muslim *Kanthas*. Usually in the form of a crescent, it is often accompanied by a star. The moon motif with a star is popular in *jainamaz Kanthas*.

The Chakra or Wheel Motif:- The wheel is a recurring symbol in Indian art, both Hindu and Buddhist. It is a symbol of order; "As spokes in the centre of a wheel, everything is established in life," says the *Upanishads*. The world is described as a wheel.

The wheel is a popular motif in *Kanthas*, even when the *Kantha* maker has forgotten what the symbol represents. Its popularity is also partly due to the ease of its embroidery. With the *Kantha* maker simply working in *chatai* around the motif, the design is quickly completed.

The Swastika Motif:- As a motif in Indian art, the swastika dates back to the Indus Valley civilization. Seals from Mohenjodaro have been found inscribed with this motif. It is, to most who embroider it, an auspicious sign, a symbol of good fortune.

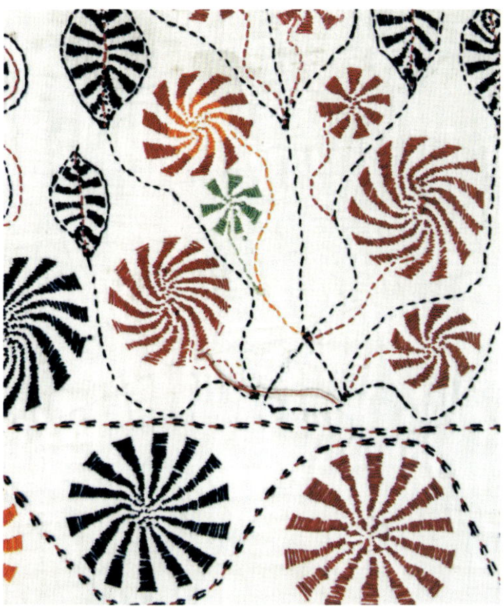

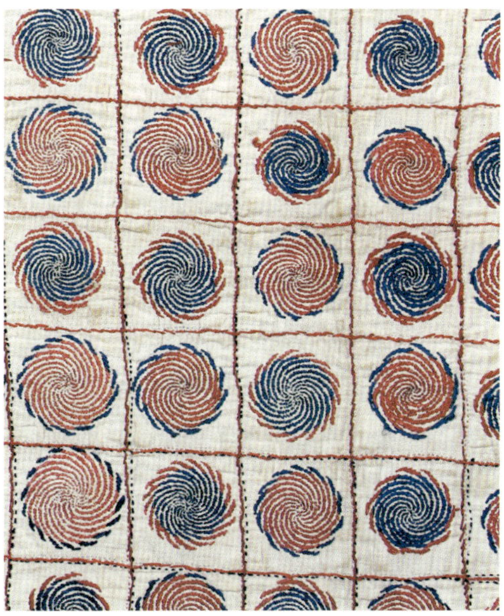

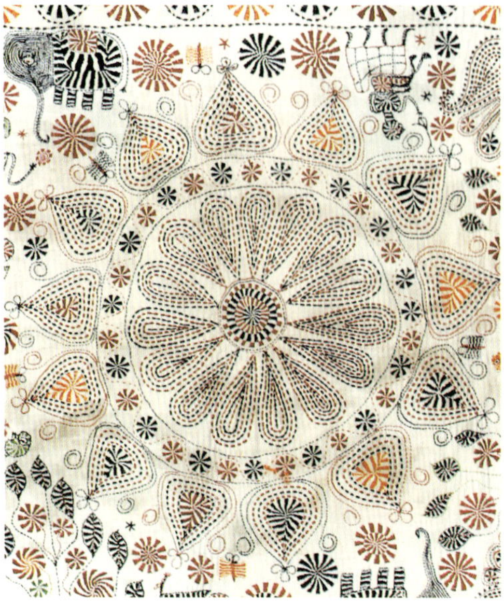
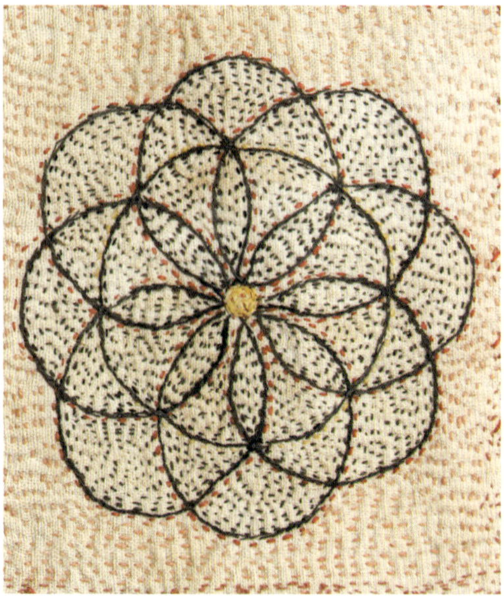
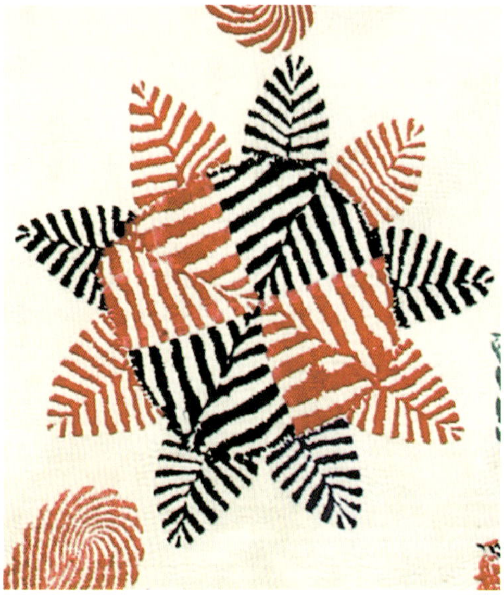
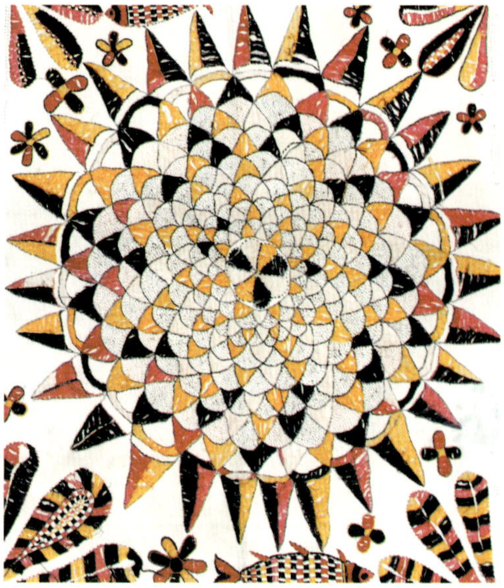
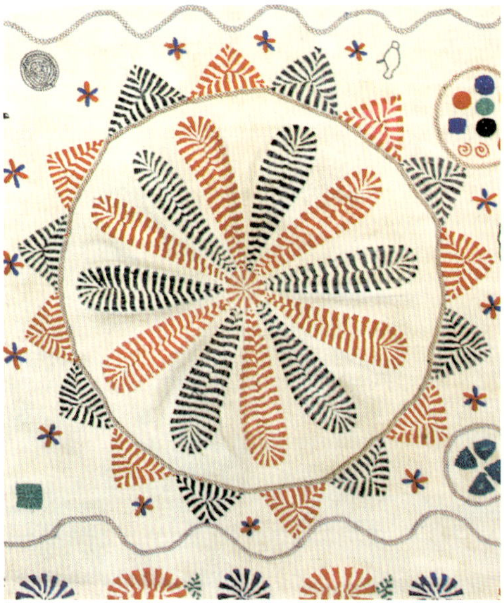
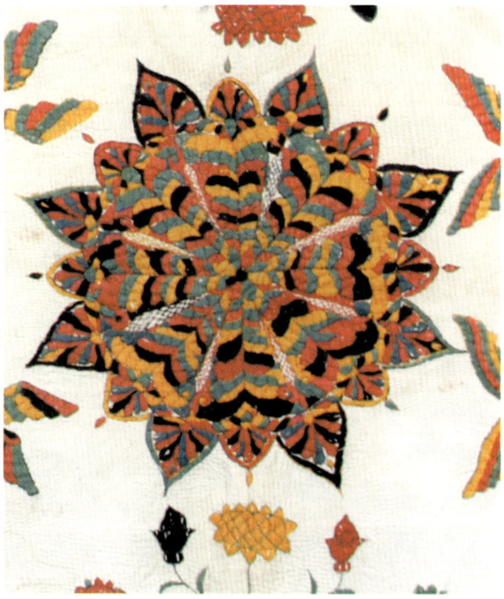

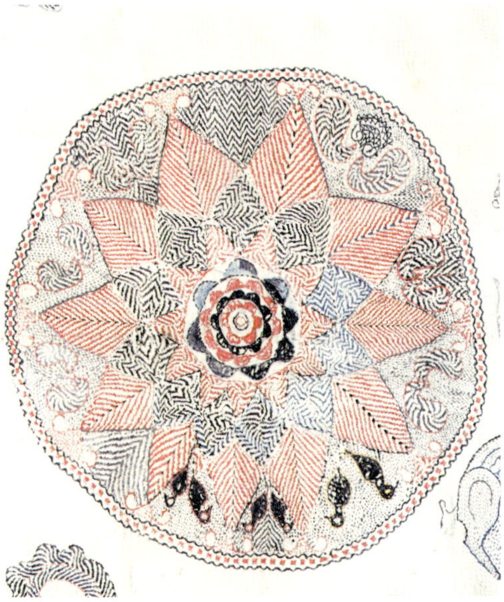
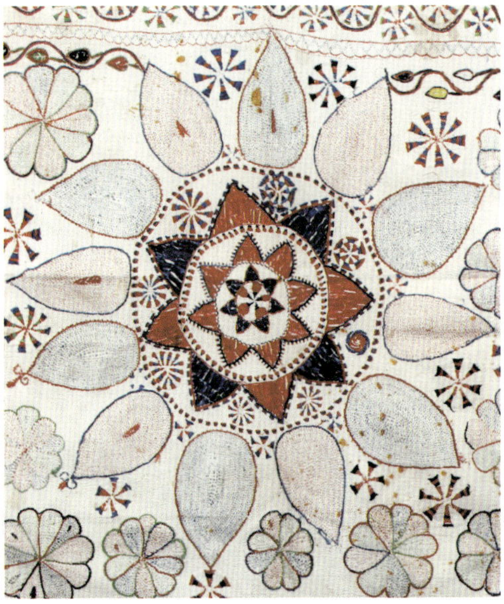
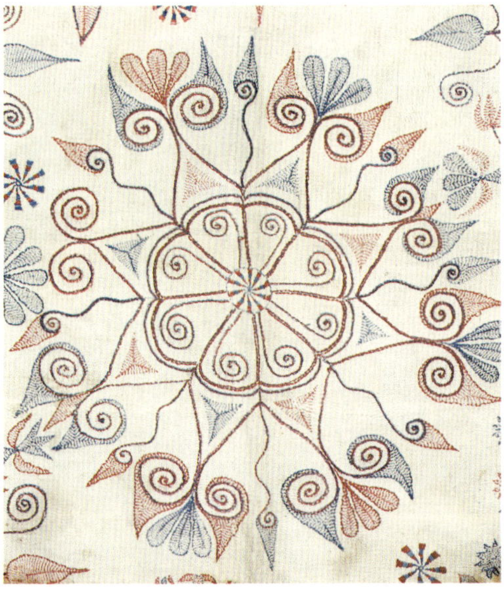
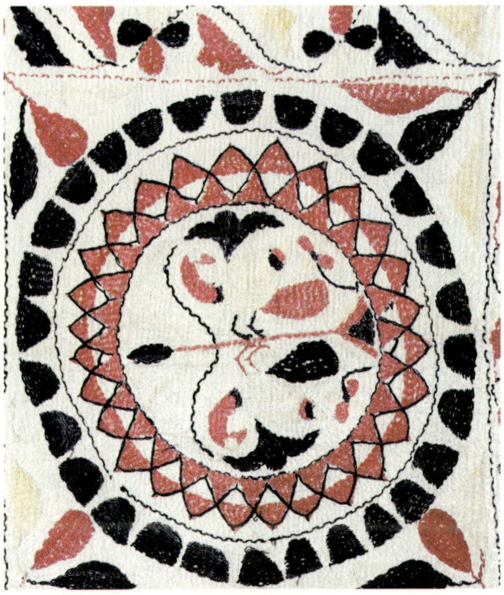
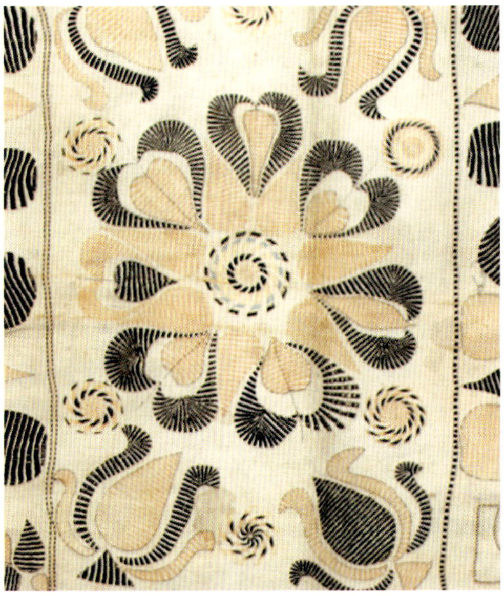
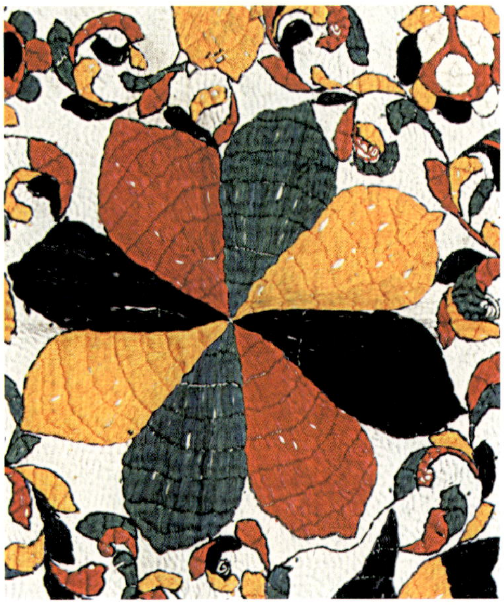

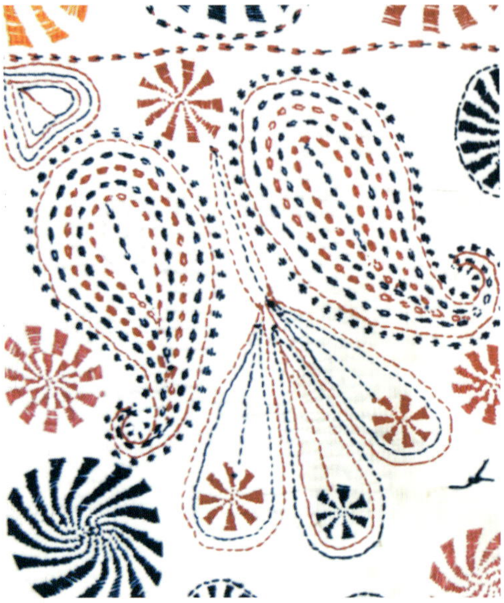
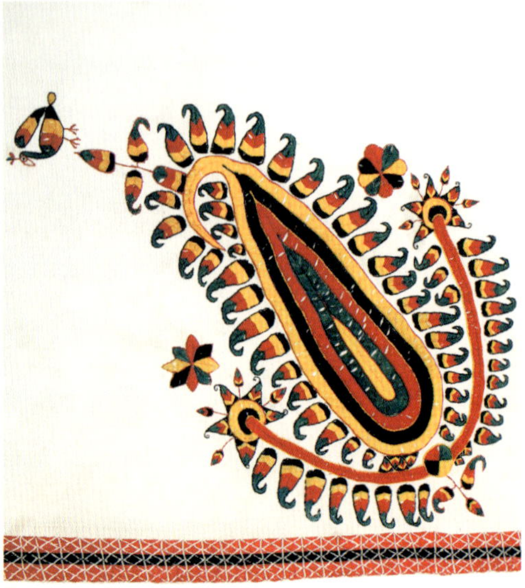
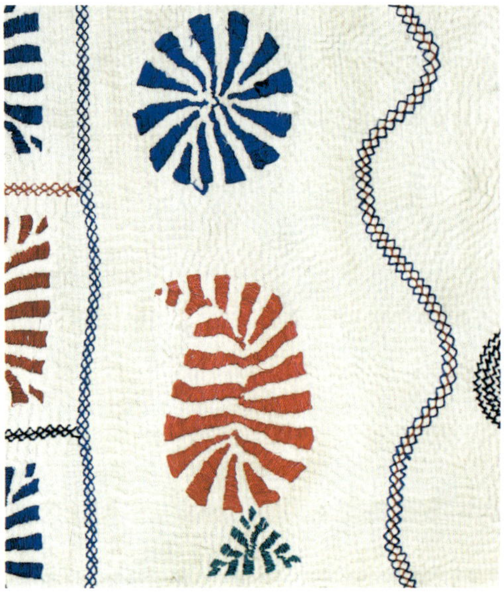
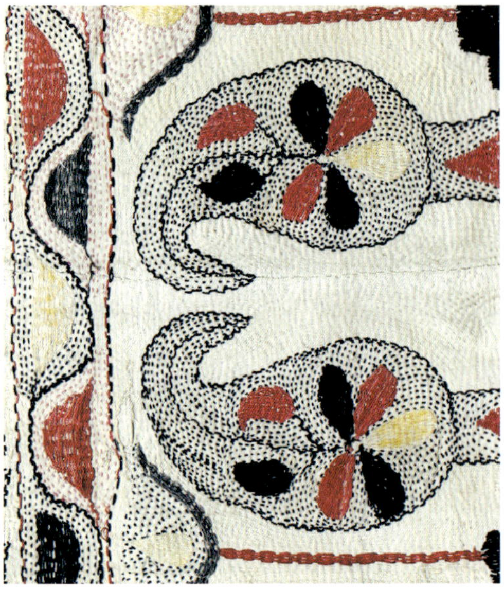
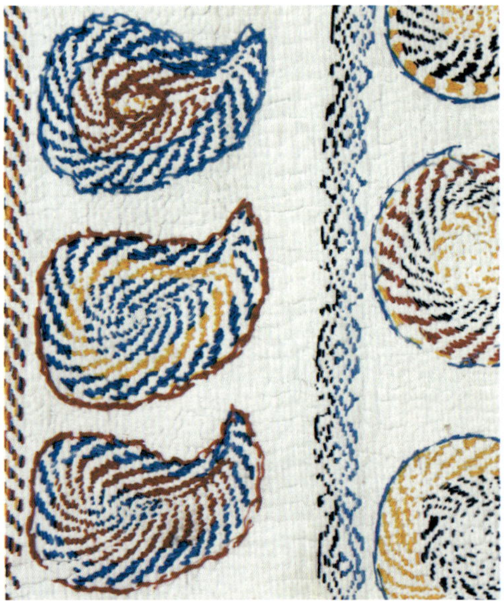
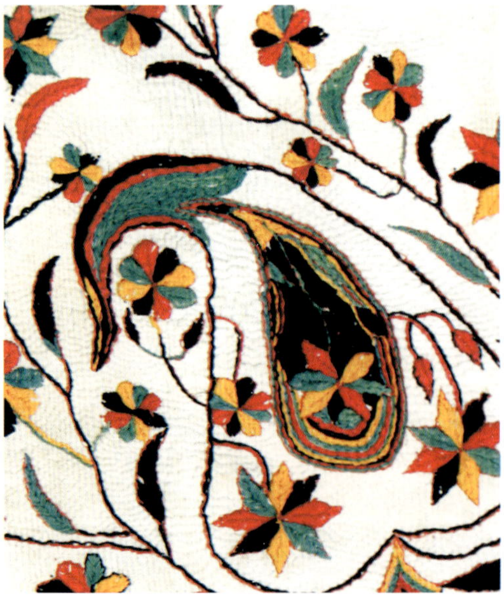

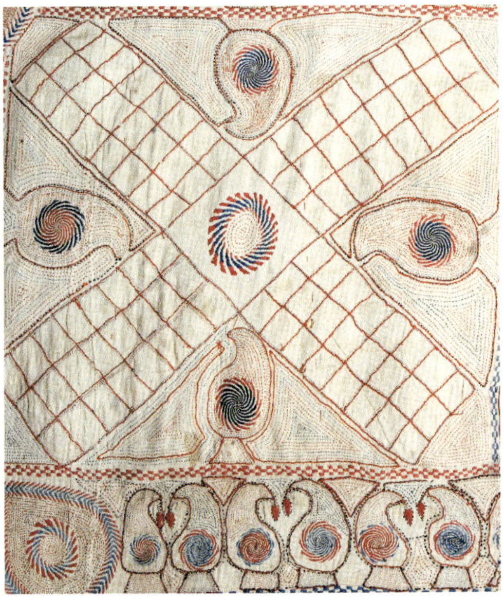
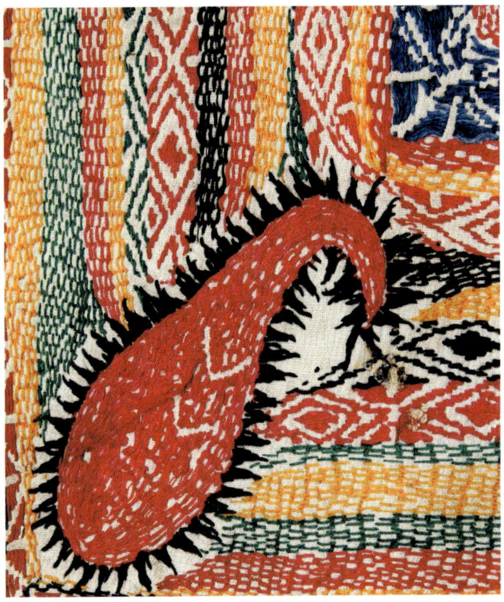
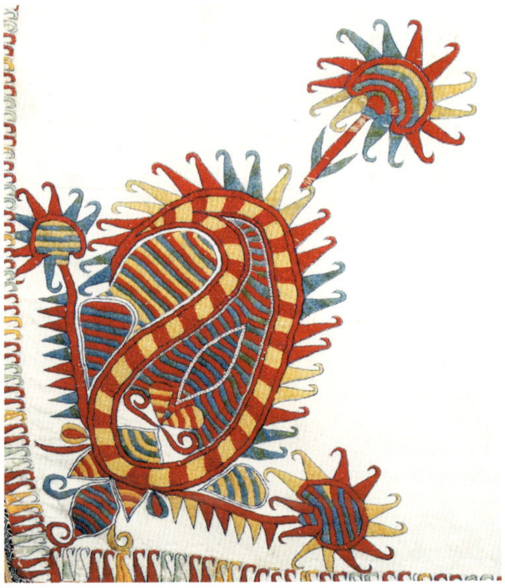
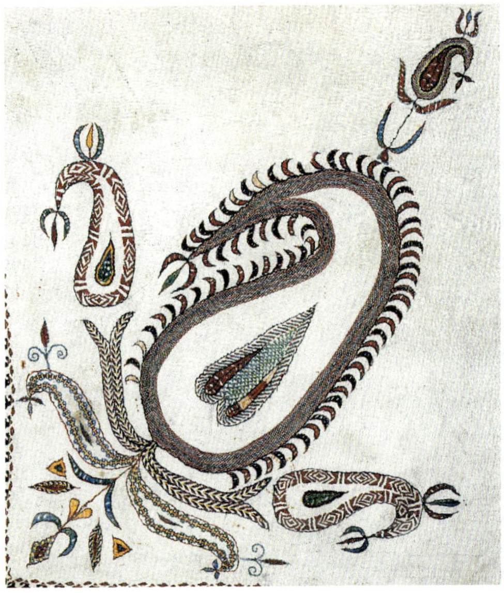
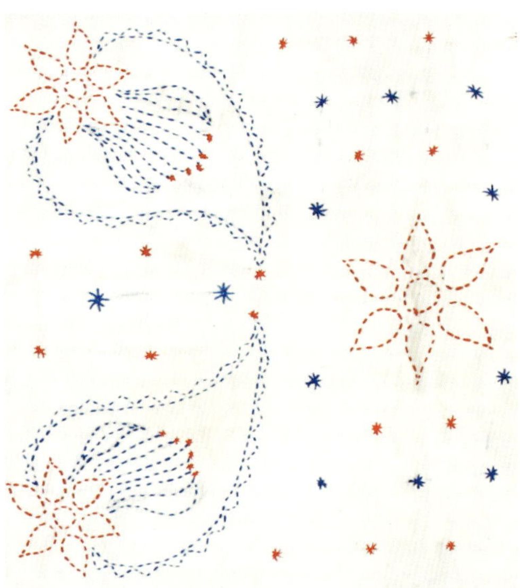
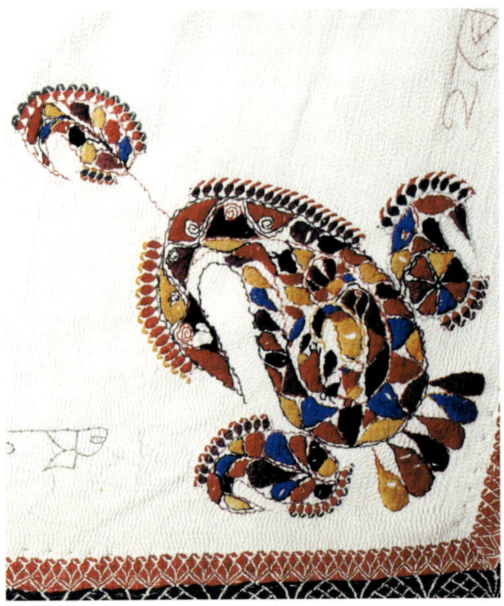

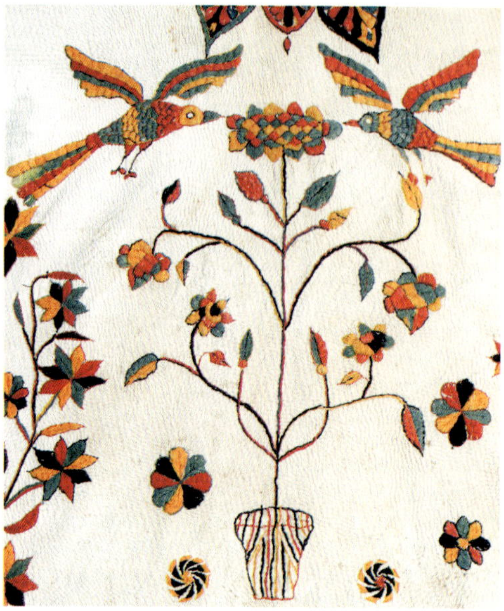 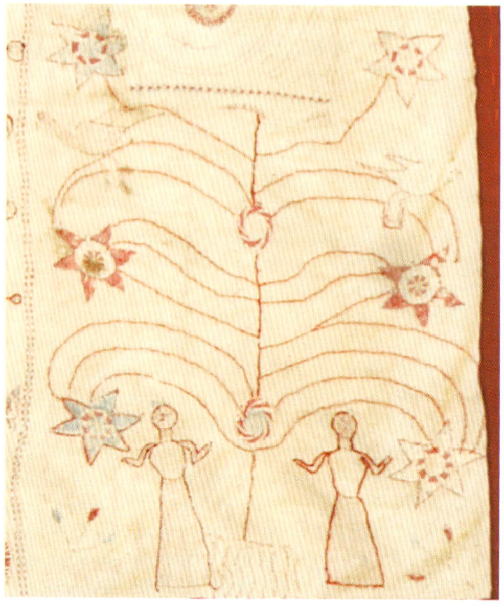

The Tree-of-Life Motif (Jeevan Briksha):- This motif may also be traced back to the Indus Valley civilization. The Indus valley culture has contributed certain permanent elements to Indian culture and art.

Even in Buddhist times this cult of trees continued, with the *pipal* being sacred to the Buddha because of the enlightenment he received in its shade. The tree-of-life motif is not exclusive to Indian art, as a glance westwards into Persian art reveals the presence of this motif in the earliest known periods.

In the *Kanthas*, as in the *alpanas,* this motif appears with great frequency. Often it is replaced by a *kalka* or a leaf motif. It is usually to be found in the four corners, representing the four directions.

The tree-of-life motif suggests the fecundity of nature and is therefore popular in an agrarian society dependent on nature. Vegetation has been associated with human fertility since time immemorial. In Indian sculptures may be seen closely entwined bodies of trees and women, as well as representations of trees sprouting from women's navels. In symbolic rites women were married to trees. In Bengal the association of fertility and trees may be seen even today. In the *lagan* ceremony, a banana sapling is still given a prominent place, not only in marriages that take place in the countryside, but also in towns.

Vines and creepers play an important part in both *alpanas* and *Kanthas*. They contain the same symbolism as that of the tree-of-life. *Pan* or betel leaves are one of the items carried with the gifts to the bride's house. Marriage *alpanas* include leaf and vine motifs as in the *Mangal charaner alpana.* In *Kanthas*, too, the betel leaf or the *pipal* leaf is often to be found, either attached to undulating vines or in single motifs. A popular non-geometrical motif of the Rajshahi *lohori* is the betel leaf.

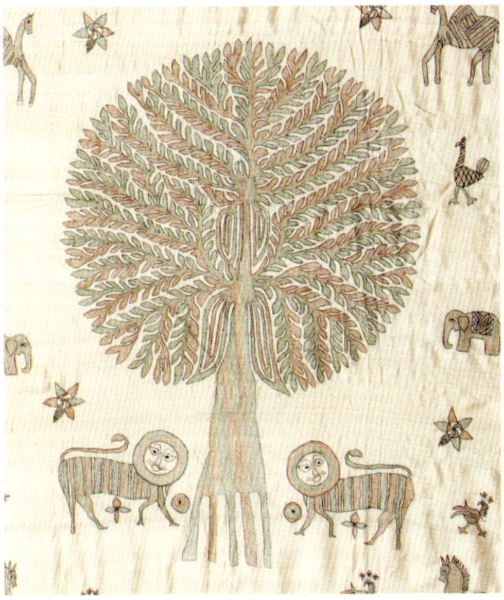
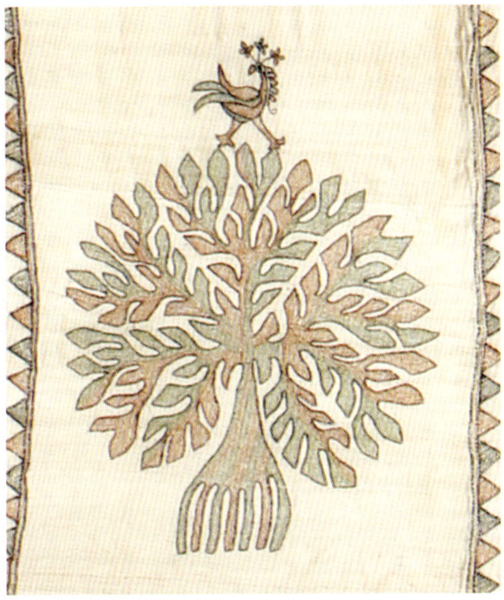
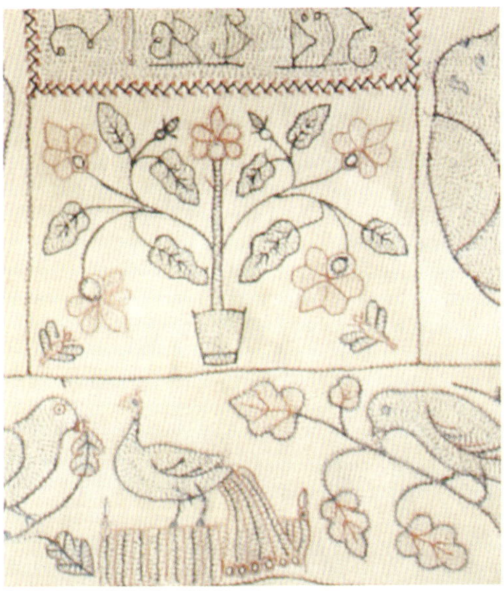
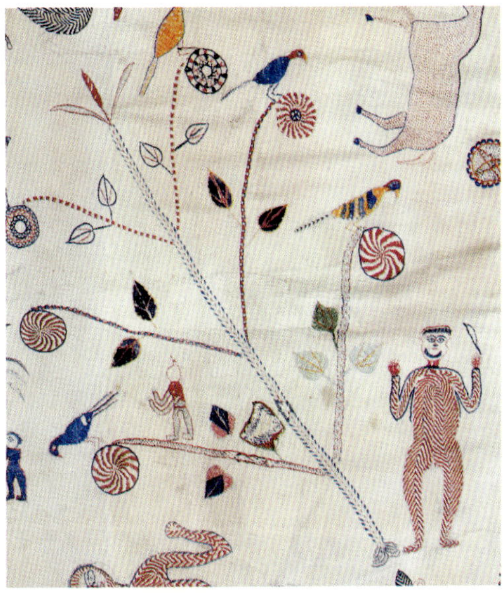
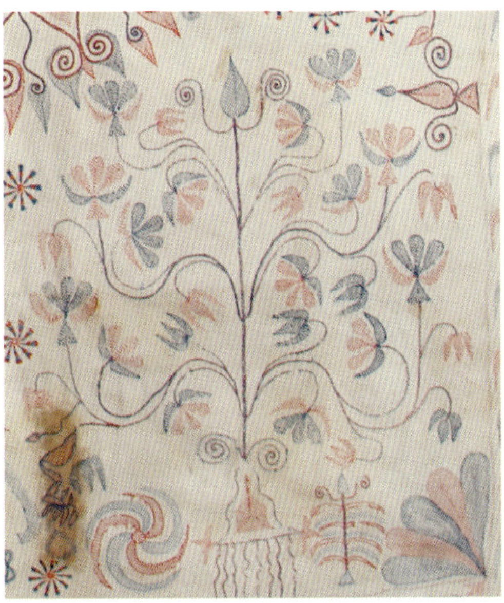
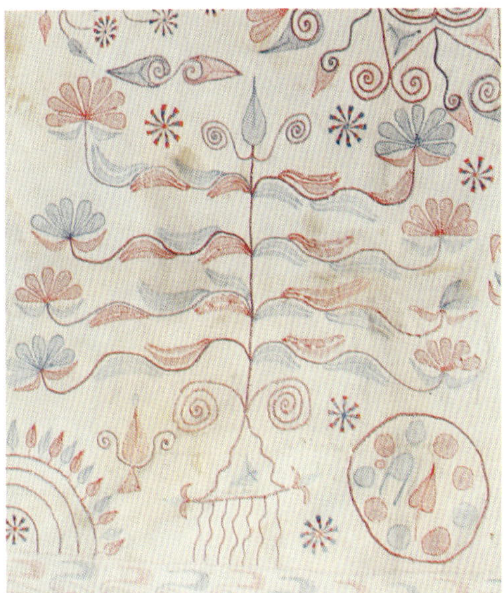

The Kalka Motif:- This is a latter-day motif, dating from the Mughal times. It has, however, become very popular in the *Kantha*. Its origins have been variously ascribed. It has been associated with pine trees, the curve representing the windswept pine tops. It has been compared to a stylized leaf; it has been compared to a mango, whose shape it resembles. Its similarity with a flame has been pointed out. It is also similar to half the Chinese symbol of Yin and Yang, representing the union of man and woman.

The *kalka* is an attractive motif and lends itself to a variety of treatments. It can be worked in *chatai* or *kaitya,* blending in with the other motifs done in a traditional stitch. But often the embroidery of the *kalka* reminds us of its ancestry. For example, it is embroidered with flowers, much in the tradition of Kashmiri shawls. Often the stitch employed is also the Kashmiri stitch.

The Water Motif:- This is an almost universal motif and is to be found in the *Kantha* as well. This motif may be found in several patterns. The rippled field of the *Kantha* surface itself symbolizes the rippled surface of water. Borders symbolic of waves such as the *beki* and the *sagar* or *shamuk taga* are popular in Jessore and Jamalpur *Kanthas*. The Rajshahi *Kanthas* are called *lohori* after the wave motif. Apart from these motifs, there are other motifs associated with water: the boat, the fish, and the lotus.

The Mountain Motif:- Mountain forms are suggested in both the *lohori* and the *kautar khupi* motifs. In some Rangpur and Jamalpur *Kanthas* as well, the division of the field of the *Kantha* into diamonds and triangles is suggestive of the mountain. The mountain is a symbol of the contact of earth and heaven.

The Fish Motif:- Fish figure prominently in marriage rites in Bengal. At the *lagan* ceremony, one of the main gifts taken to the bride's house is a large fish. The fish motif appears in both marriage *alpanas* as well as in the *Kantha.*

The reason for the popularity of the fish motif is not only its popularity as an article of food in a land of rivers, but also its fecundity. In an agricultural land, many sons are prayed for, and the fish symbolizes this prayer.

The fish portrayed in the *Kanthas* is often a simply drawn fish, but occasionally its appearance is that of the *makara* associated with the statues of religious deities. Thus, apart from being a symbol of fecundity, the fish motif also becomes an auspicious sign, a sign of prosperity.

The Boat Motif:- The boat is another popular motif in *Kanthas*. It is not surprising that it should be so in a land crisscrossed by many rivers. But the boat becomes more than a depiction of a normal mode of travel; it becomes associated with all journeys from home. Thus, in the *Bhaduli brata alpana,* a prayer for the safety of one's menfolk, the boat figures prominently.

The drawing of a boat in the *alpana* and the embroidering of it in the *Kantha* would ensure safe journeys for the men one loved, father, husband, son.

After the *Kantha* revival, one particular boat motif seems to have become very popular: the *mayur pankhi* or peacock-rowed boat. Designed for a *Kantha* of Sonargaon, this motif has been reproduced in countless wall-hangings.

The Footprint Motif:- This is a common motif in Buddhist art, with footprints representing the footprints of the Buddha. In *alpanas* and *Kanthas*, however, the footprints become symbolic of the goddess Lakshmi. The symbol has, however, become a traditional one, and continues to be embroidered even when the motif has lost all similarity with a footprint.

The Rath **Motif:-** The *rath* is associated with Vishnu or Jagannath. It is considered an auspicious sign. It is a popular motif in *Kanthas*, especially in those embroidered by Hindu women. Some of these *raths* are very elaborately made, with images of deities and with flags flying. In several, however, the representations hardly resemble a *rath*. Where the resemblance hardly exists, it is perhaps because the *Kantha* artist embroidering the motif is only dimly aware of what she is portraying. She has perhaps seen this motif in a *Kantha* and merely copies what she has seen.

The Mosque Motif:- This motif figures prominently in *jainamaz Kanthas*, occurring towards the upper portion of the *Kantha* where the forehead touches the ground in *sijda*. It occasionally occurs in larger *Kanthas* as well.

Agricultural Implements:- The *kula* and *sickle* are motifs common to many *Kanthas*. In an agrarian society, these implements are part of every household. But again, these implements become symbolic, being associated with harvests. They stand for the abundance of the fields, for the prosperity of the household.

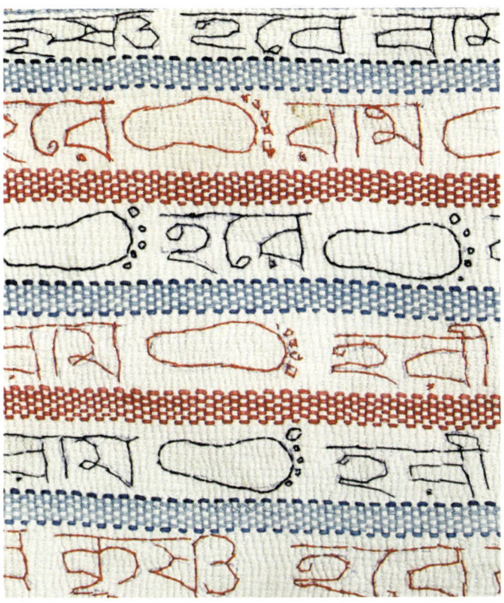

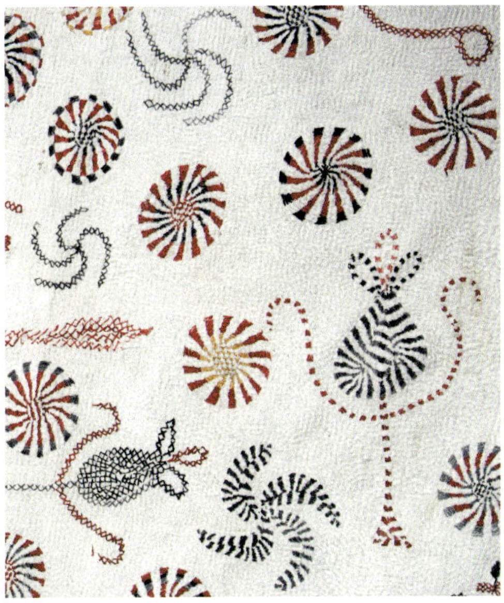

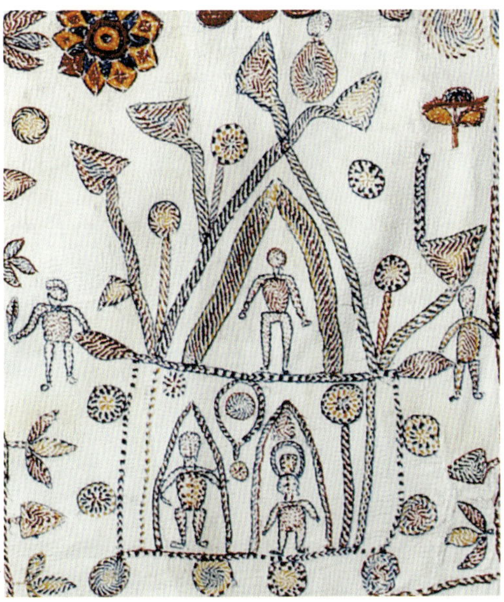

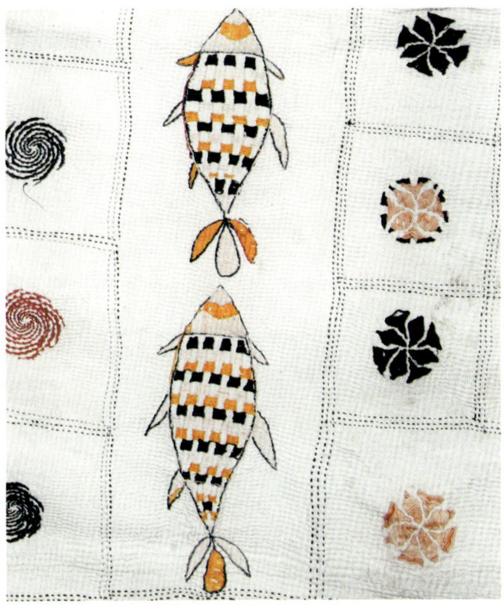

Animal Motifs:- Elephants, horses, peacocks, deer, tigers and monkeys figure in several *Kanthas*. Part of the reason for the popularity of these motifs is, of course, the presence of these animals in a land where animals still dwell in the forests. But more than being chance-met animals, many of them become symbolic motifs in the *Kantha*. The elephant and the peacock become symbols of material prosperity. Its presence in the *Kanthas* therefore is suggestive of the receptive mind of the *Kantha* maker, ready to absorb everything.

The peacock would, however, suggest the aristocracy who could afford to procure these North Indian birds. Thus, the peacock, like the elephant, would suggest material wealth. The tiger in the *Kantha* is often part of a hunting scene; thus, it is under the power of the hunter as well as of the woman who embroidered the *Kantha*.

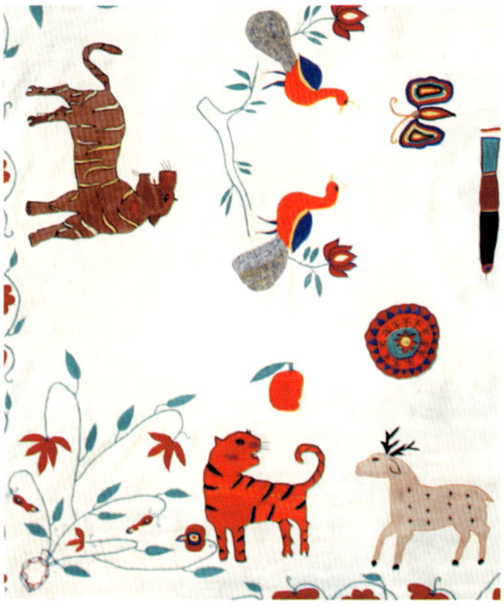

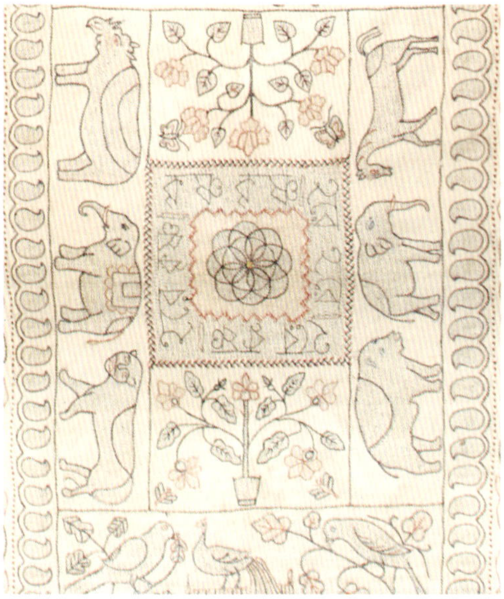

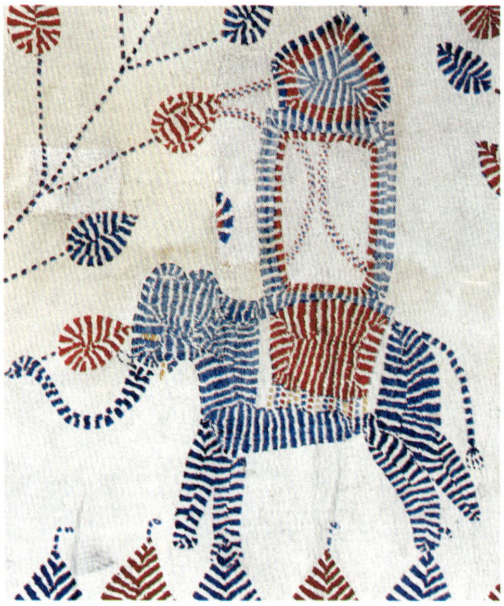

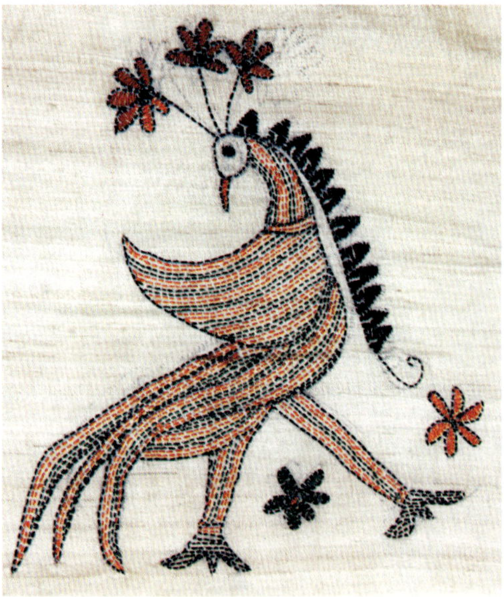

Toilet Articles:- Mirrors, combs, earrings, a *surma dani* – a container for antimony used as an eye-liner - figure prominently in large *Kanthas* as well as in *arshilata*. They are articles desired by women for themselves, but they also become symbolic of personal beauty and marital status.

Kitchen Implements:- The *beri-* tongs, the *bothi-* the curving floor knife, the *jati* or betel cutter are other *Kantha* motifs. Apart from being common household items, they represent abundance. They are symbolic of brimming cooking pots and plenty of food in the kitchen. The *jati,* for example, contains the hope that the person who uses the *Kantha* will have plenty of betel nuts to cut, and plenty of betel leaves to eat with them.

The Kantha Motif:- The *Kantha*, too, occurs as a motif in *Kanthas*. Occasionally it is a simply embroidered article, but often it is elaborately embroidered with a number of motifs. In this case the embroidered *Kantha* motif becomes a symbol of marriage.

The Palanquin Motif:- The palanquin is another traditional *Kantha* motif. Not only does it represent the mode of transport of the past, but is also associated with marriage, the bride being generally carried in it. The palanquin thus also becomes a symbol of marriage.

Apart from these traditional motifs in the *Kantha*, almost all of which tell us about the life of the people and their hopes and fears, there were several other motifs that the *Kantha* maker embroidered into her *Kantha*. Whatever she saw, she embroidered into it.

Reference: (Basak, 2007, p 46, 87, 89); (Dhamija, 2004, p 136); (Sethi, 2012, p 29, 31, 32, 141, 143, 144); (Vatsyayan, 2010, p 74, 75); (Zaman, 2004, p 64-93, 94, 95)

Present Day Scenario of Kantha Embroidery

The ever changing political scenario and the partition of Bengal brought many changes in the *Kantha* and the life of the *Kantha* maker. With the passage of time and its revival, it has ceased to be an essential part of a Bengali household as it used to be. The *Kantha*, from a simple stitch, has morphed into a fashion statement. In the mid 20th century, it has been re-introduced in a more vibrant and market-friendly form, which has brought economic independence and empowerment to thousands of poor Bengali women. Today, it enjoys the status of an art object rather than an article of utility. With brighter commercial prospects it has now broken its barriers and found a place in each household, not only country-wide but across the world. To the traditional red, blue, black threads green, magenta, mustard-yellow, and orange threads have been added. This new form can be seen in artistically embroidered garments (saris, salwar-kameez, odhanis, shawls, stoles, jackets etc), accessories, and other items (bags, purses, file folders, pen cases, etc.) that have replaced patched garments and spreads or coverlets in popularity. The *Kantha* is now a fashionable textile, embraced by style conscious urban women. *Kantha* embroiderers have introduced new fabrics (silk, wool, and cotton), silk threads, and an array of floral, geometric, and figurative patterns and designs in response to the tastes and demands of new patrons. One of the earliest forms of embroidery in India, the *Kantha* has been transformed from an ascetic's patched garment employing the simple darning stitch into a modern and fashionable attire for urban Indians.

Reference: (Sethi, 2012, p 57, 76, 94, 105, 117, 181)

IGNCA collection

Bed Cover

Acc. No. IV/1C971/JS-KAN-1

Rectangular bedcover with lining, embroidered in *Kantha* stitch with a large tree in the centre and smaller trees on all four sides. Each tree has stylized roots. The roots of larger trees are flanked by two mythical lions.

Each small tree is surmounted by a mythical stylized bird having three flowers on its head. The central big tree has two stars on two sides and one in the centre, which is flanked by two mythical lions. The rest of the field has peacocks, camels, hens, elephants, horses, and mythical birds with stars in between.

There are two enclosures comprising of line and triangular motifs. Colours used are green, red, and black.

Material - Tussar

Condition - Stable

Size - 270cmx224cm

Period - 21st Century

Place - West Bengal

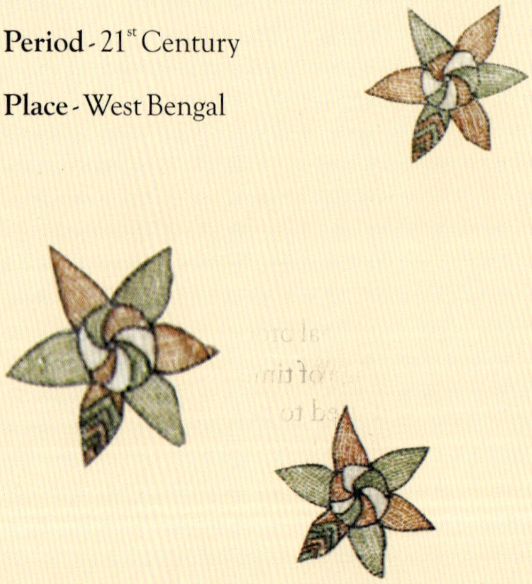

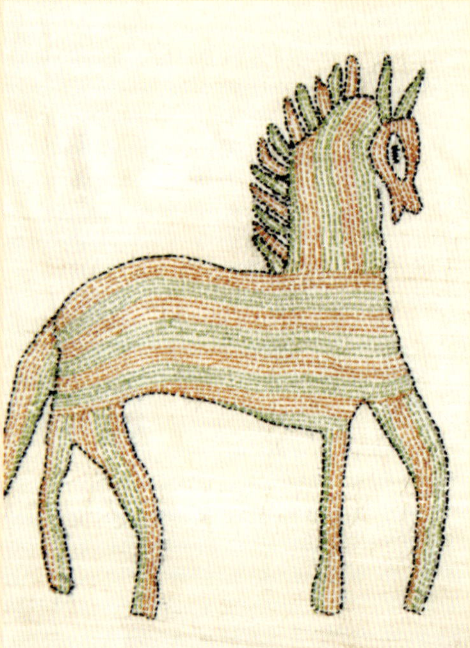

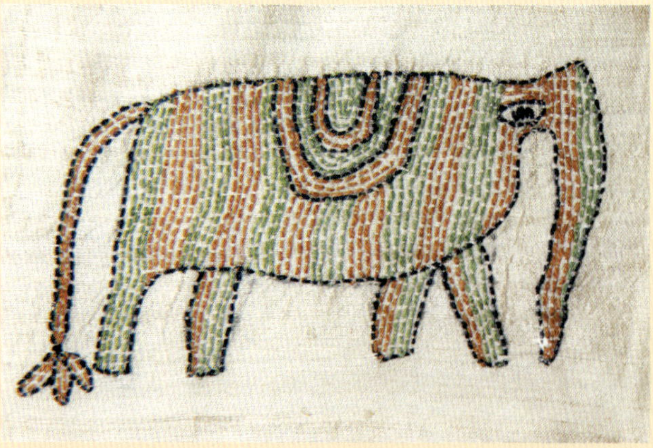

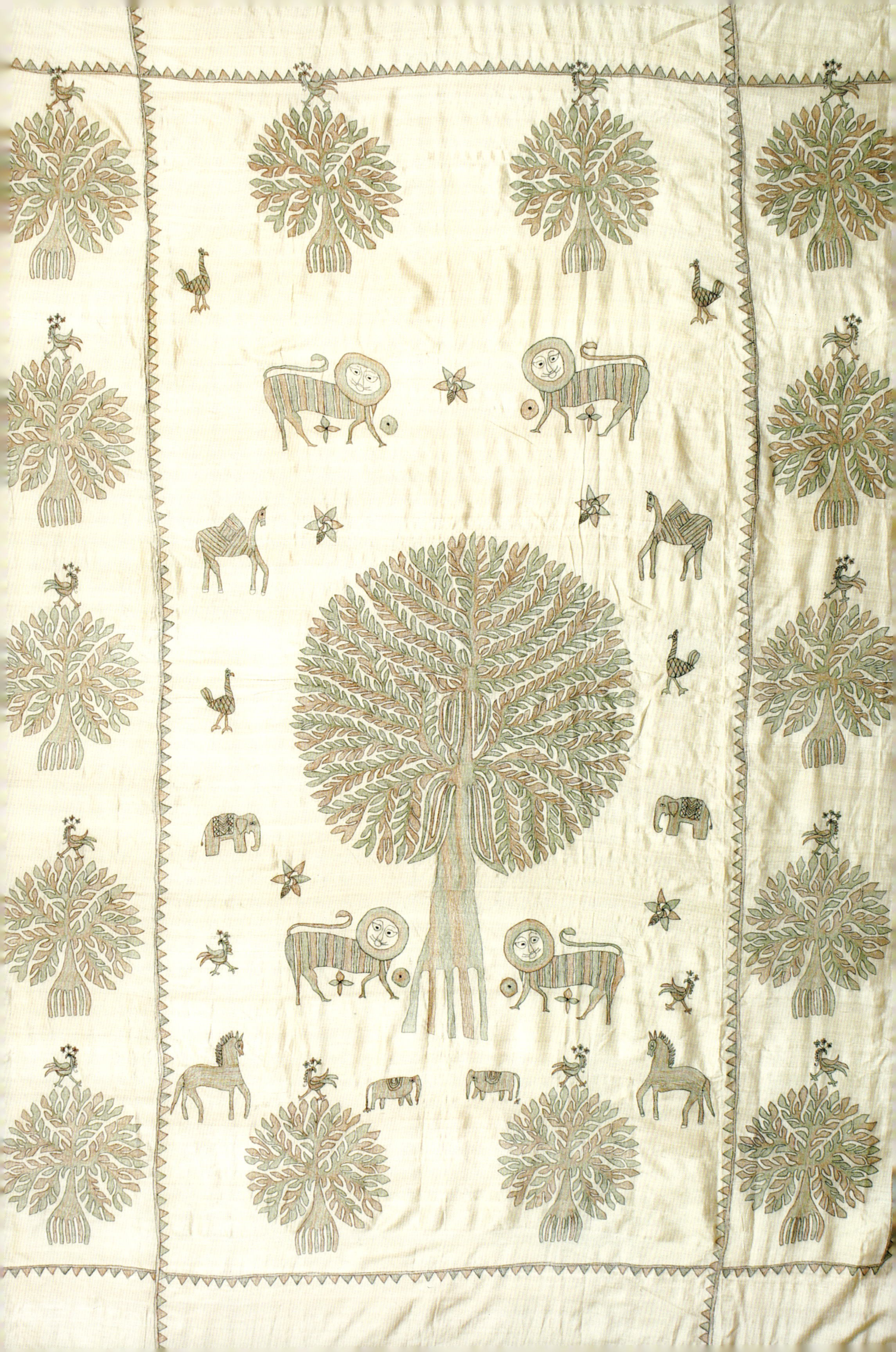

Bed Cover

Acc. No. IV/1C971/JS-KAN -1 (CONTD)

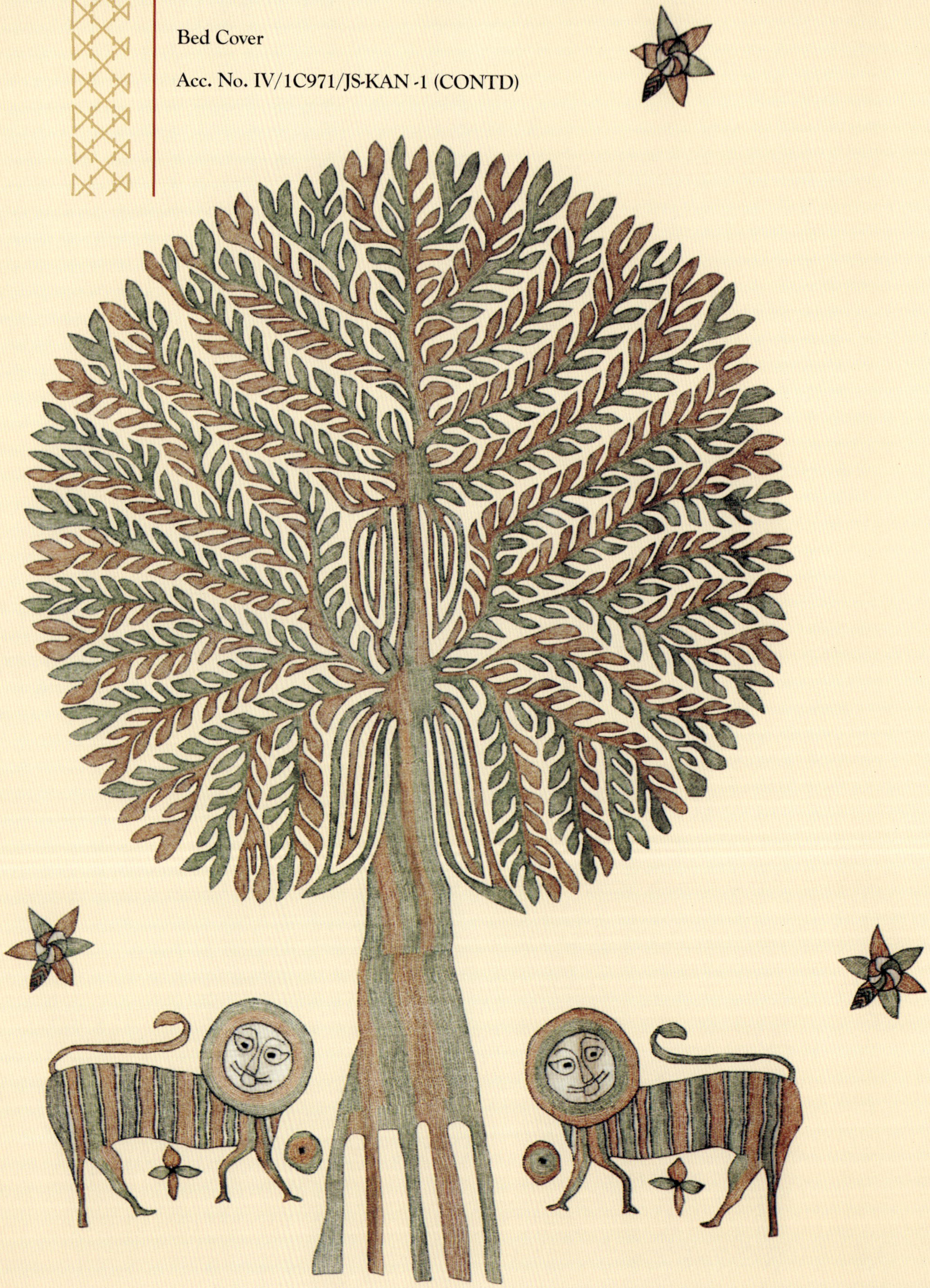

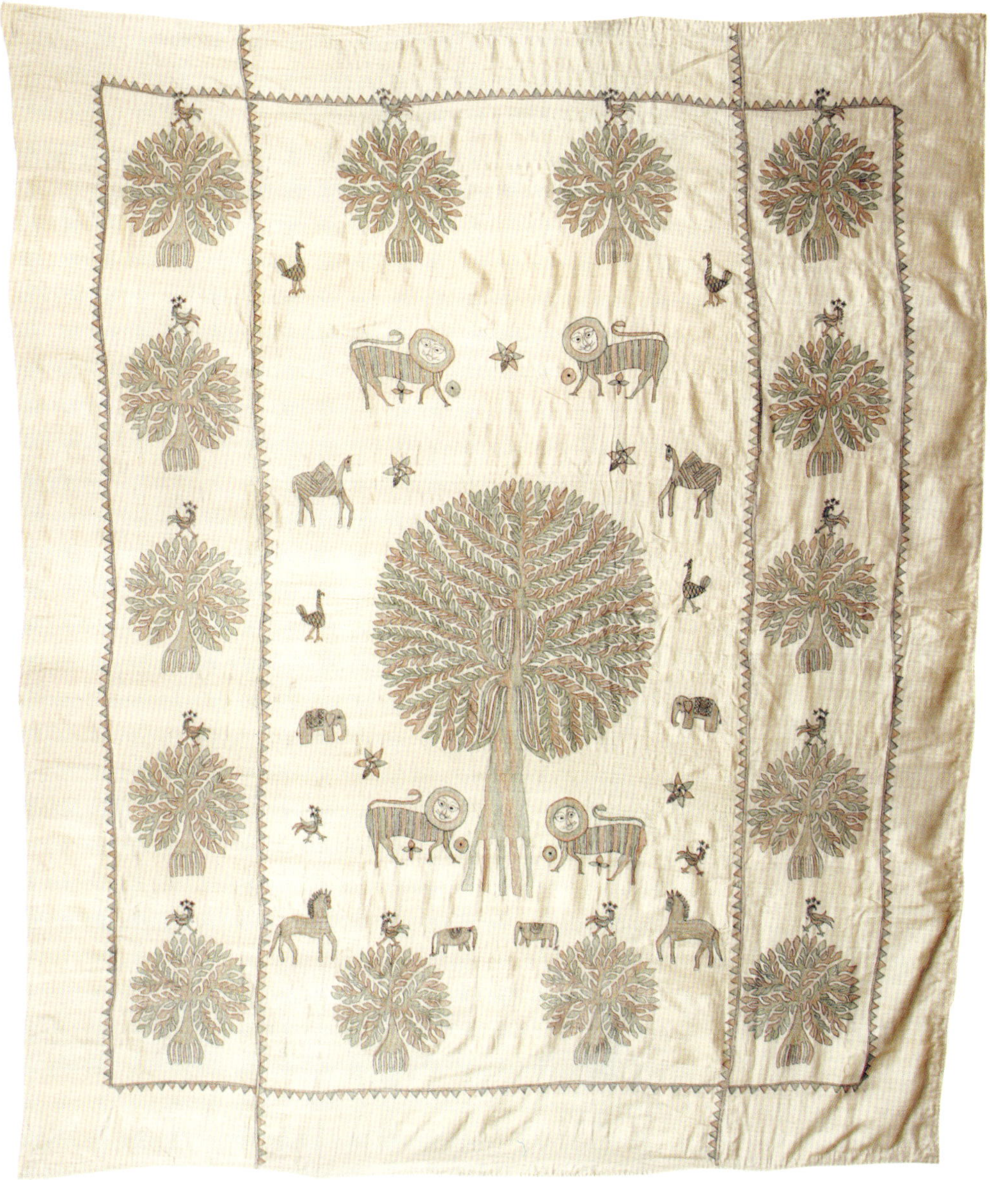

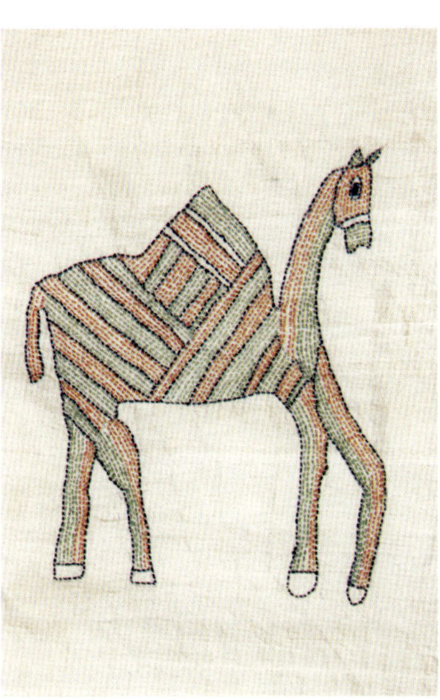

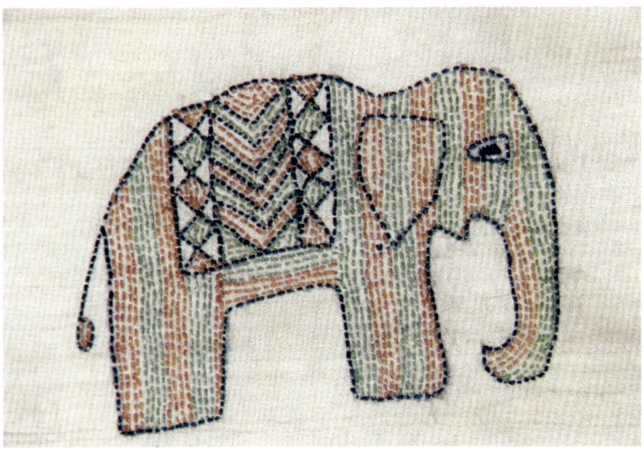

Bed Cover (King Size)

Acc. No. IV/1C971/JS-KAN-2

Big rectangular bed cover (king size) with lining embroidered in *Kantha* stitches. There is a big stylized tree in the centre, having fourteen small trees on all four sides. Each tree, small and big, is surmounted by a pair of sparrows. Each tree, big and small, is enclosed with triangular motifs. The roots of all trees are stylized and the roots of the central tree are flanked by two elephants.

There are six stylized large birds on the side of the big central tree. Each bird has three flowers on its head and triangular creepers on the back. Small sparrows are also embroidered in between the large birds.

Colours used are black, red, green, and rust.

Material - Tussar

Condition - Good

Size - 271cmx222cm

Period - 21st Century

Place - West Bengal

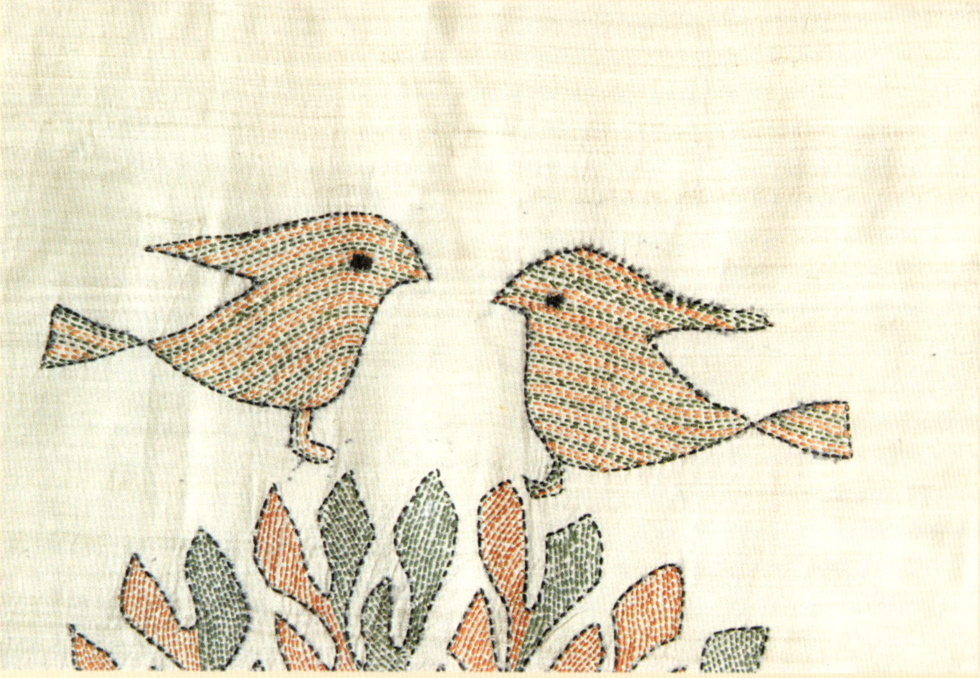

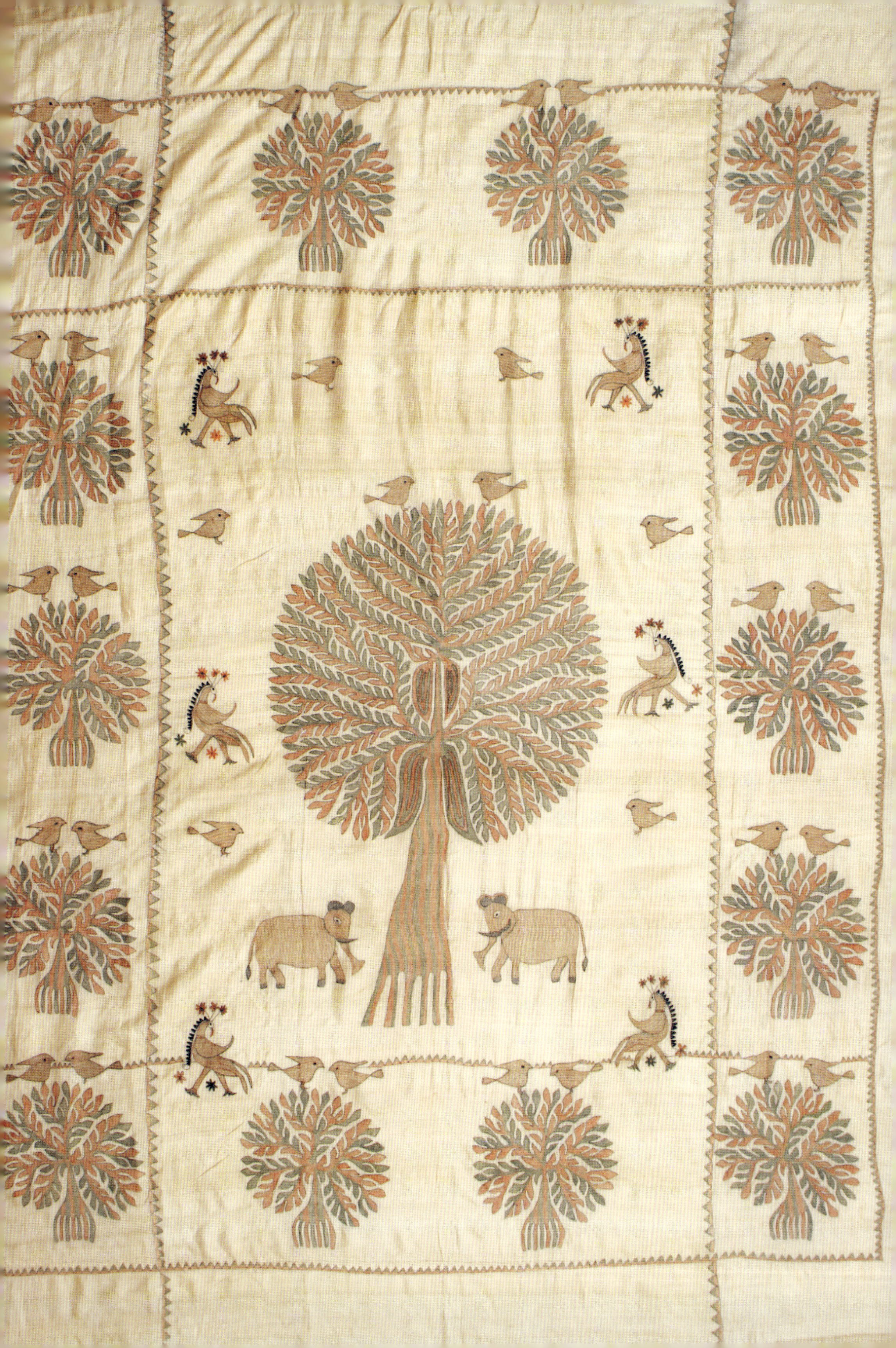

Bed Cover (King Size)

Acc. No. IV/1C971/JS-KAN-2 (CONTD)

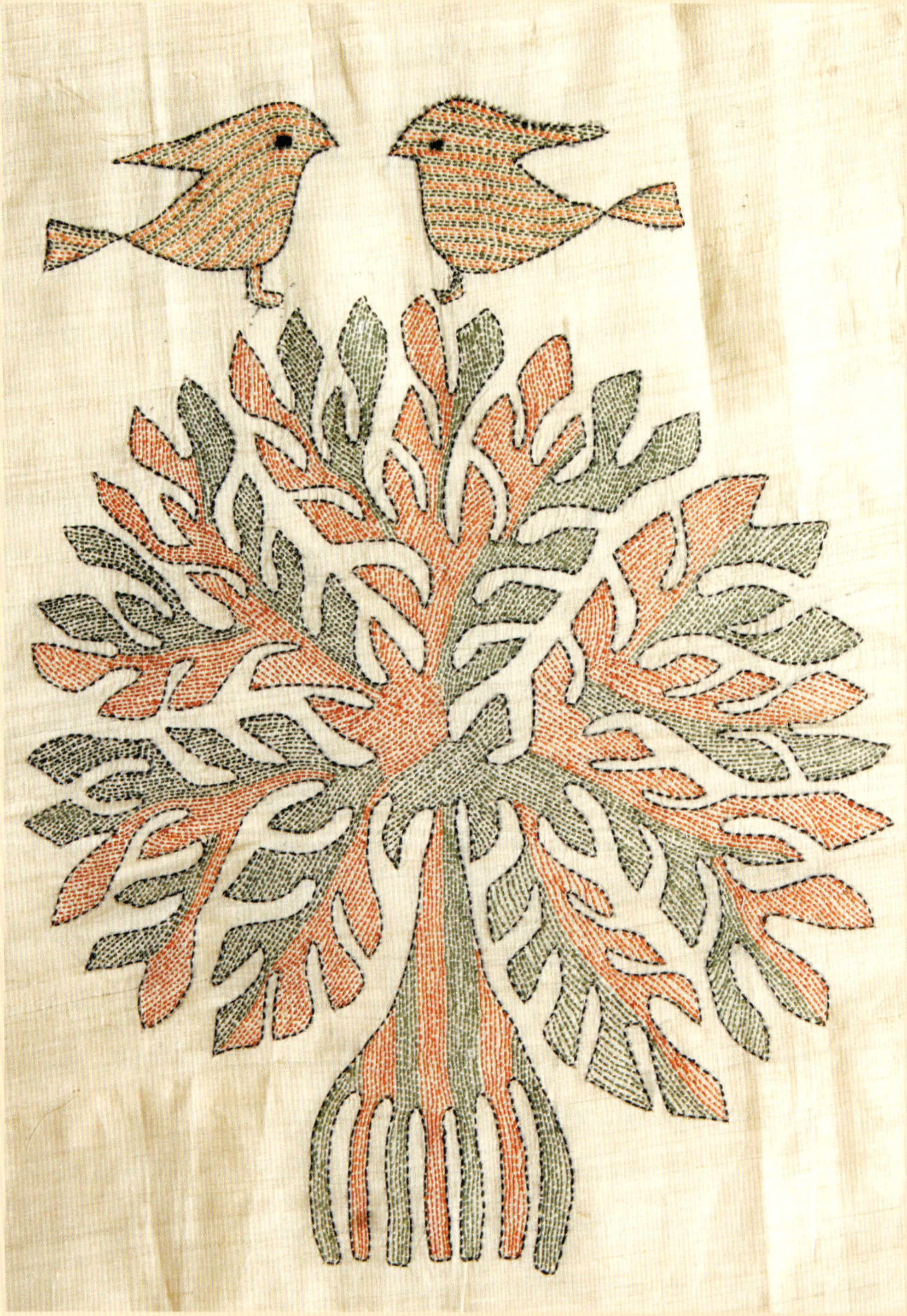

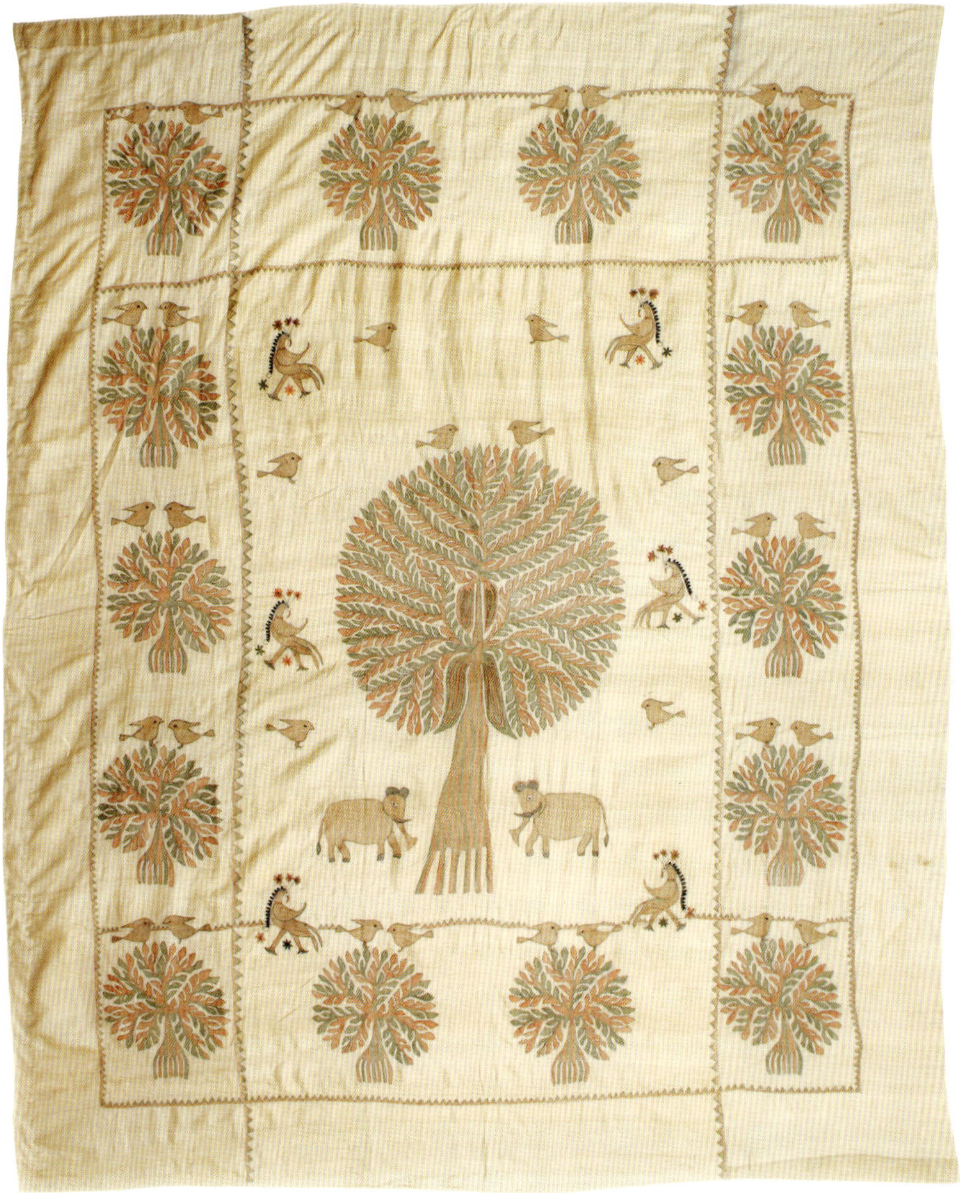

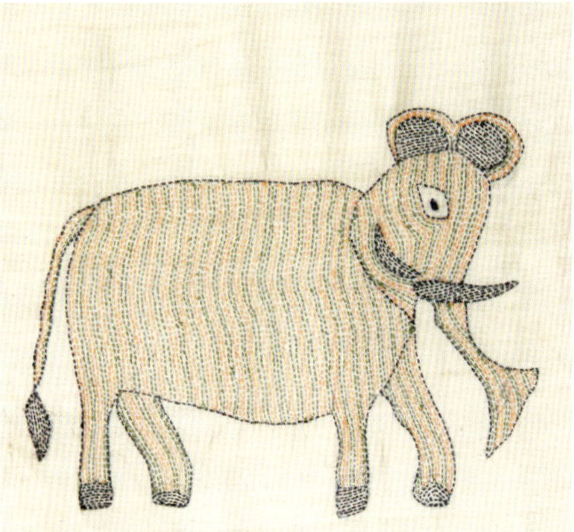

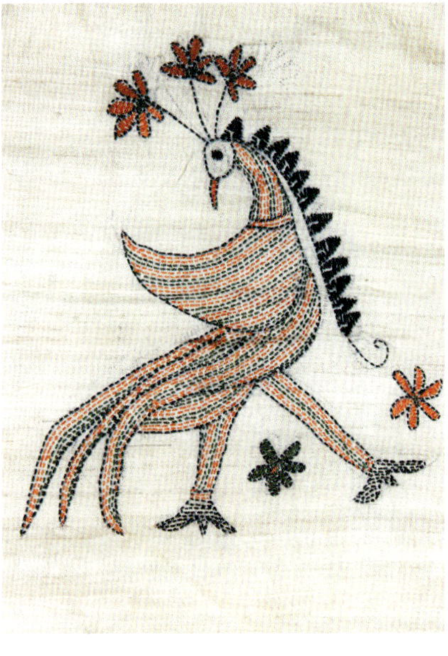

Kantha

Acc. No. IV/1C971/JS-KAN-3

Square *Kantha* having a stylized lotus in two circles in the centre, which again has a small circle inside, decorated with wheel like motif and embroidered in *chatai* (mat) like pattern. In between the two circles around the lotus, there are small wheels embroidered at equal distances, and around the outer circle there are a number of stylized betel leaves each having trefoil patterns on top and spiral motifs on either side.

There are two *kalkas* surmounted by three long and rounded leaves in each of the four corners.

Around the lotus, there are four *Butas* with wheels, elephants, standing and sitting human figures, peacocks, bees and *shosti chinha* scattered over the entire field.

There are two borders in which the inner one has wheel motifs in between the curved line, while the outer border is made with an old saree added to it.

Colours used in embroidery are red, blue, yellow, black and green.

Material - Cotton

Condition - Stained

Size - 110cmx92cm

Period - Late 20th Century

Place - West Bengal

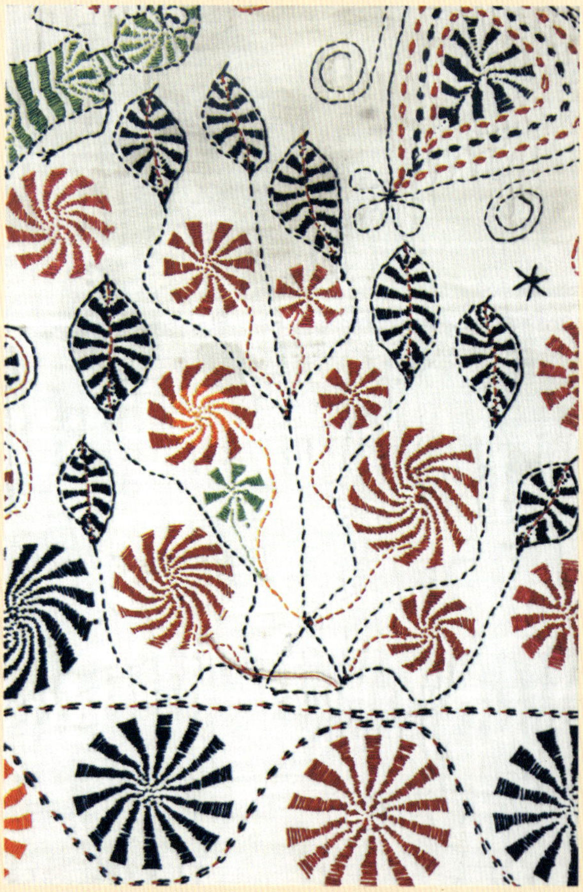

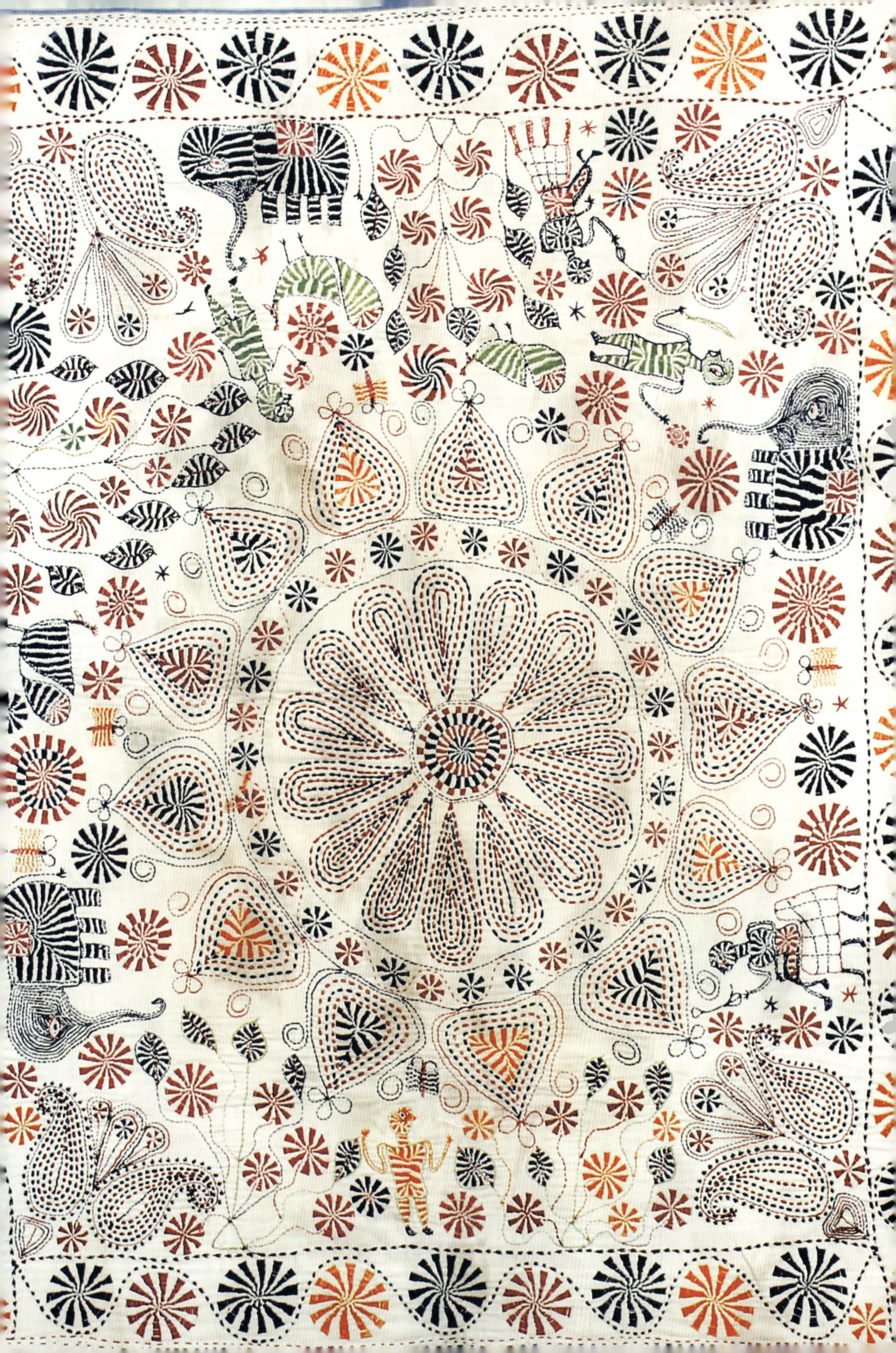

Kantha

Acc. No. IV/1C971/JS-KAN-3 (CONTD)

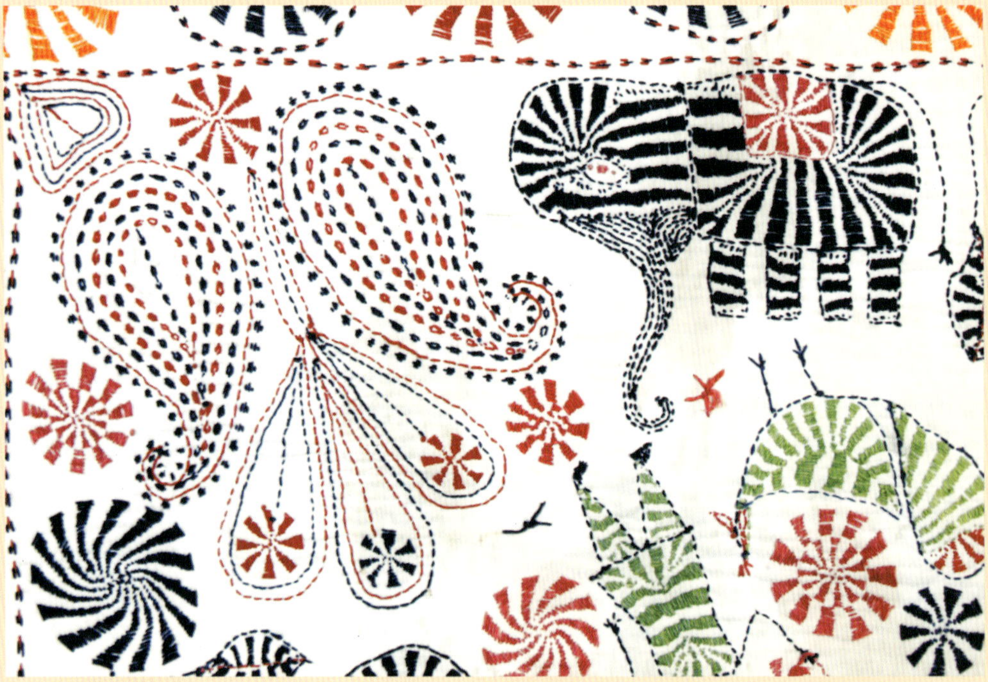

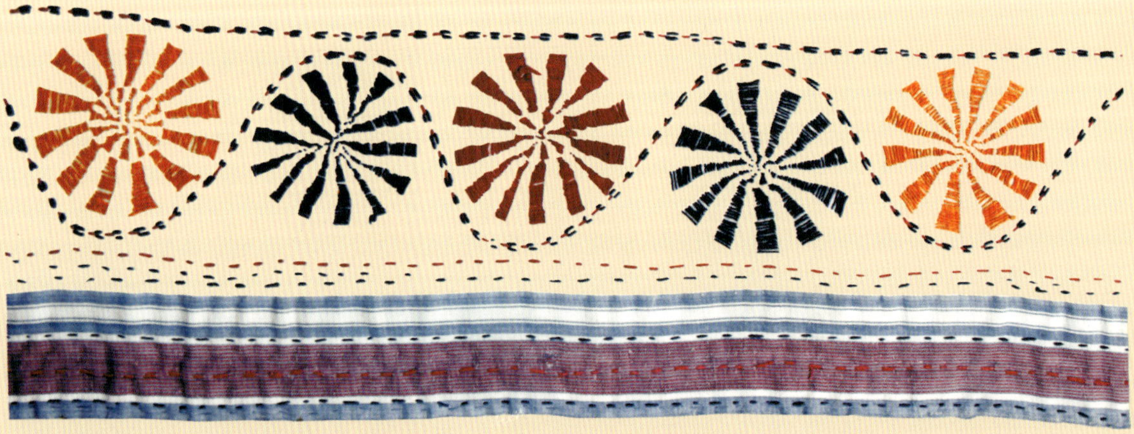

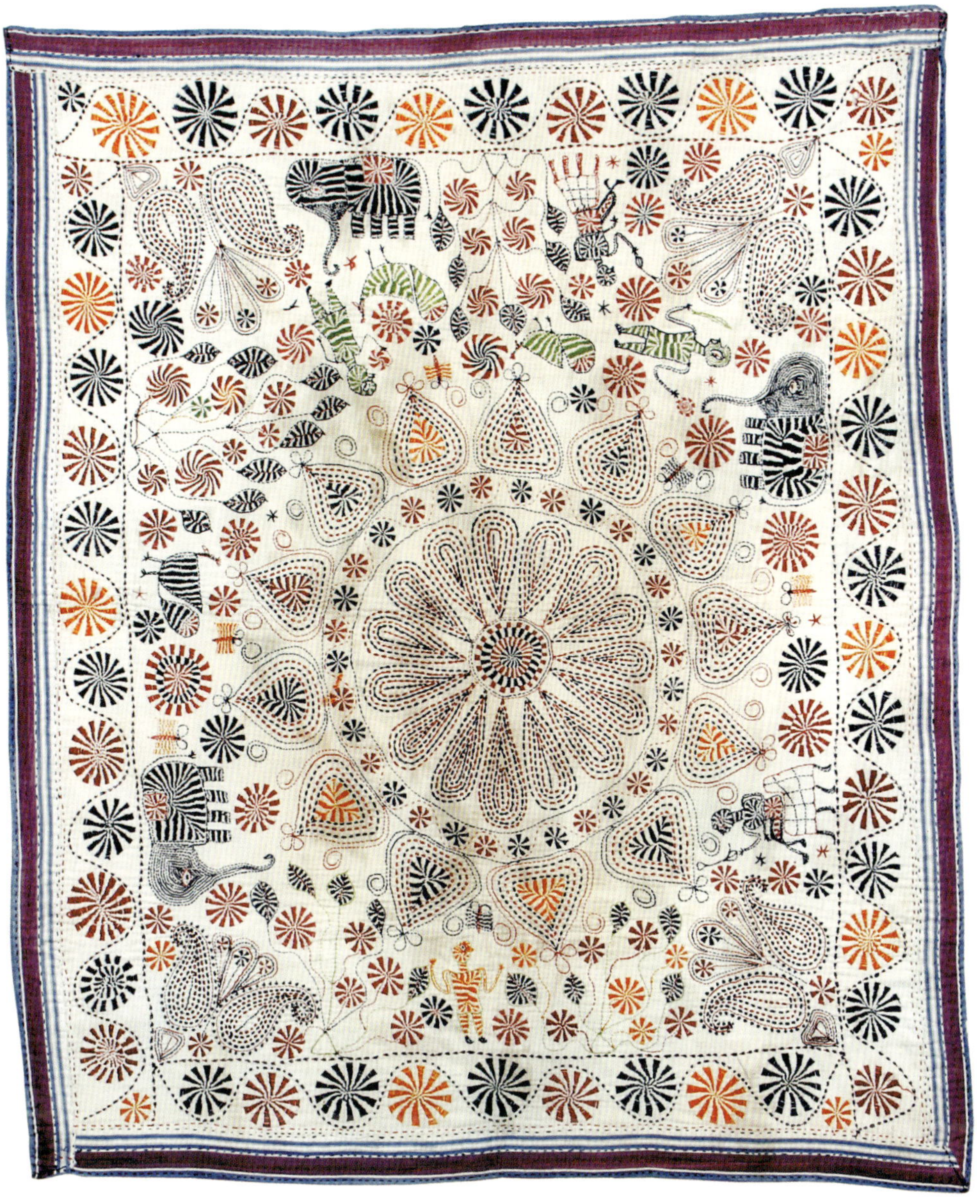

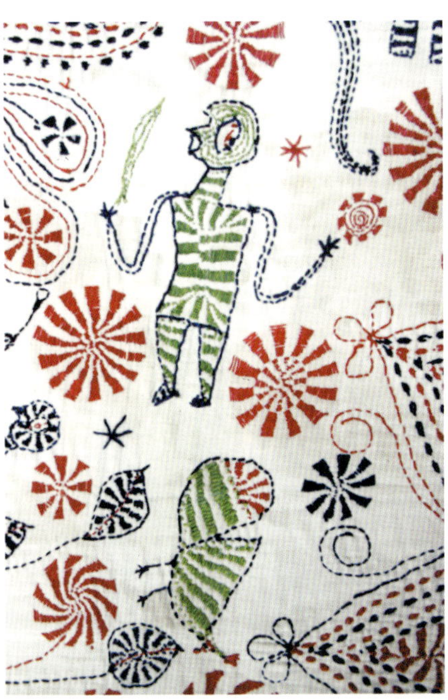

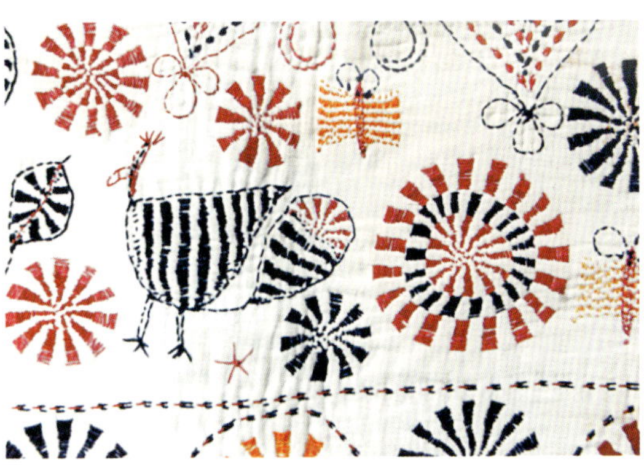

Kantha

Acc. No. IV/1C971/JS-KAN-4

Small *Kantha* having nine rectangular enclosures, the central enclosure has a small circular lotus in the centre with spiral edges. The four corners are richly embroidered, each having two leaves on a balloon-like flower in the centre. In between the two corners, there is a betel leaf with a small stem on either side.

The central flower has two floral motifs, one bird and a fish and two small dots around it. This enclosure has a double border, half of it is embroidered in herring bone stitch pattern, while the inner border has a chess soldiers like motif with a dot in between.

Rest of the eight enclosures have different types of *Pars* (borders) with different designs like herring bone, *chok paar* etc.

The borders on all four sides have *chok paar* pattern with button hole stitches at the edges.

The ground has very fine running stitches with self colour.

Colours used in embroidery are red, blue, mustard, green, yellow, rust, orange, light peach and different shades of green.

Material - Cotton

Condition - Stained at places.

Size - 95cmx78cm

Period - 19th Century

Place - West Bengal

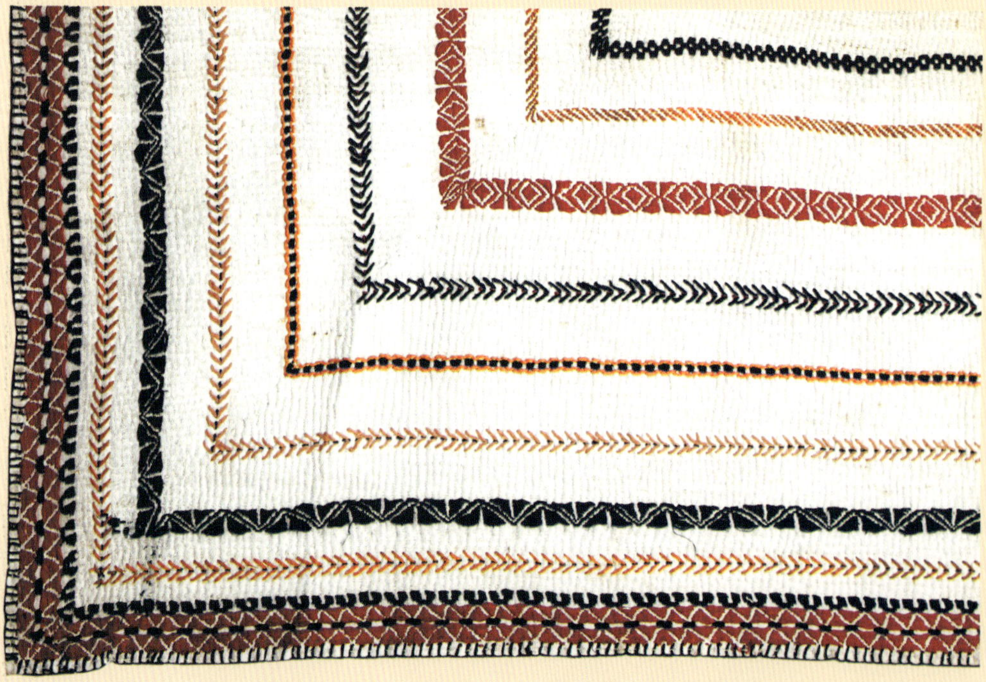

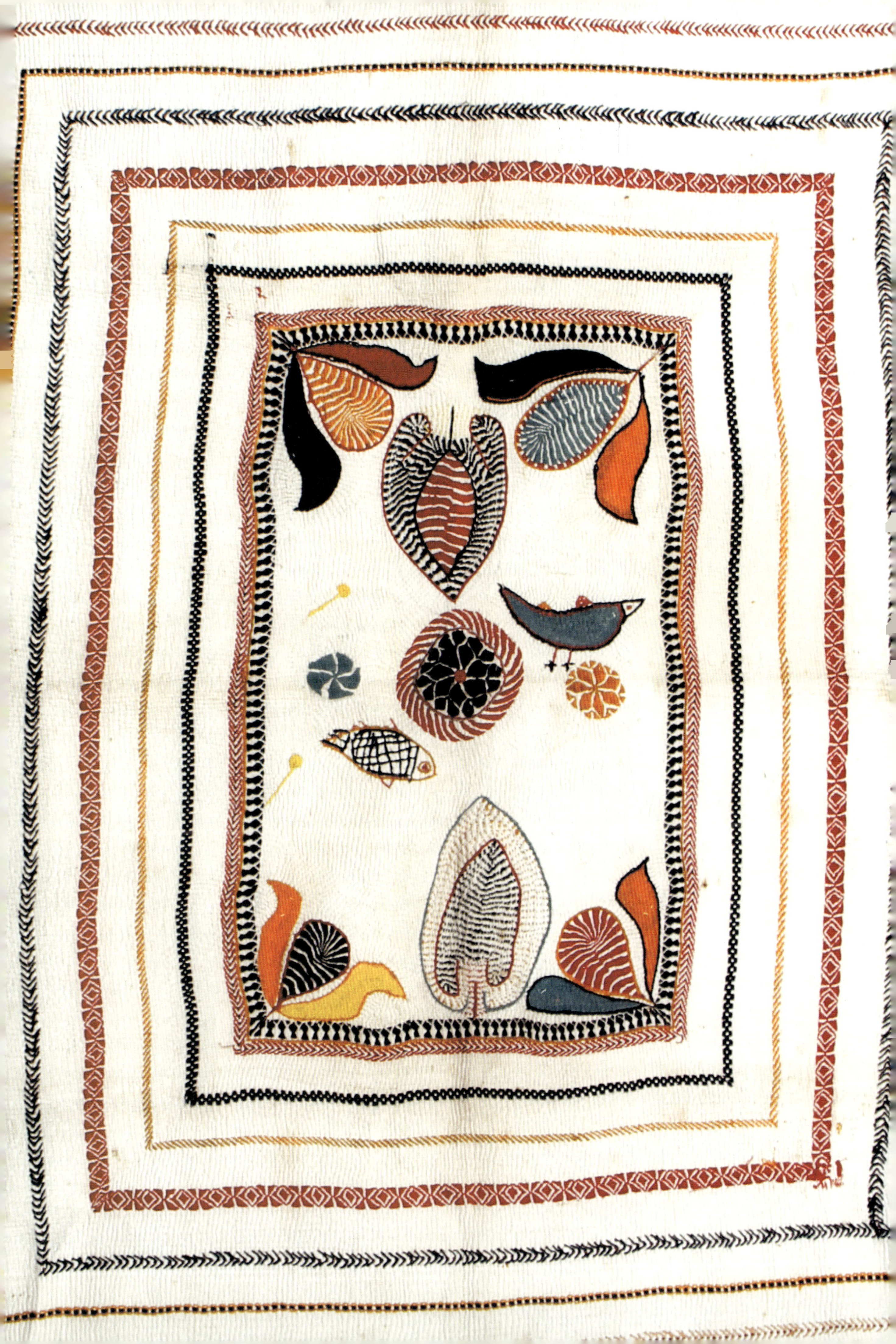

Kantha

Acc. No. IV/1C971/JS-KAN-4 (CONTD)

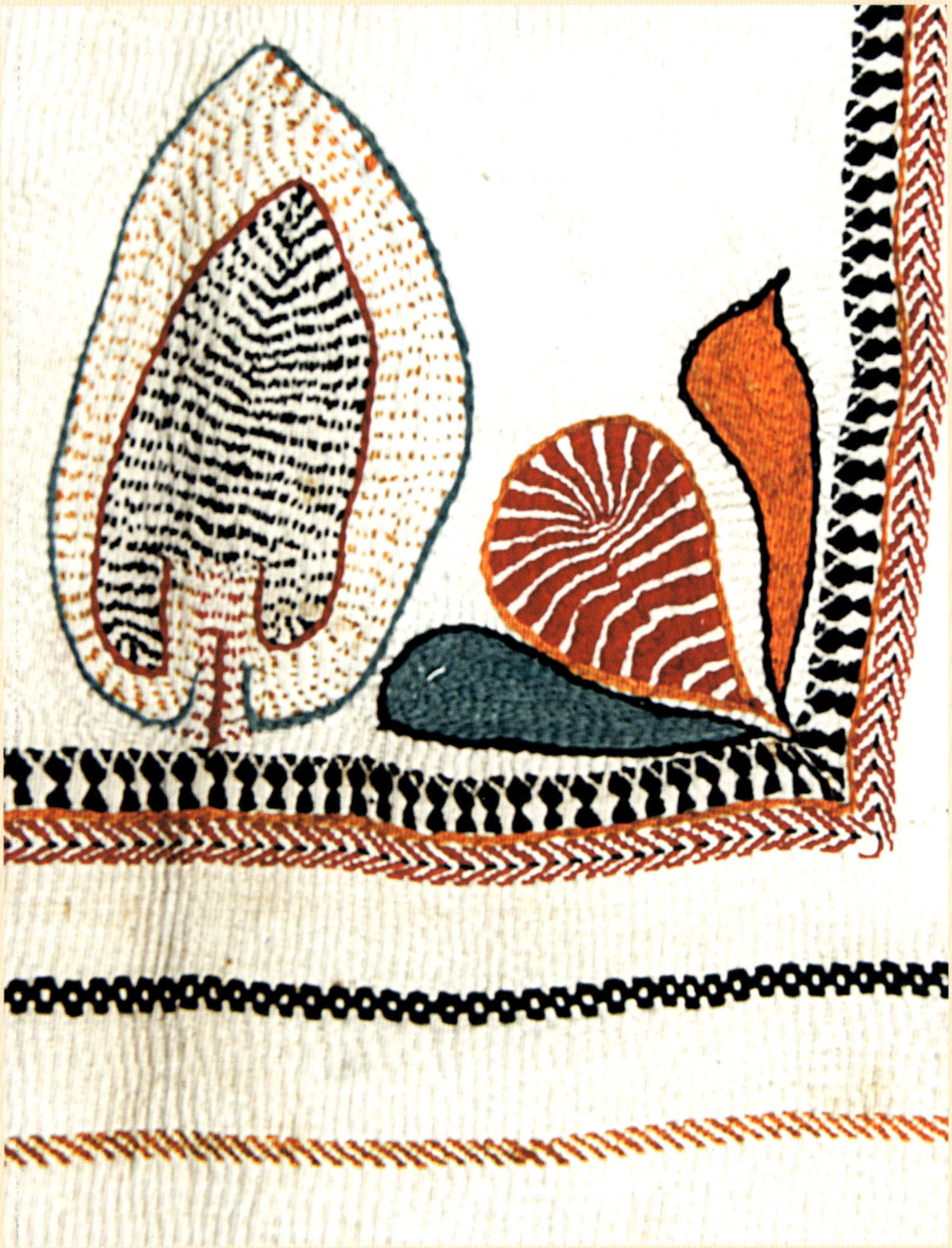

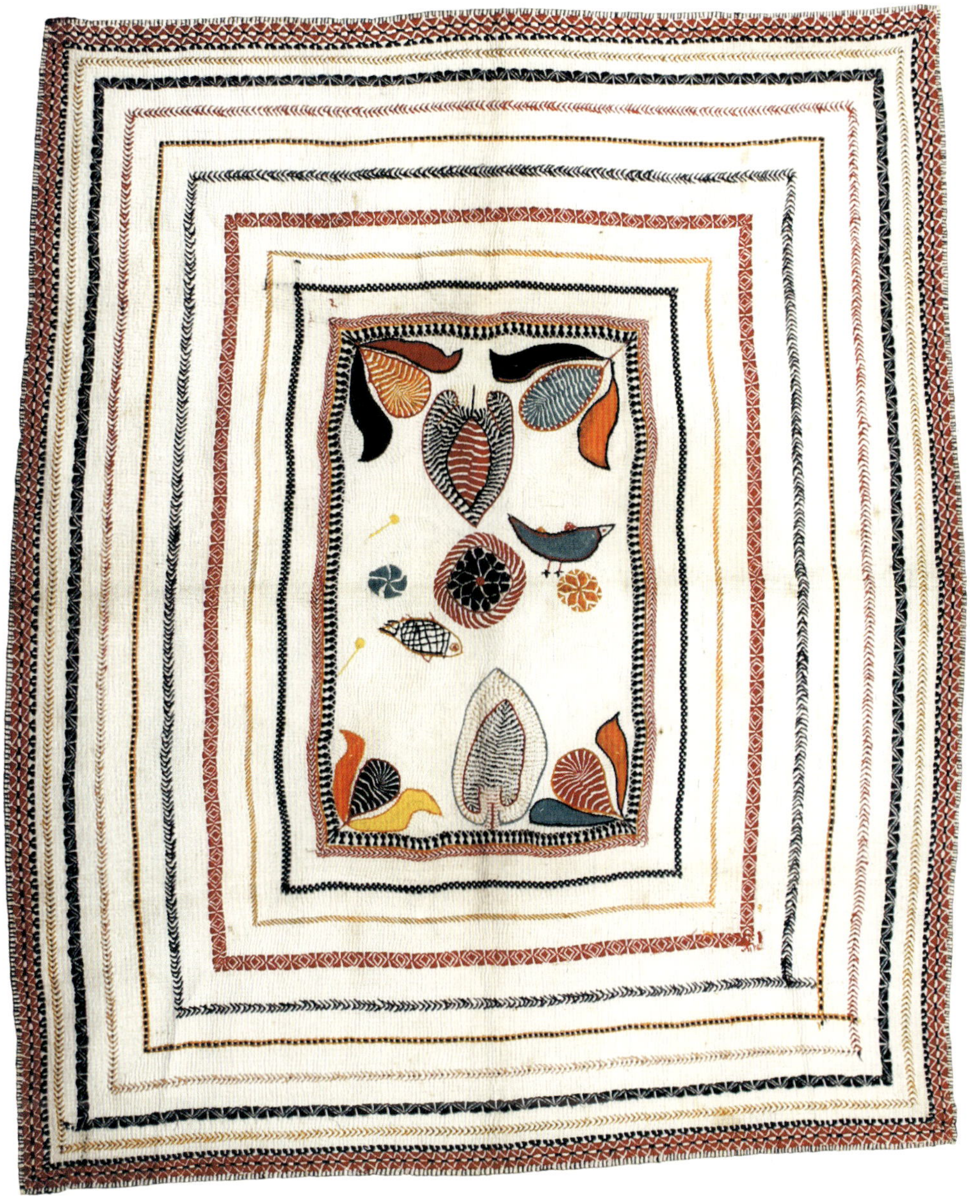

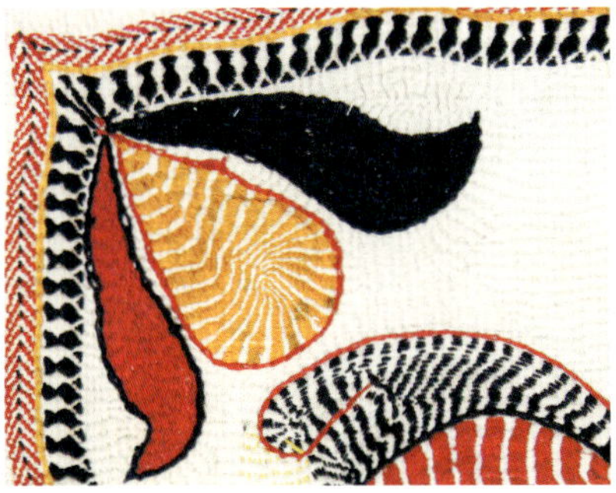

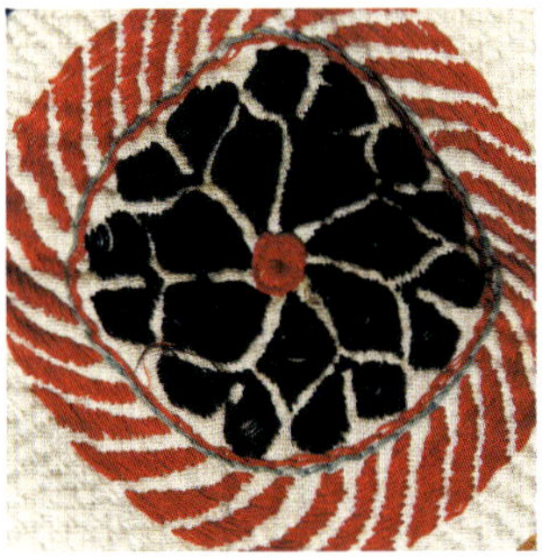

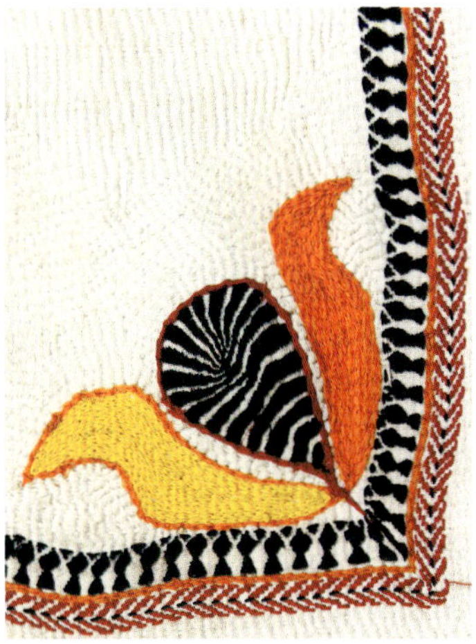

Kantha

Acc. No. IV/1C971/JS-KAN-5

Off-white *Kantha* having multi-coloured running stitches all over the field, which has been divided into various enclosures. The central enclosure is square, having a lotus enclosed in another square with button-hole stitches in faded red colour and zigzag pattern, while the four corners of the square are straight.

The next enclosure has been embroidered with Bangla script in black colour. The words are- *Hare Krishna, Hare Krishna, Krishna Krishna, Hare Hare.*

This square has been embroidered in herring bone stitches with pink dots on both sides. On two sides of the central enclosure (lengthwise) there are two plants each in a pot placed opposite each other. Each plant has stylized flowers and foliage motifs, which are embroidered with different types of flowers and leaves in between. In one pot, there are two butterflies while in the other there are bees.

On the other two sides (lengthwise), there are animals. One side has a pig, elephant, and a horse, while on the opposite side there is a rhinoceros, elephant and a tiger. On both the sides, elephants are in the centre.

The next two enclosures have a parrot sitting on one side, with a pigeon on the other; both are sitting on the branches. In the centre, there is a duck sitting with a bee in its beak.

The next opposite enclosure has a stylized plant with three big flowers, four small flowers and leaves in a pot flanked by one female and one male figure each standing under an arch. The male figure has curly hair while the female figure is richly adorned. Both the figures are in a dancing pose.

On the other side, there is a peacock sitting on the terrace with a flared tail having six eyes. It has two birds sitting on branches on either side.

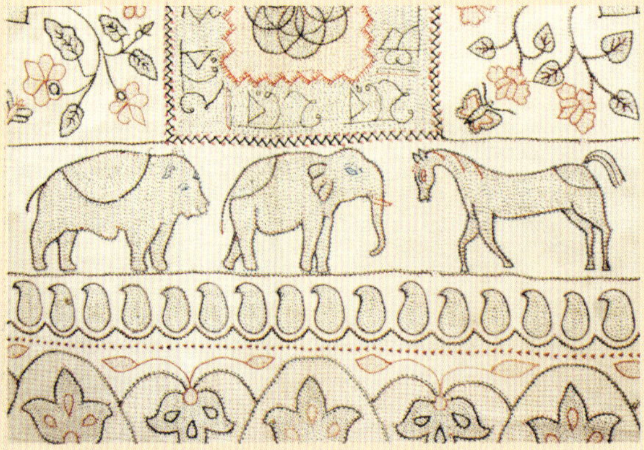

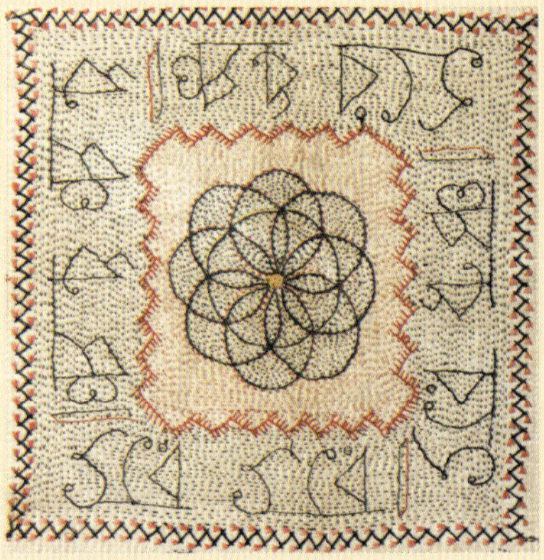

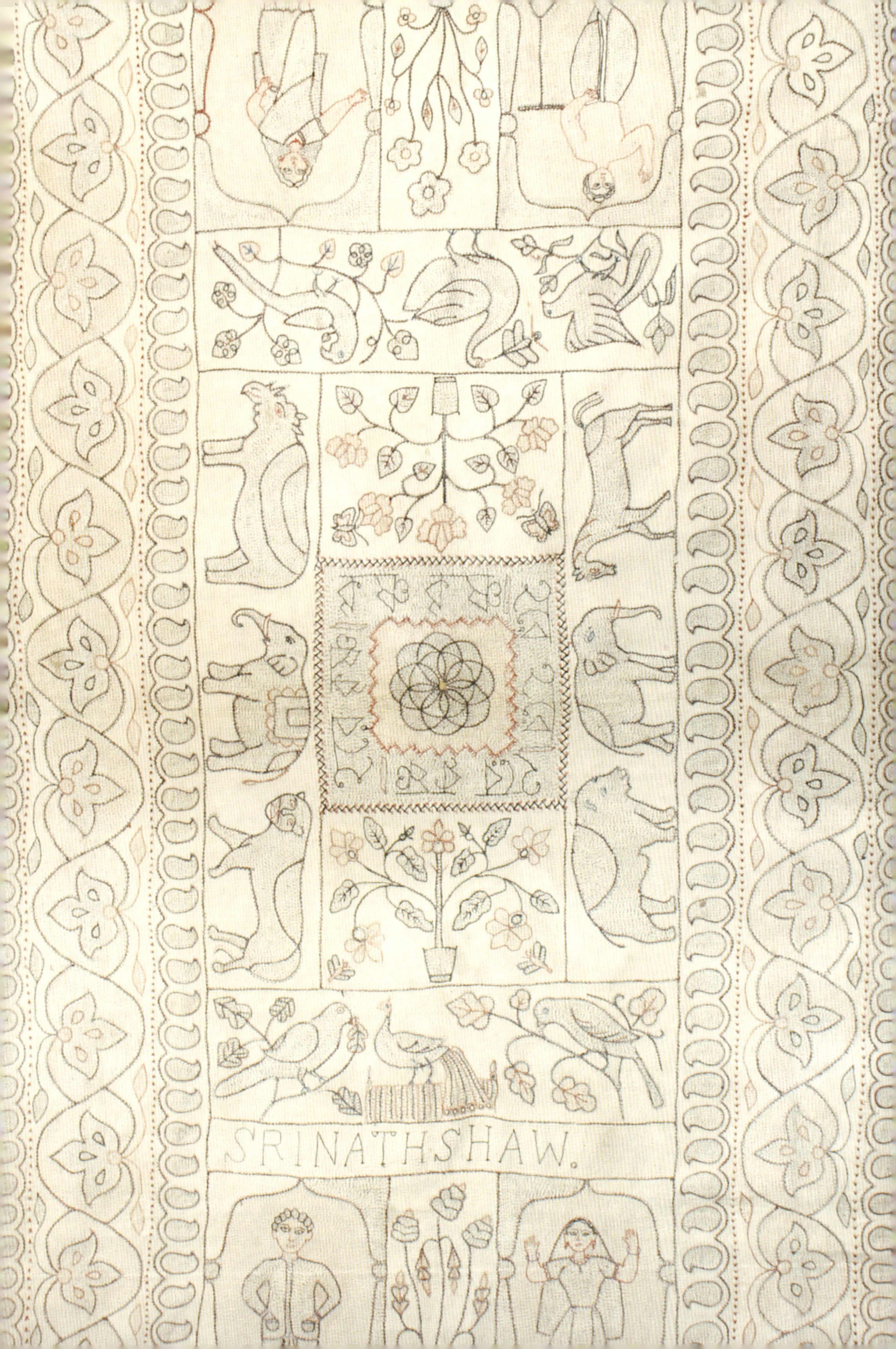
SRINATHSHAW.

Kantha

Acc. No. IV/1C971/JS-KAN-5 (CONTD)

There is a small panel below which has been embroidered with a name - SRI NATH SHAW.

Below this name there is a plant having very stylized flowers in a *pot,* flanked by one male and one female figure standing under an arch.

The female figure is in a dancing pose with head covered, while the male figure has curly hair, wearing a kurti with his hands in his pockets. He is also wearing dhoti and shoes.

There are three borders; the inner and outer borders have *kalka* patterns arranged in a row, while the central one has a trefoil pattern in enclosures.

The two diagonally opposite corners of the *Kantha* are embroidered with stylized *buta*, one having two birds, while the other one has two peacocks with curved necks.

There is a red piping on all the four edges. All the embroidery has been done in running stitches with stem stitches on the edges.

Colours used in embroidery are black, different shades of pink, blue, and orange.

Material - Cotton

Condition - Stained at places.

Size - 197cmx100cm

Period - Late 19th Century

Place - West Bengal

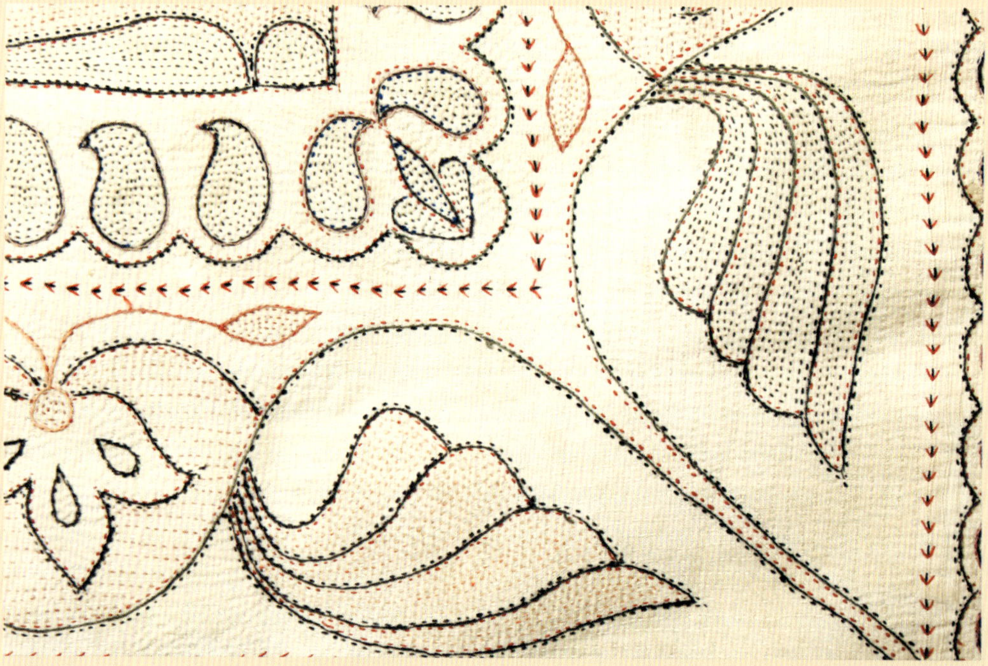

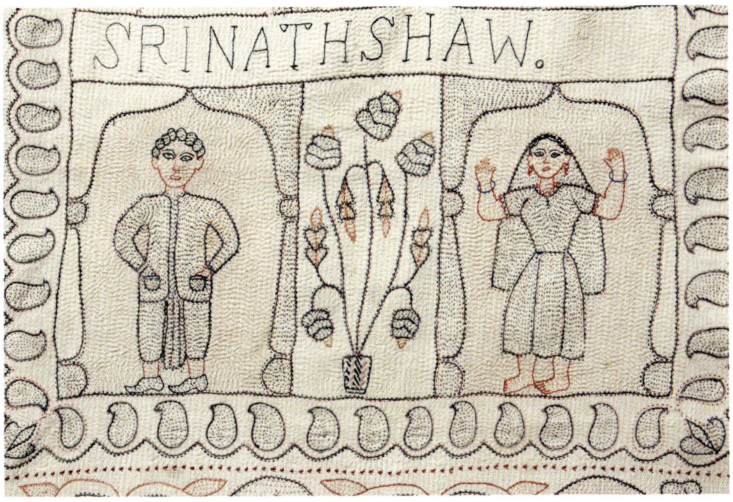
SRINATHSHAW.

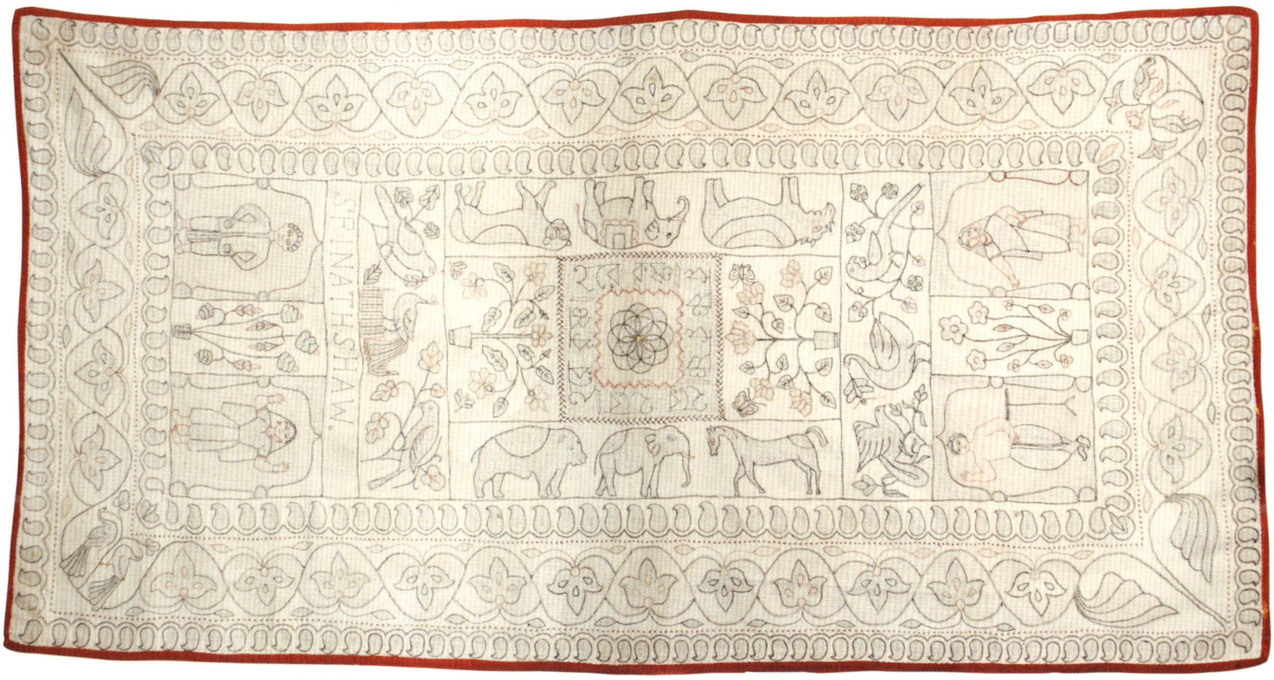
SRINATHSHAW.

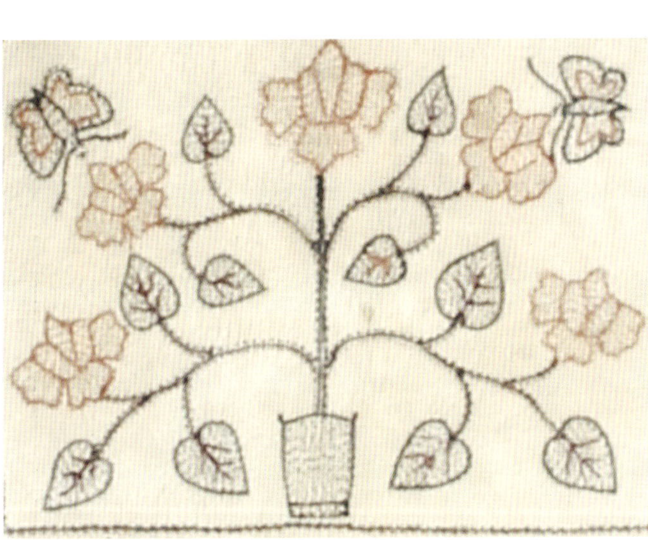

Kantha

Acc. No. IV/1C971/JS-KAN-6

Small rectangular *dorukha* (double-sided) *Kantha*, having six petalled flowers in the centre with a lotus flower on the right and another lotus flower on the left just below the centre.

One horizontal side of the *Kantha* is embroidered with a long branch having stylized *paan* (betel) leaves on both sides. The entire field has very close running stitches with many figures and motifs of day to day scenes like birds in a row on one side, stylized elephant with a rider, *pankha* (fan), *sheesha* (mirror), *kanghi* (comb), many *sarotas* (nut cutters), winnowing fan, birds, animals, fish etc. *Shostichinho* and wheel like flowers are scattered in between various motifs.

There are two borders, the inner one has a row of wheel like flowers and *shosti chinho* arranged alternately on opposite sides (length wise), while the other two sides have pyramid like structures; the outer border has button hole stitches on the edges and *chatai* pattern in the middle of the two borders.

Most of the embroidery has been done in *katiya* stitches with satin stitches in between. The rest of the field is rippled by self-running stitches.

Colours used are green, black, different shades of blue, brown, pink, red, and grey.

Material - Cotton

Condition - Stained at places.

Size - 115cmx83cm

Period - 20th Century

Place - West Bengal

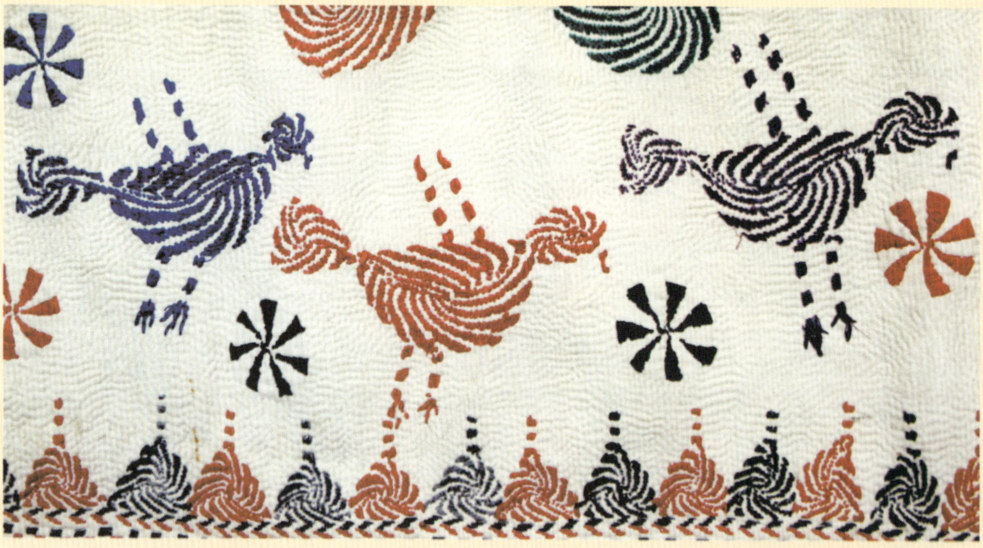

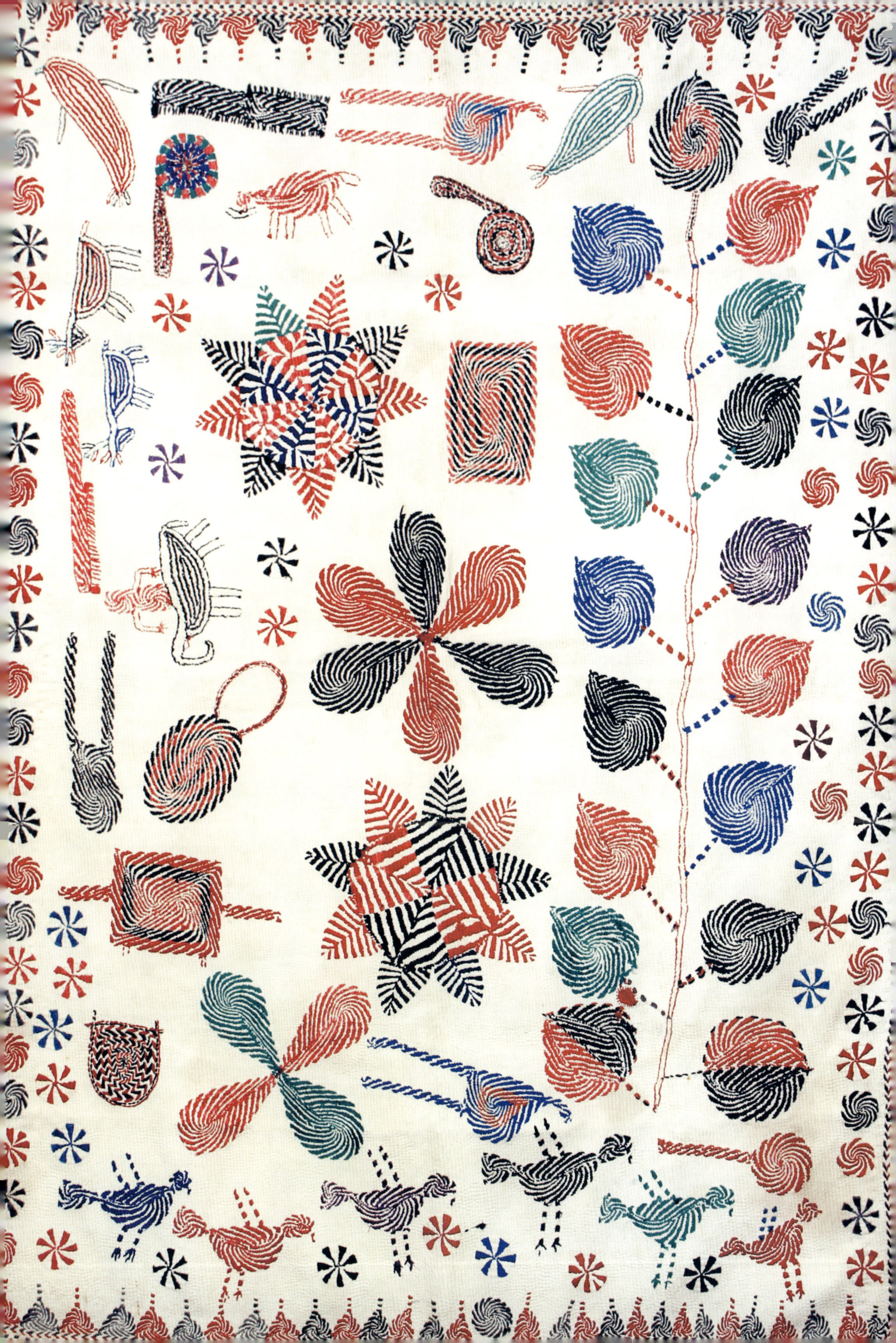

Kantha

Acc. No. IV/1C971/JS-KAN-6 (CONTD)

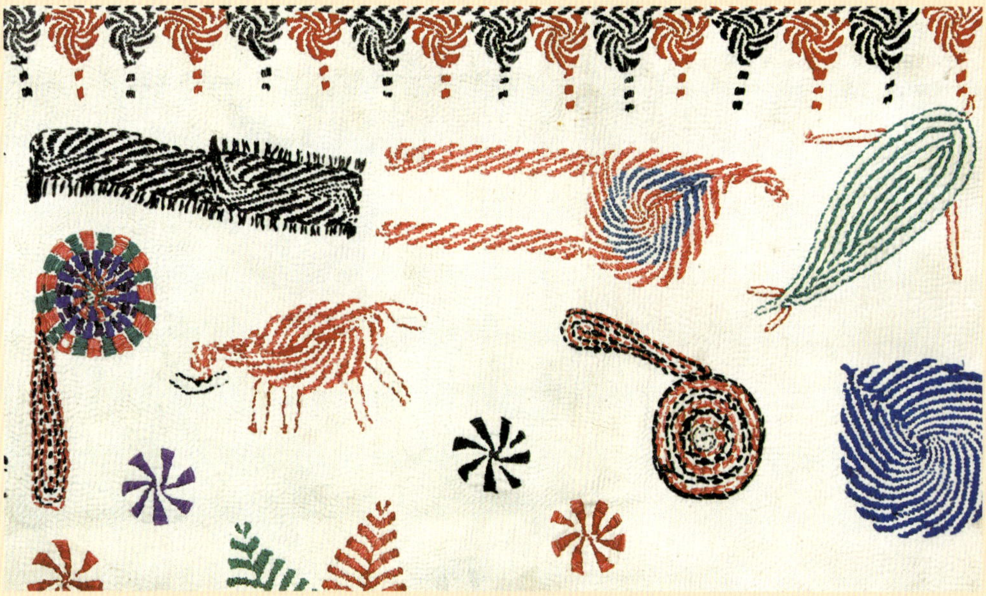

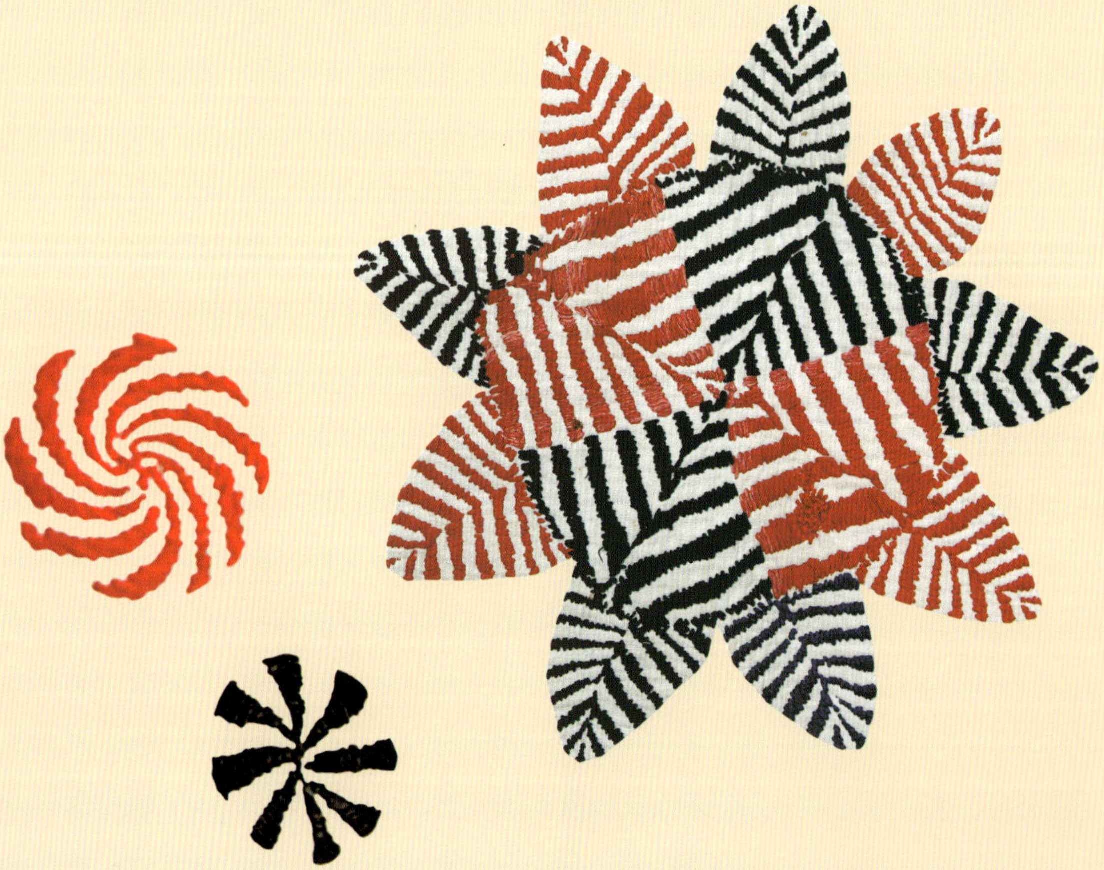

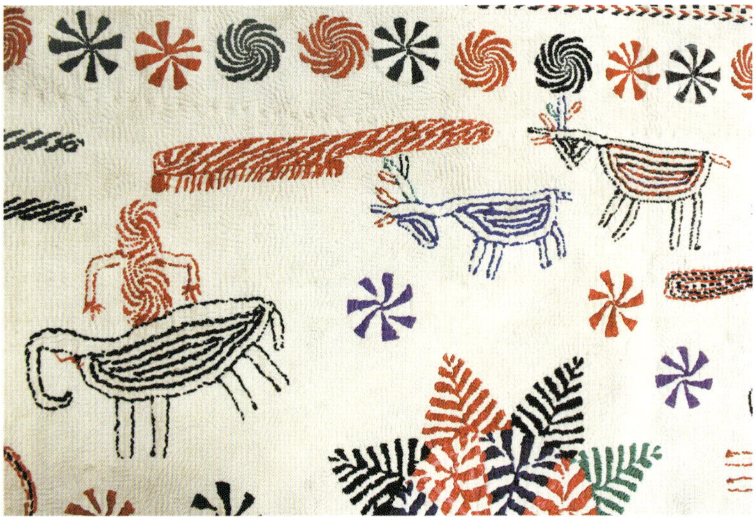

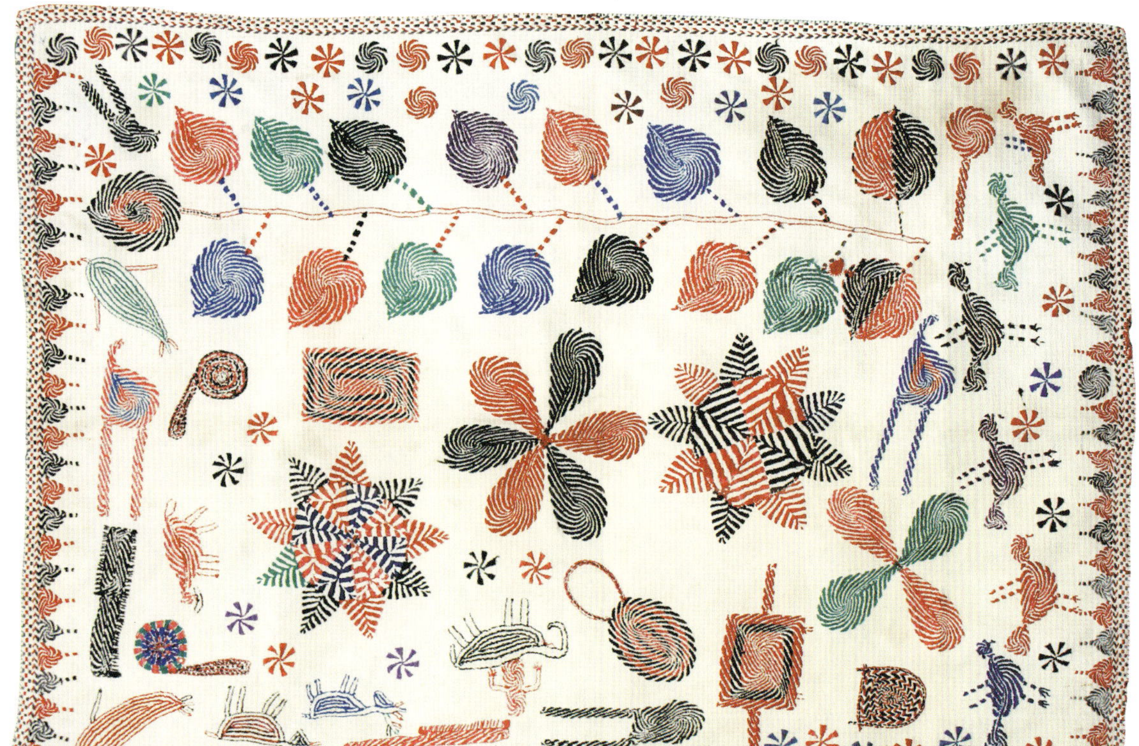

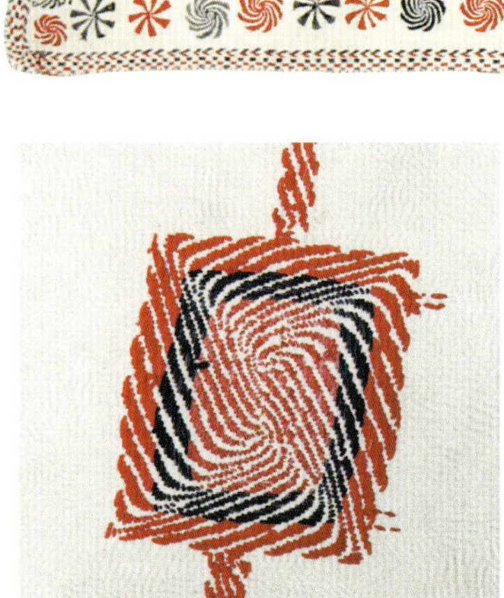

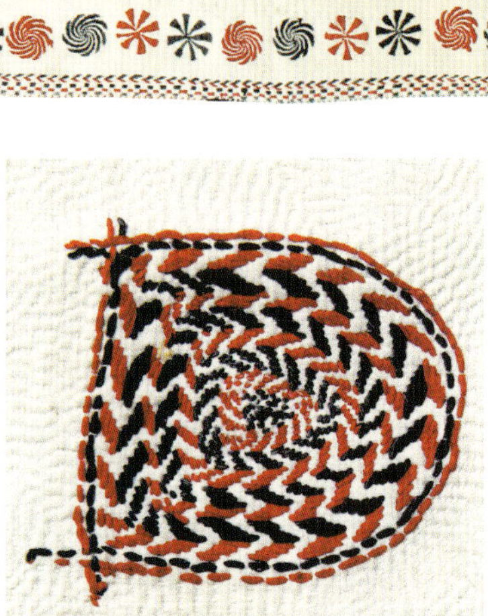

Kantha

Acc. No. IV/1C971/JS-KAN-7

Rectangular *Kantha* having four stylized *kalkas* (paisley) motifs, one in each corner, which has been embroidered with a multi-coloured leaf like pattern.

The *kalkas* are surrounded with miniature *kalkas*, which have a semi-circular rope-like motif which is attached to each end, having an unfinished stylized star and foliage motif in between the centre of the semi-circle.

Diagonally opposite *kalkas* have two flowers on either side; one is in the shape of a lotus, and the other has a circular pattern, while the other two diagonal *kalkas* have only one flower on each of them. One is in the shape of a lotus, while the other has a circular motif.

Each *kalka* has been surmounted by trefoil patterns with a peacock on the top. On all the four edges, there is a geometrically designed beautiful border with black colour in the centre, flanked by red colour. Embroidery is mostly done in satin stitches with mustard, red, black, and green.

The field of the *Kantha* is plain and richly rippled with running stitches.

Material - Cotton

Condition - Badly stained.

Size - 212cmx146cm

Period - Early 20th Century

Place - West Bengal

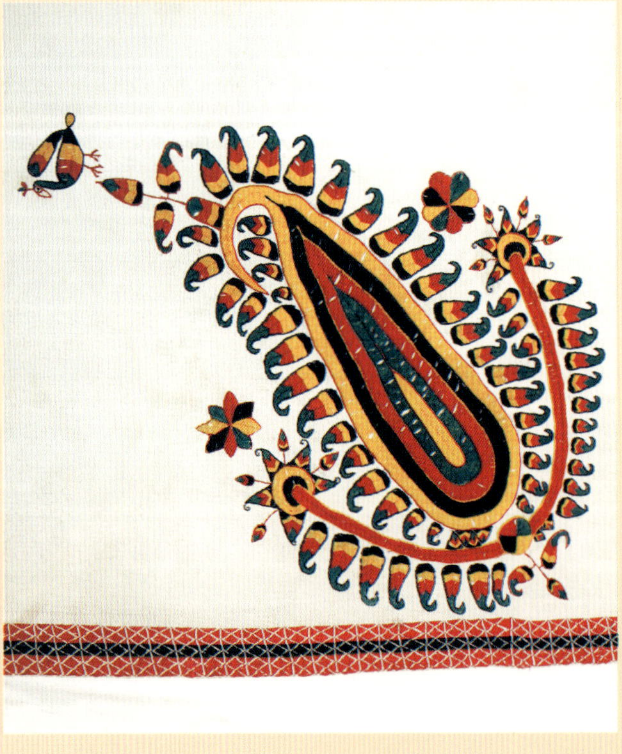

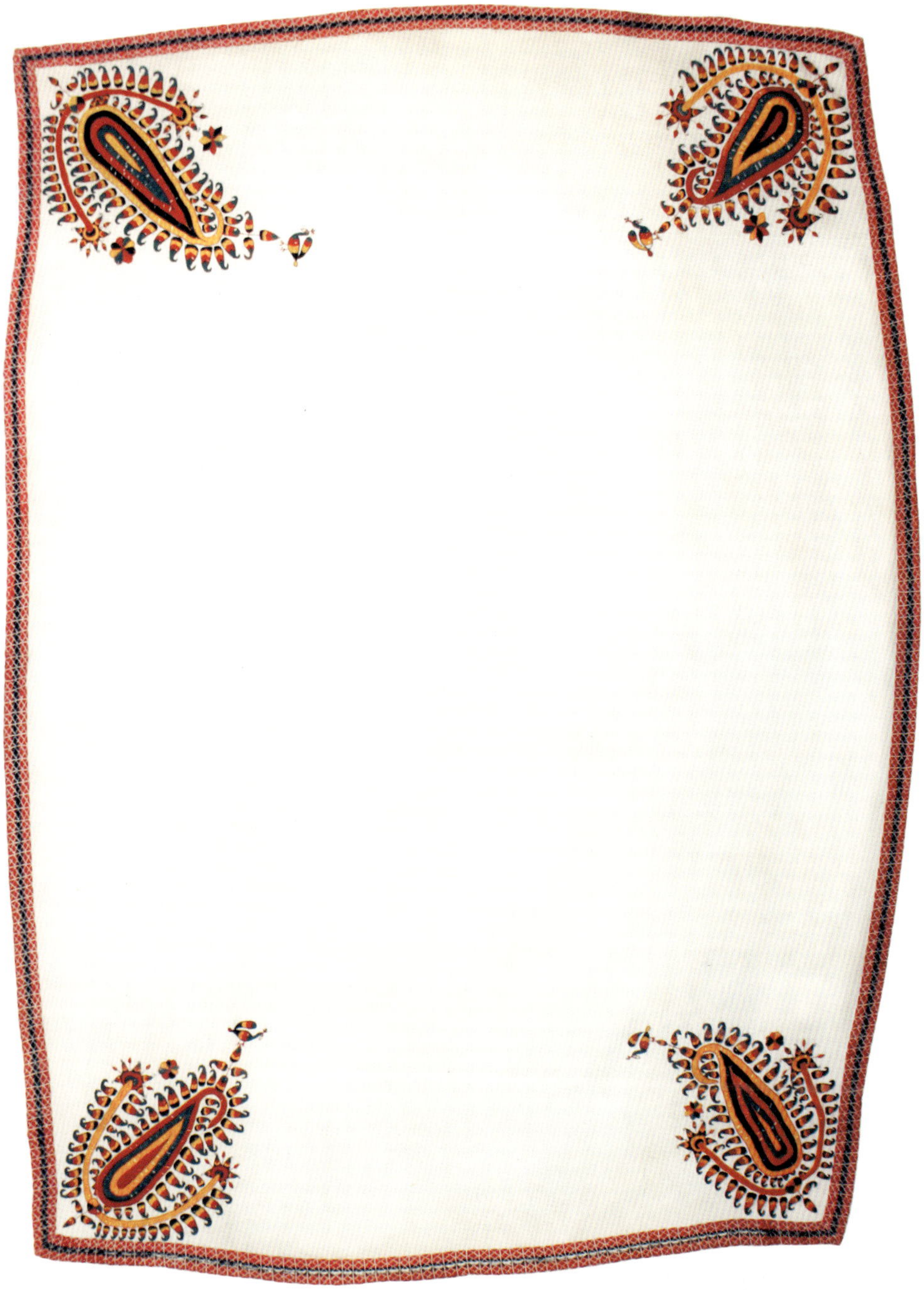

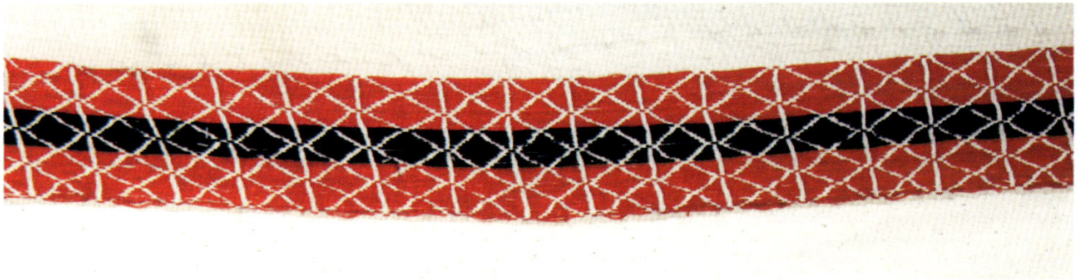

Kantha

Acc. No. IV/1C971/JS-KAN-8

Rectangular *Kantha* having a decorated lotus motif in the centre and arranged in a circle with a small flower in the middle surrounded by four tiers. Three have stylized diamond shaped patterns while the outer-most tier has triangular leaves with two pairs of birds, stylized *kalkas* in pairs and a zigzag pattern. In each of the four corners there is a big *buta* having double *kalkas* with elongated leaf patterns at the bottom. The tree is flanked by two male figures (one holding a small knife like object in his left hand while the other has a fisted hand) and has different types of birds sitting on branches, leaves, flowers, wheels, shosti chinha and a child playing in between. The other corner again has a plant flanked by two standing male figures and small flowers at the end of the long branches. There is a very stylized bird with flared wings and a long tail sitting on top of the plant. The bottom also has similar *Kalkas* as the other one. The third corner has similar *kalkas* at the bottom, with only one male figure on one side, while the other side has three musicians; one of them is holding an *Ektara*(one string musical instrument). Behind this, on the lower part of the plant there are small flowers with birds at the end of the branches. In between two plants, on one side of the *Kantha,* there are three small standing human figures. One of them is clad in peculiar clothes, wearing shoes and holding a gun like-object in his hands.

There is an inscription in Bangla which reads:-

Shri Kunj Bihari Dutta, Jagvaishnavikrit, Keetpara

There is also a very beautiful figure of a tiger on top of the inscription.

The rest of the field has very fine running stitches having a small shrine with windows in one corner, each window having a human figure. The dome of the shrine is decorated by two birds, while the opposite side has a fish with a long curved tail and an elephant like head. There is a god like figure sitting on the back of the fish, it could be a stylized form of the *Matsya Avtara.*

The entire field is covered with various types of animals, human figures, and peacocks in various forms. There is a coconut tree under which a man is standing and catching the falling coconuts.

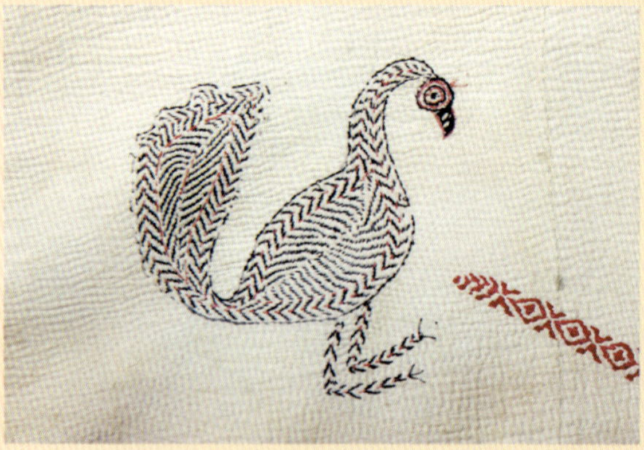

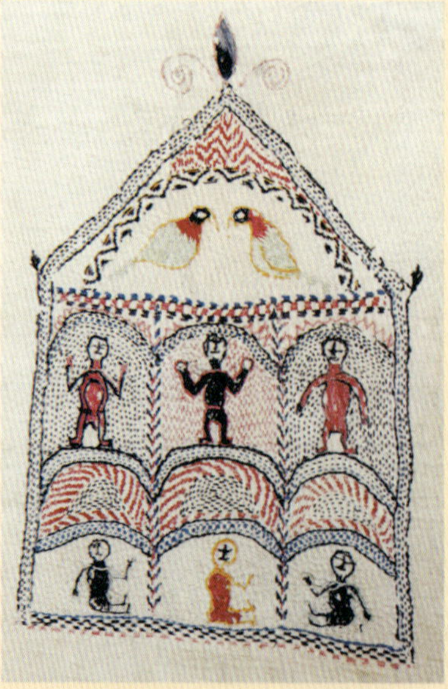

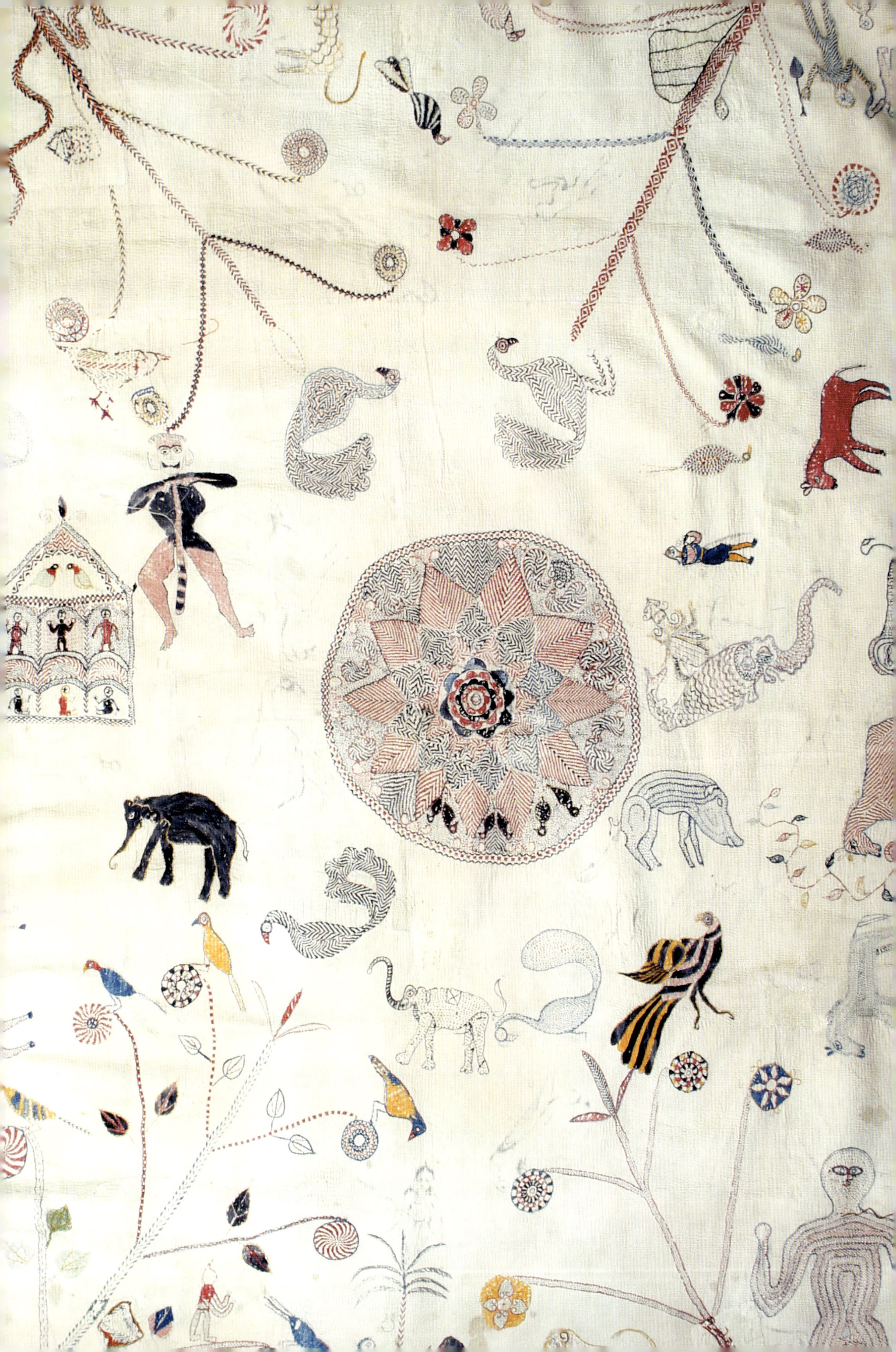

Kantha

Acc. No. IV/1C971/JS-KAN-8 (CONTD)

The border on all four sides has geometrical patterns. The rest of the field is rippled by running stitches.

Colours used are red, blue, black, orange, yellow and green.

Material - Cotton

Condition - Torn, repaired and stained at places.

Size - 195cmx118cm

Period - 20th Century

Place - West Bengal

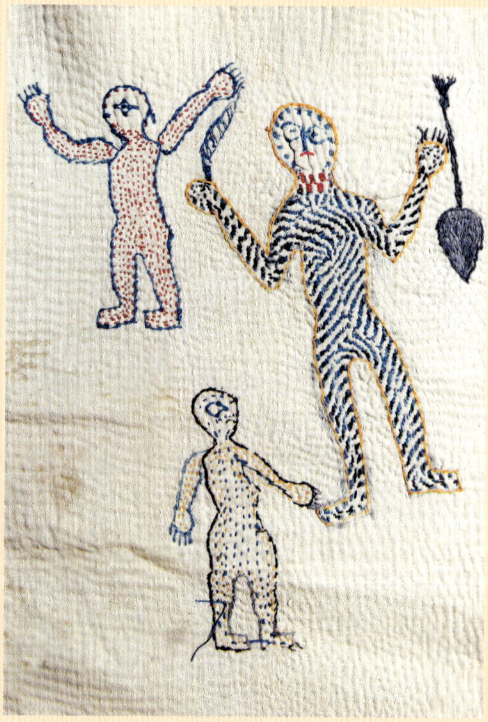

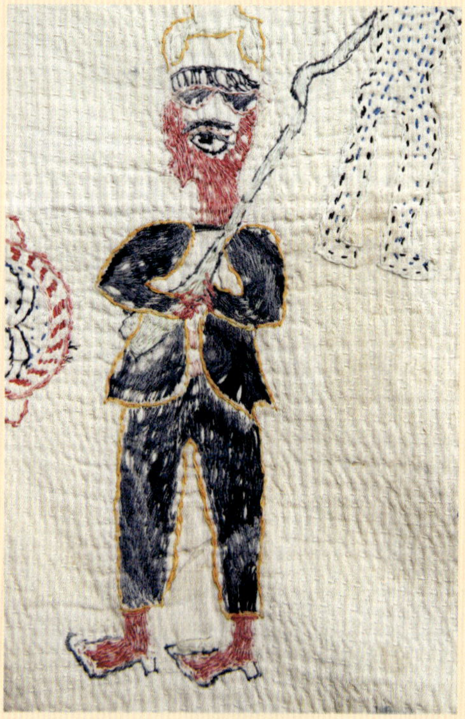

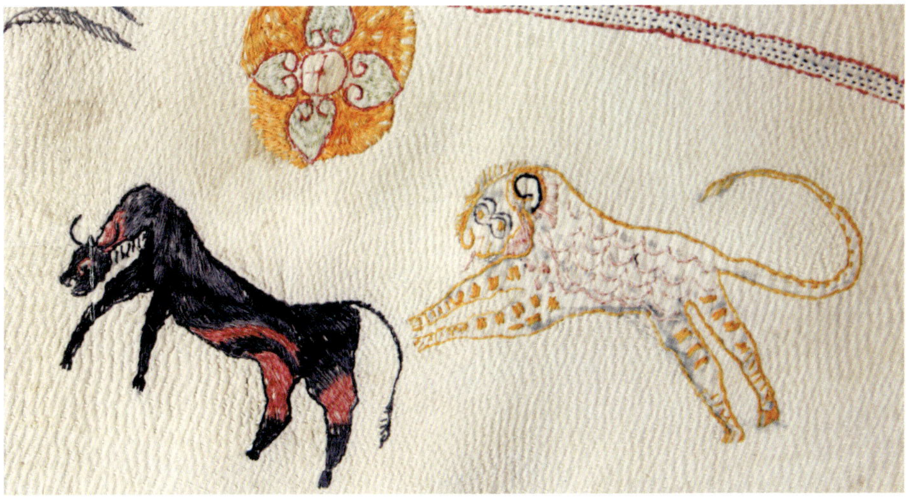

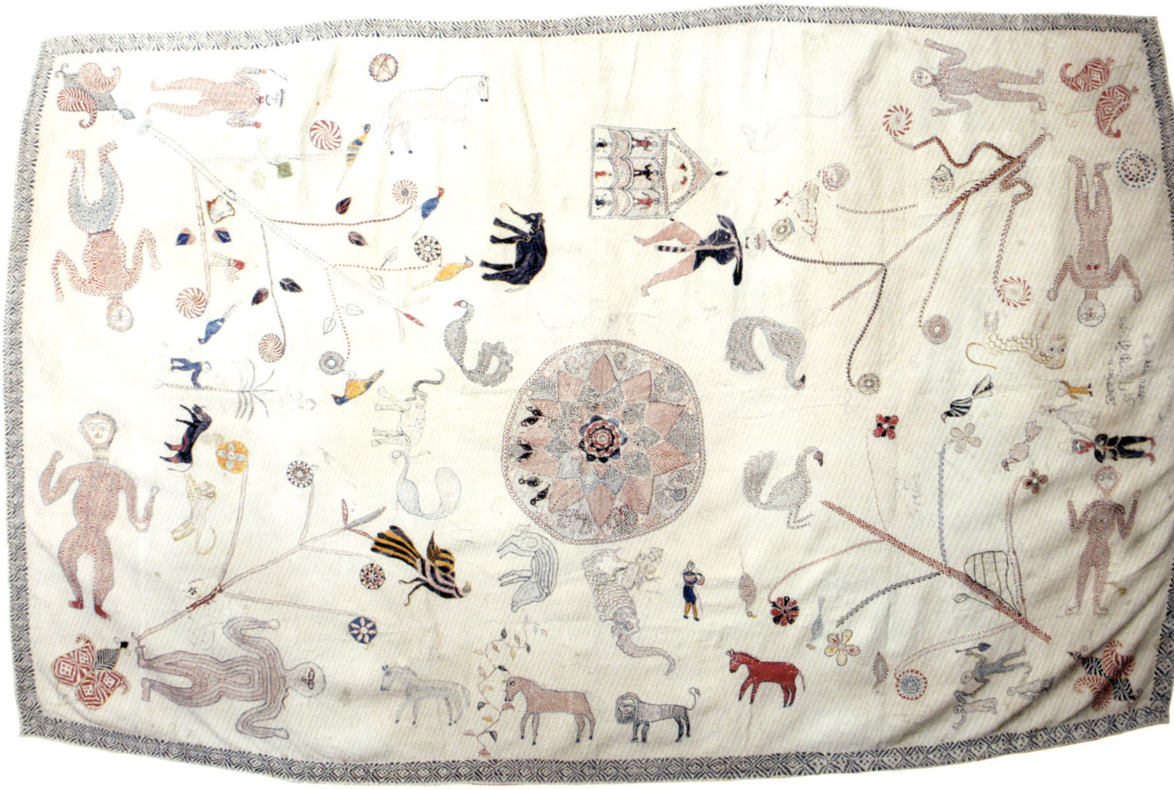

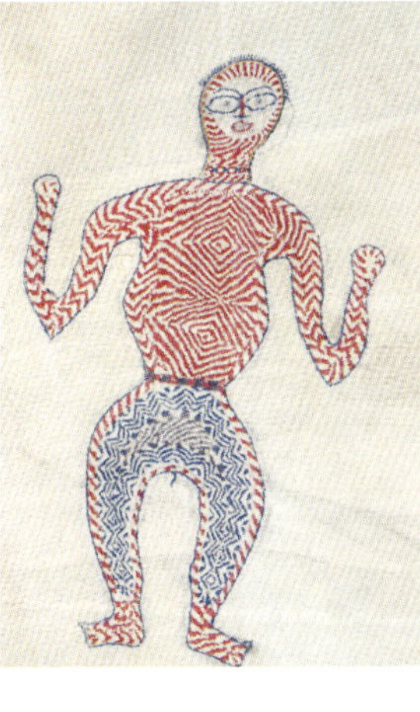

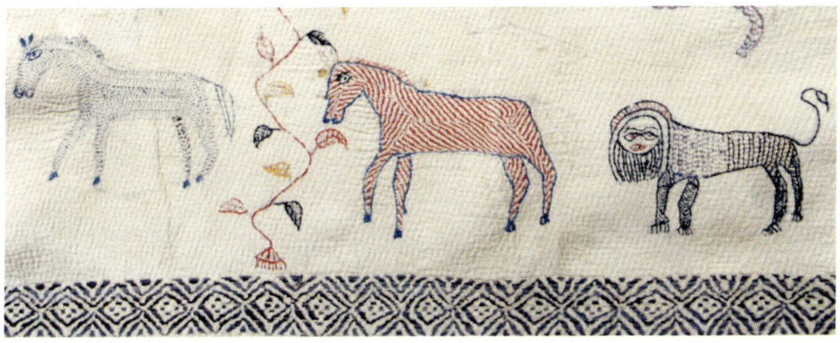

Kantha

Acc. No. IV/1C971/JS-KAN-9

Rectangular *Kantha* embroidered with small leaves in rhomboid patterns all over the field. There is a small stylized lotus flower only in one corner.

Border on four sides of the *Kantha* is divided into three parts. The central border is decorated with rows of wheels and curved lines while the outer and inner borders have pyramid-like designs with red and black colours arranged alternately.

Colours used in embroidery are red, blue, black, mustard and green.

Material - Cotton

Condition - Torn, stained and embroidery missing at places.

Size - 200cmx142cm

Period - 19th Century

Place - West Bengal

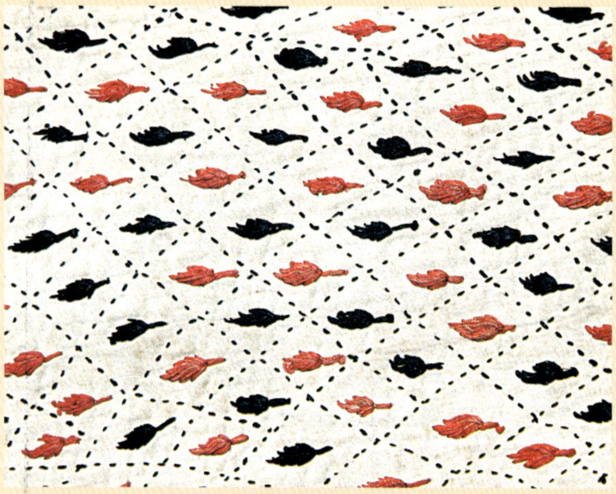

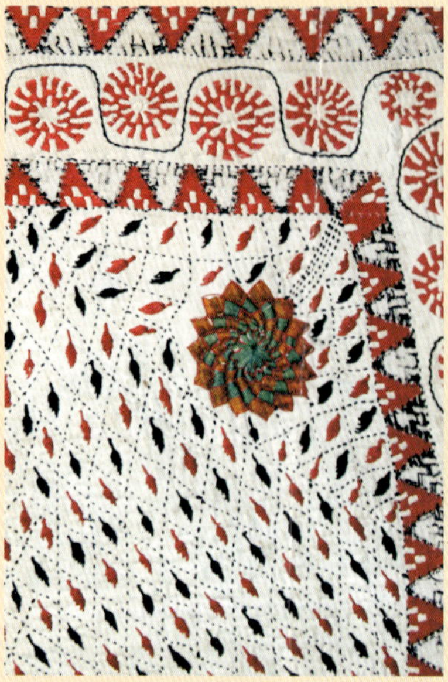

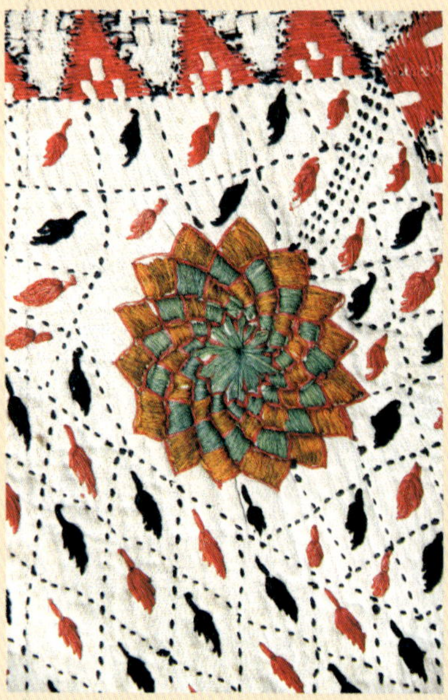

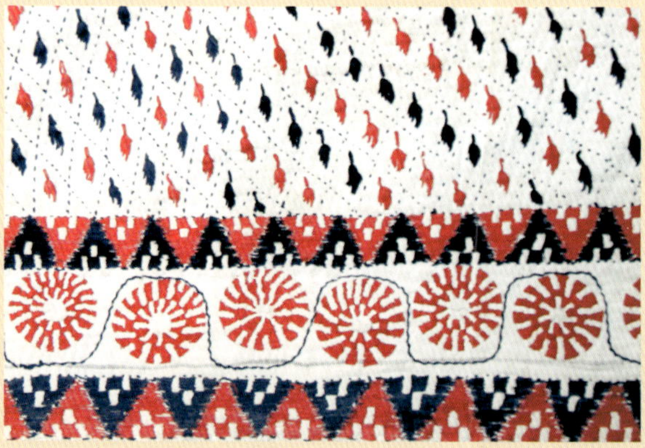

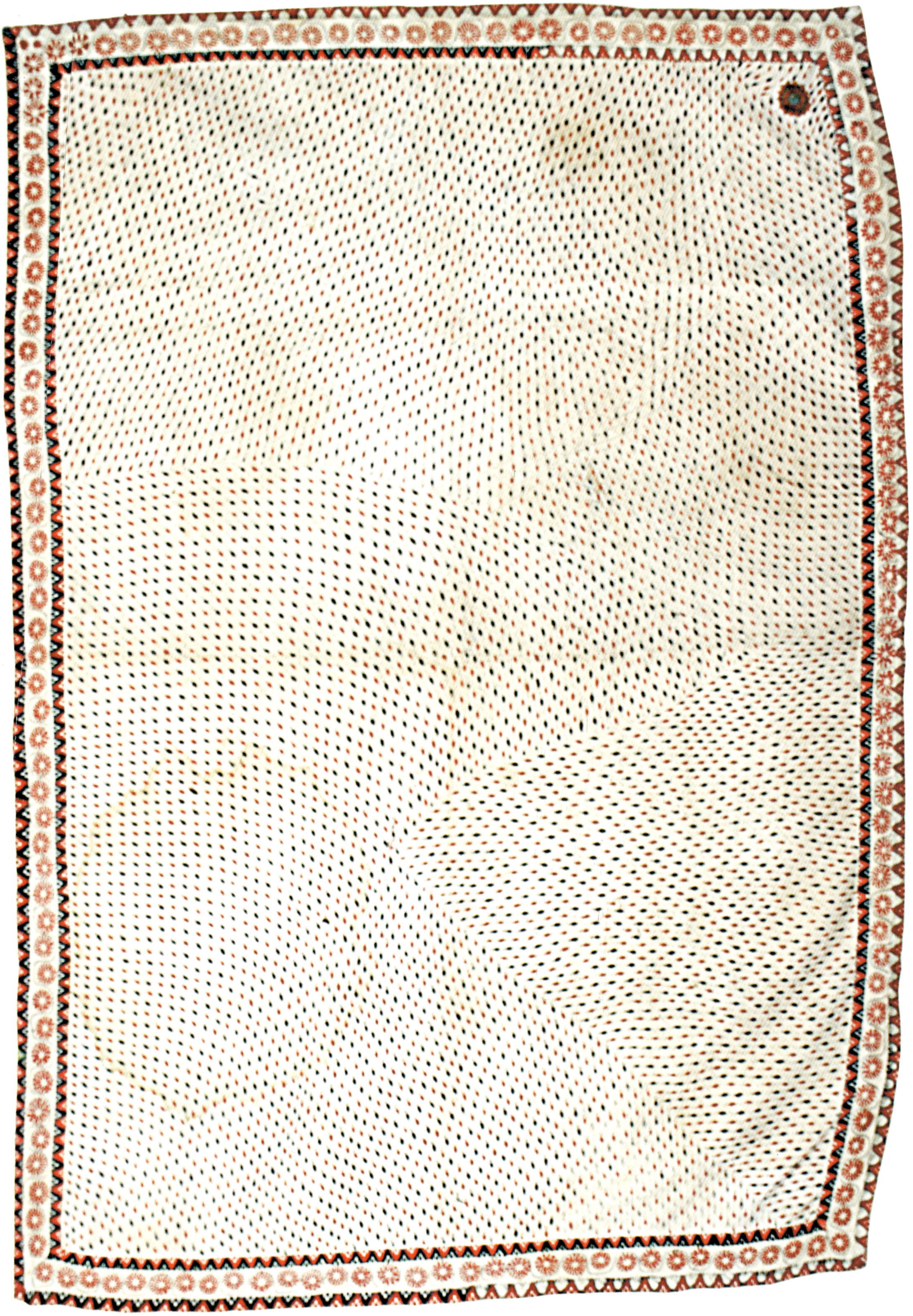

Kantha

Acc. No. IV/1C971/JS-KAN-10

Rectangular *Kantha* having a large lotus in the centre. The lotus has round edged leaves, enclosed in a circle with triangular leaves on the outer side. This central lotus has been enclosed with a curved creeper like pattern having double herring bone stitch. This enclosure has a large trefoil pattern, one in each corner, and two circular plate-like motifs on one side of the lotus. One plate has multicoloured objects on it, while the other has four petalled flowers. The rest of the field is filled with different figures like elephant, horse, duck, fish, crow, mouse, birds and stag with small floral motifs in between. Space in between the enclosure and border is decorated with a row of *kalkas* and wheels arranged alternately. There are two borders divided into squares, each having one stylized floral motif. The dividing lines of the squares are made of double herring bone stitches, while the edges of the border are in *chatai* pattern.

Most of the embroidery has been done in *katiya* stitches barring the small flowers in between. The rest of the field has self-running stitches.

Colours used are black, blue, red, different shades of green, turquoise and grey.

Material - Cotton

Condition - Stained and embroidery missing at places and edges are torn.

Size - 195cmx12cm

Period - Late 19th Century

Place - West Bengal

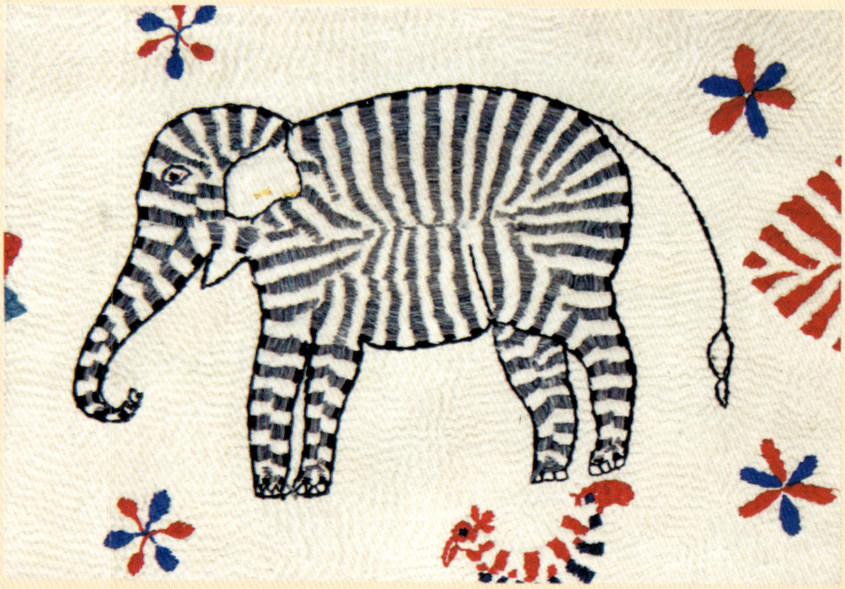

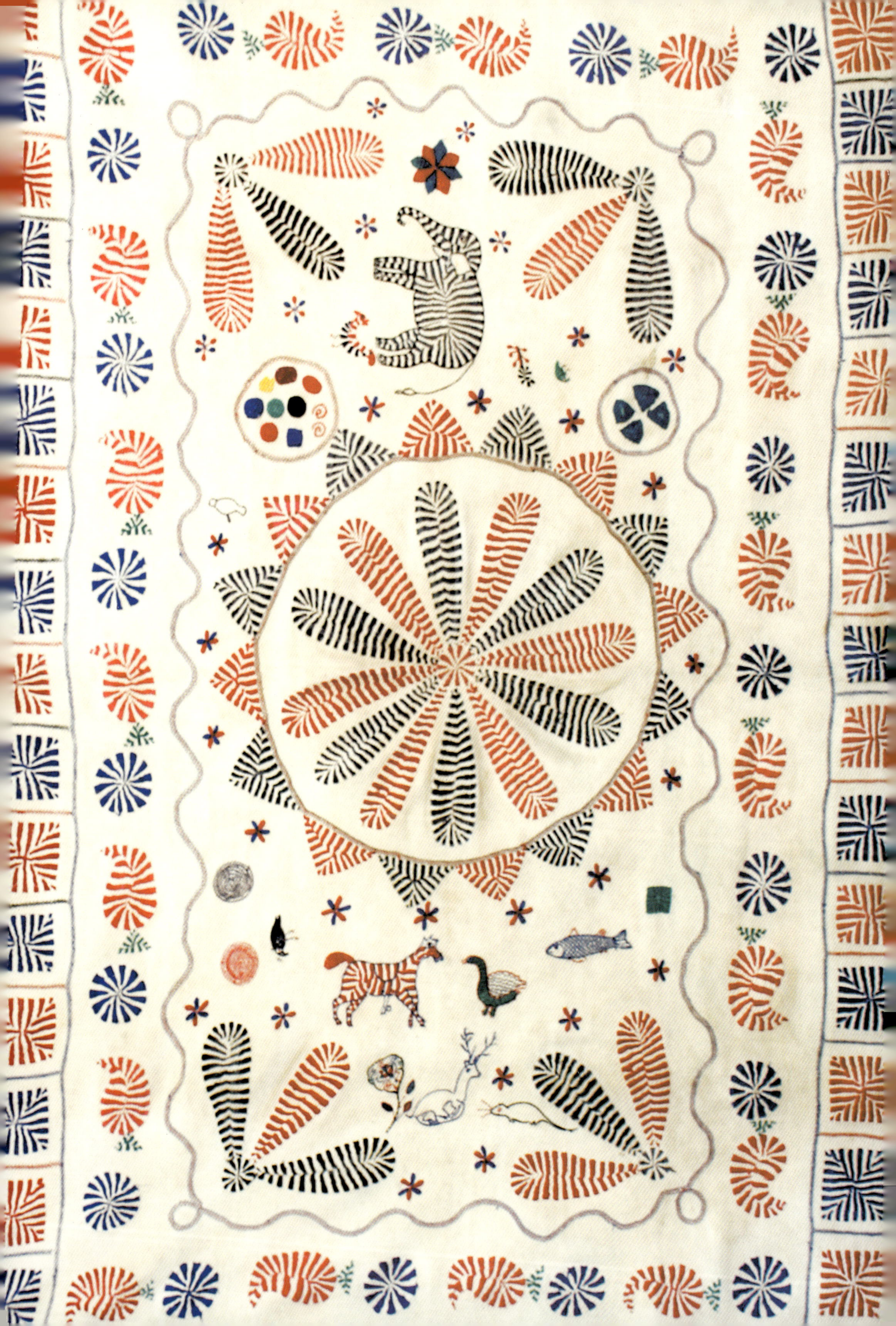

Kantha

Acc. No. IV/1C971/JS-KAN-10 (CONTD)

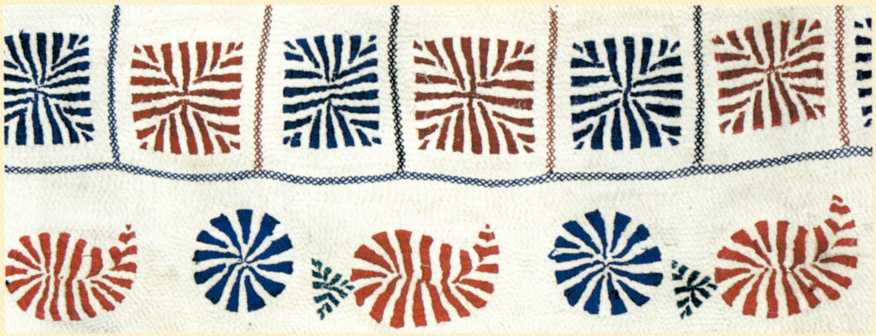

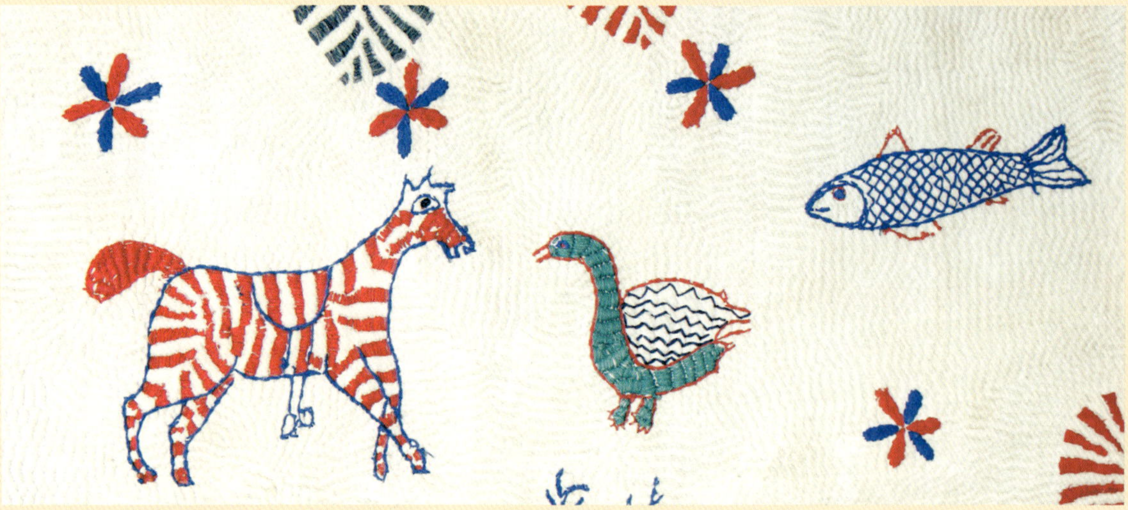

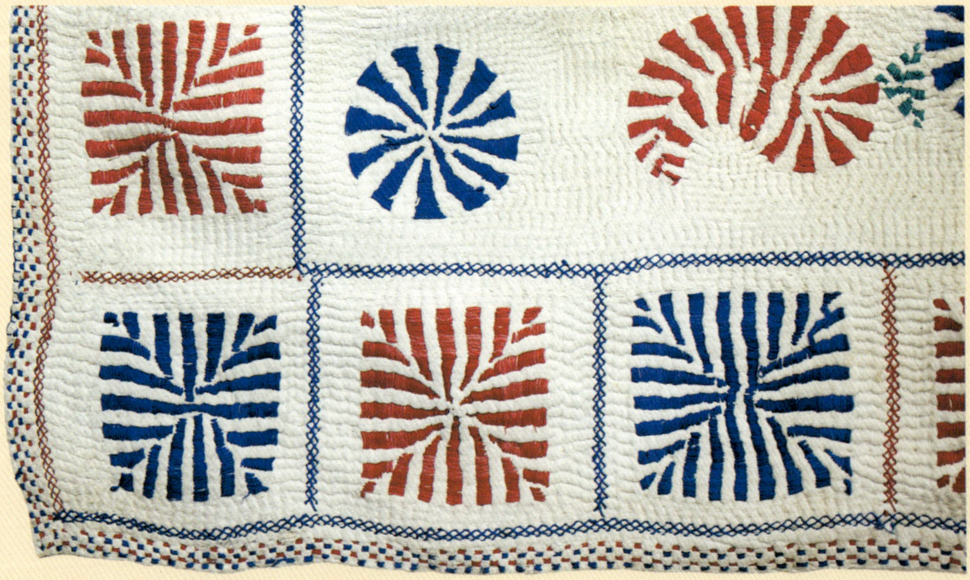

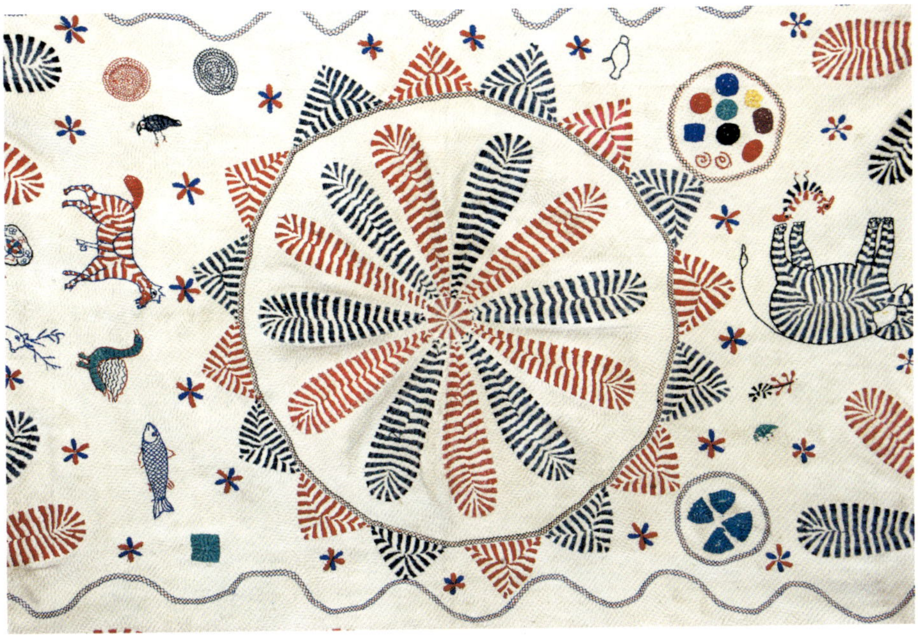

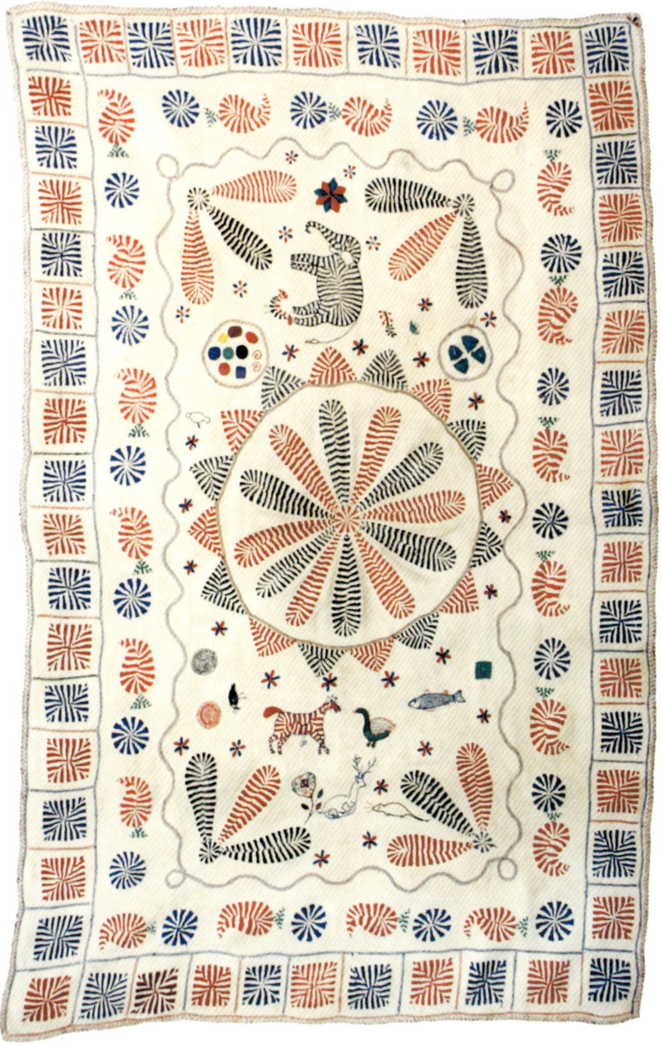

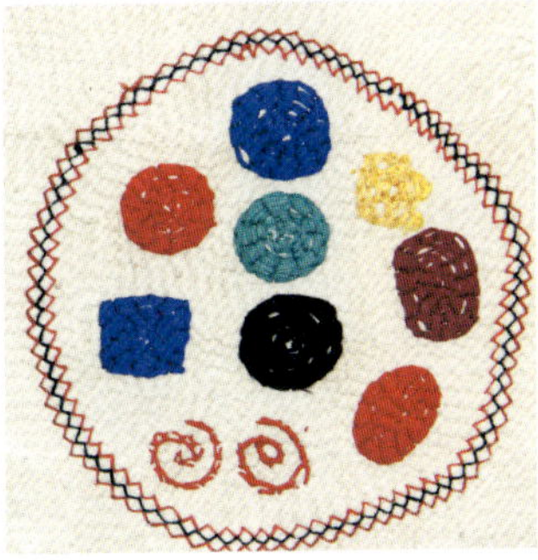

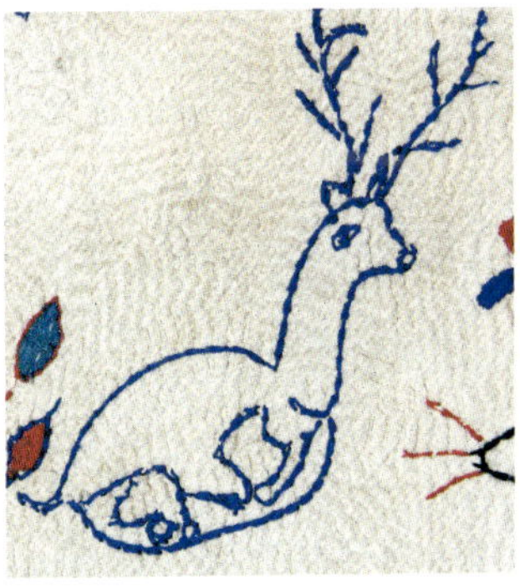

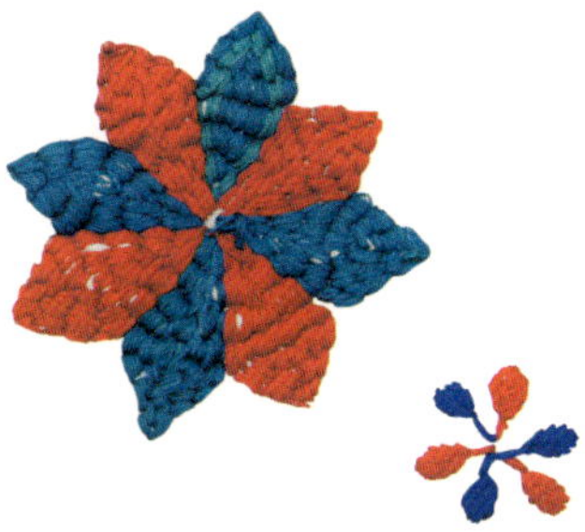

Kantha

Acc. No. IV/1C971/JS-Kan-11

Rectangle *Kantha* has a stylized lotus in the centre with trefoil motifs in all the four corners. The lotus in the centre has a square enclosure which has been embroidered with floral and foliage creepers. The square motif has a rectangular enclosure which has trident motifs arranged in a row on four sides. The inner side of the trident pattern is decorated with two enclosures on both sides; the outer sides have two plants in a pot and the inner portion has anthromorphic figures. There are four borders on the trident enclosure, the first one has a row of elephants, the second one has a half-moon pattern arranged in the creeper, the third enclosure has *kalka* pattern and the outermost side is decorated with a half lotus pattern in the enclosure.

It has a thin cotton lining. Colours used in embroidery are red, blue, yellow, black and grey. The field is rippled by self-running stitches.

Material - Cotton

Condition - Stable

Size - 186cmx124cm

Period - 20th Century

Place - West Bengal

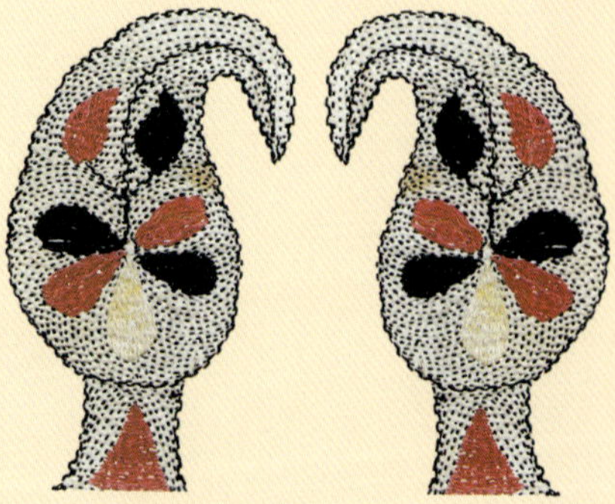

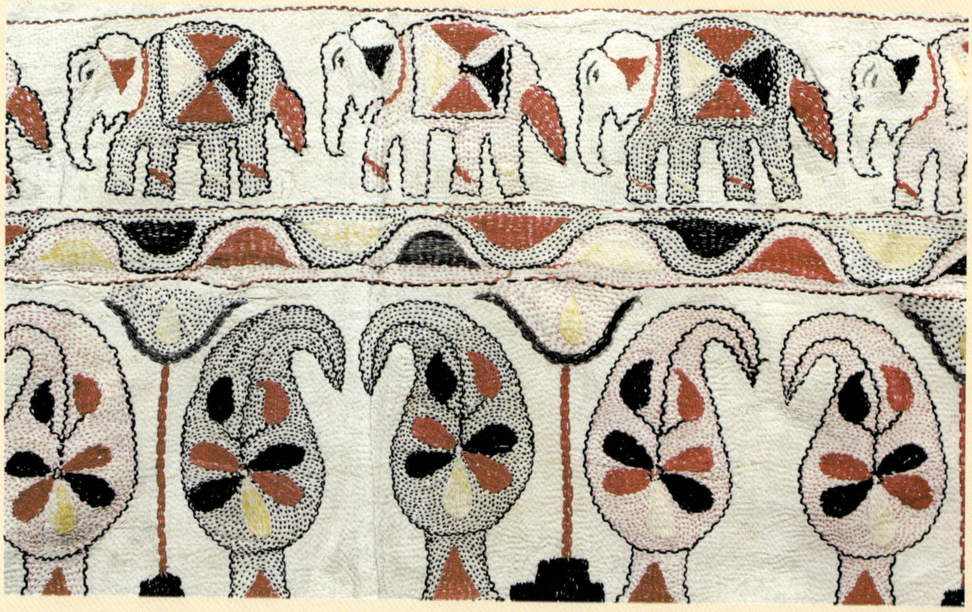

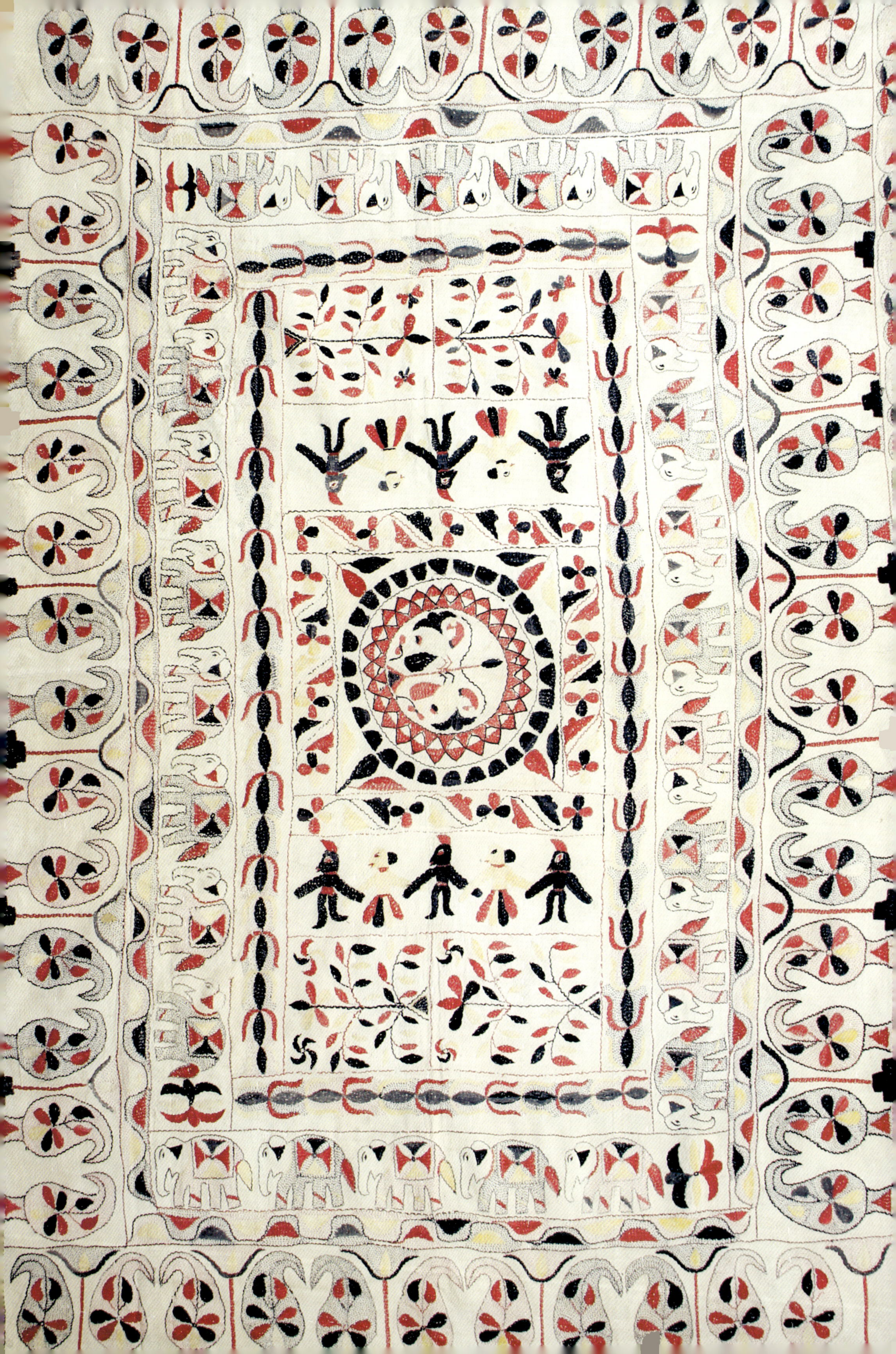

Kantha

Acc. No. IV/1C971/JS-Kan-11 (CONTD)

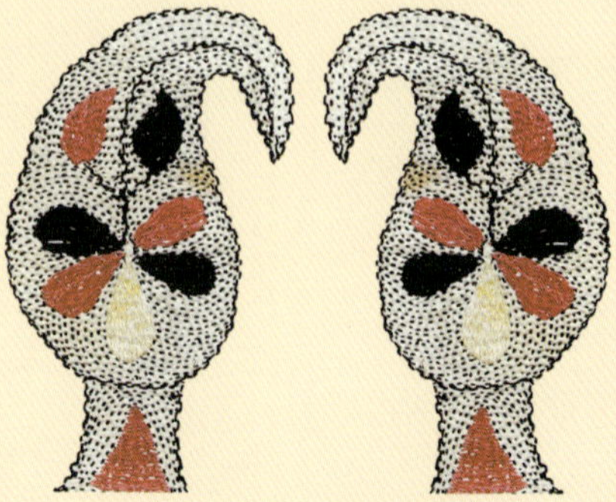

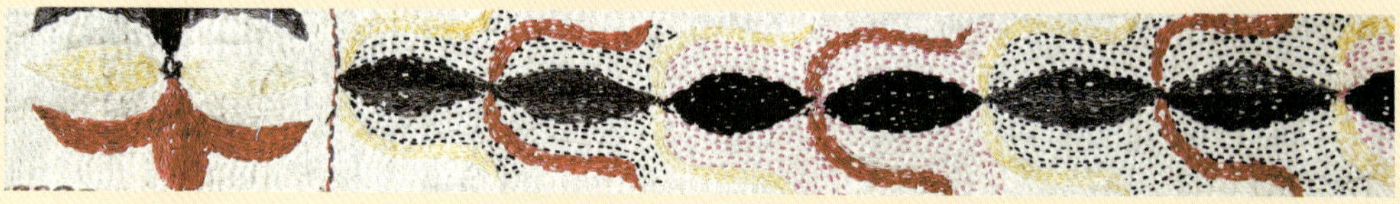

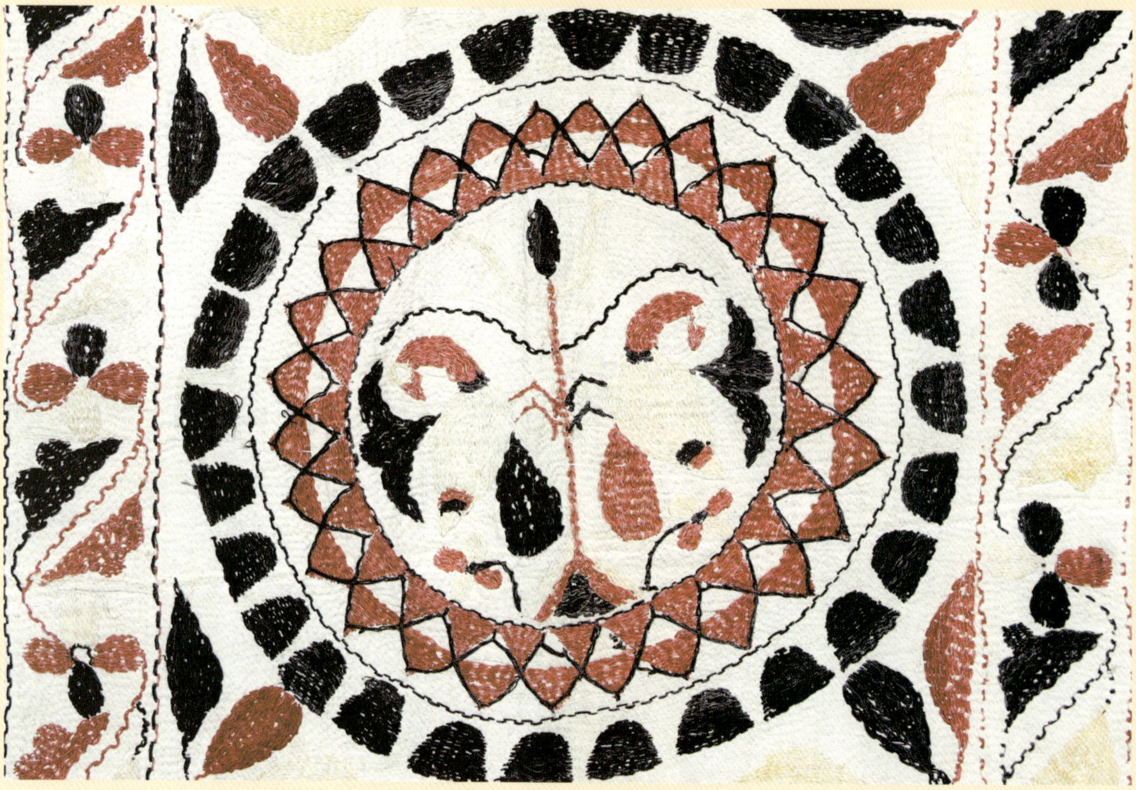

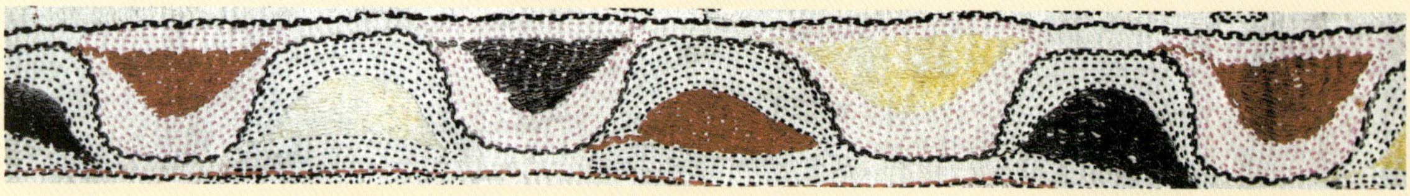

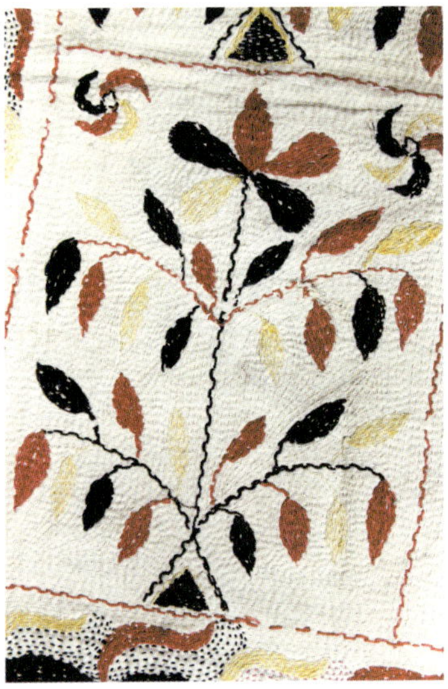

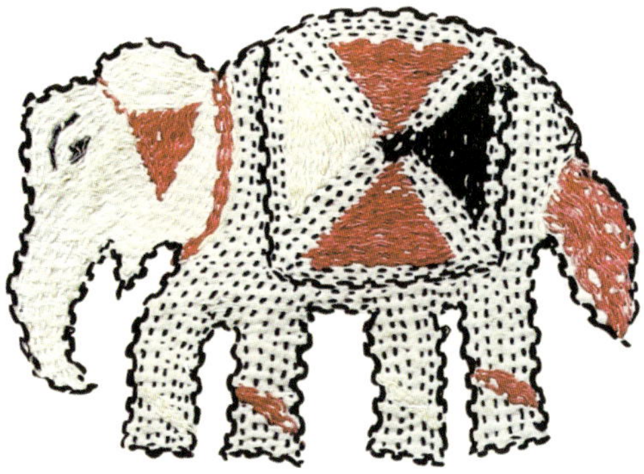

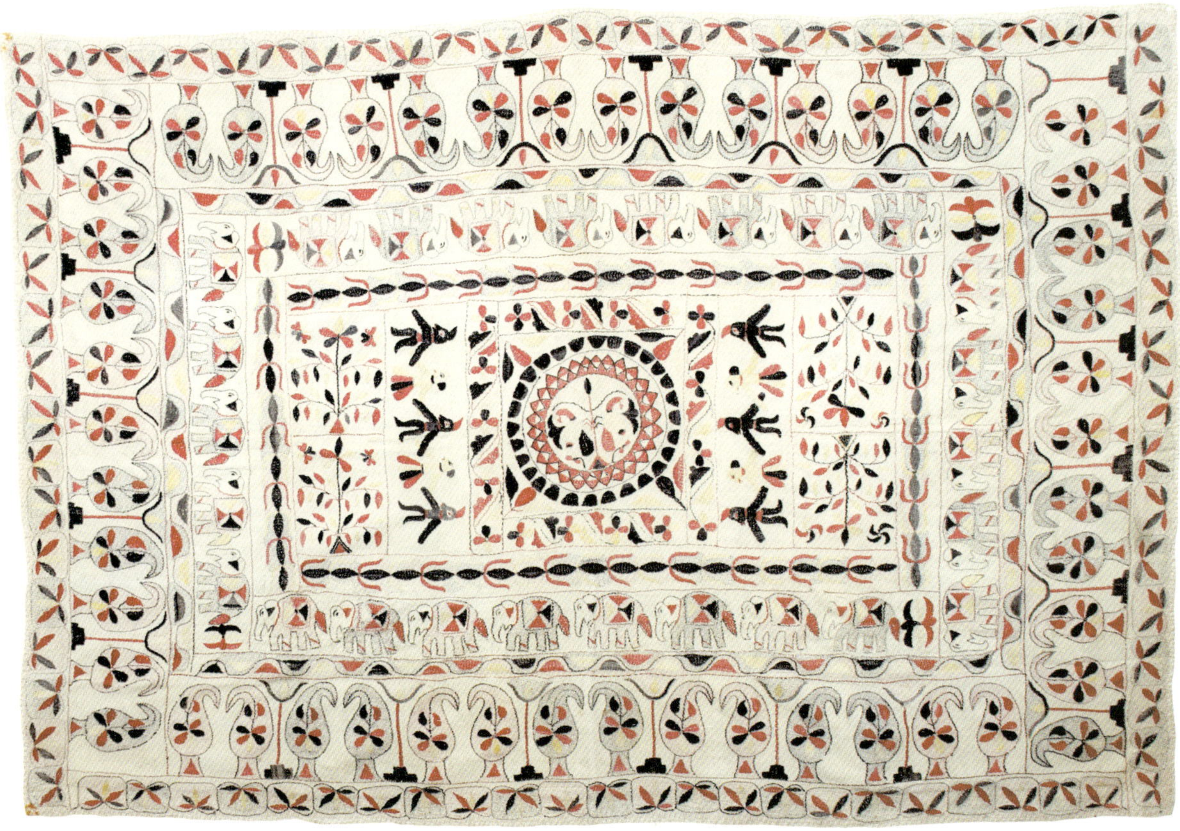

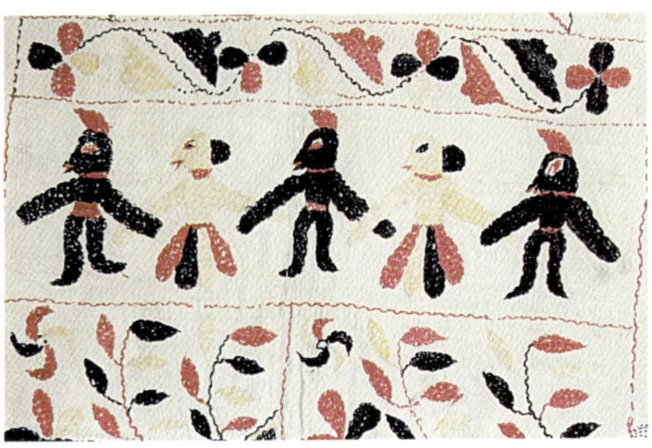

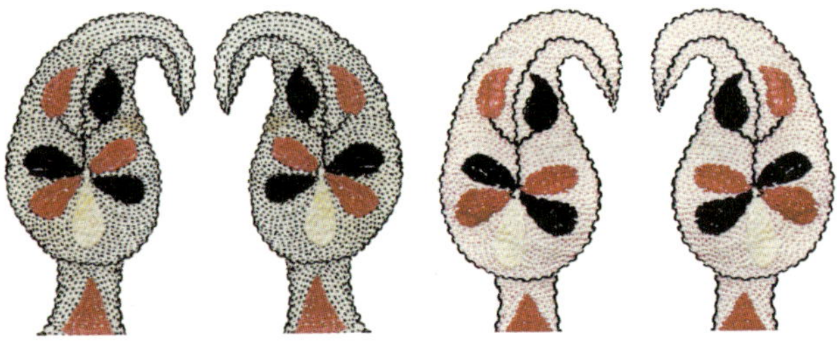

Asana

Acc. No. IV/I(97)/JS-KAN-12

Square *Kantha* (*asana*) having four layered lotus motif in the centre. The first layer has seven triangular leaves with tiny flowers in the middle. The second layer has eight red coloured triangular leaves which have blue edges with tiny creeper-like design on the edges. Next is a circular layer having tiny bud-like motif on the edges. The outer layer has eight triangular leaves in red and navy blue colours arranged alternately.

On the outer side, there are eight different wheels with *shosti chinha* in between two petals of the outer layers. The circle is surrounded by twelve betel-leaves, each filled with coloured running stitches.

The area around the lotus motif has eight and ten petalled stylized floral motifs with small multicoloured wheels in between. Around this floral motif, there is a foliage creeper on three sides, leaving fifteen centimetres on the fourth side.

The *Kantha* has another creeper as a border with wheels. There is a triple border on the edges having buds in a zigzag pattern and dotted designs on all four sides. The four corners again have stylized single leaf motifs. Colours used in the embroidery are red, yellow and multi shades of green and blue.

The ground has running stitches which is so fine that it looks rippled.

Material - Cotton

Condition - Edges have been torn and the field stained at places.

Size - 78cmx72cm

Period - 19th Century

Place - West Bengal

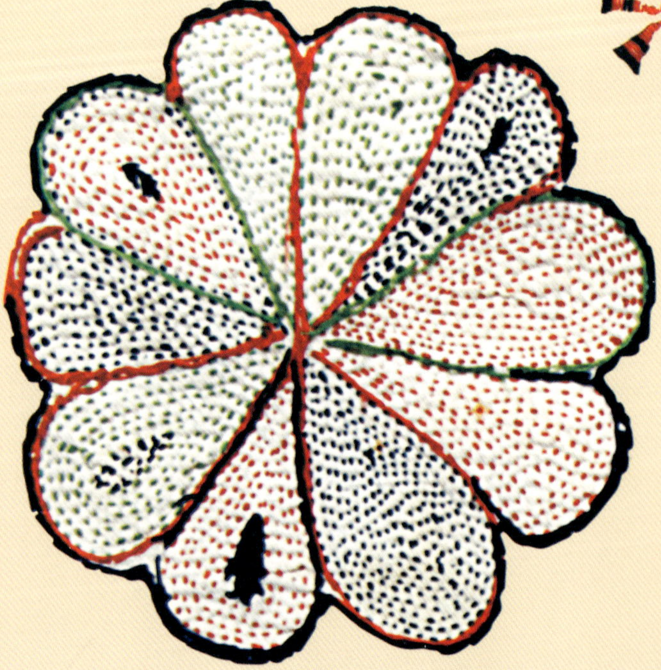

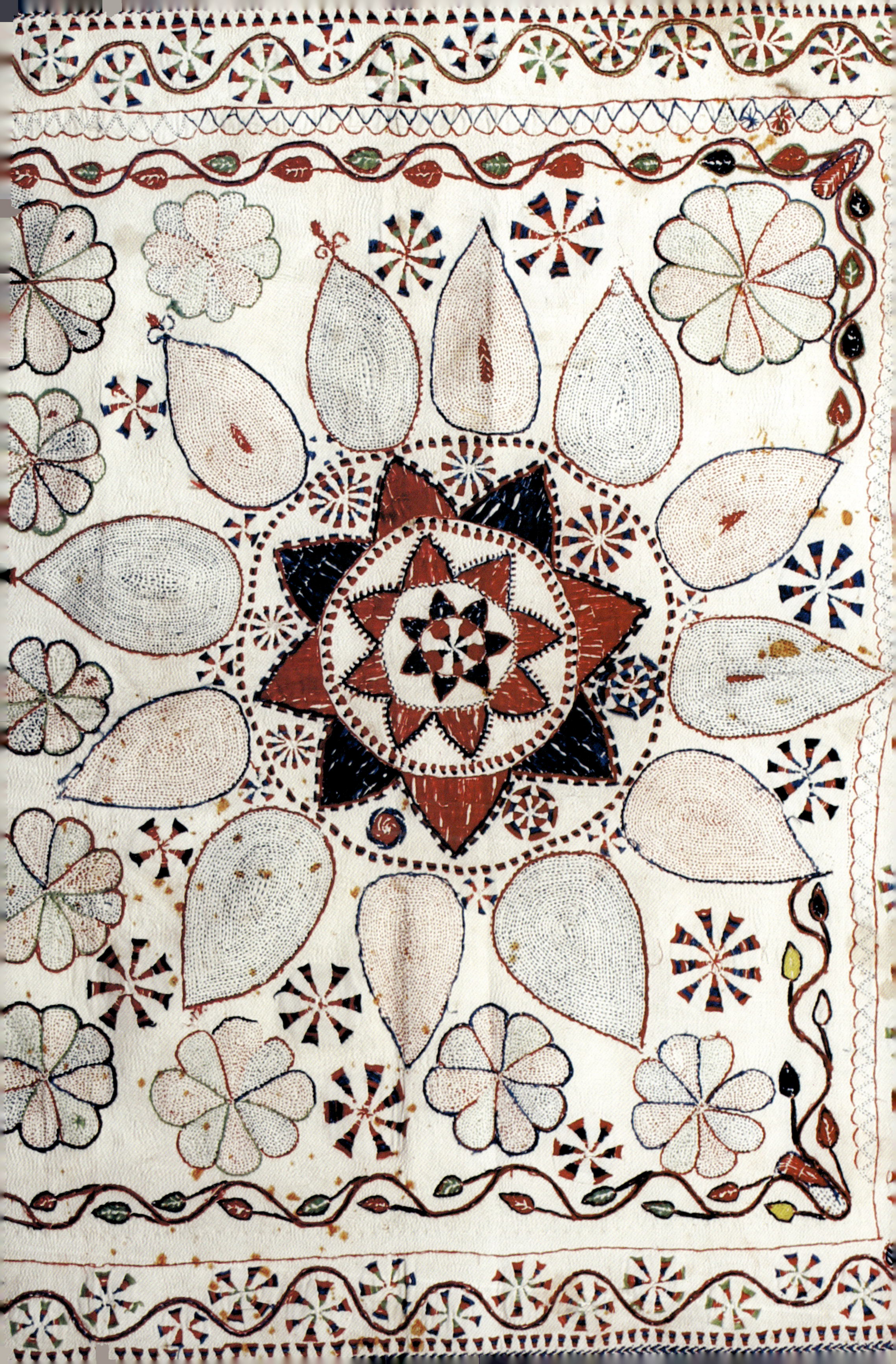

Asana

Acc. No. IV/I(97)/JS-KAN-12 (CONTD)

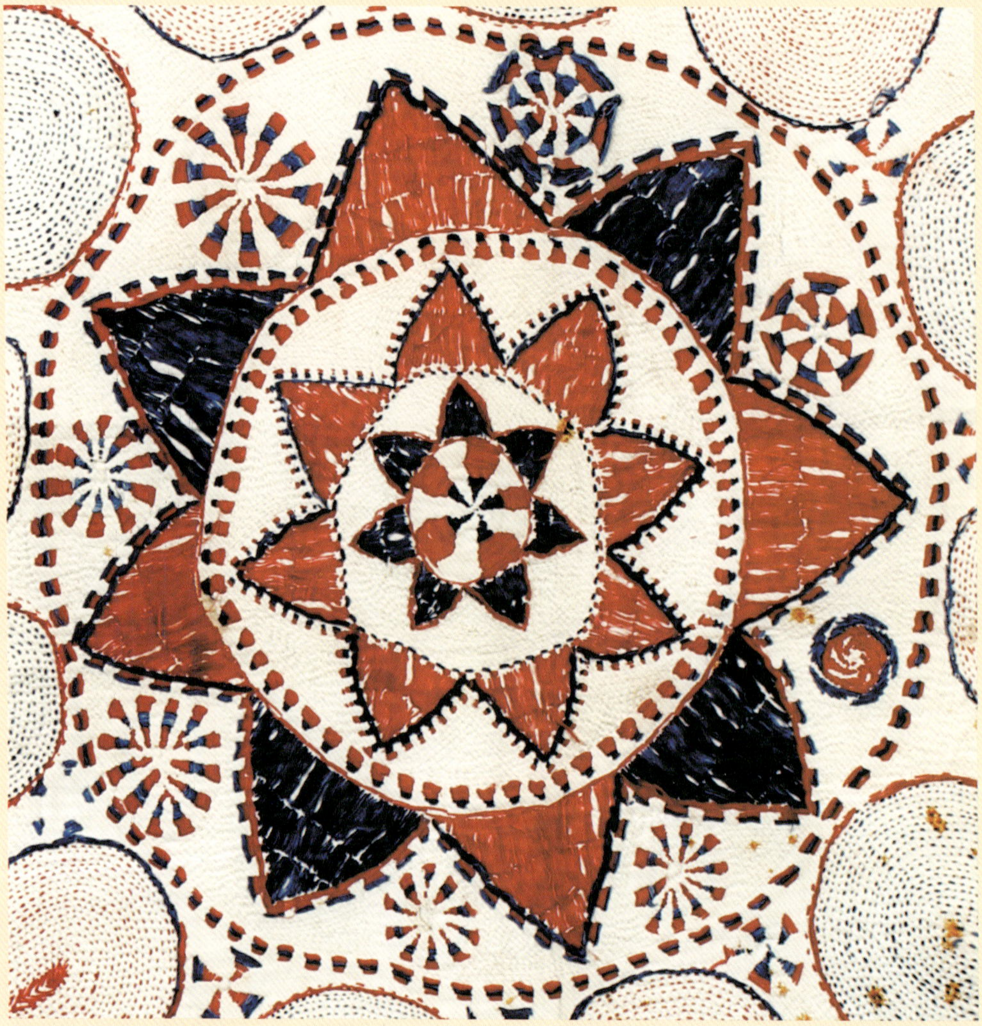

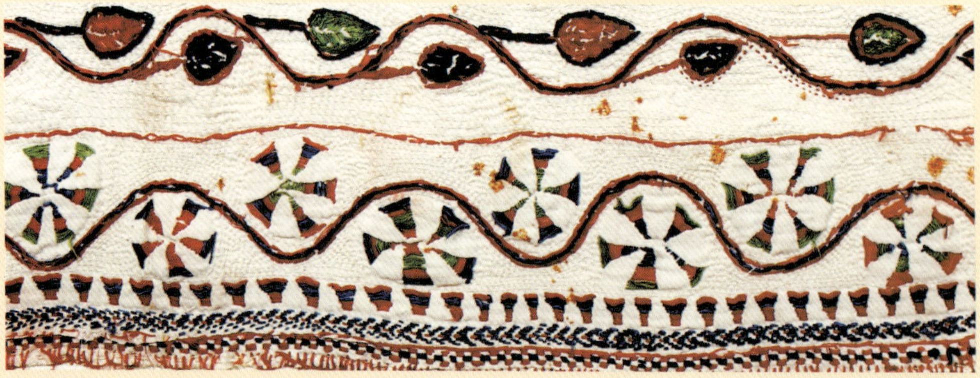

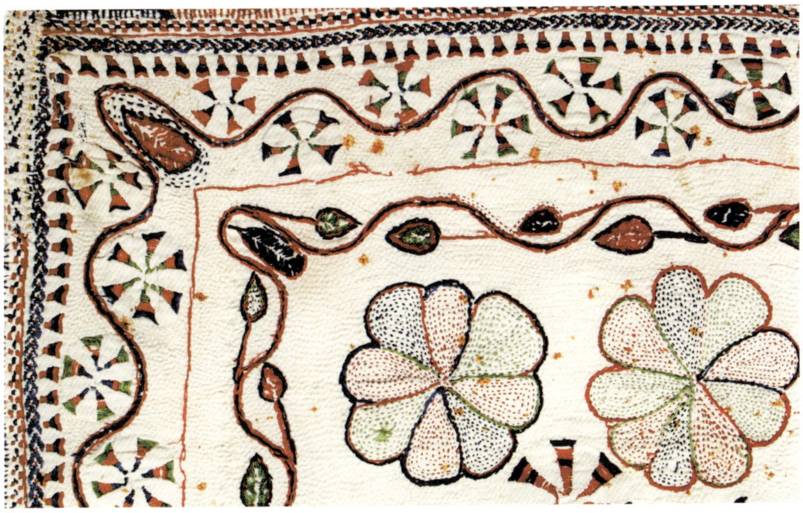

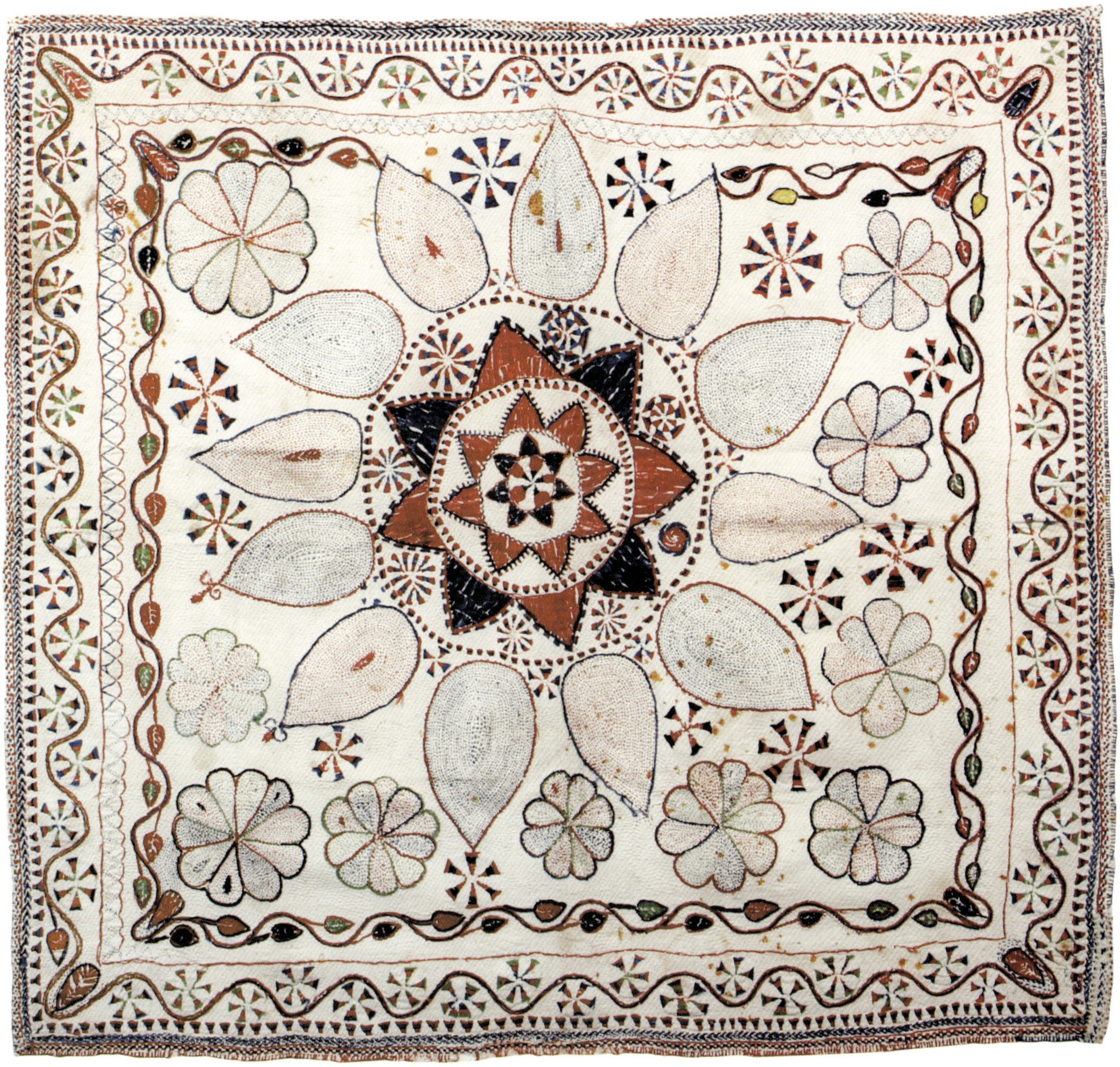

Kantha

Acc. No. IV/1C971/JS-KAN-13

Rectangular *dorukha* (double sided) *Kantha*, having a colourful lotus motif in the centre and the circular enclosure surrounded by *kalka*, wheel and miniature lotus etc.

One side of the central enclosure has a chariot decorated with wheels, flowers, flags and trefoil pattern. There are fine human figures in and around the chariot.

Below the chariot there are two columns which have human figures and motif like *shosti chinha*, wheel, trefoil and other geometrical figures. The other side of the enclosure has human figures, floral motifs and animal figures such as bull, donkey and cow; in the field, animals and human beings are seen together.

Outer part of the *Kantha* has two enclosures. The first enclosure has a row of wheels and *shosti chinha*, while the second enclosure is decorated with stylized *kalkas*.

The border of the *Kantha* is made of geometrical figures.

The background base is completely rippled by self-running stitches.

The colours used in embroidery are red, blue, yellow and black.

Material - Cotton

Condition - Stained at places.

Size - 20cmx90cm

Period - 19th Century

Place - West Bengal

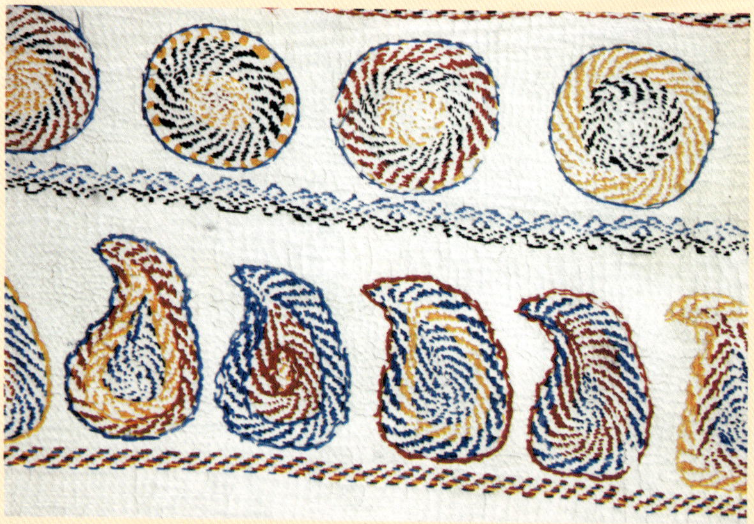

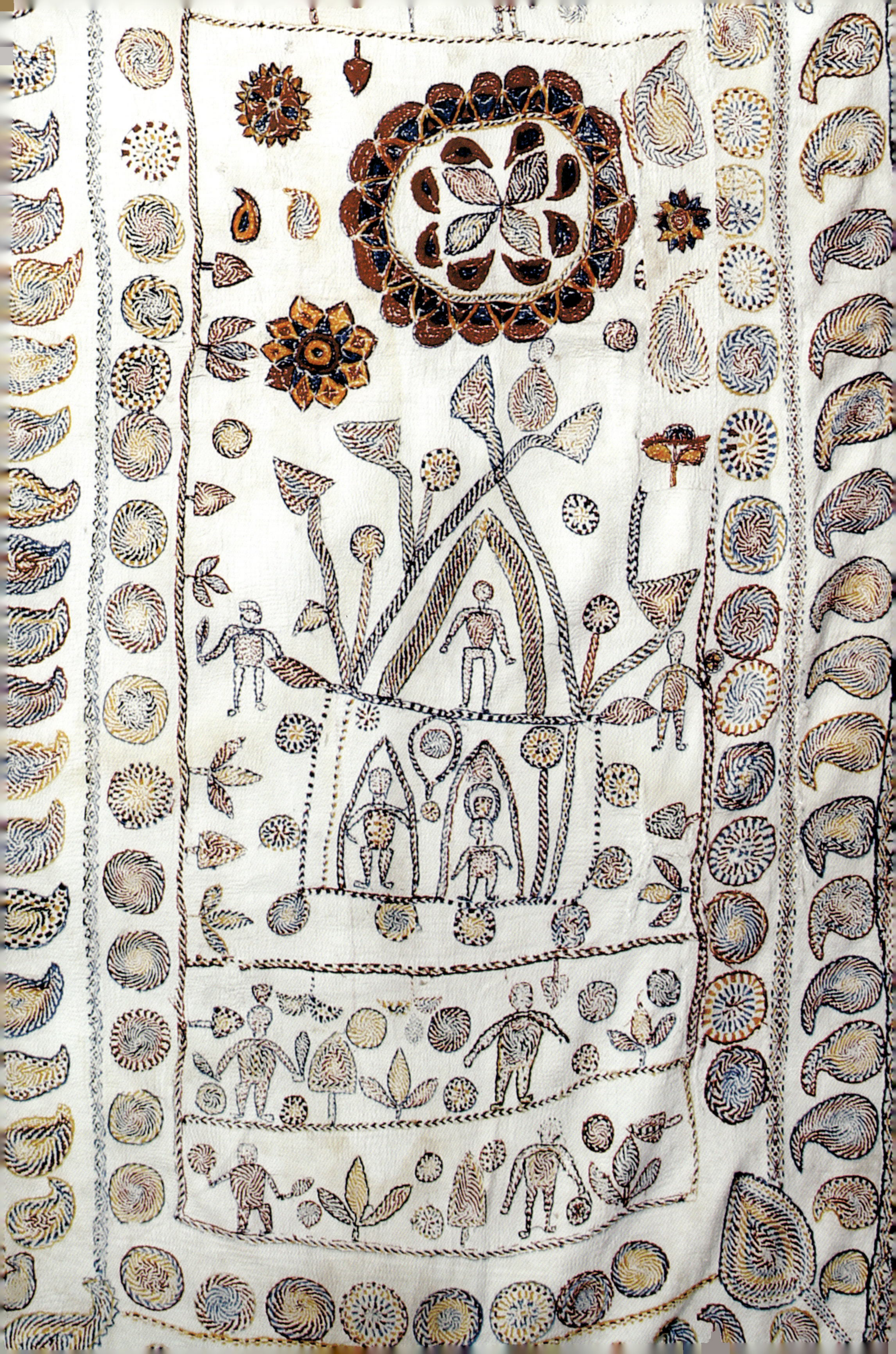

Kantha

Acc. No. IV/1C971/JS-KAN-13 (CONTD)

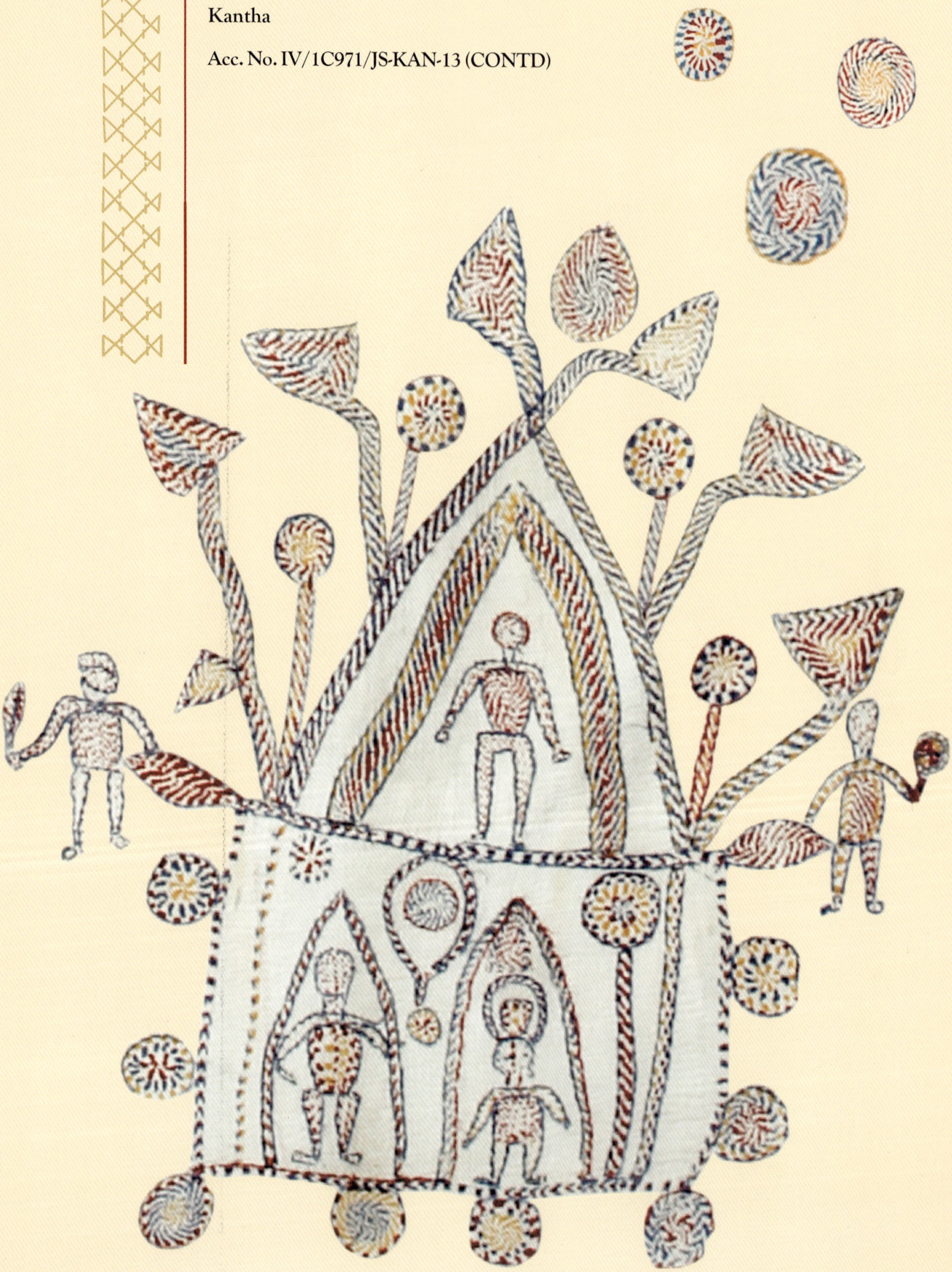

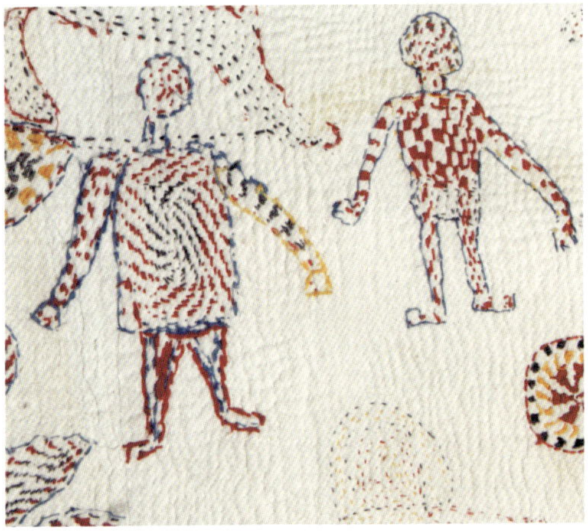

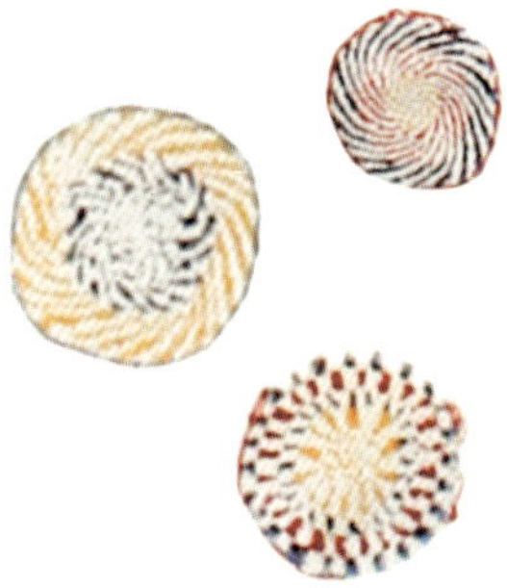

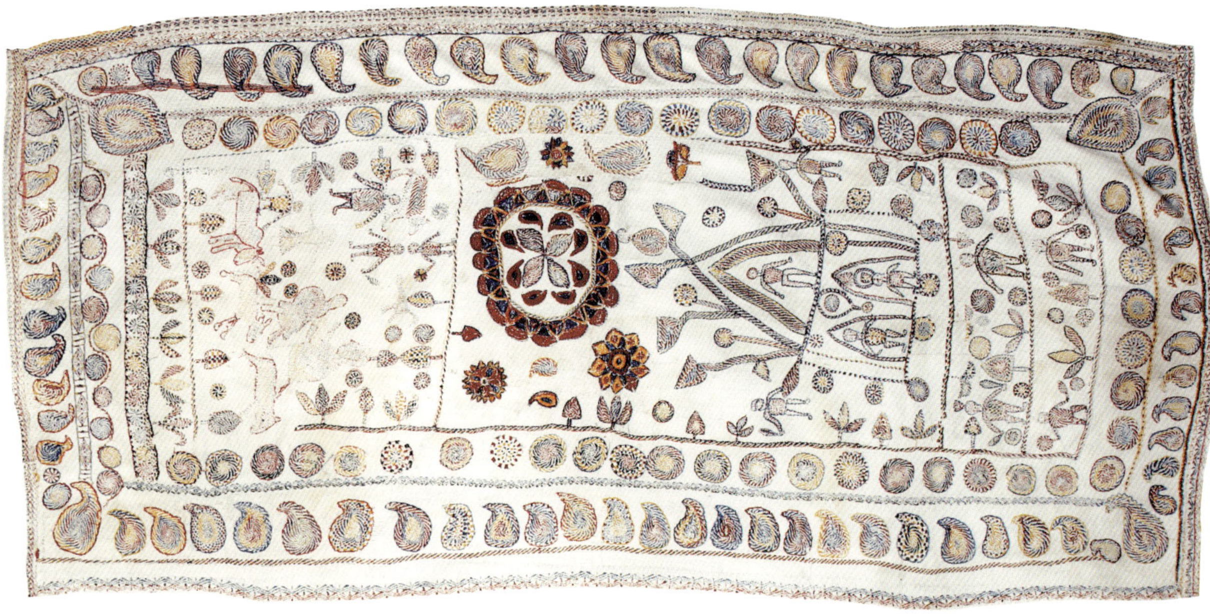

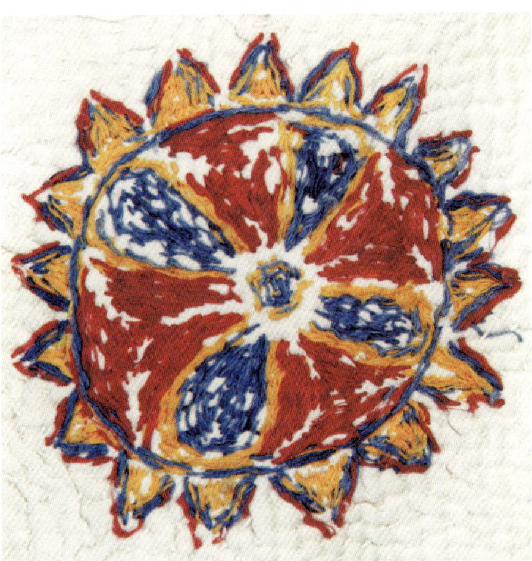

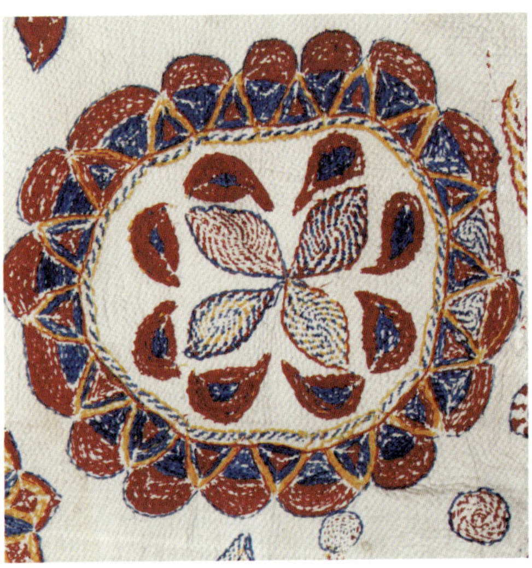

Kantha

Acc. No. IV/1C971/JS-KAN-14

Large *dorukha* (double sided) *Kantha* adorned by a large sized lotus with scattered spiral and foliage patterns. On the two diagonal corners there are big plants in ornamental pots having foliage patterns. Some have round while some others have pointed tips. Near these plants, in the two corners, there are five leaf patterns in each. There is a large elephant with *houda* (seat), which is surrounded by foliage creeper, wheel, small lamps (*diya*) and *shosti chinha* (swastika).

In the other two corners, each has one wheel with four semi-circular lines surmounted by twelve leaves, each having a small stem. Next, there is a small lamp like figure and a plant in an ornamental pot having a curved line below (perhaps roots).

The plant has flowers and very ornamental curved leaves. Next to the plant, there is a small circle, perhaps a betel box containing a *sarota* (nut cutter), betel leaf with a stem, and *areca* nuts (*supari*). (Eight big *suparis* and one small *supari*).

On one side of the *Kantha* are sea organisms like snails, jelly fish etc.

Small wheels have been embroidered at places. Borders on the four sides have buttonhole stitches at the edges with stylized foliage pattern on the surface.

The field has very fine running stitches in self colours.

Colours used in embroidery are red, blue, pink, orange and green.

Material - Cotton

Condition - The *Kantha* is badly stained and repaired and embroidery is missing at places.

Period - 19th Century

Size - 181cmx125cm

Place - West Bengal

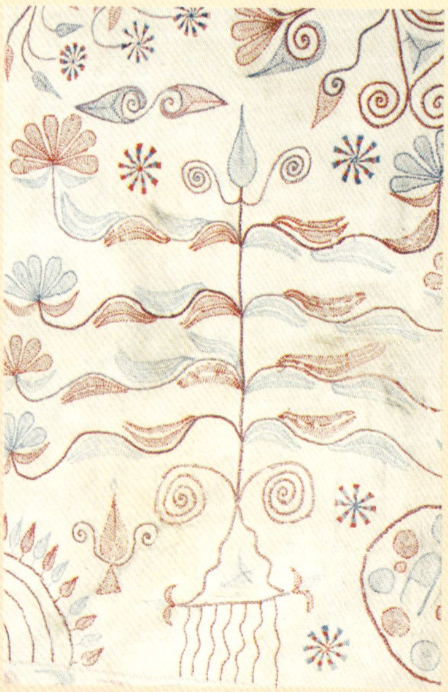

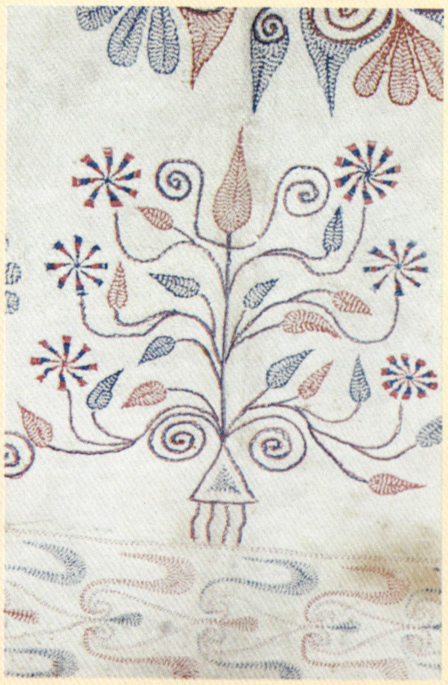

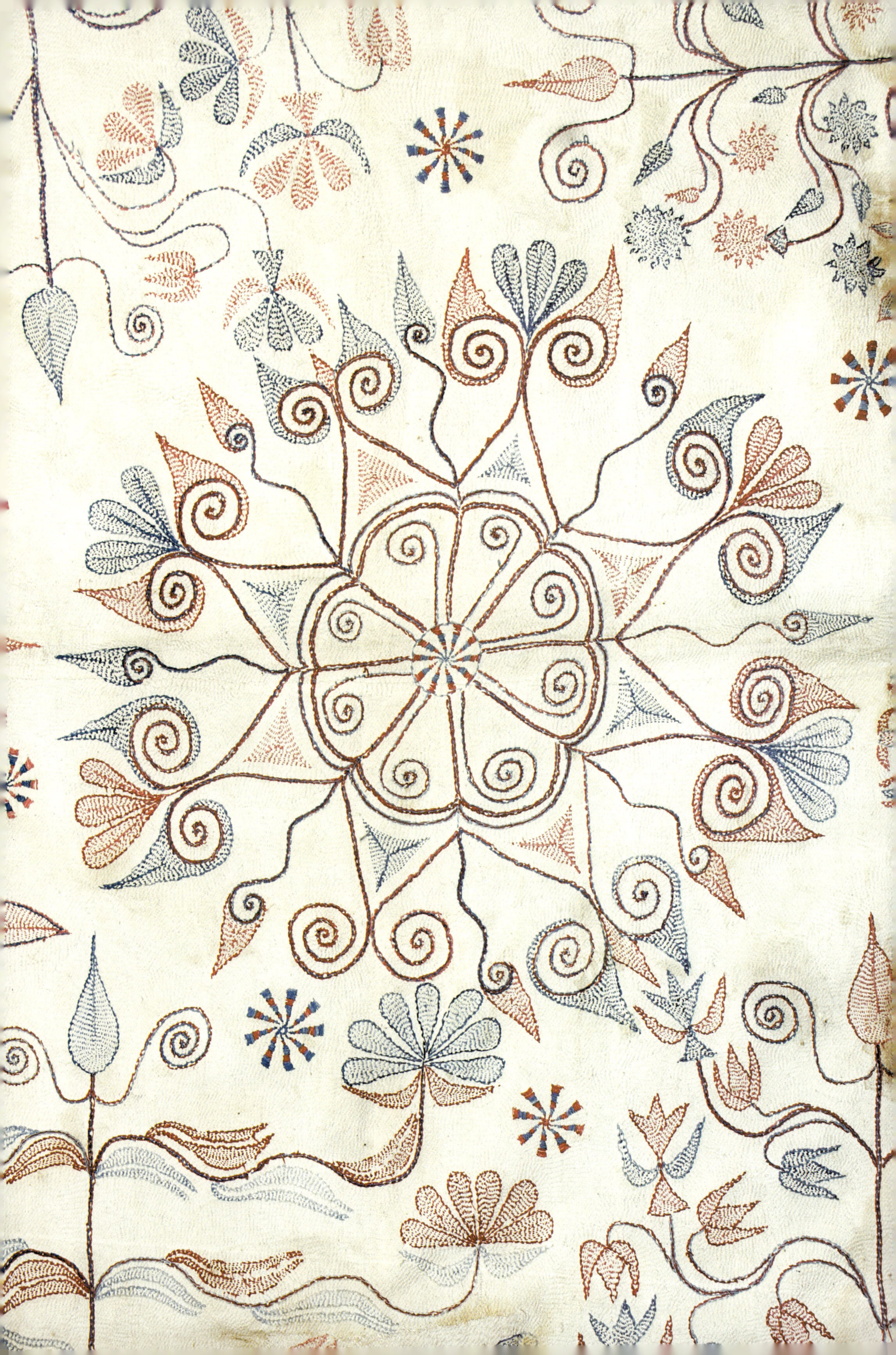

Kantha

Acc. No. IV/1C971/JS-KAN-14 (CONTD)

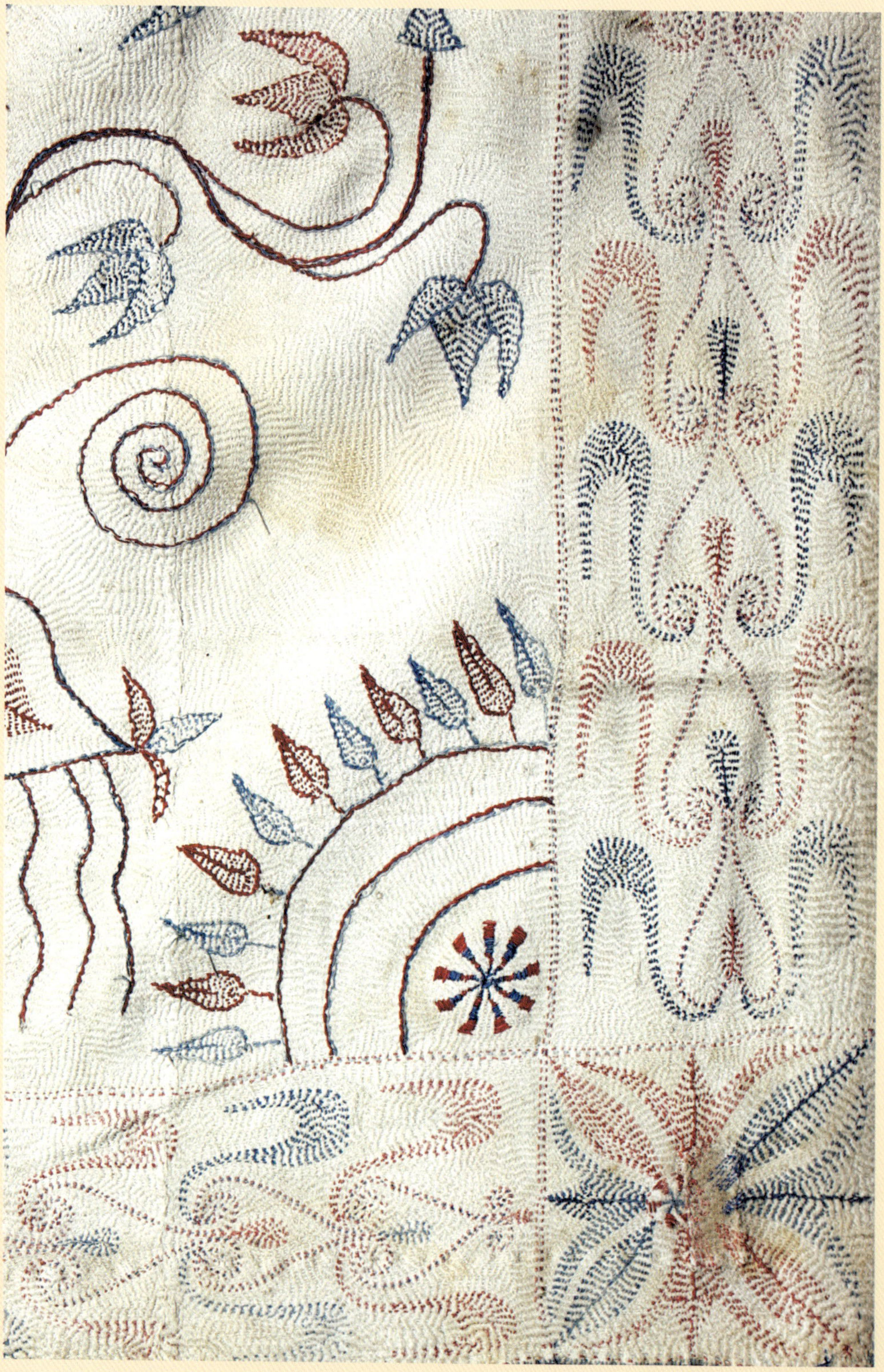

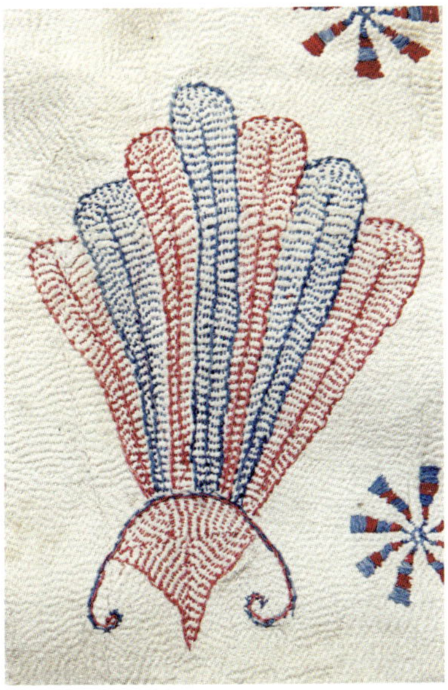

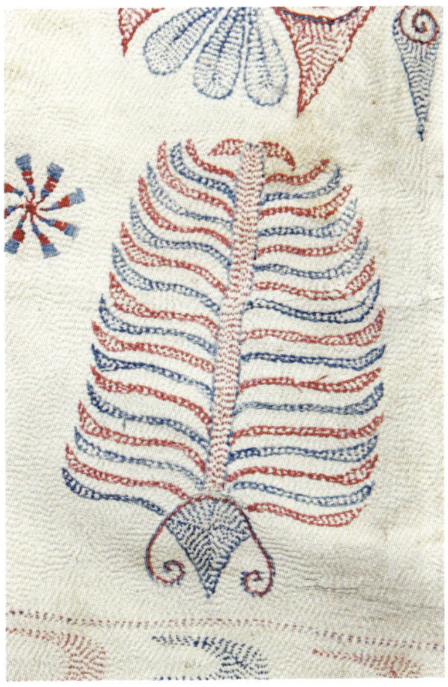

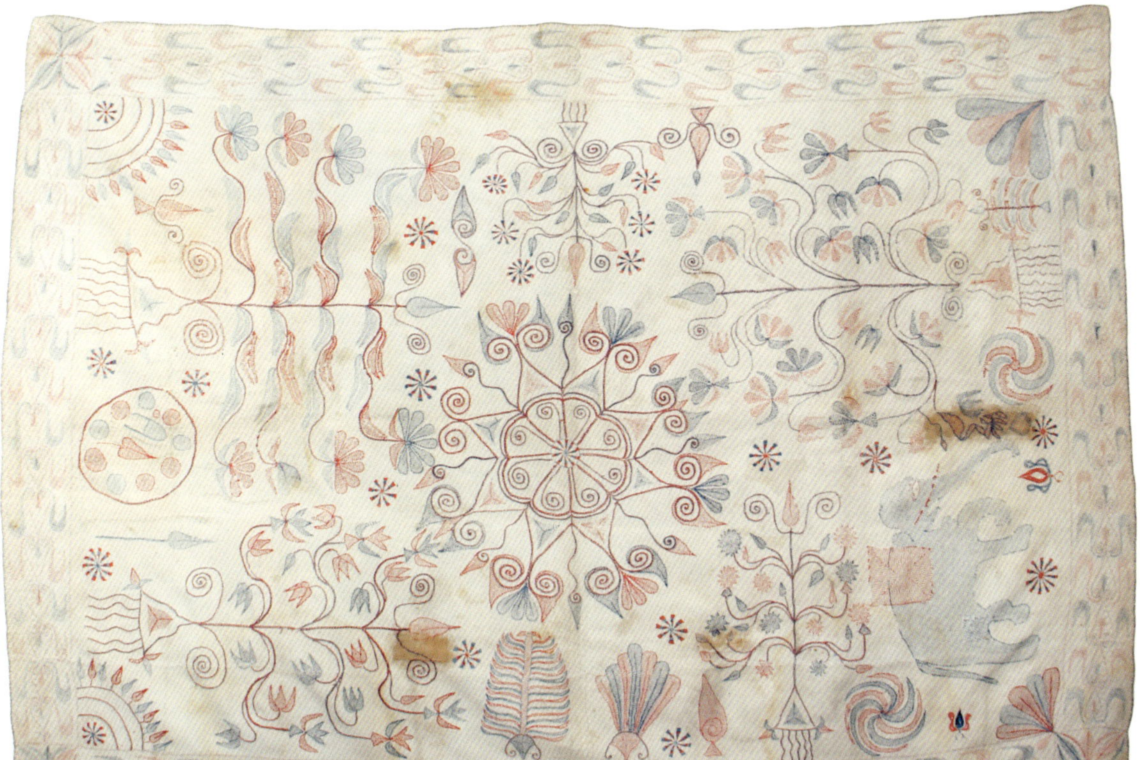

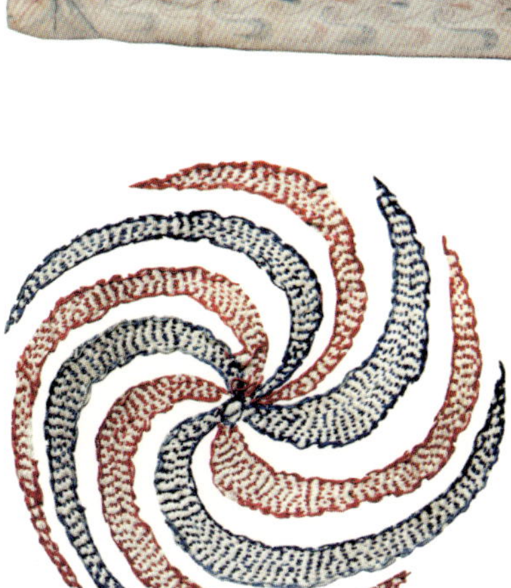

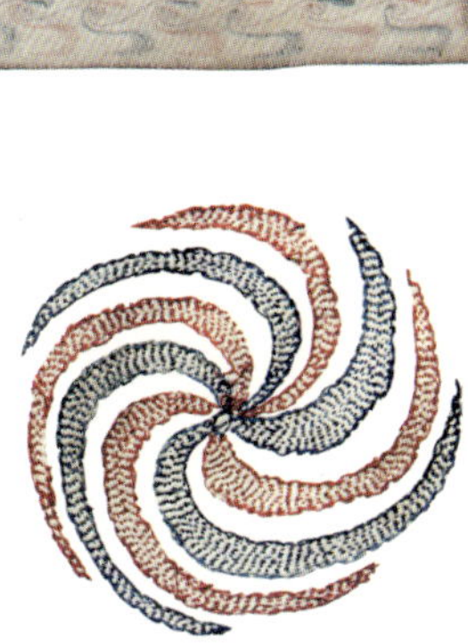

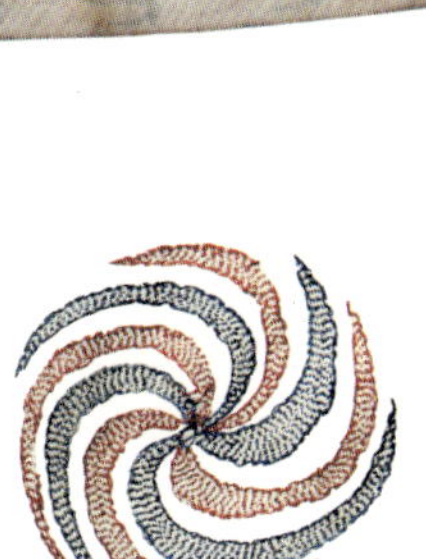

Kantha

Acc. No. IV/1C971/JS-KAN-15

Rectangular piece of *Kantha* having a lotus in the centre, enclosed with a line in *chatai* pattern which has a half leaf pattern in a row arranged inwards. It has eight round shaped petals. The outer circle of lotus is decorated with triangular leaves and curved lines.

In each of the four corners, there is a trefoil *buta* surmounted by a triangular pot having foliage leaves with long stems and with a bird on top.

The central lotus is flanked by two elephants (lengthwise). One elephant has a rider, while the other has an ornamental shrine-shaped *houda* on its back. The other side of the lotus has a tiger in the centre and a horse-rider and elephant- rider on either side. Between the tiger and horse-rider, there is a *sarota* (nut-cutter) in the centre, flanked by a sitting tiger and a man riding on an ornamental horse. On the other side (length wise), there is a tiger pouncing on an elephant with a rider and there is also a horse-rider by its side.

There are three broad borders on all the four sides, each demarcated with broad lines of *chatai* patterns.

The first inner border has a betel leaf pattern arranged in a curved enclosure. The middle border has a single row of wheel-like motifs. The corner most border is embroidered with wheel patterns in the centre, with an elongated side.

The entire field has running stitches while the embroidery has been done in the *katiya* stitch. Colours used are red, mustard, black and different shades of blue.

Material - Cotton

Condition - *Kantha* has holes and stains at places.

Size - 189cmx136cm

Period - 20th Century

Place - West Bengal

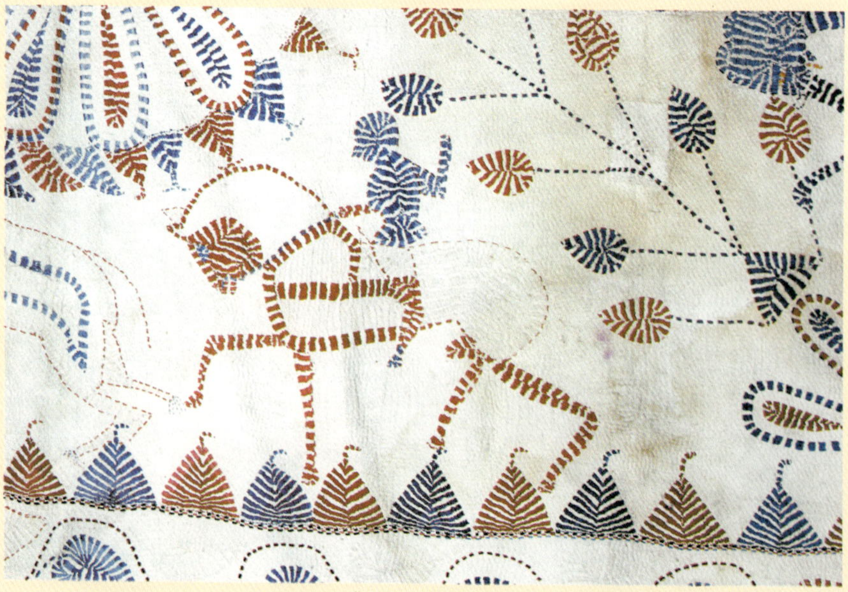

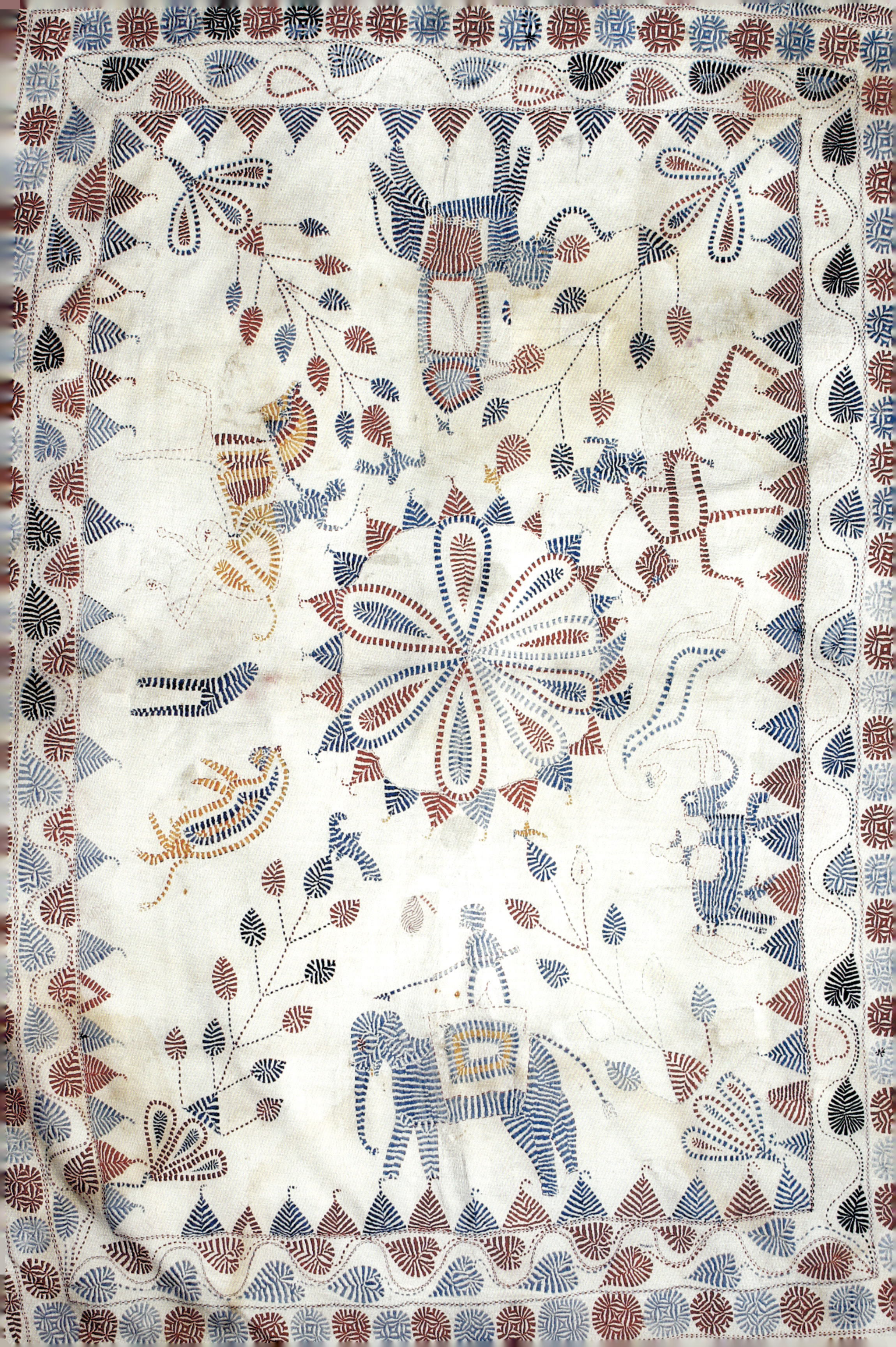

Kantha

Acc. No. IV/1C971/JS-KAN-15 (CONTD)

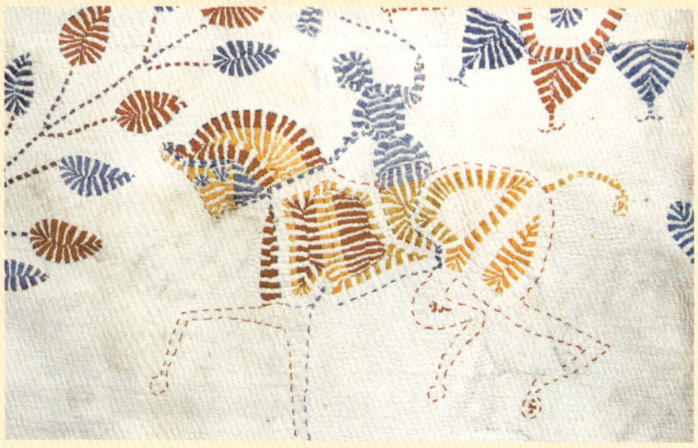

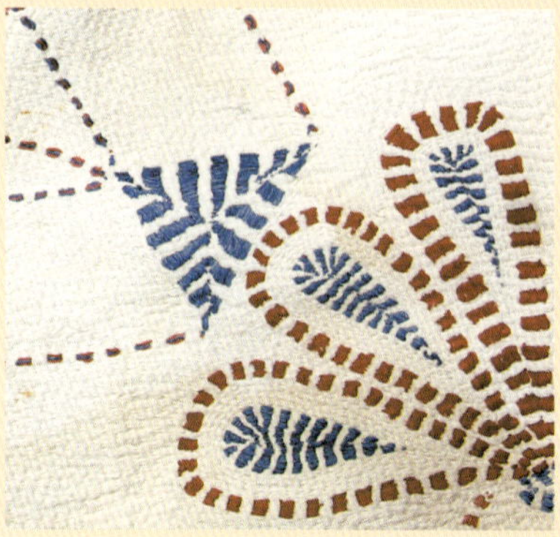

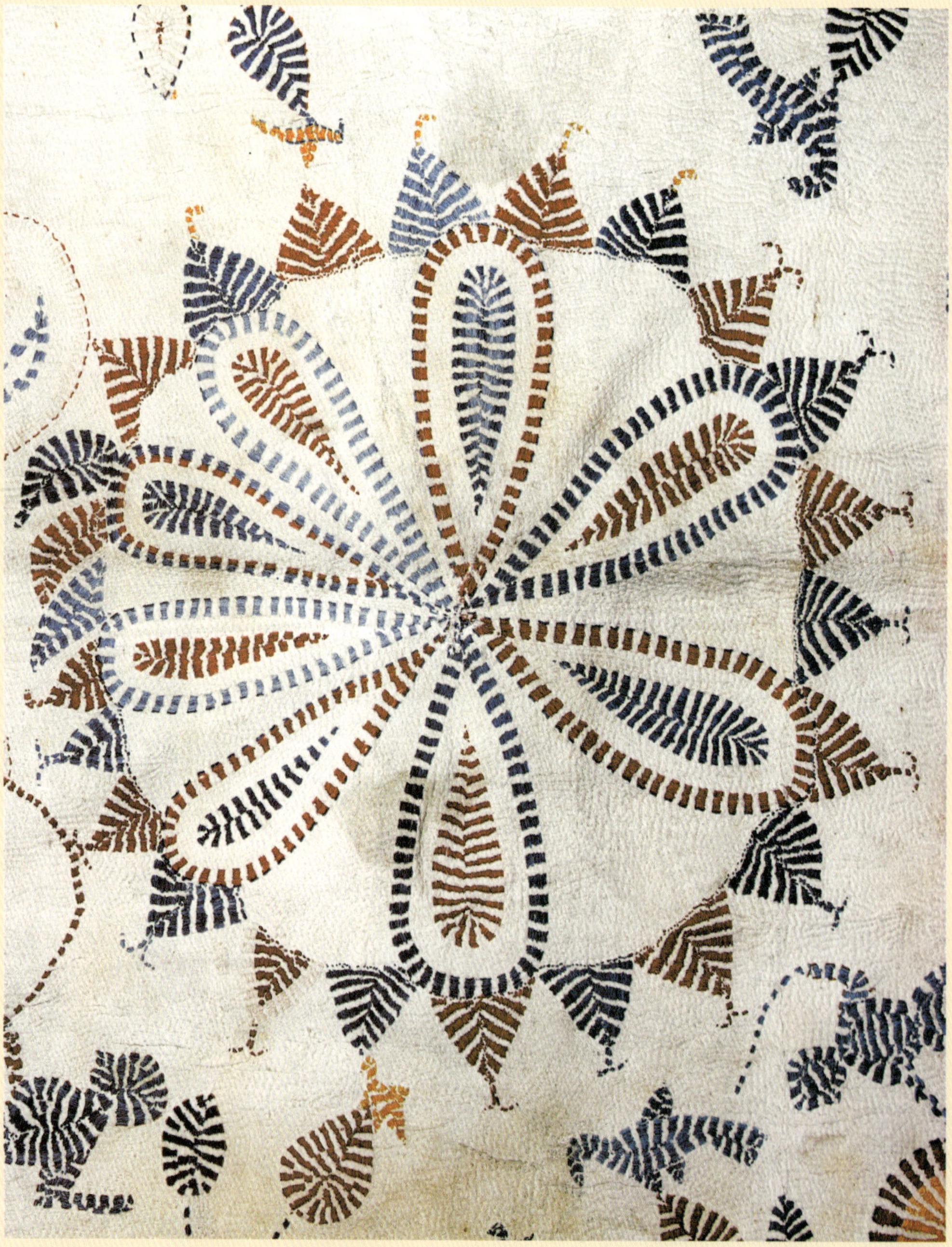

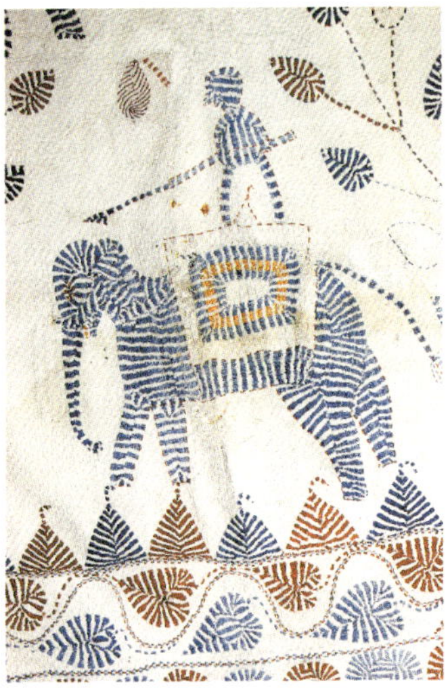

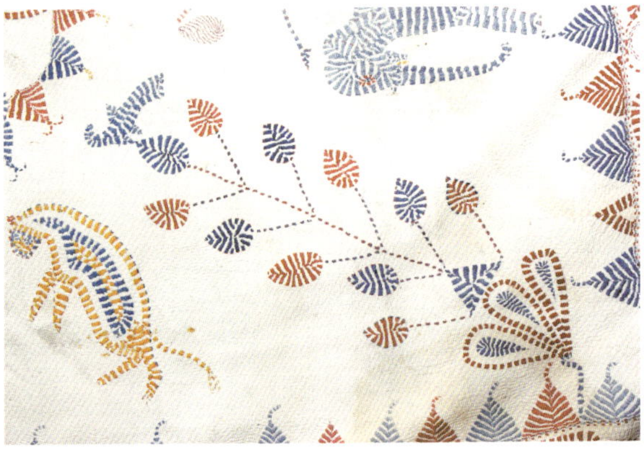

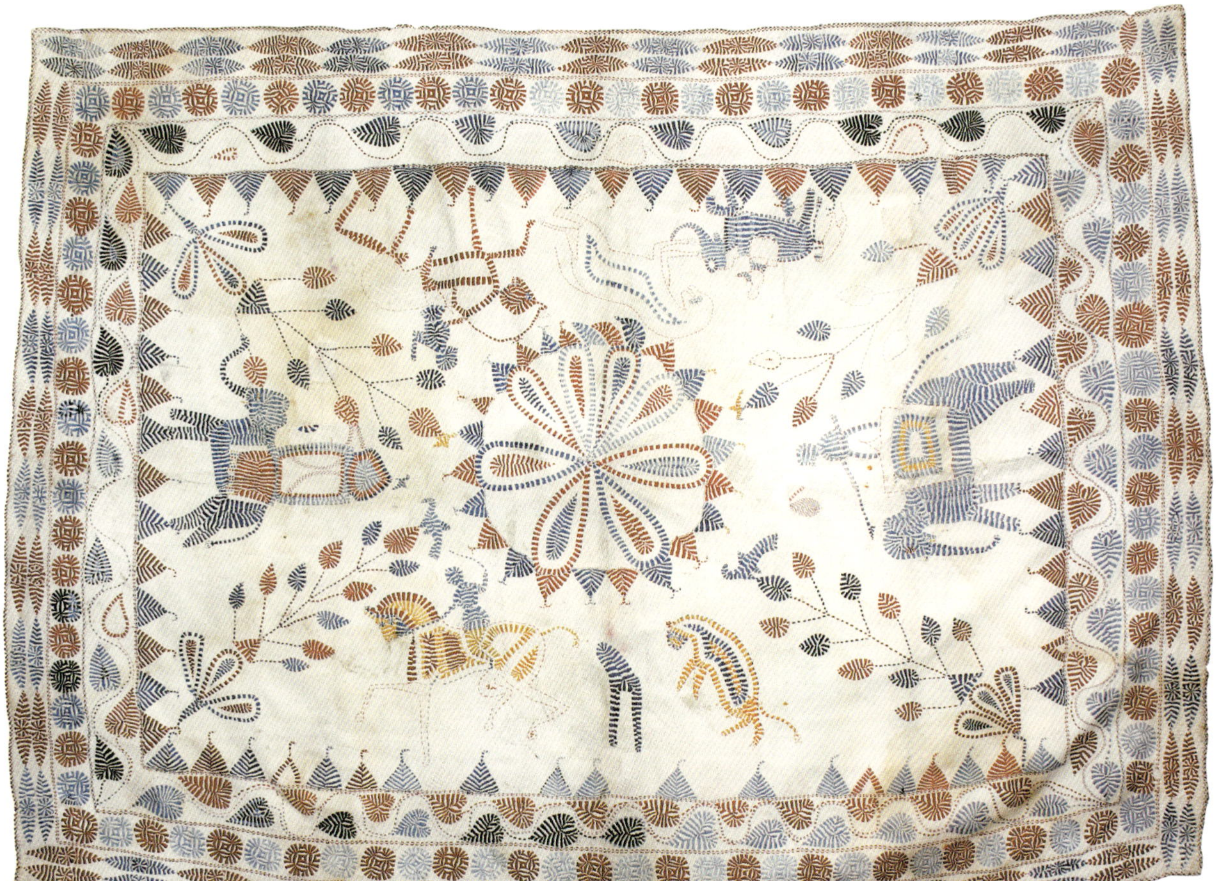

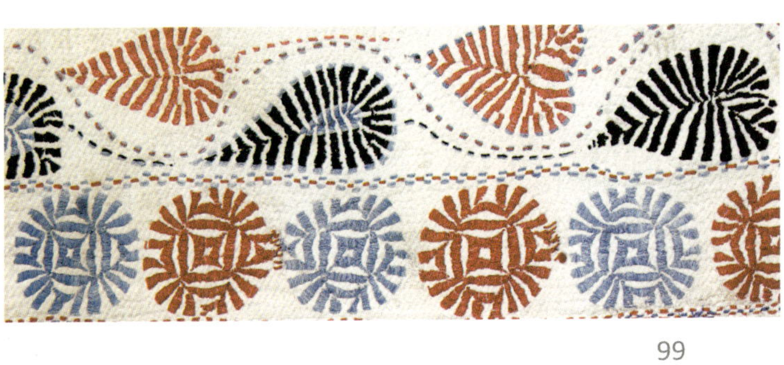

Kantha

Acc. No. IV/1C971/JS-KAN-16

Rectangular *Kantha* with its entire field embroidered with multi coloured borders arranged horizontally. These borders are decorated with geometrical designs like *Taa'l biz* (amulet), *Chok* (diamond shaped) *Bichche* (scorpion border) and *Beki* (wavy and bent) etc.

There are two enclosures in this *Kantha*. The inner enclosure has been decorated with *Chok* (diamond shaped) pattern, while the outer border has geometrical designs enclosed in a zigzag pattern and having vessels on all the four corners.

The gaps in between the embroidery have been filled by running stitches. Colours used are blue, red, black, green, and grey.

Material - Cotton

Condition - Stained and holes at places.

Size - 148cmx104cm

Period - Late 19th Century

Place - West Bengal

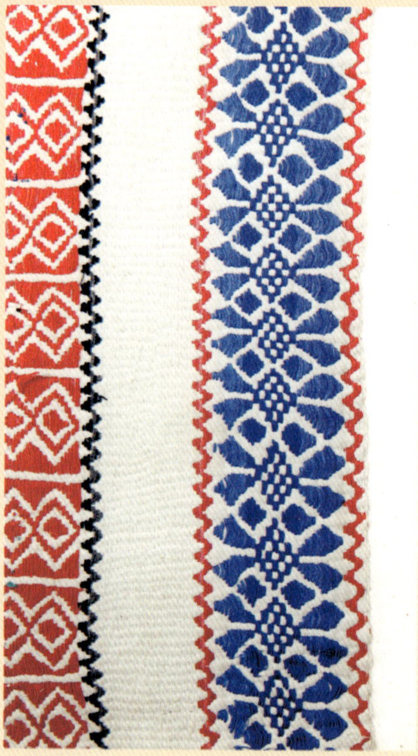

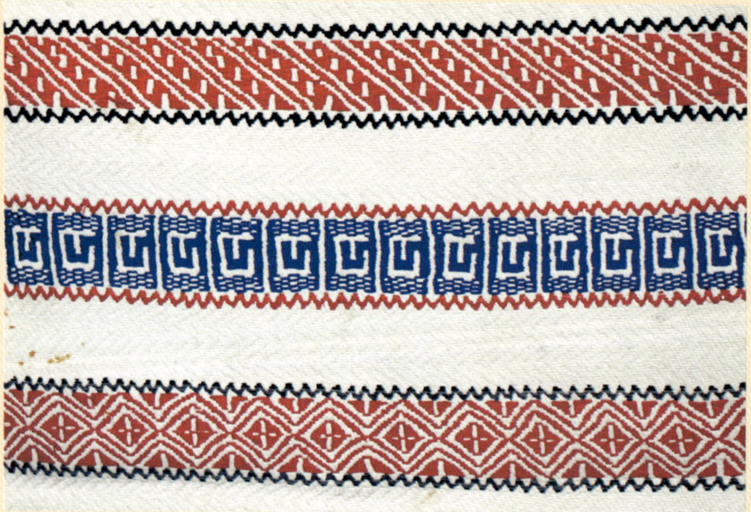

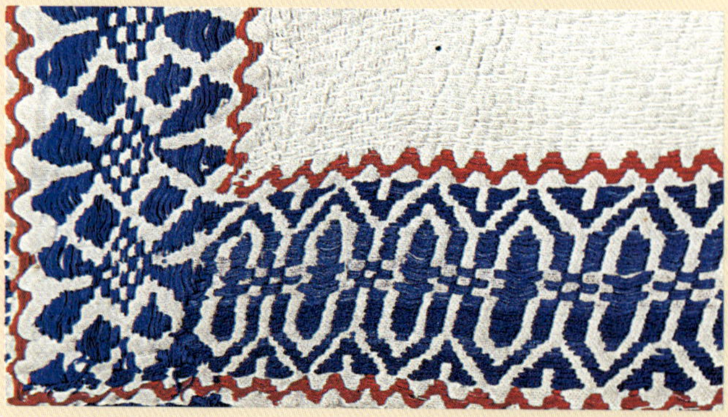

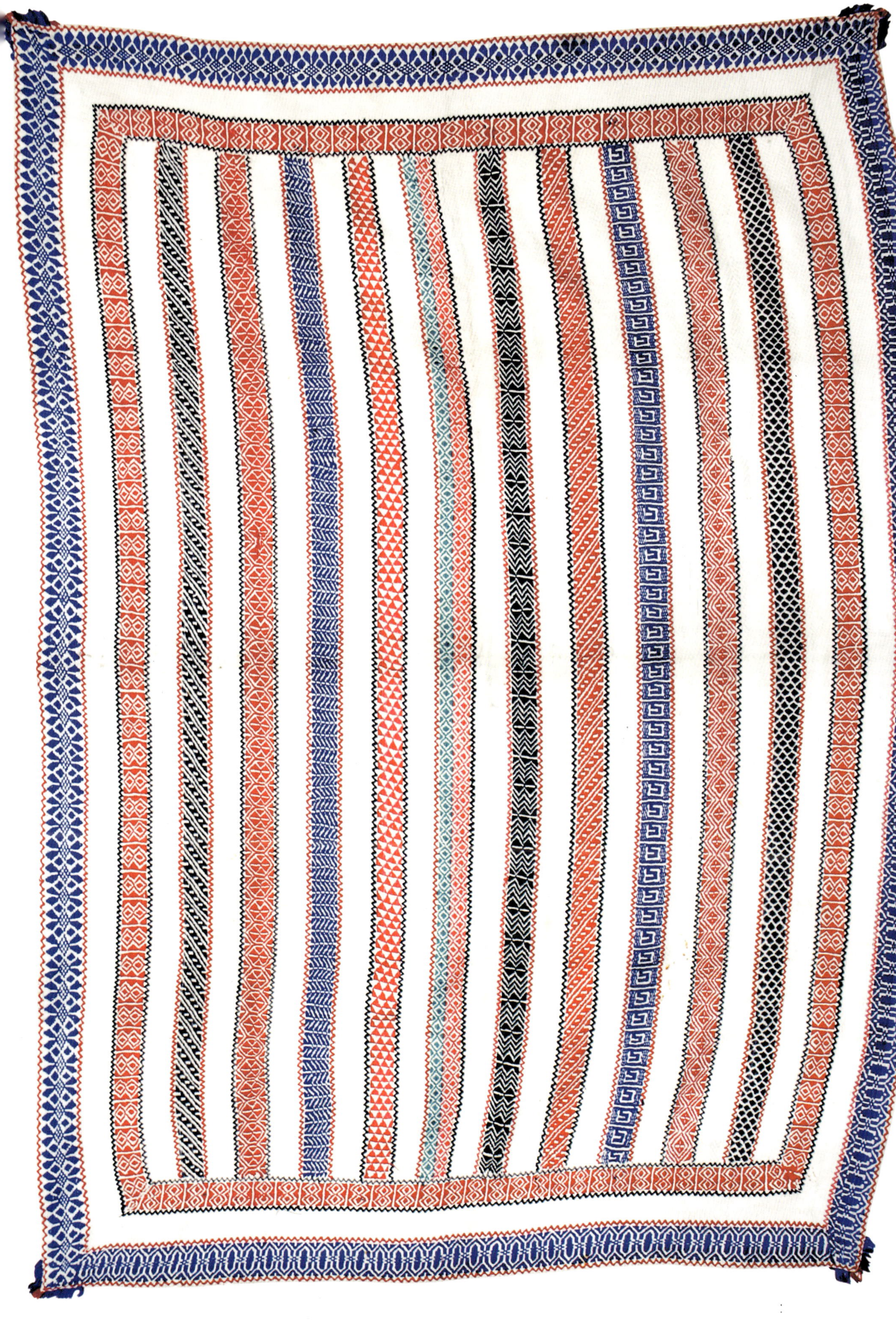

Kantha

Acc. No. IV/1C971/JS-KAN-17

Rectangular *Kantha* having a big stylized lotus in the central enclosure, which has three rows of running stitches as the border. The lotus is very elaborately embroidered with triangular petals of fish scale pattern in the centre of the curved edges. The lotus is circular in shape with spikes on the edges. The four corners have long trefoil pattern (one in each corner). There are two fish on two sides of the lotus with small flowers all around it at places.

The rest of the field is divided into squares barring two rectangular enclosures on both sides of the lotus, each having rows of fish (four fish on each side) the rest of the squares have small single motifs like star, flower, shosti chinho and geometrical-cum-floral motifs.

The small borders on all four sides have been embroidered with geometrical designs. The field has very fine running stitches because of which the entire field looks rippled.

Colours used are red, black, yellow, light orange and different shades of pink.

Material - Cotton

Condition - Stained all over with tiny holes in between.

Size - 146cmx104cm

Period - Late 19th Century

Place - West Bengal

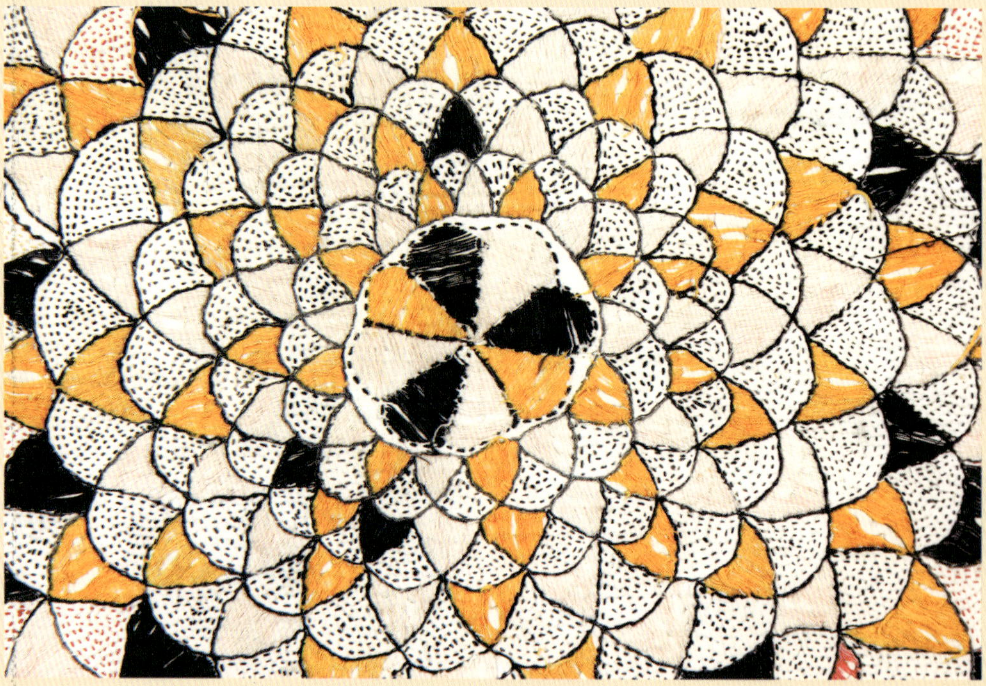

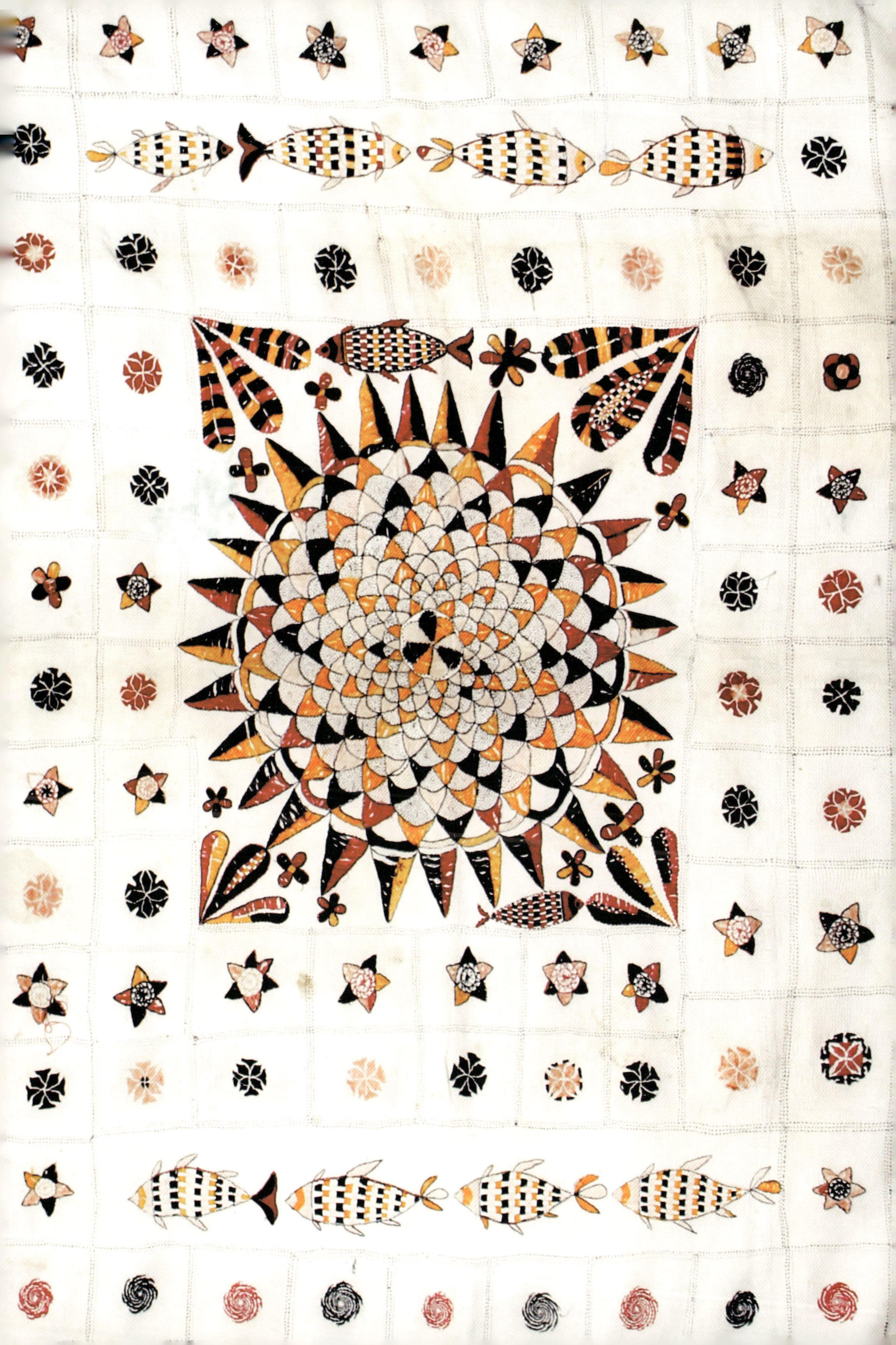

Kantha

Acc. No. IV/1C971/JS-KAN-17 (CONTD)

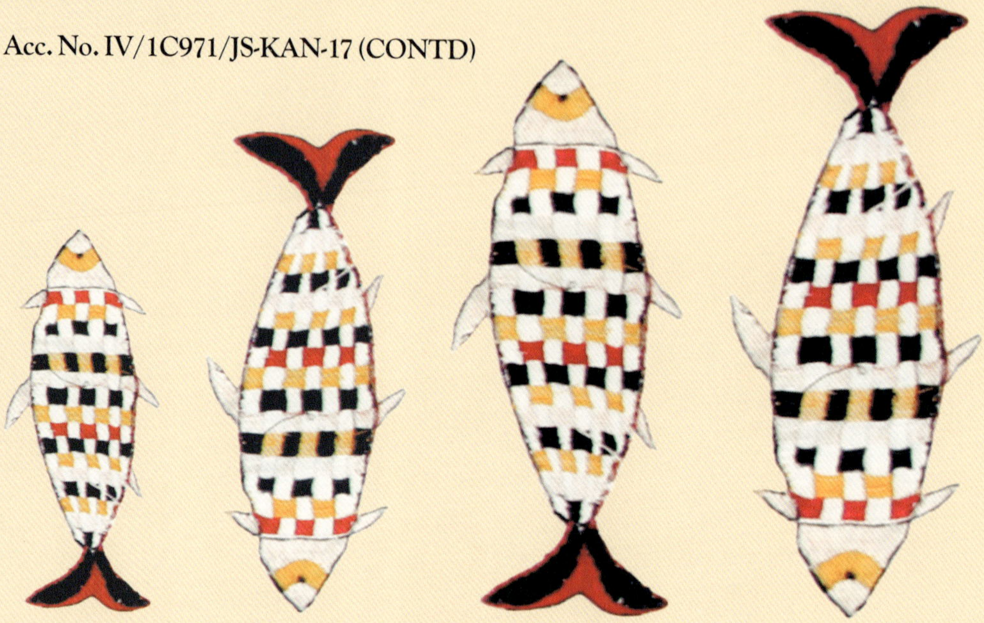

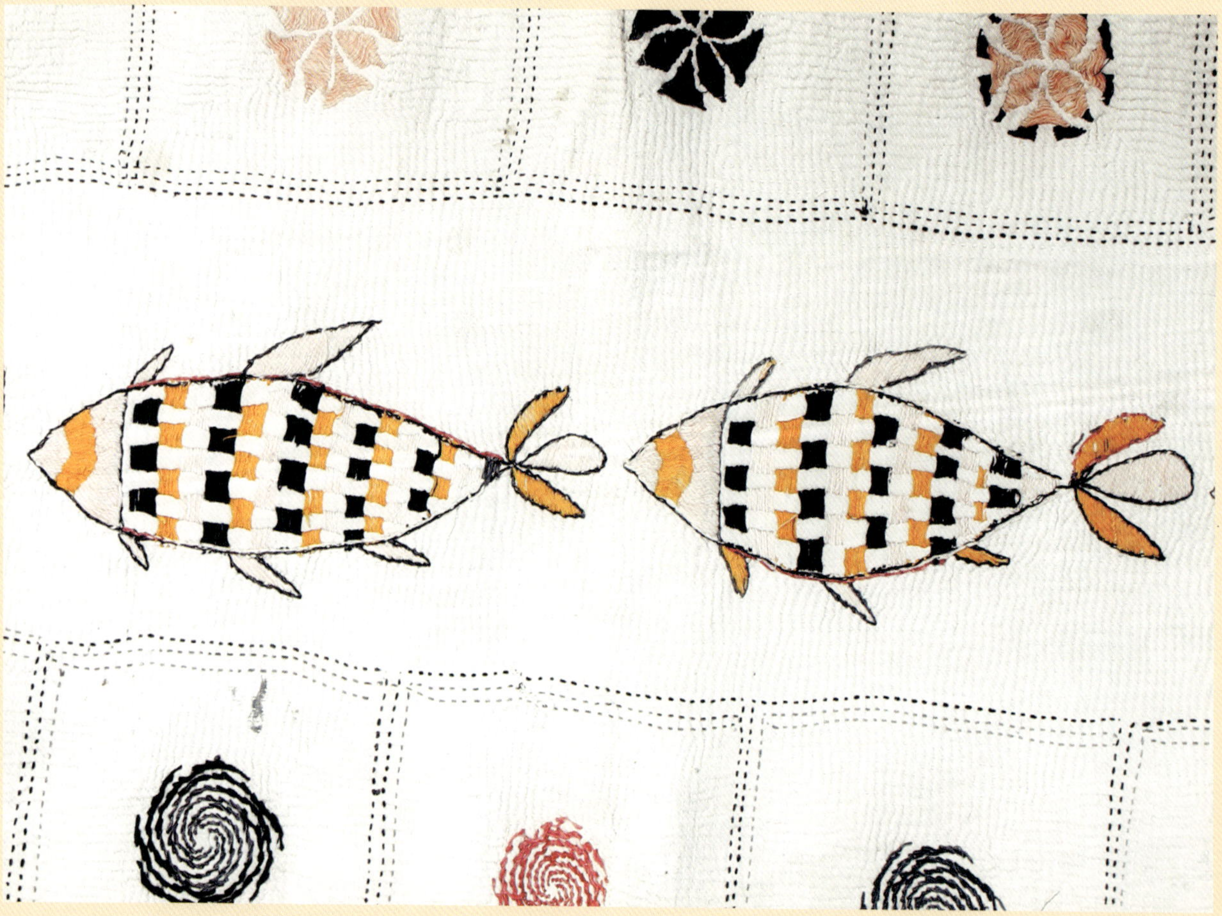

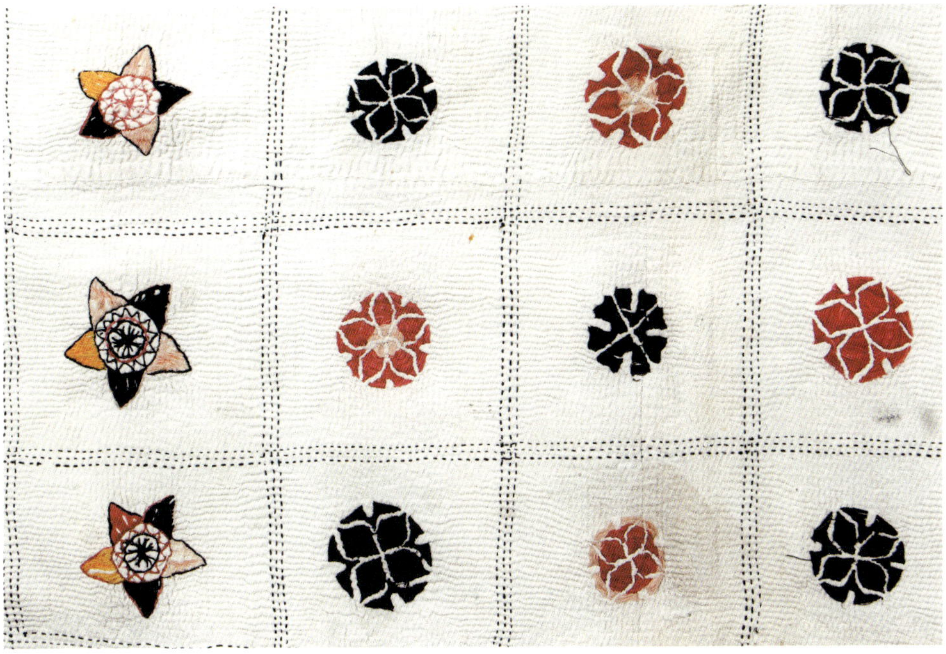

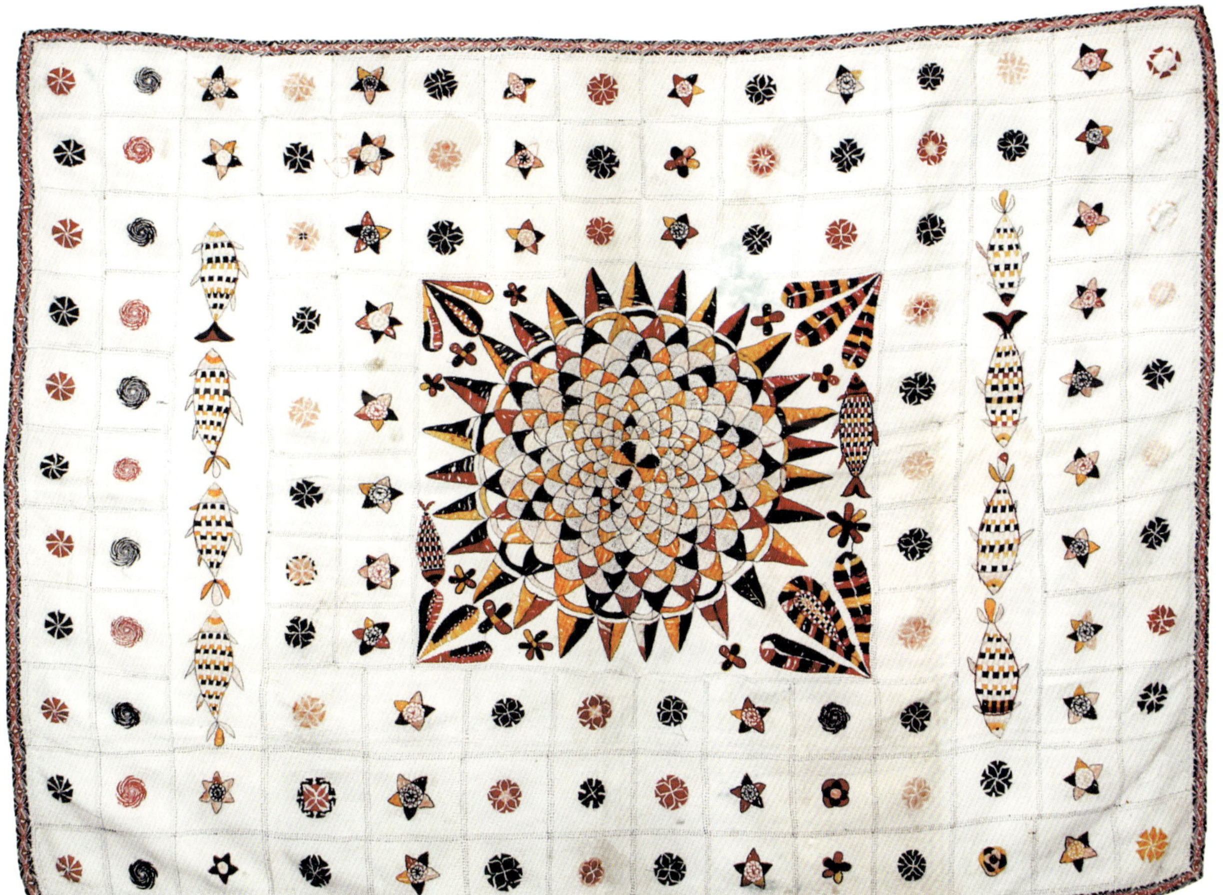

Kantha

Acc. No. IV/1C971/JS-KAN-18

Small rectangular *Kantha*, which has a very elaborately embroidered lotus in the centre. Each of the four corners has a *kalka* surrounded by floral creepers. The *kalka in* each corner is very richly embroidered, except one which has a single lotus flower. There are four plants in pots on the four sides in between the corner decoration. Two opposite plants (length wise) are similar, except the two on the other side, which have a pair of flying birds each on either side. One plant on the other side is flanked by two peacocks.

The *Kantha* is very colourful and most of it has been embroidered in satin and stem stitches.

The ground has very fine running stitches. The small border has four rows of very tiny diamond shapes, embroidered in red and blue colours.

The rest of the field is rippled by self-running stitches. The colours used in embroidery are red, black, green, yellow, grey, light orange, blue.

Material - Cotton

Condition - Stained all over.

Size - 104cmx82cm

Period - 19th Century

Place - West Bengal

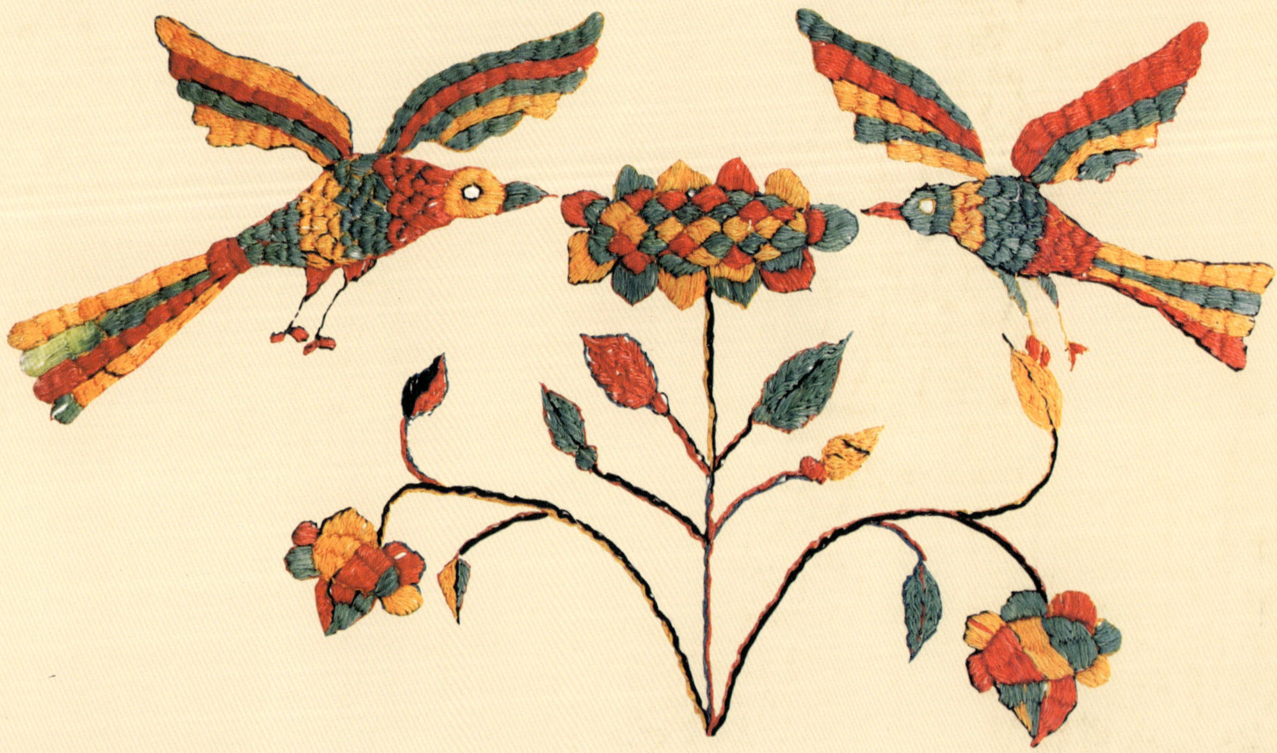

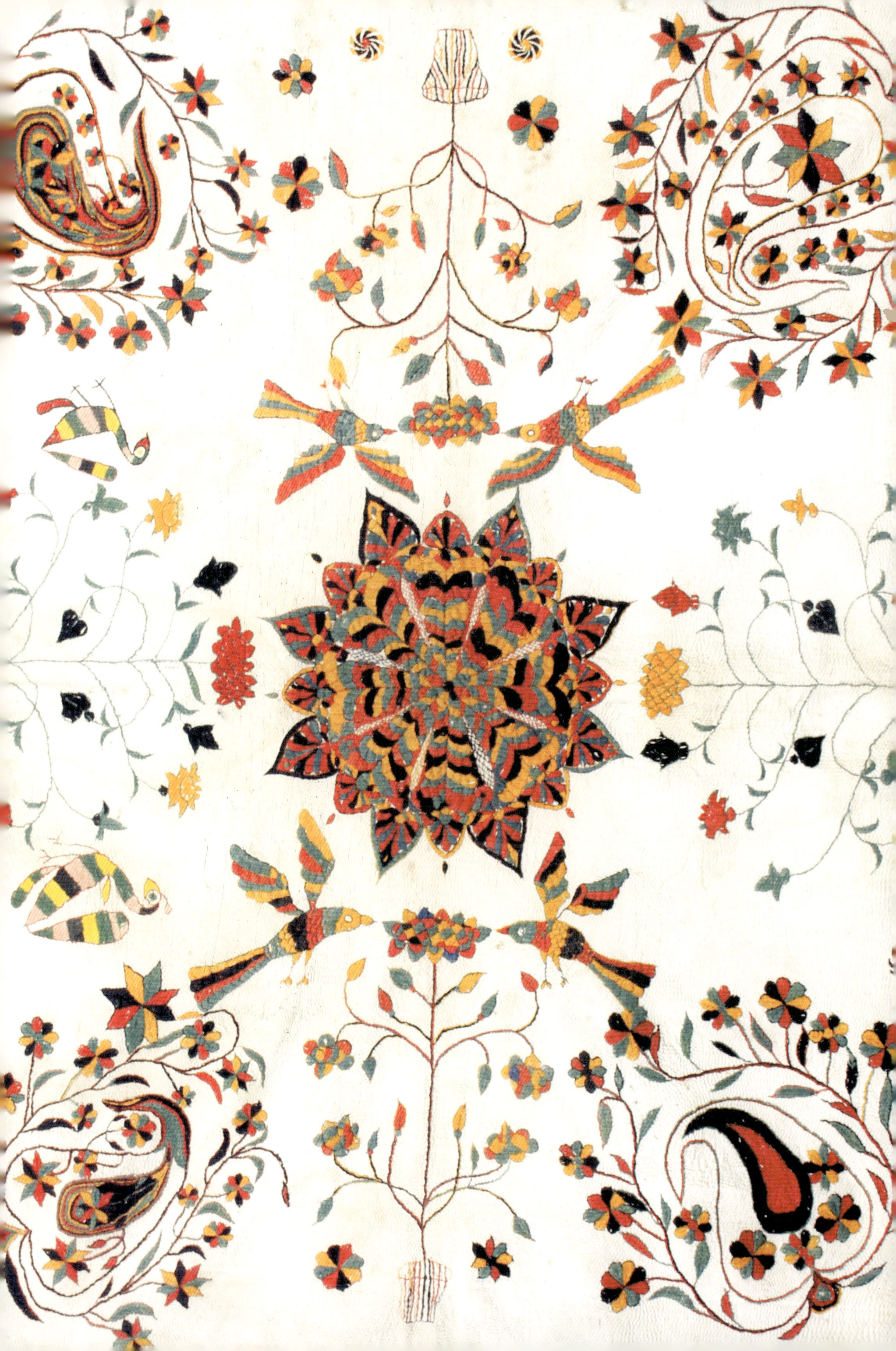

Kantha

Acc. No. IV/1C971/JS-KAN-18 (CONTD)

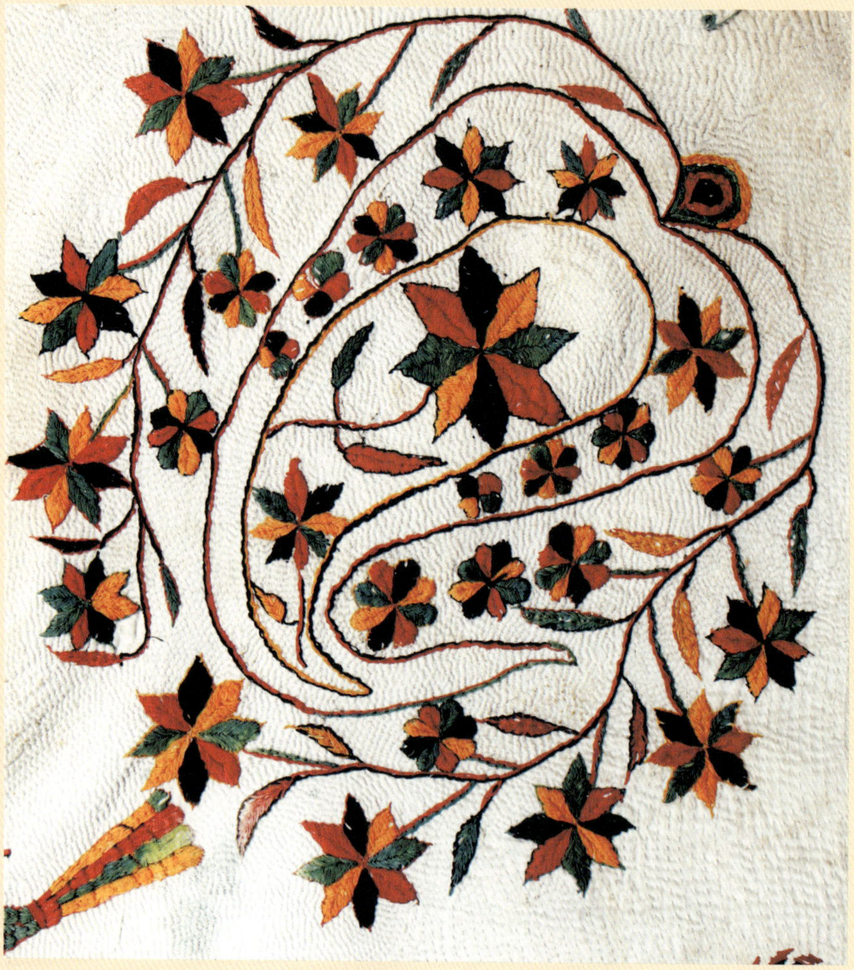

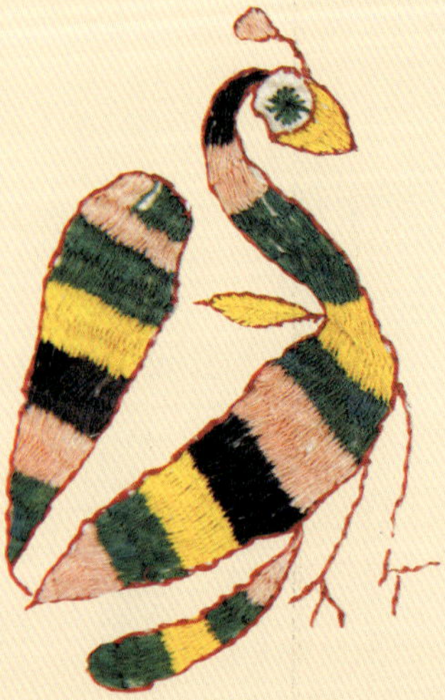

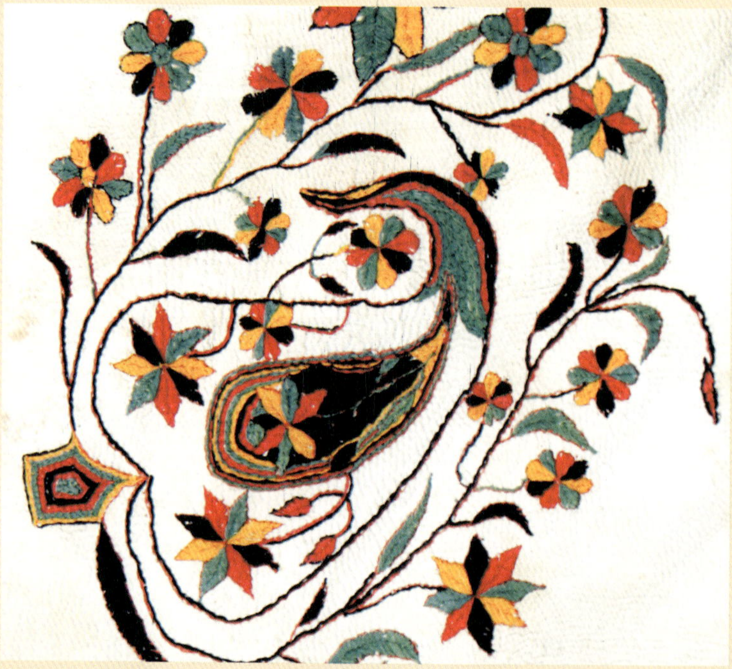

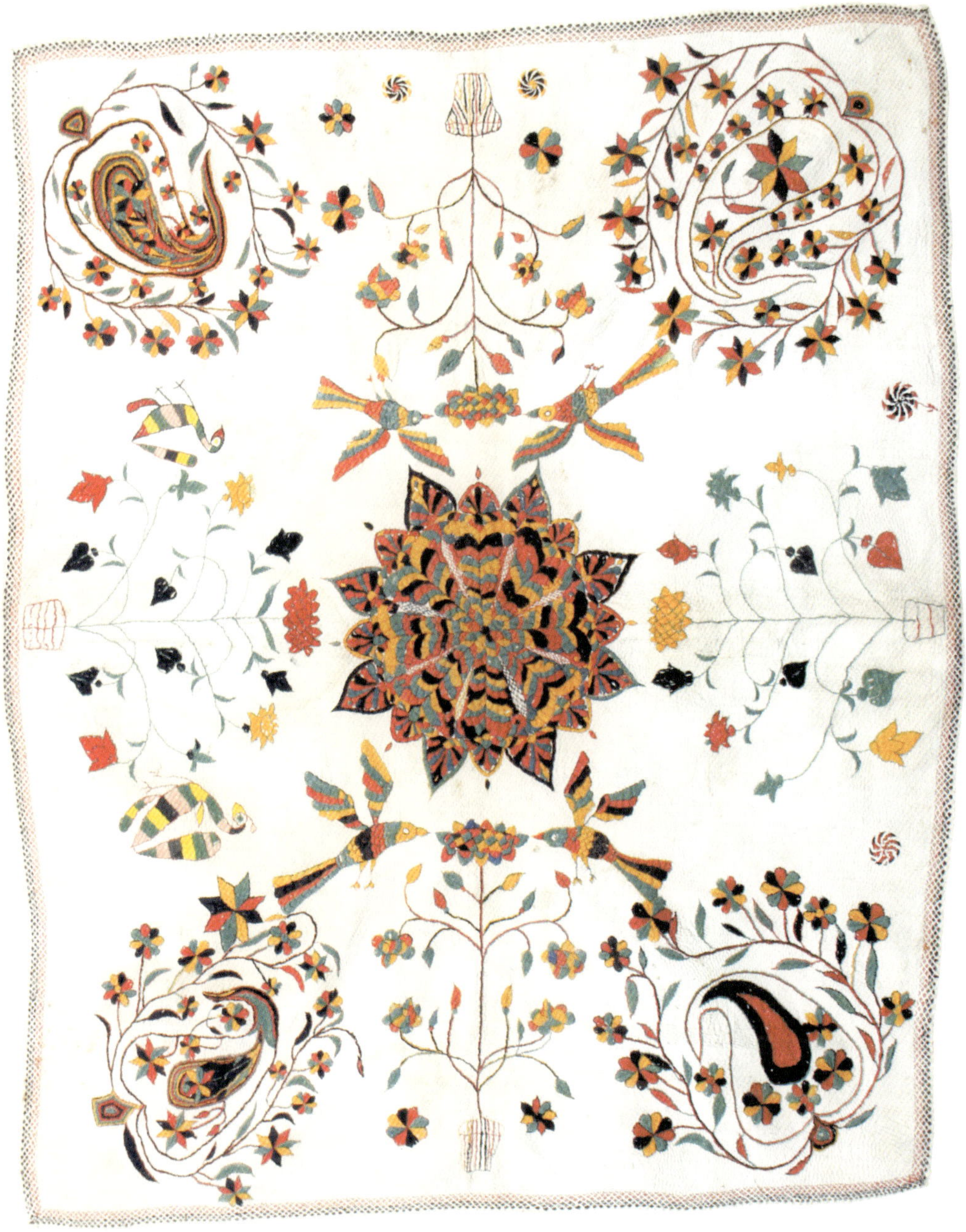

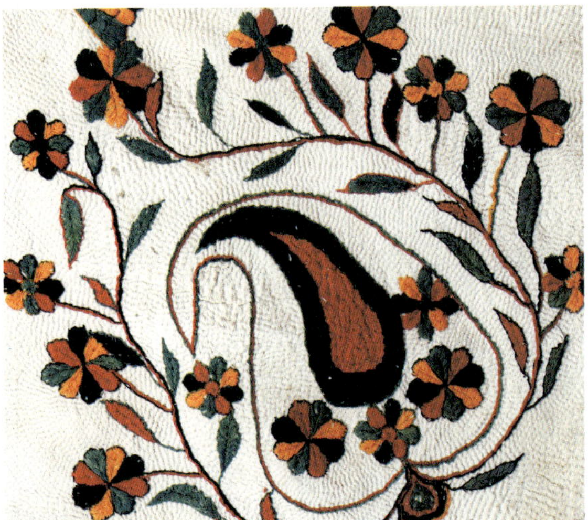

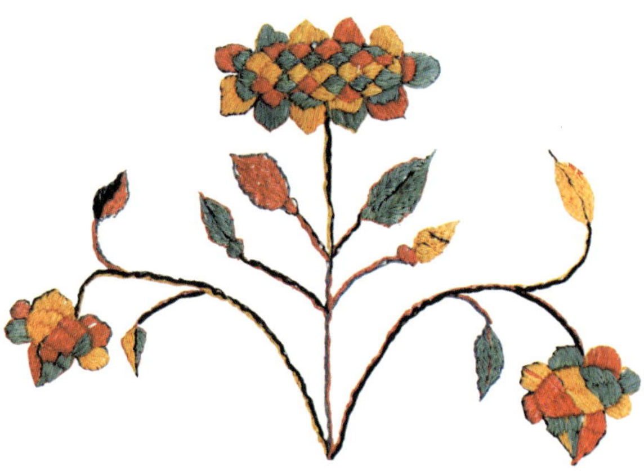

Kantha

Acc. No. IV/IC971/JS-KAN-19

Rectangular small *Kantha* having four stylized *butas* in the four corners (one in each corner). Each *buta* has a *kalka* like motif at the bottom, out of which different types of flowers shoot out with trefoil pattern in between. These flowers are very richly embroidered with satin stitches.

On one side, in between two flowers, there is an unfinished male figure, while on the opposite side there is a well adorned female head wearing nose-ring, long earring, and black head gear surmounted by trefoil pattern.

These floral *butas* are enclosed with a red geometrical border. The edges are very richly embroidered with a geometrical border in black colour.

The field is rippled.

The colours used in the embroidery are black, red, mustard, white, green, and orange.

Material - Cotton

Condition - Stained, repaired and embroidery is missing at places.

Size - 105cmx77cm

Period - 19th Century

Place - West Bengal

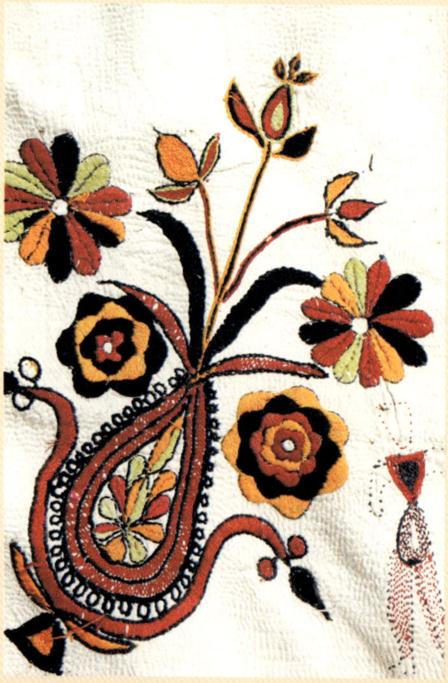

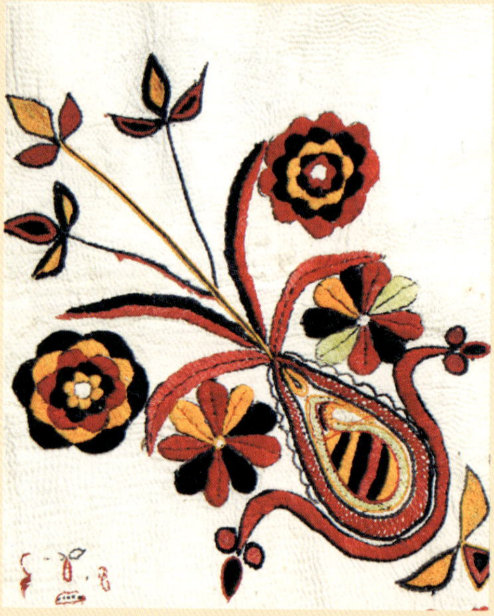

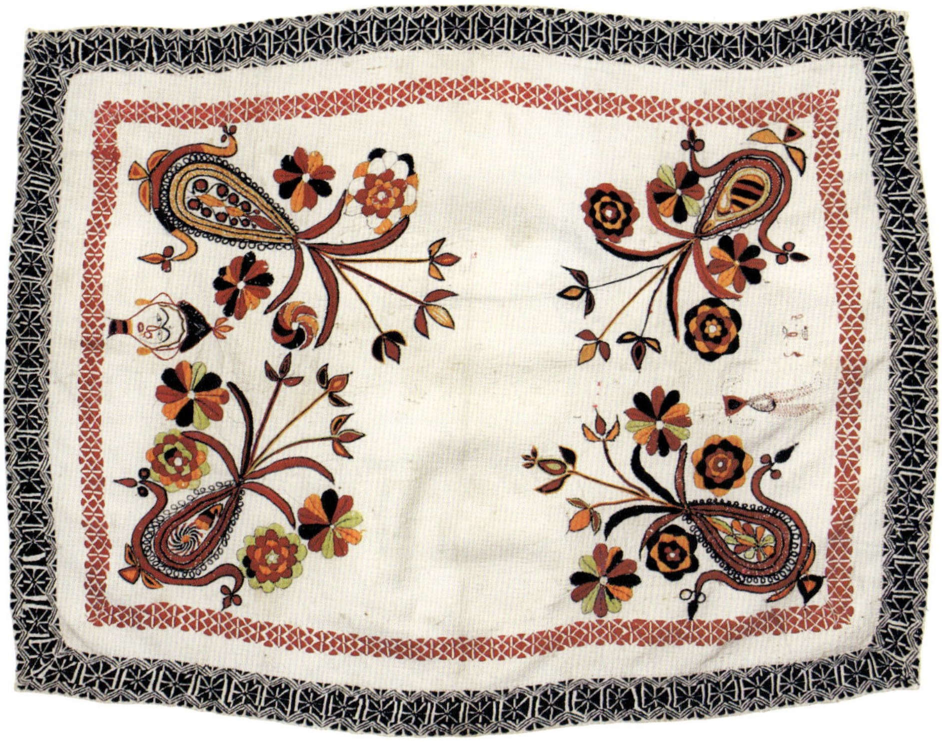

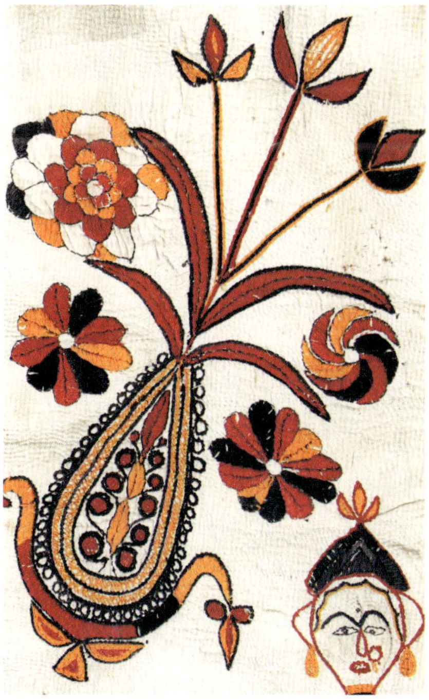

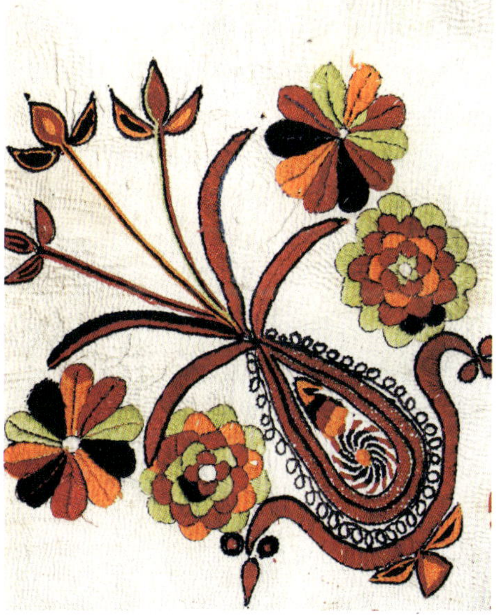

Kantha

Acc. No. IV/1C971/JS-KAN-20

Rectangular small *Kantha* having golden colour silk cloth lining and red cotton piping on all the four side edges. The central enclosure has stylized lotus motif having two layers of zigzag lines with *shosti chinha* and wheel motifs arranged alternatively on the outer side of the zigzag pattern. There are four stylized peacocks at the four corners of the middle enclosure surrounding the lotus flower.

On the four sides of the central motif there are two elephant-riders, two horse-riders, a man smoking a *hookah* sitting on a chair, a male figure sitting on a stool and a dancing human figure. There are four wheels in each corner. On the two extreme panels there are plants with birds, dancing figures and small stylized lotus motifs in between.

Colours used in embroidery are red, blue and grey.

Material - Cotton

Condition - Faded and repaired.

Size - 132cmx69cm

Period - Early 20th Century

Place - West Bengal

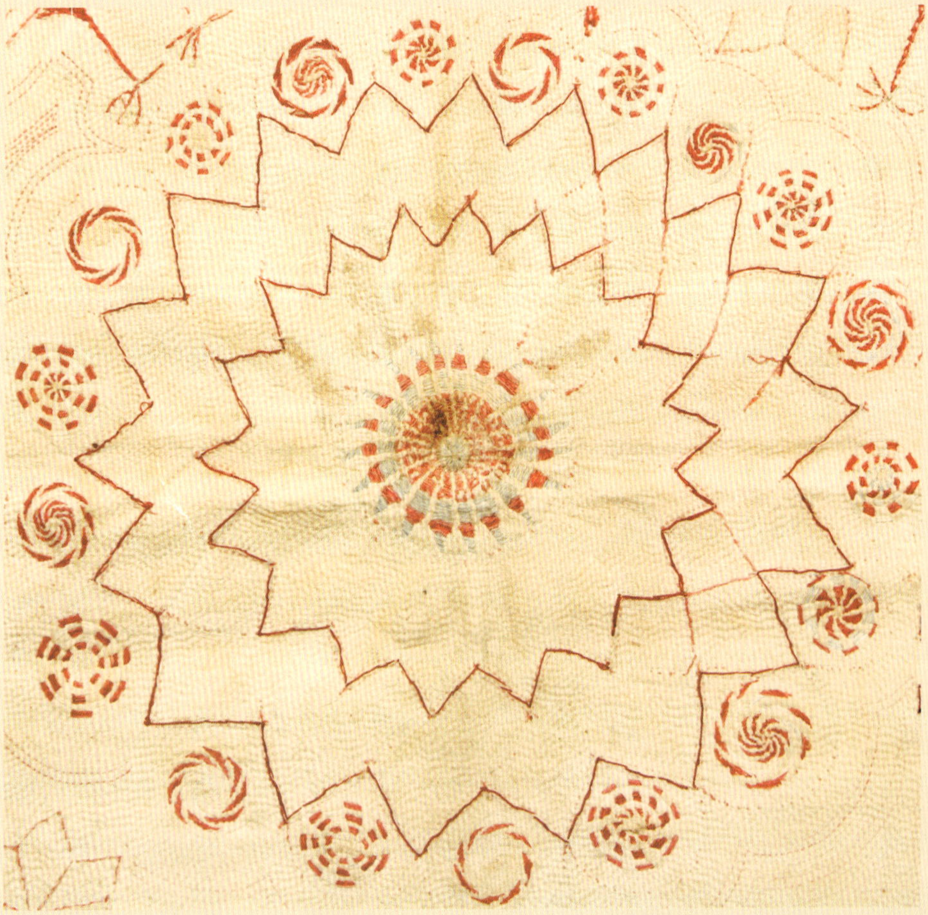

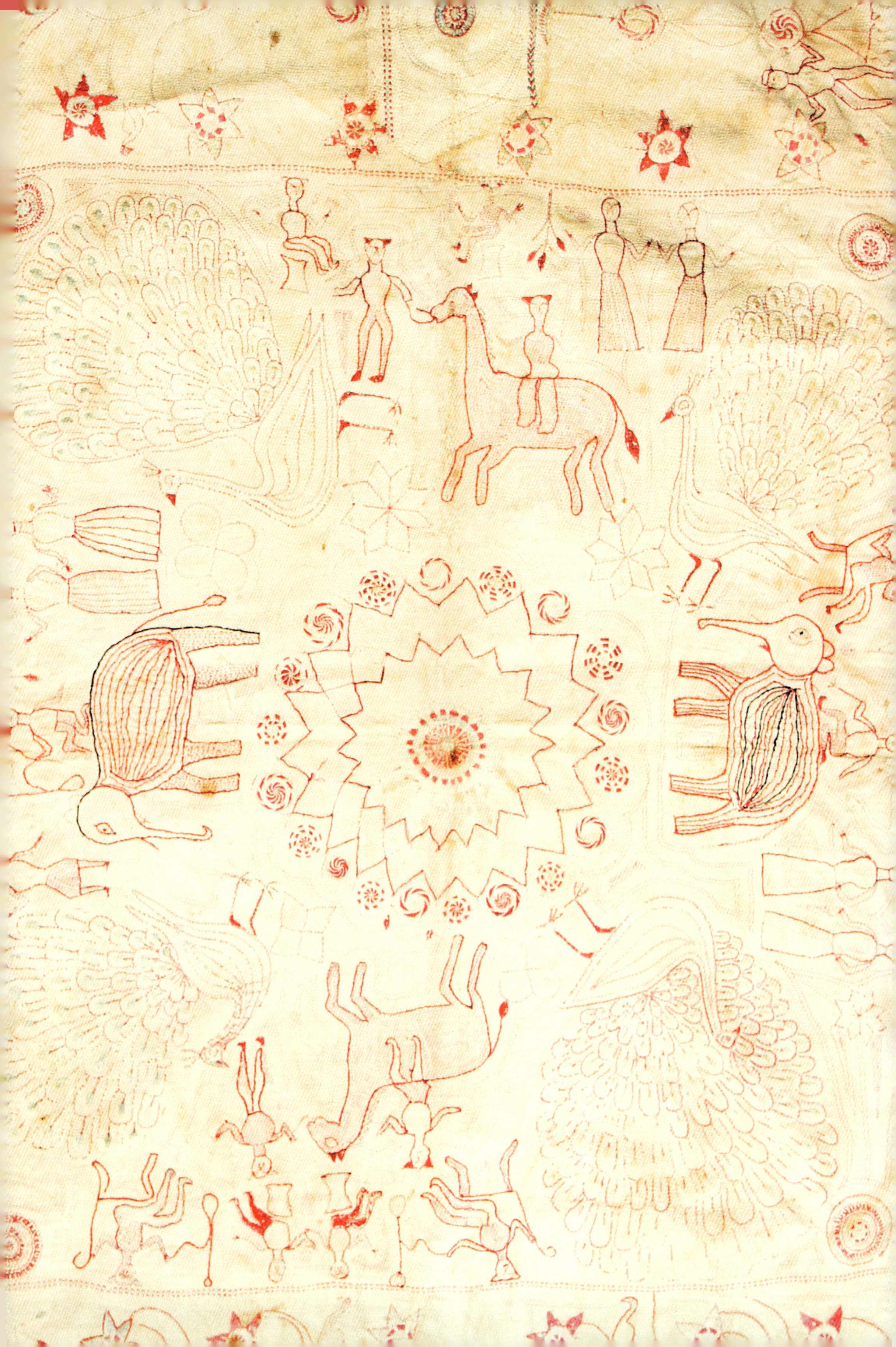

Kantha

Acc. No. IV/1C971/JS-KAN-20 (CONTD)

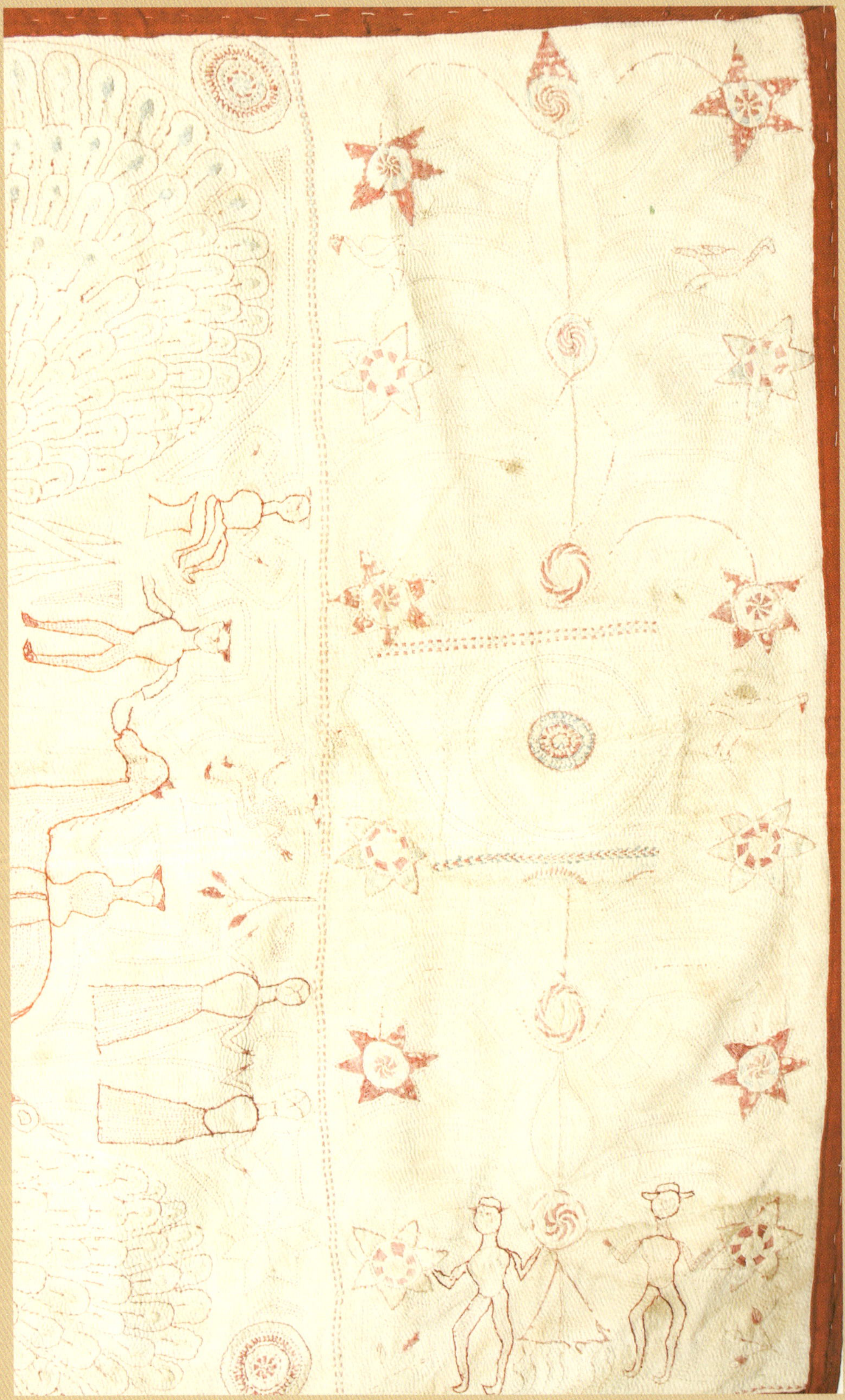

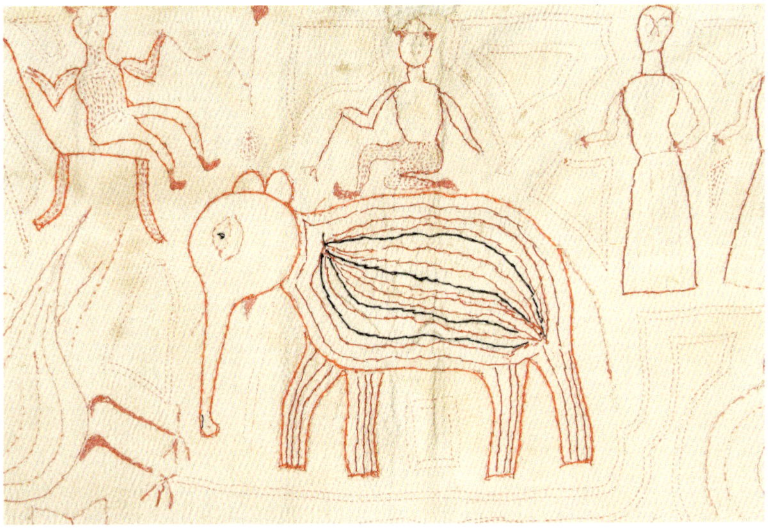

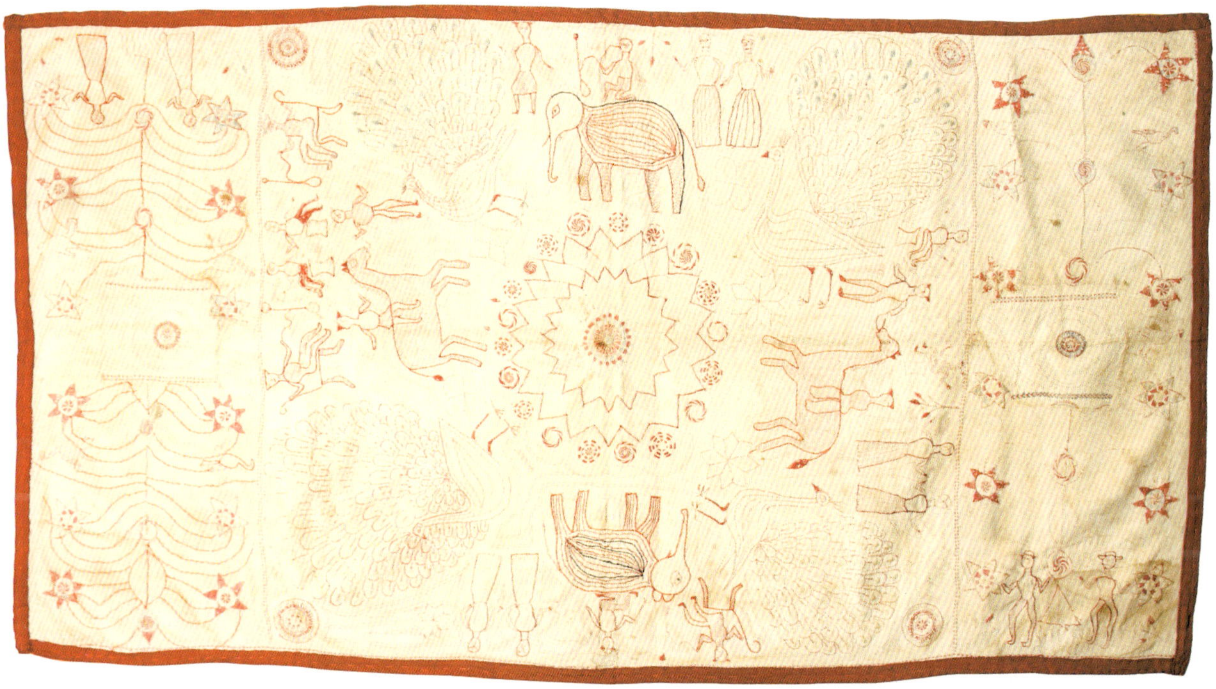

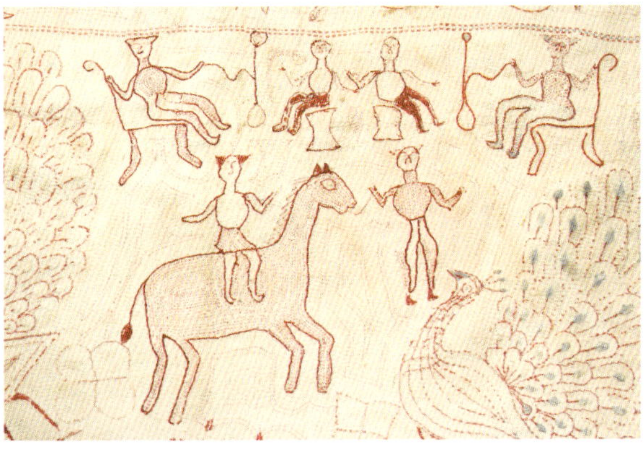

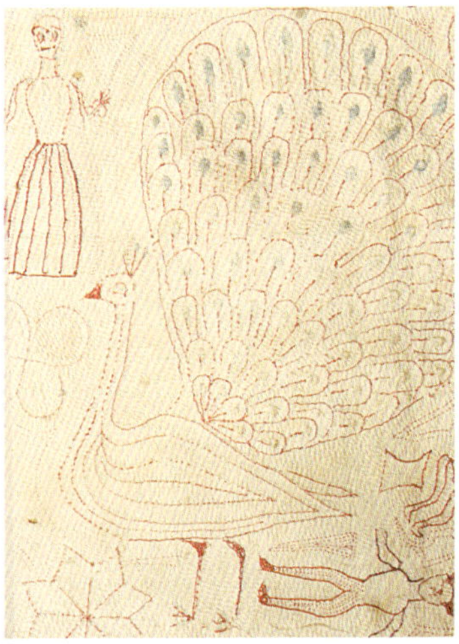

Kantha

Acc. No. IV/1C971/JS-KAN-21

Small *Kantha* (asana) very richly embroidered in the centre with eight petalled lotus motifs surrounded by foliage creepers with flowers all over the ground. In between this floral motif, there is a mythical figure and flying birds.

In the four corners there are four *butas*, each having small flowers and leaves and on the top there is a big betel-like leaf which has been embroidered in *Katiya stitches* (zebra pattern). There are two elephants and eight horses. Both the elephants have *shosti chinha* (swastika) near their necks, all embroidered in *Katiya* (zebra like) patterns. The elephants on both sides are flanked by horses. On all the four corners, there are herring bone stitches and a woven old red saree border forming the double border.

Besides the *Katiya* stitches, most of the *Kantha* has been embroidered with satin and stem stitches.

The colours used are red, blue, black, yellow, mustard, white, green, grey and purple.

Material - Cotton

Condition - Stained and torn at places. Border is missing at places.

Size - 87cmx71cm

Period - 20th Century

Place - West Bengal

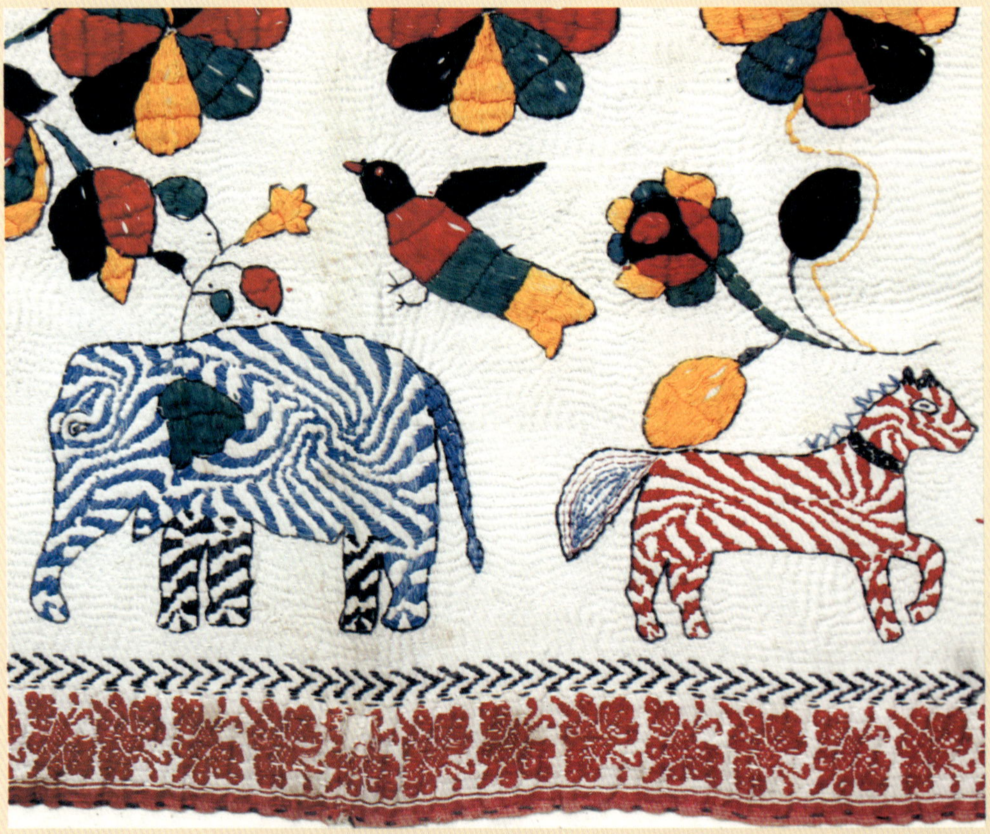

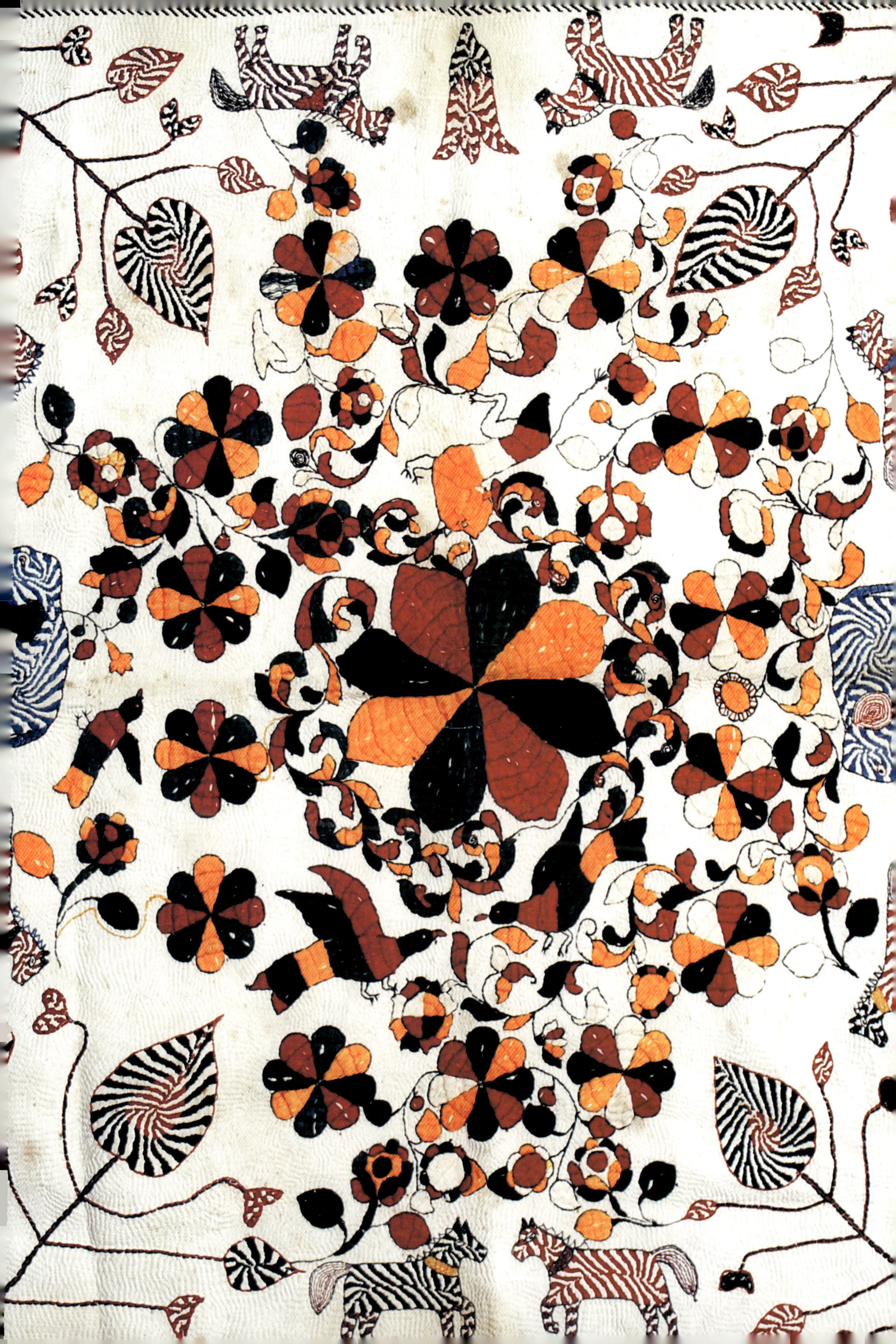

Kantha

Acc. No. IV/1C971/JS-KAN-21 (CONTD)

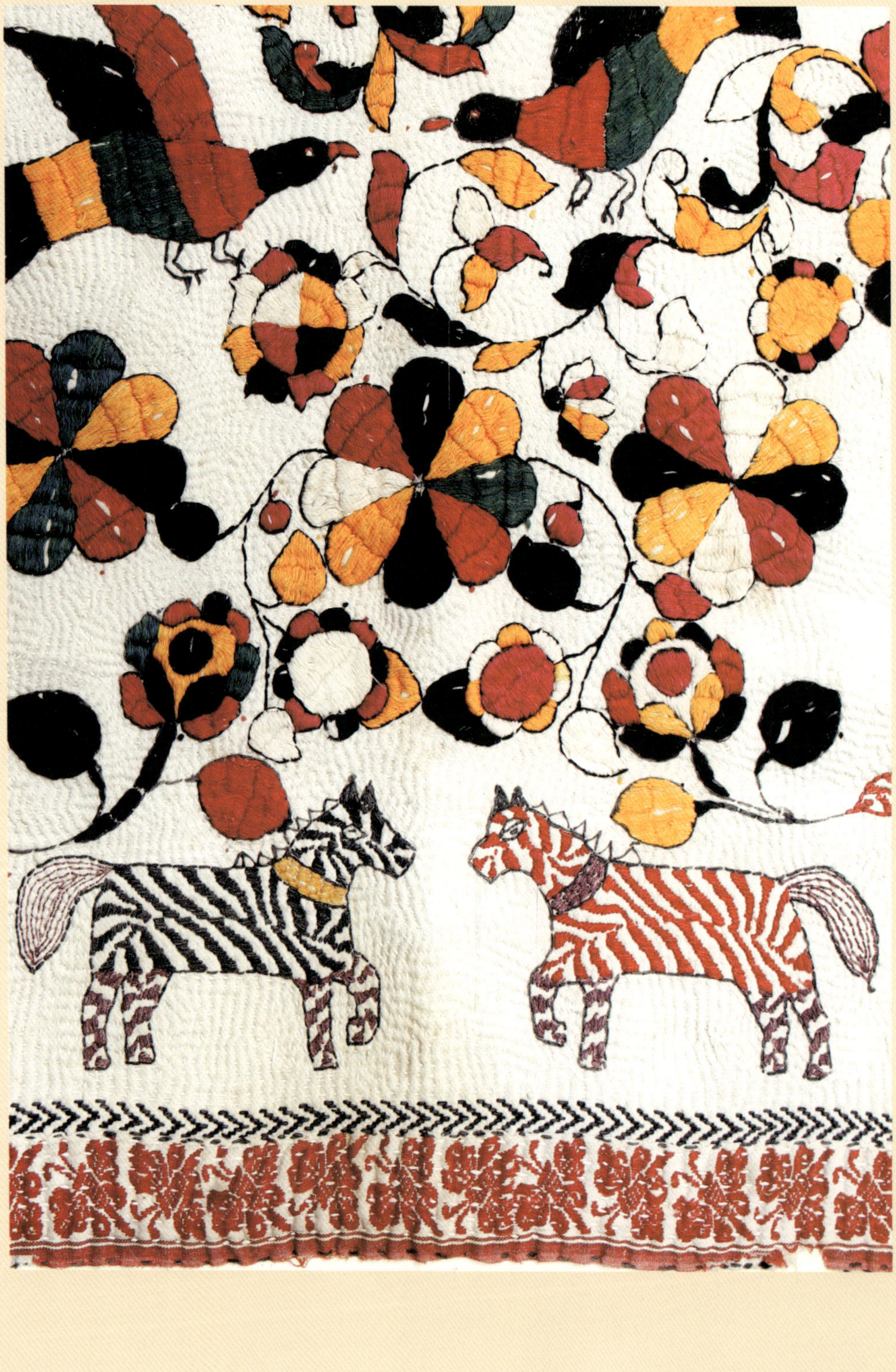

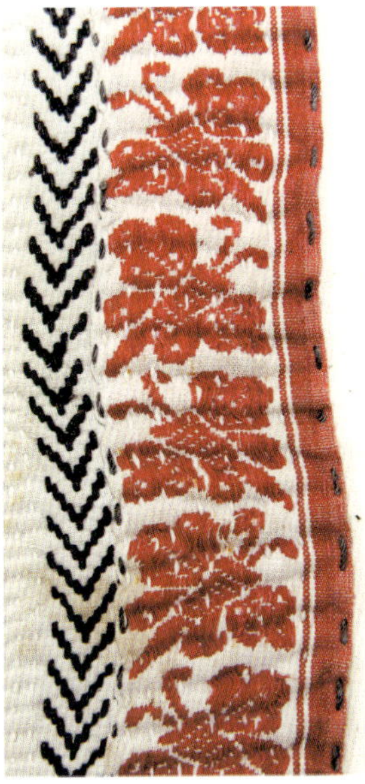

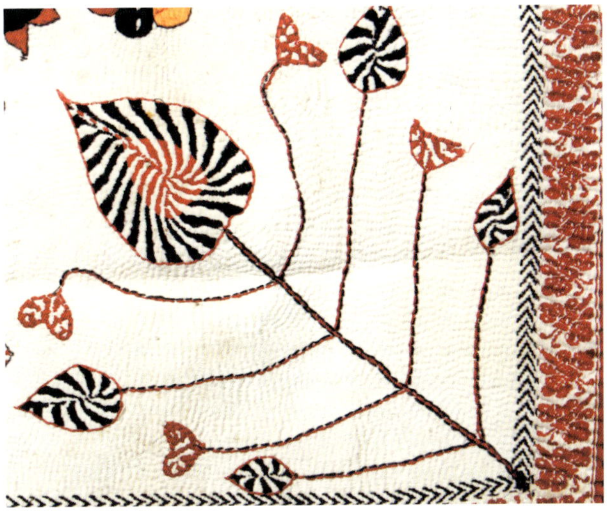

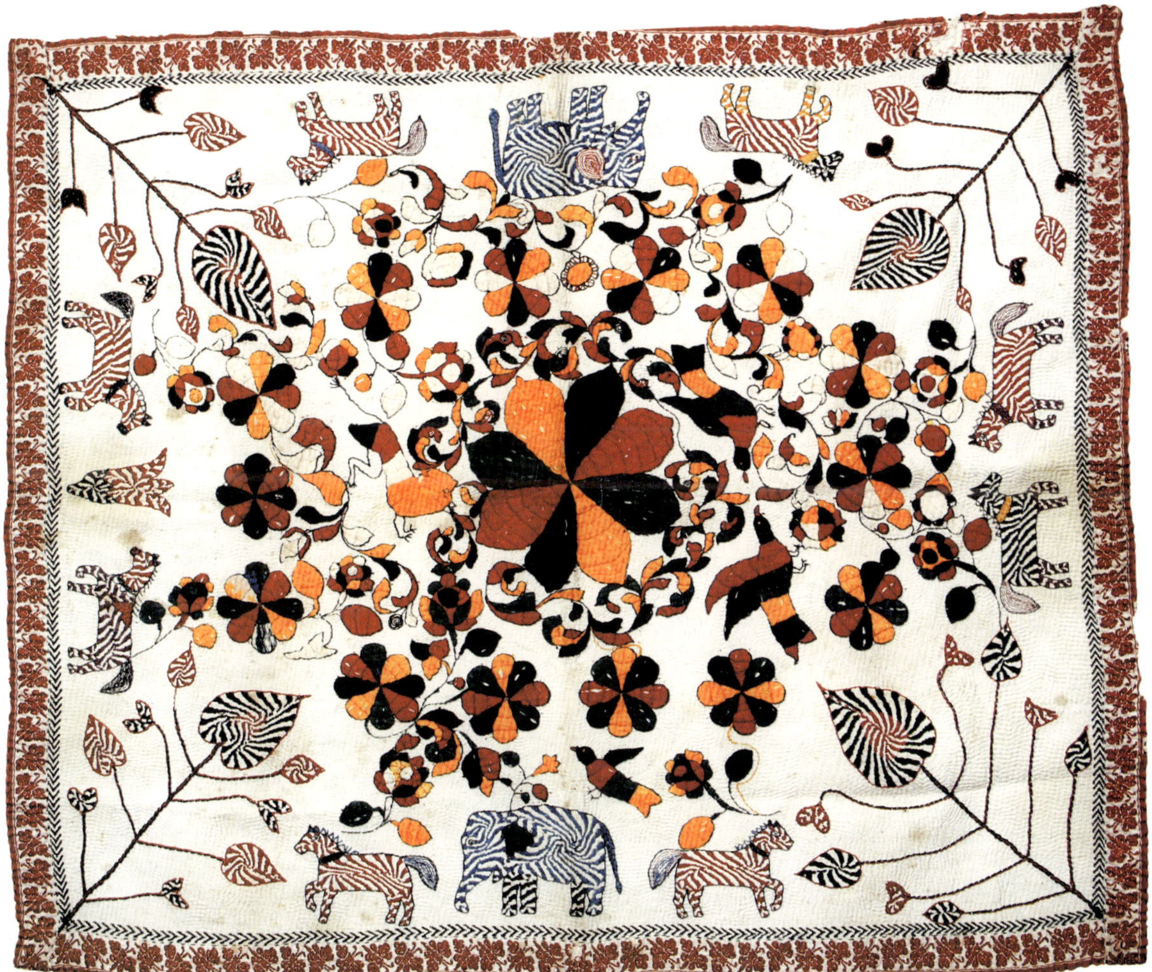

Kantha

Acc. No. IV/1C971/JS-KAN-22

Rectangular *Kantha* having sixty four small squares in the centre like a chess board. Each square is embroidered with *shosti chinha* (swastika). The four corners of the chess-board have four *butas* with *shosti chinha*.

On the two sides, opposite each other, there are two elephants on each side, while on the other two sides there are two tigers, one bigger than the other. The bigger tiger is preying upon a baby elephant. On the other side, there is foliage pattern surmounted by two horses. This enclosure has a small border in *chatai* pattern. The border around the central square has four stylized leaves on all four corners (one in each). Each leaf has a *swastika chinha* in the centre and herring bone type of border on the sides.

The border has a pair of *kalkas* in a row, part of which has been embroidered with a different foliage and floral pattern with a male figure standing in one corner.

The other side has a *chatai* shaped small border and has been divided into three parts. The centre part has two female figures, in conversation, standing under a pavilion which has three leaves on top. There is also a script in Bangla which reads:-

Shri Sharda Sundry Chodhu Vahan

The right portion is embroidered with a *chauper spread* with a *shosti chinha* in the central enclosure. There are four *kalkas* around the *chauper* board each having a *shosti chinha*, one in each of them.

On the left side there are foliage motifs on top with a large circle below. Within this large circle, there are eight smaller circles, the centre one being bigger.

There is a foliage design. There are borders on all the four sides with each corner having a leaf pattern with a *shosti chinha* in the centre.

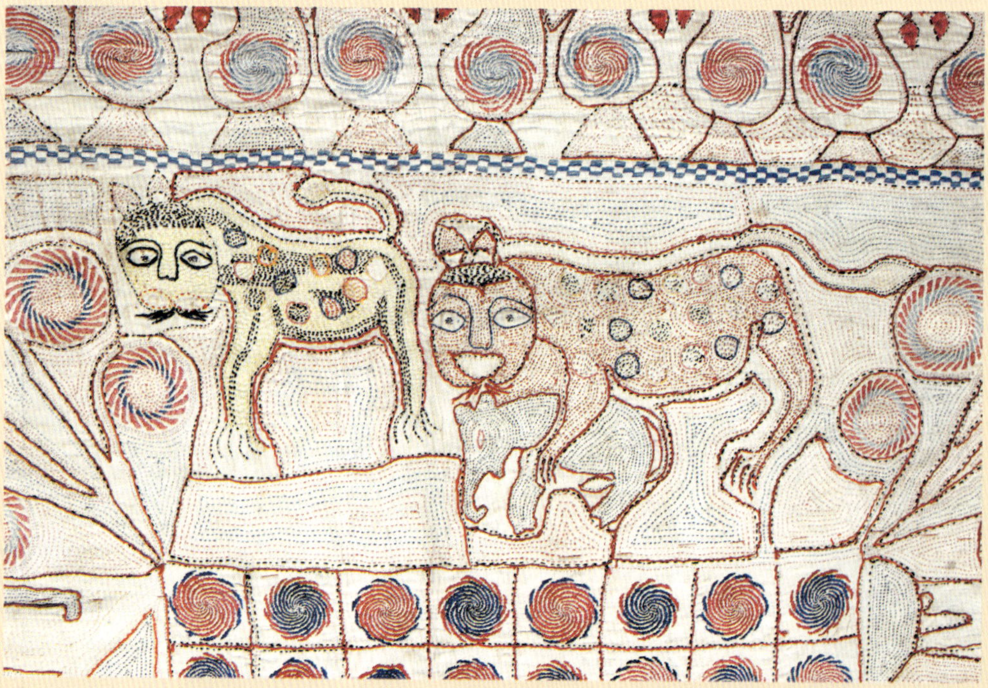

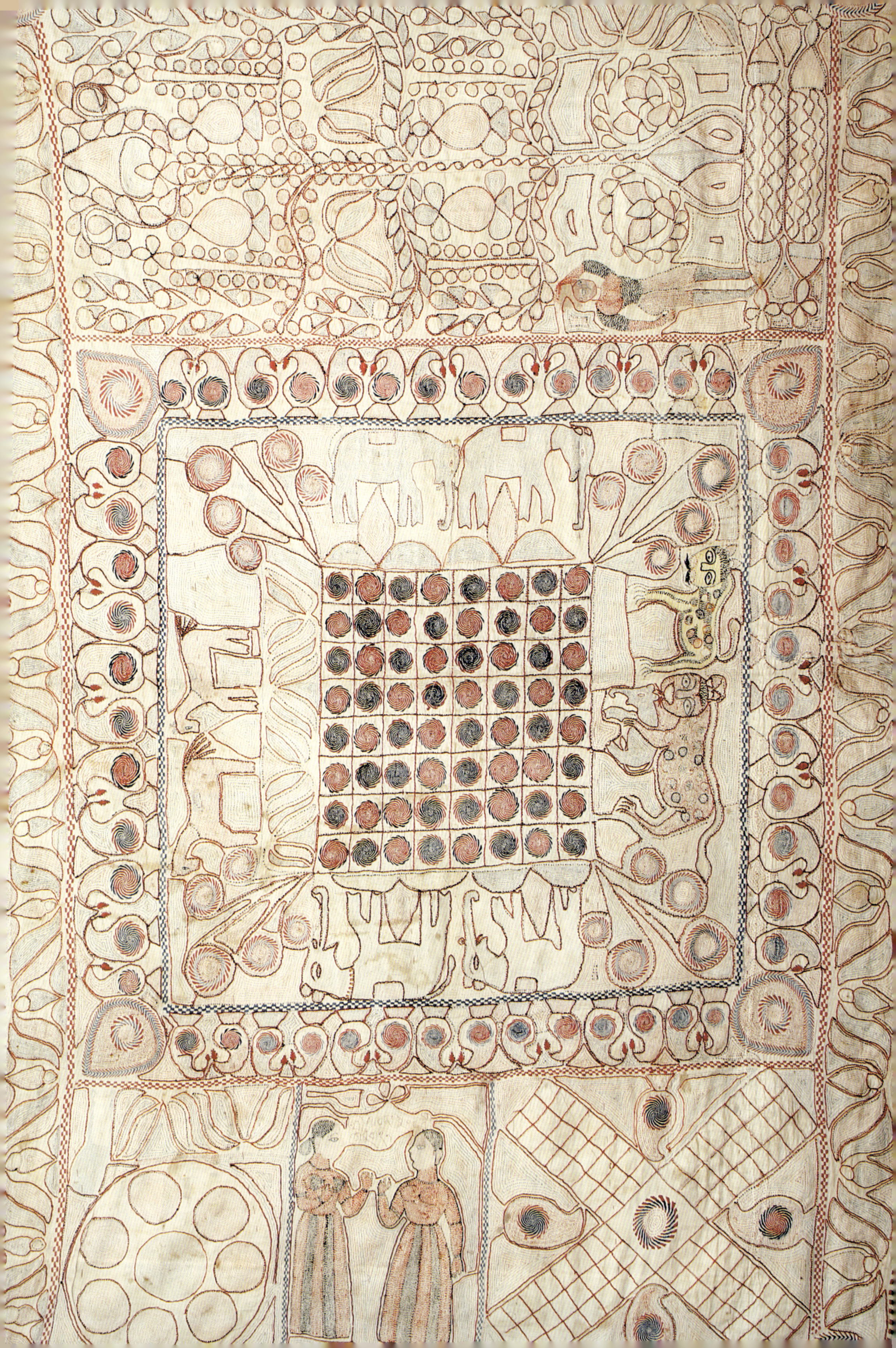

Kantha

Acc. No. IV/1C971/JS-KAN-22 (CONTD)

There is an orange coloured printed lining, with small uniform flowers and leaves. Colours used in embroidery are different shades of blue, red, green and orange.

Material - Cotton

Condition - Stained and embroidery missing at places.

Size - 186cmx121cm

Period - 19th Century

Place - West Bengal

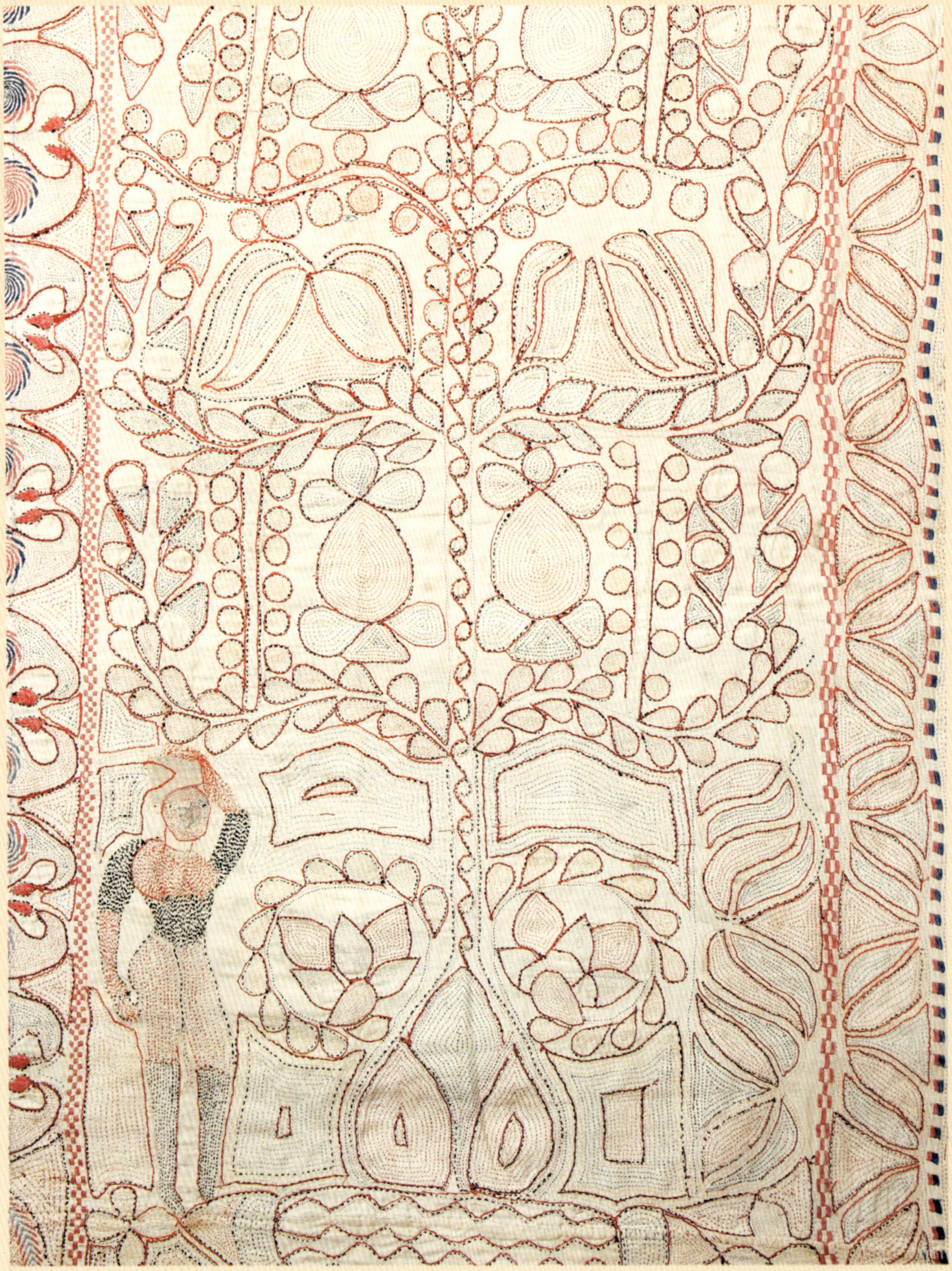

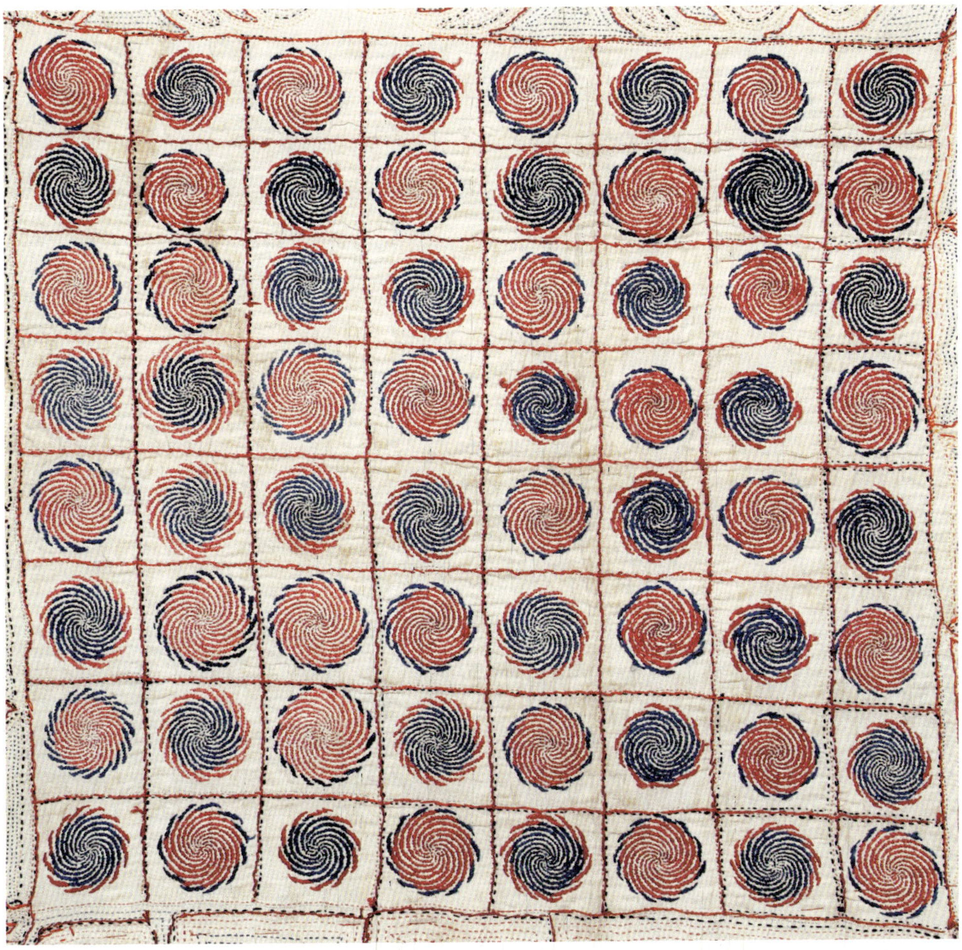

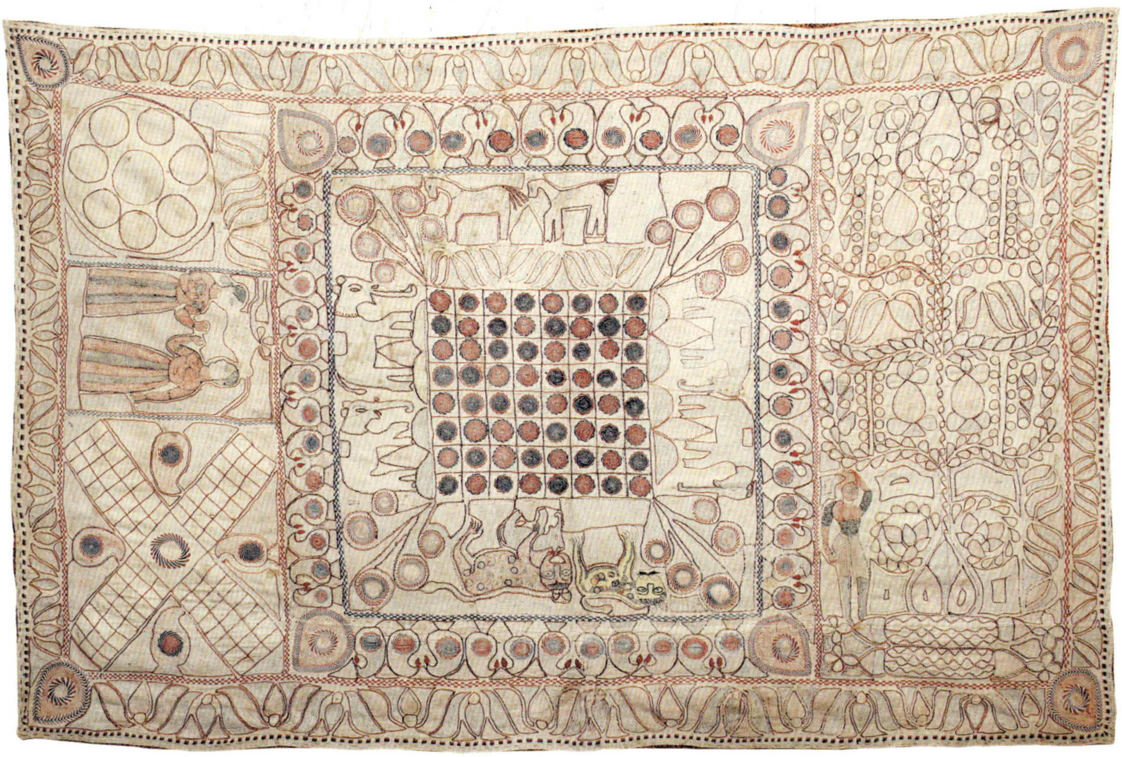

Asana

Acc. No. IV/I(97)/JS-KAN-23

Square *Kantha* in the shape of an *asana*. It has a stylized circular lotus motif in the centre with small *butas* in all the four corners. Each *buta* has three different floral types of motifs, for example, wheel, *shosti chinha* etc. One flower has a star in the centre and the others have thick rounded and dotted centres.

In three corners, there are *kalkas*, embroidered in red colour, having flame like edges in black colour.

The rest of the field has different types of multi-coloured borders with different designs. In between the borders on all four corners, there are single floral motifs.

The colours used are red, green, black, mustard, white, pink, orange, yellow and blue.

The ground has very fine multi coloured running stitches.

Material - Cotton

Condition - Slightly damaged and stained at places.

Size - 69cmx74cm

Time - Early 19th Century

Place - West Bengal

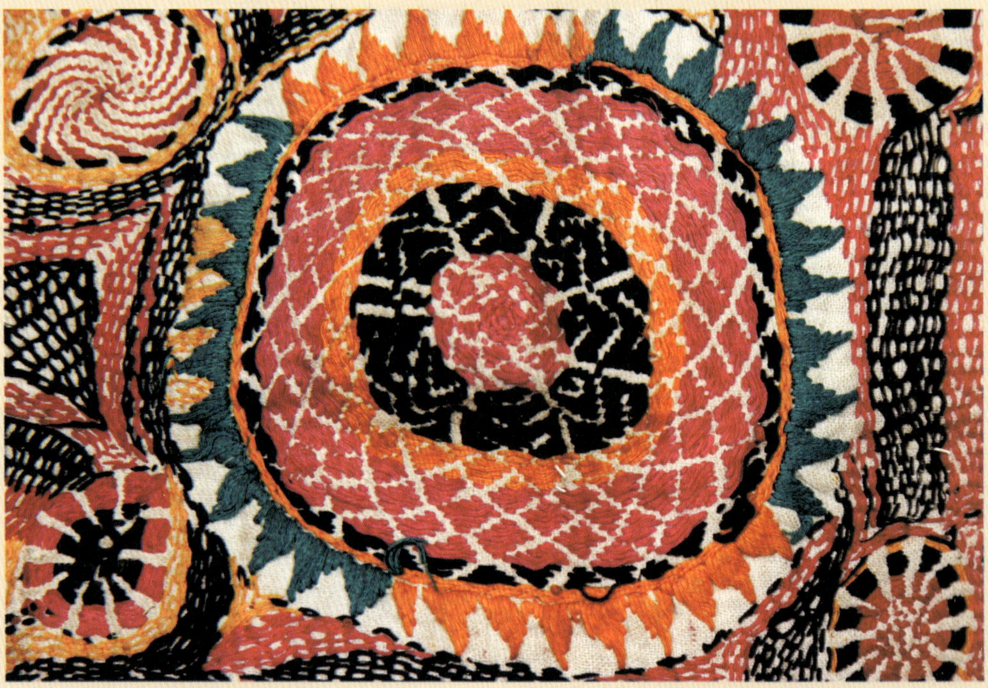

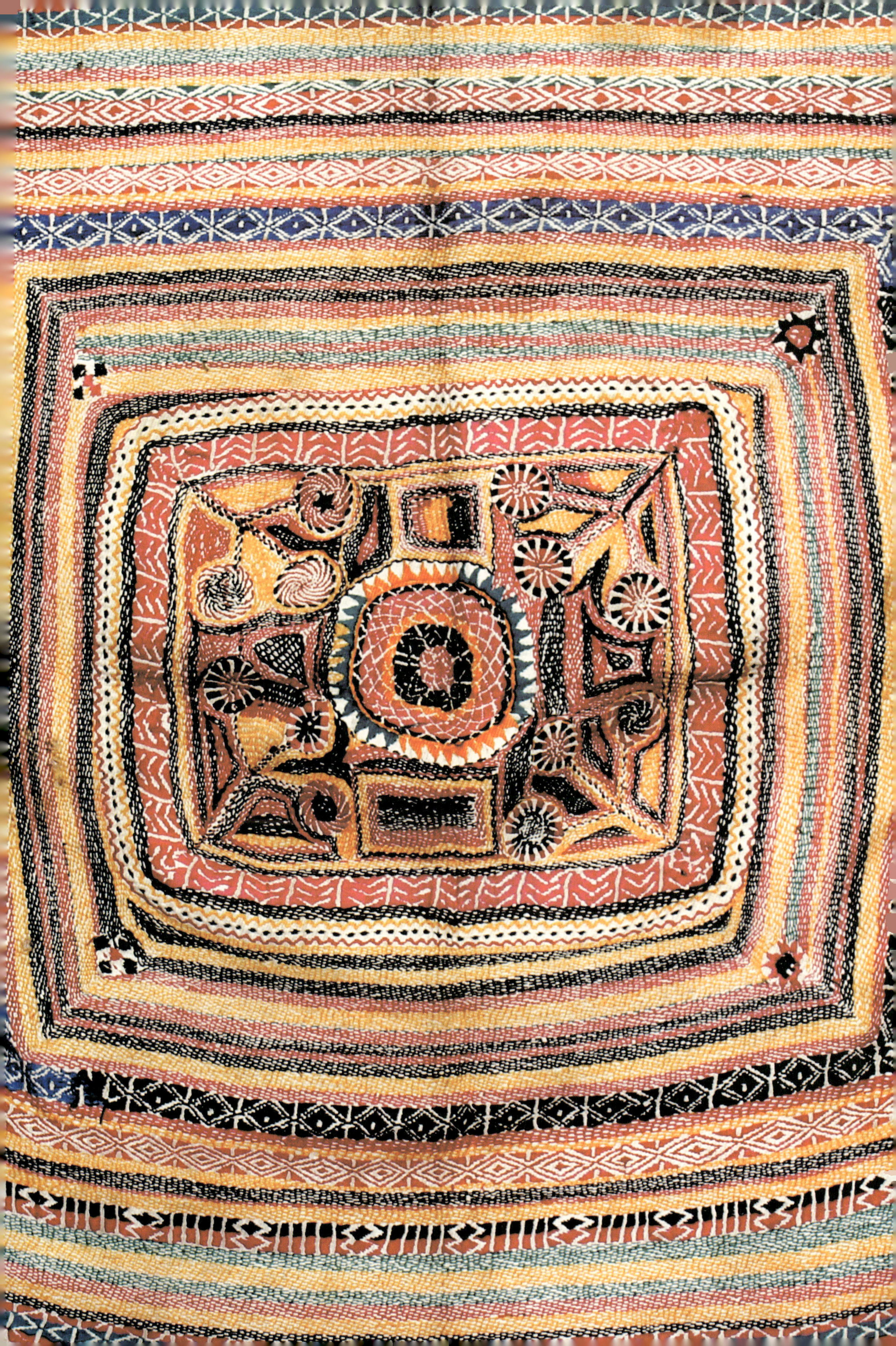

Asana

Acc. No. IV/I(97)/JS-KAN-23 (CONTD)

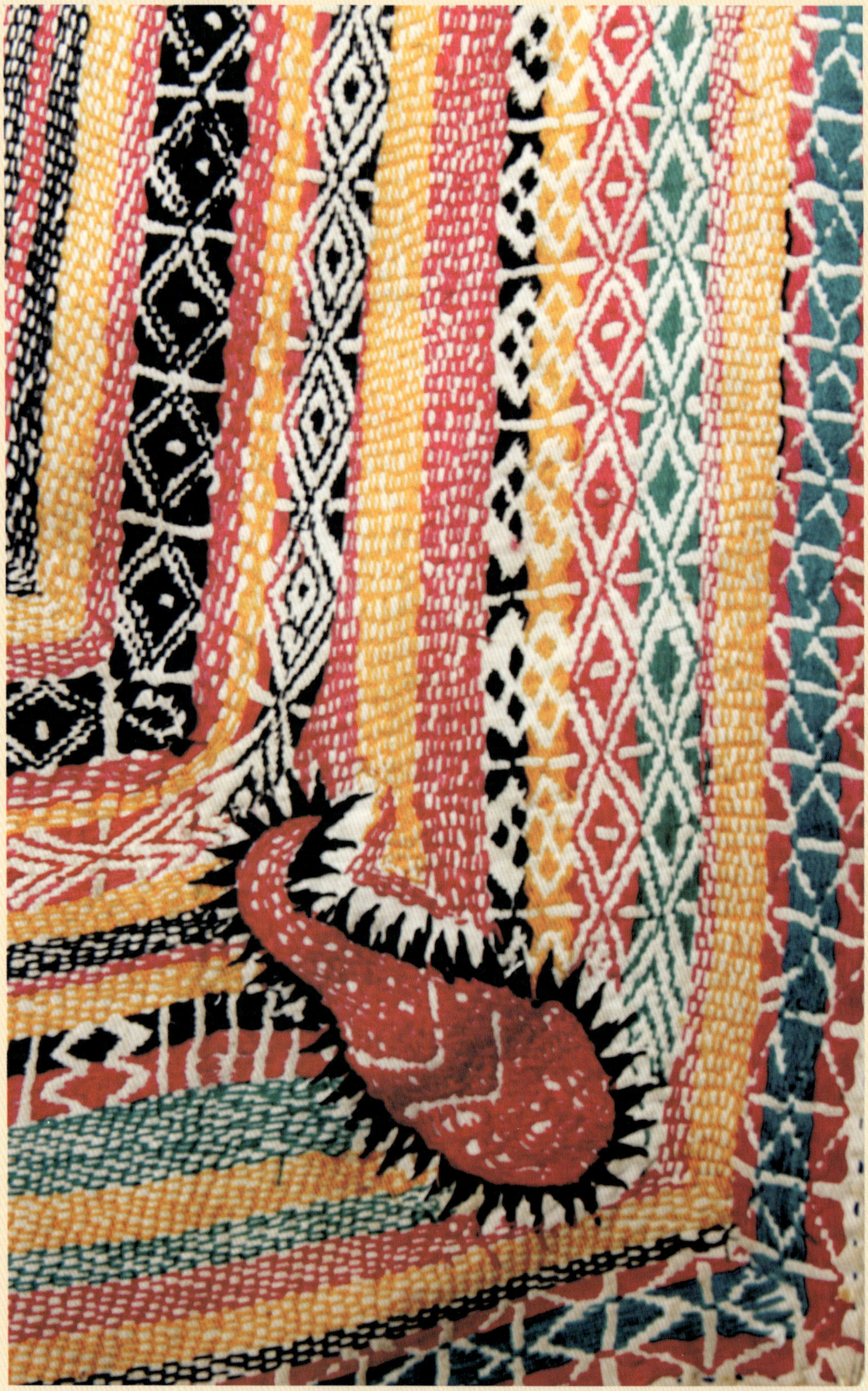

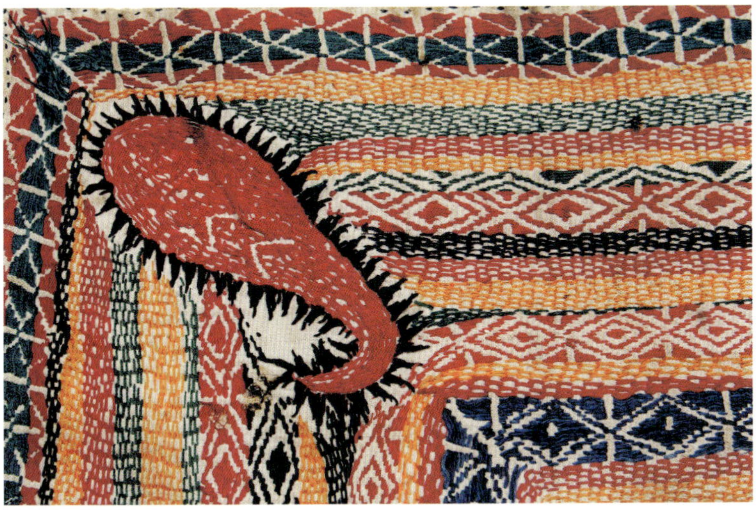

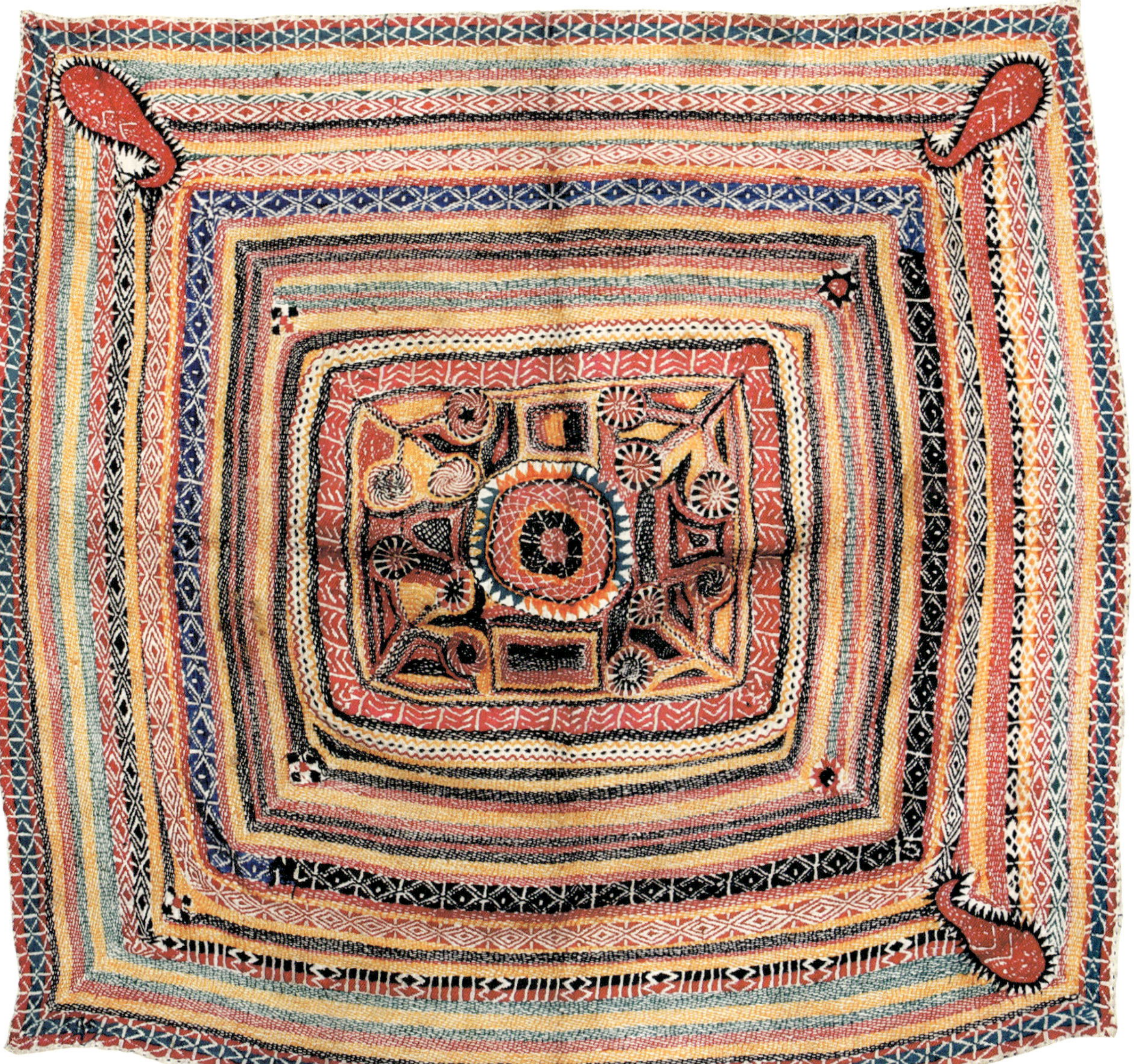

Bharany Collection-Kantha Textiles

Bh-1

Namavali Kantha having horizontal narrow panel embroidered in Bangla script in two colours, blue and red. The first panel has inscriptions which read as below :-

First row

Blue- *Hare Ram, Hare Krishna*

Hare Ram, Hare Krishna

Second row

Red-Foot print, *Ram*, Foot print, *Hare*, Foot print, *Ram*, Foot print, *Hare*.........

Third row

Blue-*Hare*, Foot Print, *Ram*, Foot Print, *Hare*, Foot Print, *Ram*

Fourth row

Red- *Hari Om Shri Ram*, Foot print

" " " " "

Fifth row

Blue- Same as fourth row

Sixth row

Red-Same as First row

Seventh row

Blue-Same as above

The five upper and lower rows are the same.

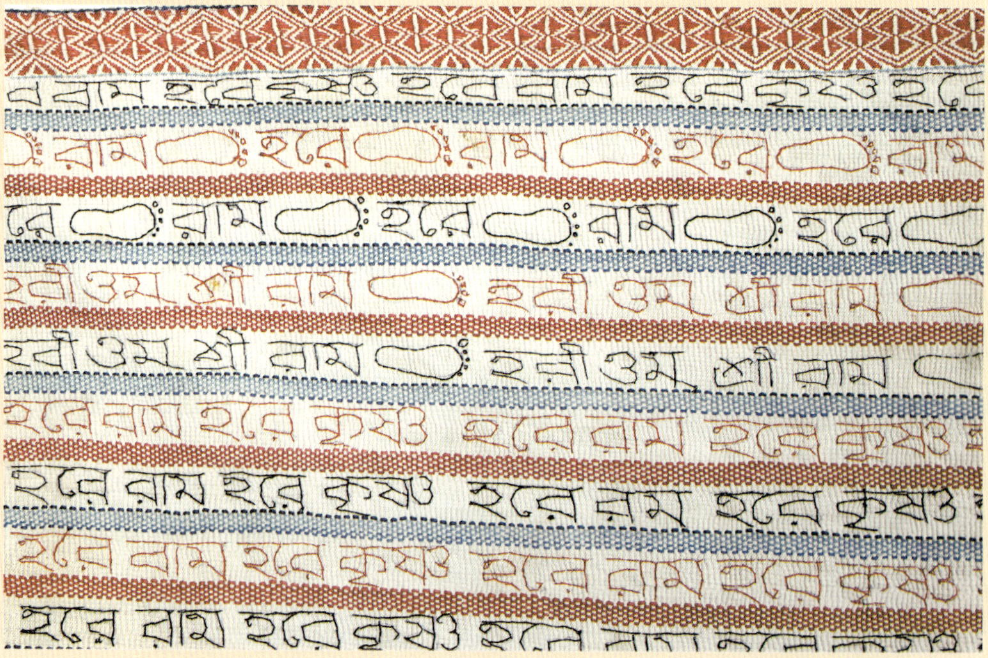

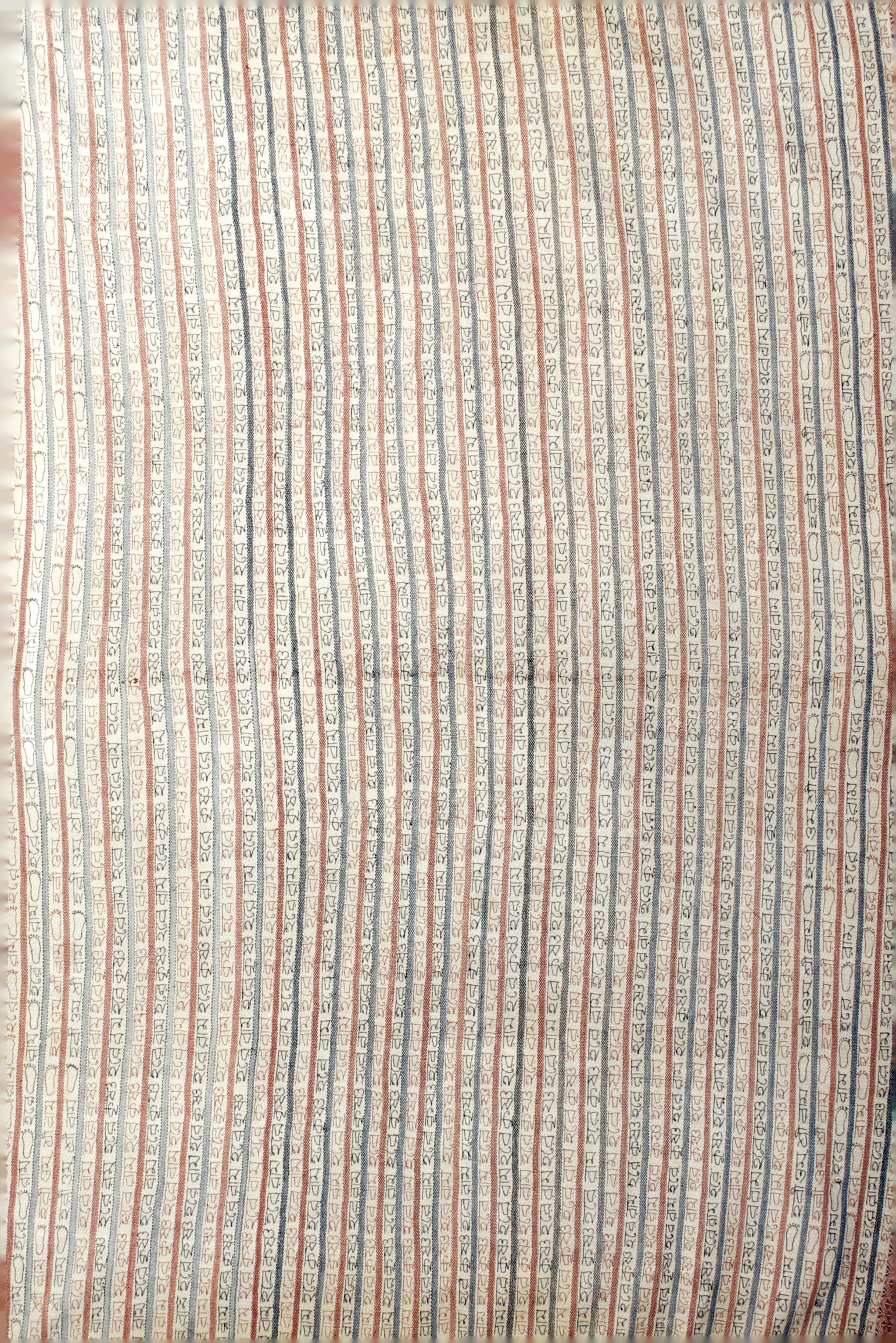

Bh-1 (CONTD)

While the other panel has been embroidered in *chatai* pattern which has been arranged alternately, the sacred feet have been embroidered in between inscriptions at places.

There is a very fine self *bakhiya* pattern all over the field which forms small squares. There is a red border on all four sides with a green edge on the inner side and blue on the outer.

Chatai pattern is very finely and symmetrically done. Colours used in embroidery are red, different shades of blue, black, orange, and green.

Material - Cotton

Condition - Borders are damaged.

Size - 224cmx147cm

Period - 19th Century

Place - West Bengal

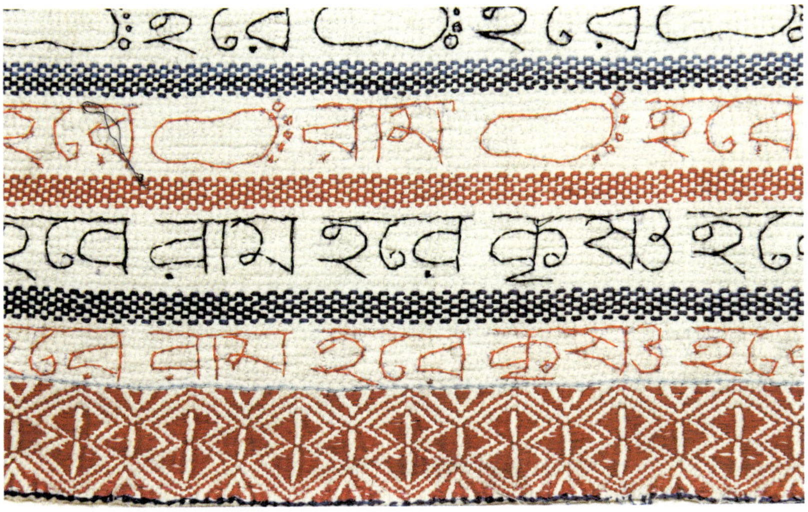
হরে রাম হরে কৃষ্ণ

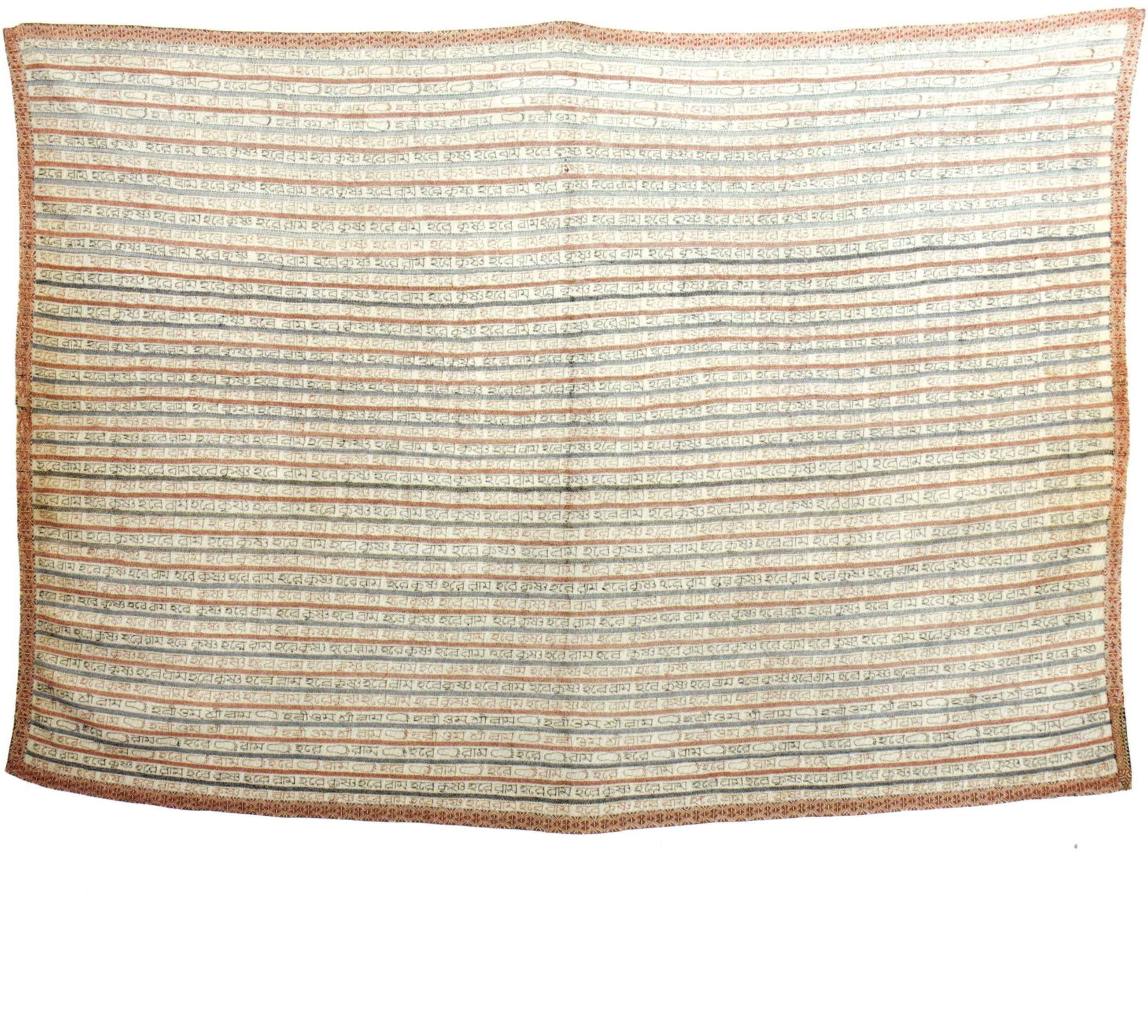

Bh-2

Namavali Kantha with squares arranged in the centre Perhaps it is a *rathyatra patta* (curtain) having flags, one on each outer side of the square. All around this *patta* there are musicians. On one side there are three male figures with two central dancing figures. One is playing on a *mridanga*, while the other is wearing a designed tunic. Of the two figures on either side, one is holding a rosary in his hand while the other one is playing a trumpet and wearing a patterned skirt.

On the second side (width wise) there are three musicians, the central one having a gong in one hand and a hammer in the other. This figure is flanked by a *mridanga* player and a *shehnai* player. On the third side (width wise), the central figure is *Chaitanaya Maha Prabhu* or *Gorang* in a dancing pose with his two hands raised upwards. He is wearing a tunic which has two branches with foliage motifs. On one side of this figure there is a man standing, holding a flag in his hands, while the figure on the other side is playing a *manjira* (cymbals) with his two hands.

On the fourth side (length wise), there are again four musicians. One is playing a trumpet wearing a designed skirt; the second is playing a dhol (drum) with a stick in his hand. The third is playing a mridanga and the fourth is playing a *manjira* (cymbals).

All the fourteen figures are round faced, each having a *tilak* on his forehead and a big *chutia* (standing pigtail) on the head. Besides wearing designed tunics and skirts, some are wearing designed dhotis.

On all the four sides near the border, there are scattered inscriptions in Bangla language which read:

(Width wise) Two Sides

Hare Rama, Hare Krishna

Krishna Krishna, Hare Hare.

(Length wise) Two Sides

Hare Ram, Hare Krishna, Krishna Krishna, Hare Hare.

Inside the centre, (*Radha* is referred to as *Krishna*)

First box

Hare Krishna, Hare Krishna

Krishna, Krishna, Ram, Ram

Hare Krishna, Hare

Hare Ram, Hare Ram

Krishna, Krishna, Ram, Ram

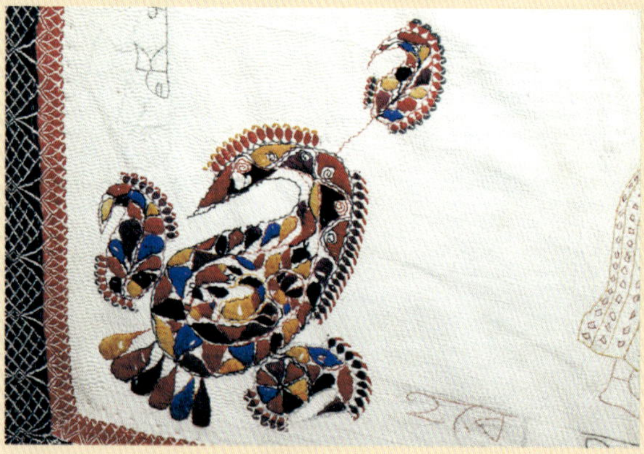

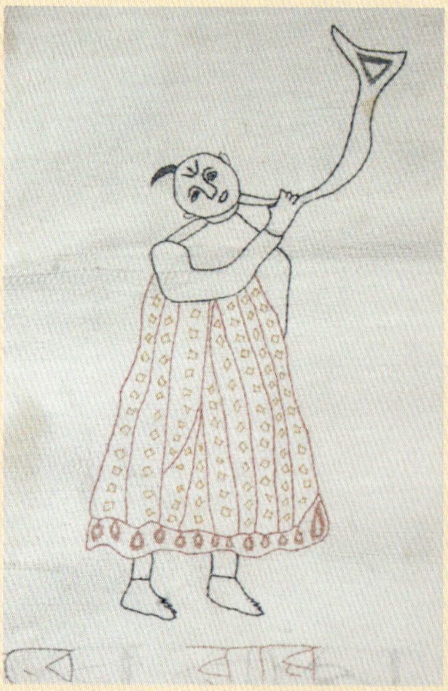

This pattern is repeated in the other boxes also.

There are four stylized *kalkas* in each corner, the central one is bigger than the others; one has six rounded leaves at the bottom and the other two diagonally opposite *kalkas* have multiple leaves at the bottom. The fourth *kalka* has a seven petalled flower with a stem stitch at the bottom. This particular *kalka* has been enclosed with a foliage border all around. The field of the four *kalkas* has been richly embroidered with foliage patterns, some having flowers in between.

Part of the edges of the three *kalkas* have foliage motifs with curved tops. It seems that these three *kalkas* have been added at a later stage.

The *Kantha* has two borders on all the four sides. One border is smaller than the other. The inner border which is of red colour has geometrically designed foliage motifs, while the outer black border has stylized geometrical diagonal squares in enclosures. The field has fine running stitches all over.

The colours used are blue, rust, black, red, mustard, dark blue, orange, purple, and dark green.

Material - Cotton

Condition - The border is damaged and stained at places.

Size - 186cmx137cm

Period - 19th Century

Place - West Bengal

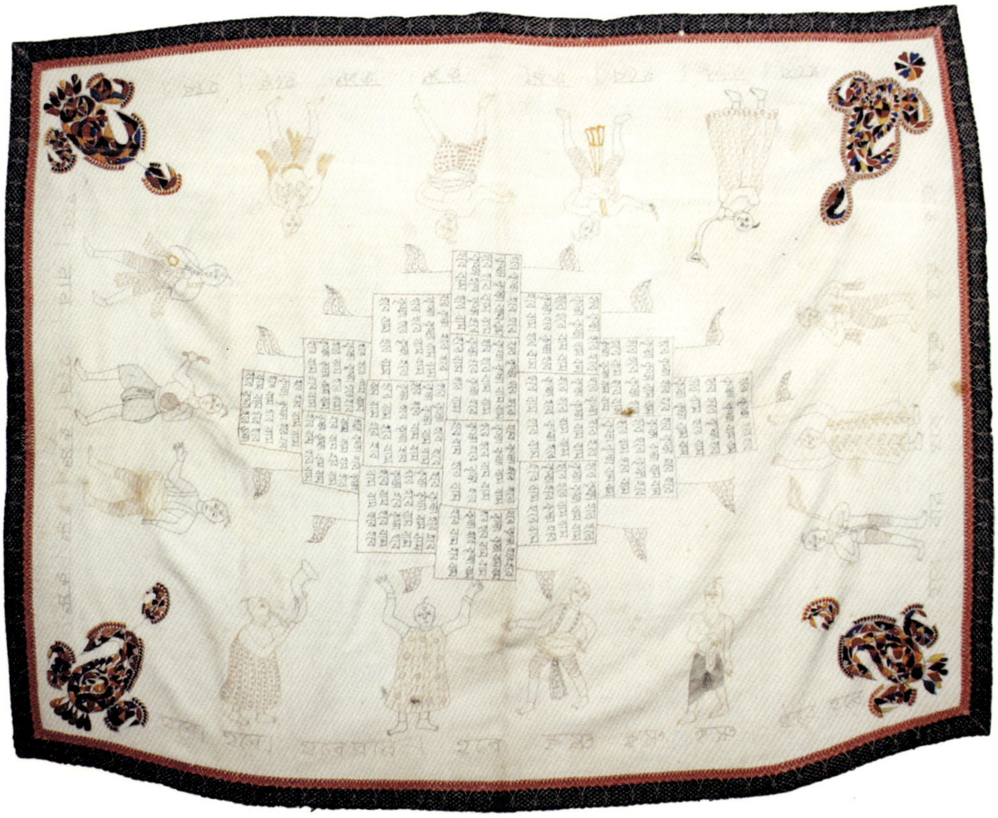

Bh-3

Rectangular off-white coloured *Kantha* having a lotus flower in three layers in the centre. The first layer has eight rounded petals enclosed in a circle while the next layer has half semi-circle enclosures, each having a small flower in the centre. The third layer has leaves in pyramid shape.

The rest of the field, barring the three borders on all four sides, is very richly embroidered mostly with small *butas*, each enclosed in a circle. In between these circles, there are various motifs like wheels, *shosti chinha*, *swastika* motif, small and big *butas*, fish etc embroidered all over the field.

There are three borders on all four sides. The first inner border has single leaves with a small stem arranged in a row, while the middle border has zigzag patterns, each pattern having a small leaf in the centre. The last border has rows of sitting birds. Besides these three borders, there are four embroidered corners, each having a stylized *buta* with an elongated leaf in the centre, curved branches and three birds sitting on them. Each corner also has a wheel on the sides, except one.

All the enclosures and the borders are enclosed in *Ma-taga* stitches, some single and some double.

Most of the embroidery has been done in the *katiya* stitch. Colours used are red, black, grey, pink and different shades of blue.

Material - Cotton.

Condition - Good, but stained at places.

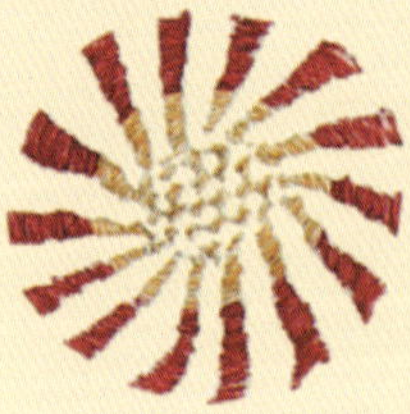

Size - 196cmx160cm

Period - 19th Century

Place - West Bengal

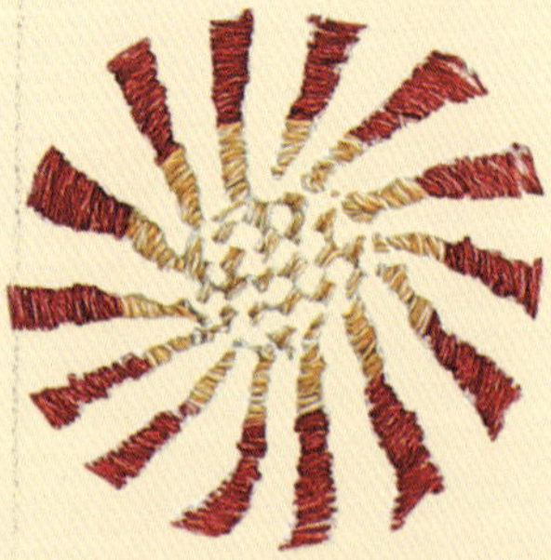

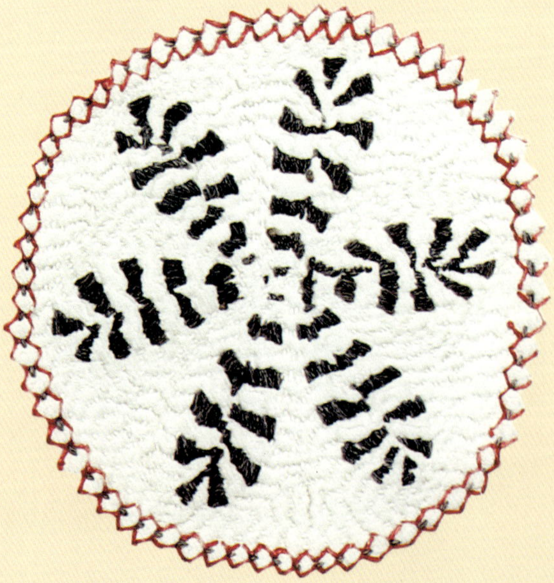

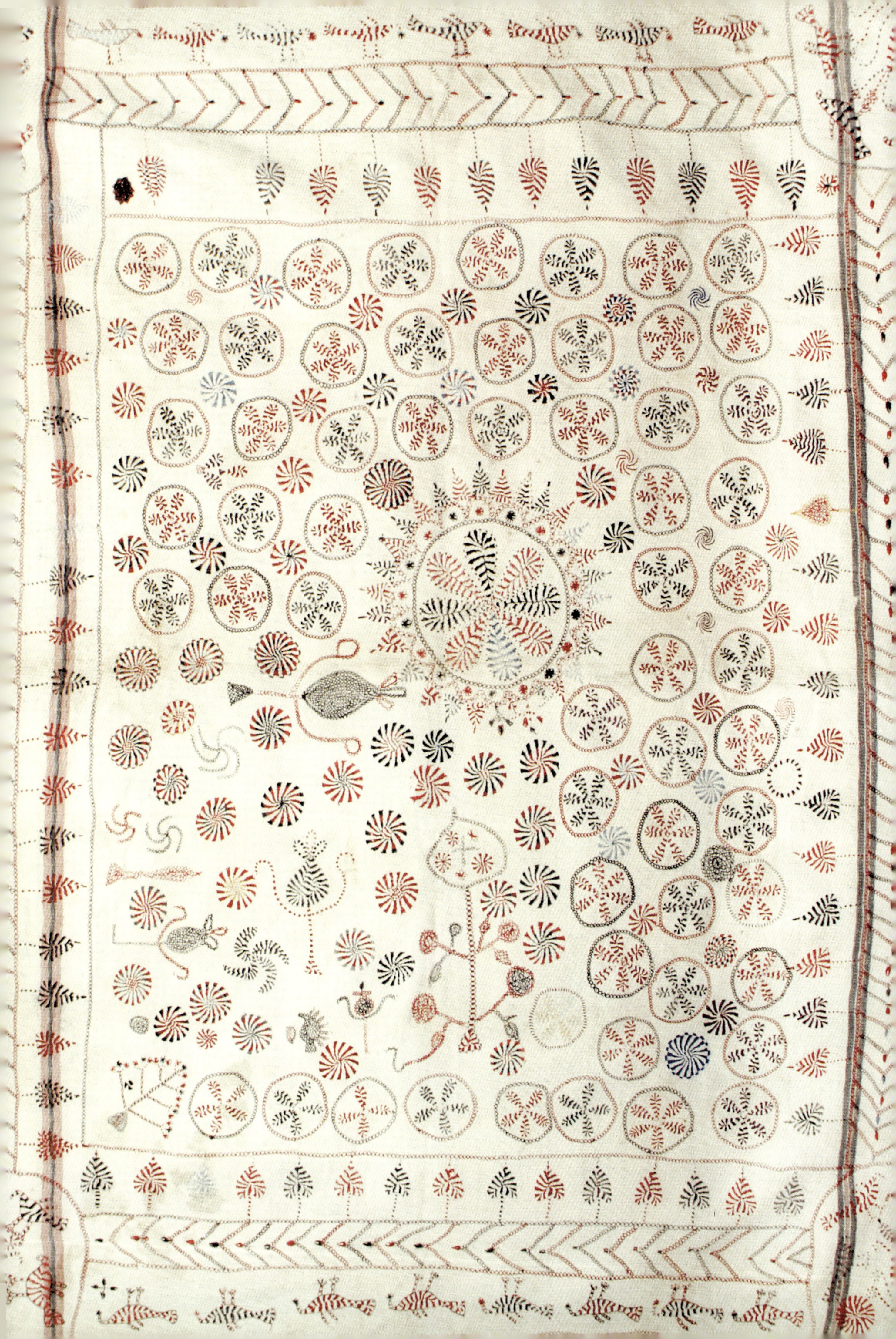

Bh-3 (CONTD)

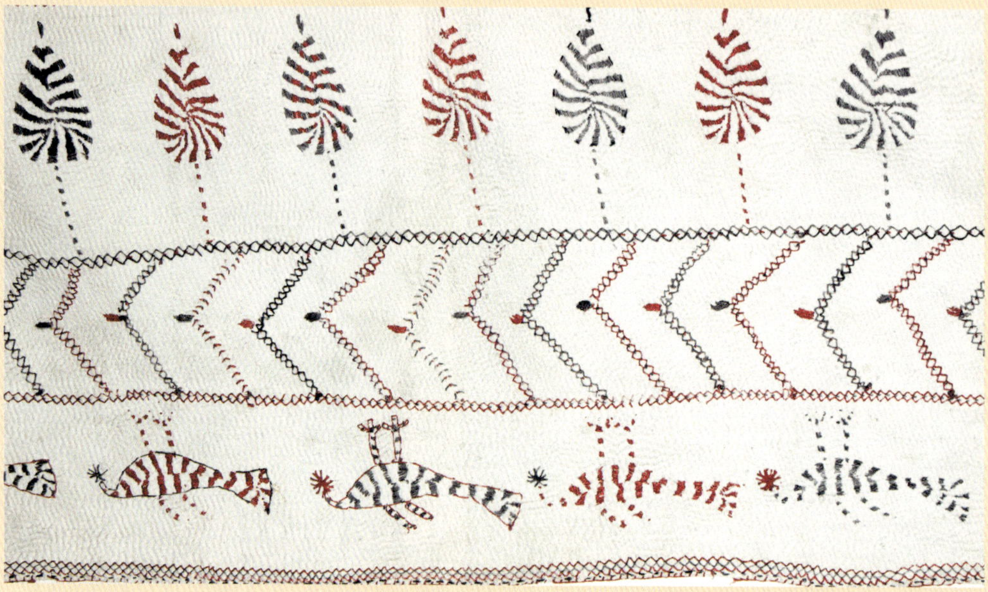

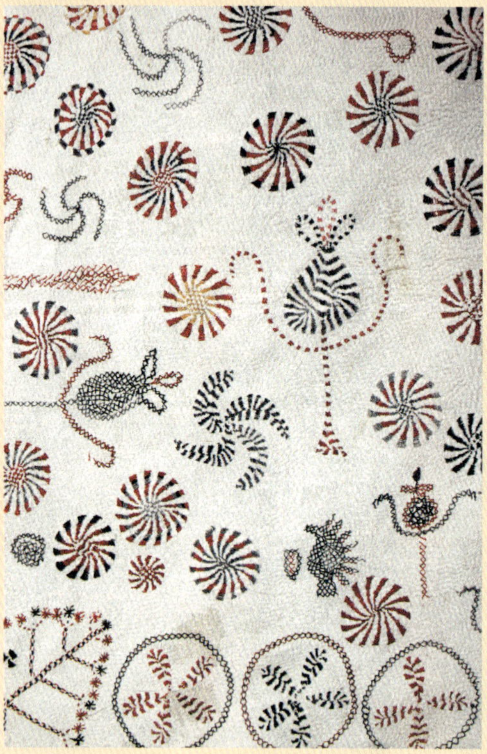

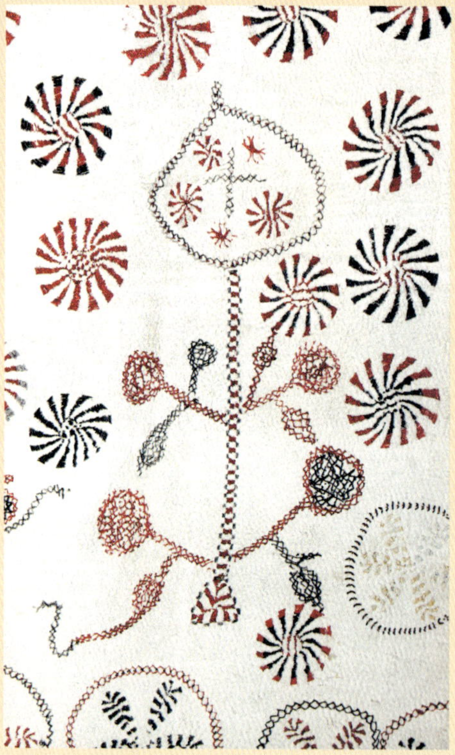

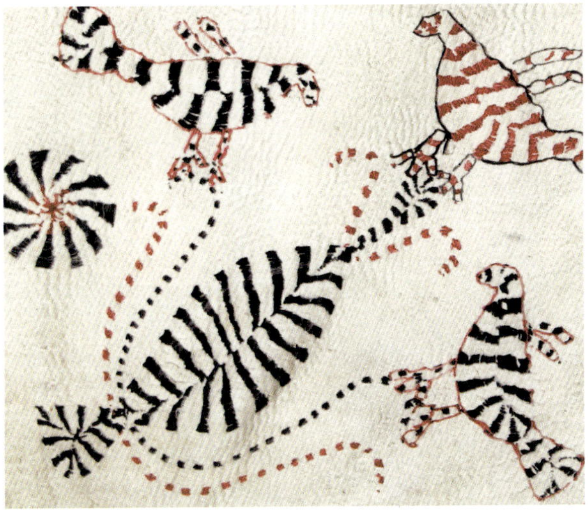
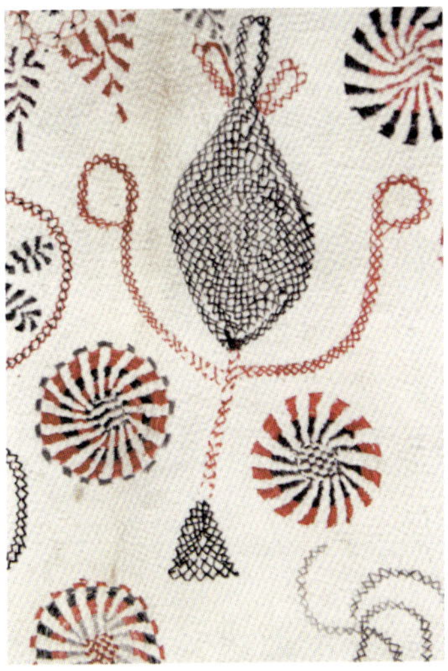
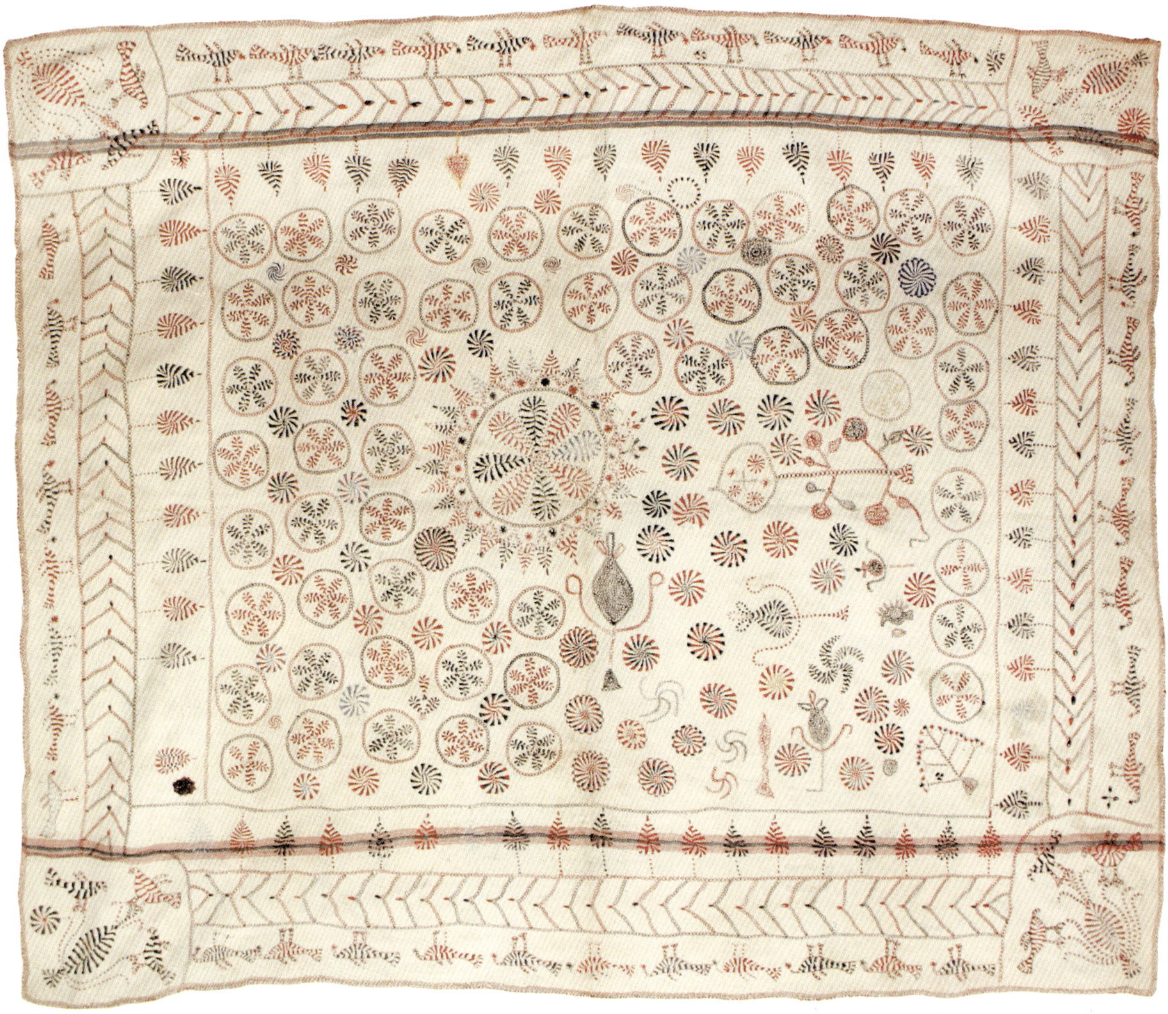

Bh-4

Rectangular *Kantha* embroidered with four female figures each carrying a pitcher on her head and each of them wearing a *ghagra*, *choli* and *odhni*.

There are four *kalkas* (one in each corner), embroidered with a broad line joined together in *chatai* pattern forming its outline. The centre of the kalka again has a stylized betel leaf enclosed with lines in *chatai* pattern. The centre of the *kalka* is embroidered with diamond motifs. The edges of each *kalka* have foliage motifs of different shapes and sizes. Four *kalkas* have been embroidered in different colours. The main *kalka* is surmounted by a smaller *kalka* with leaves resting on two stylized *kalkas* at the bottom.

There is a triple border on all four sides. The outermost has diamond shaped motifs arranged in diagonal squares. The middle border has a betel leaf and a candle stand arranged alternately. The inner most border has stylized floral and tree motifs with a foliage pattern arranged in line and with a curved top. Each *kalka* has been embroidered in different colours and the central part of the borders on two sides (length wise and width wise) has been embroidered in pink colour.

It appears that the figures of the village women have been embroidered at a later stage than the original *Kantha*, because the embroidery does not synchronize with the other work. A small bird can be seen on one side of the *kalka*, while there is a drawing of a village woman on the field.

The body has very fine running stitches. Colours used in embroidery are red, black, green, mustard, yellow and different shades of blue.

Material - Cotton

Condition - Stained, repaired and edges torn at places.

Size - 199cmx123cm

Period - Late 19th Century

Place - West Bengal

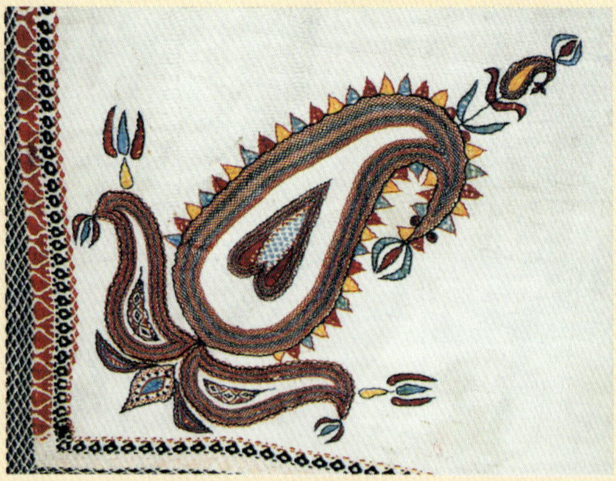

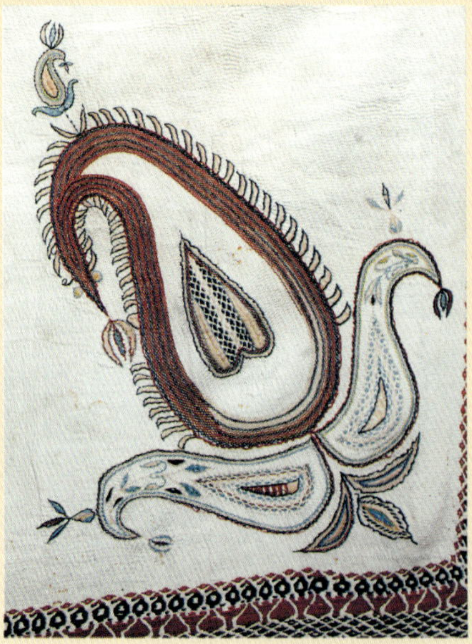

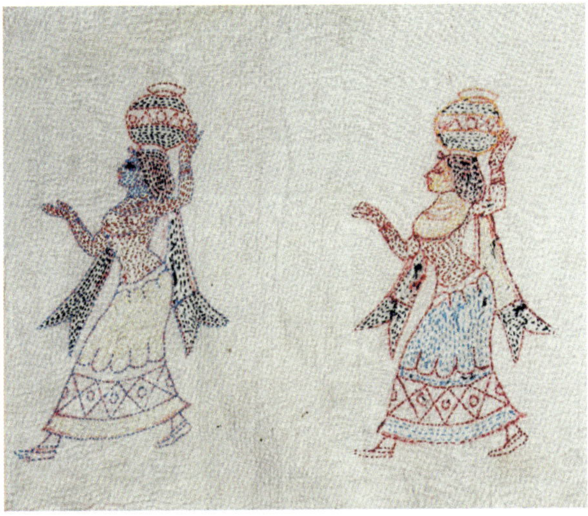

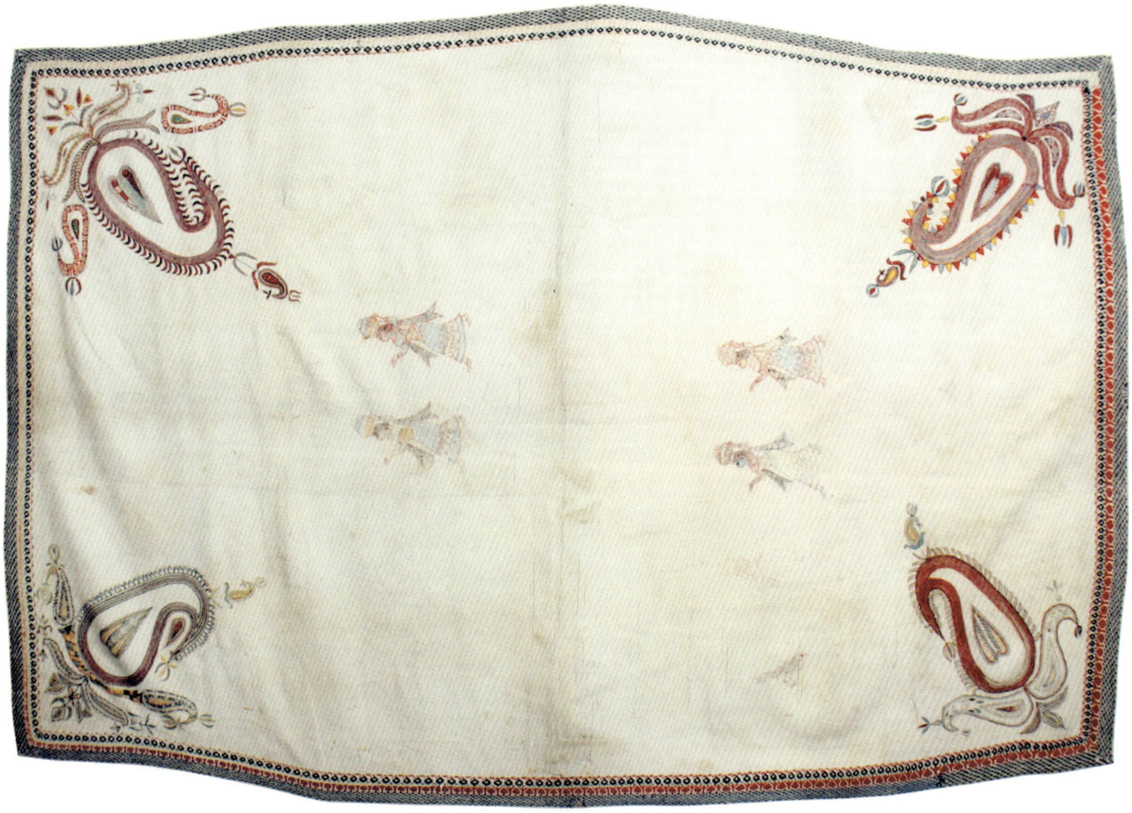

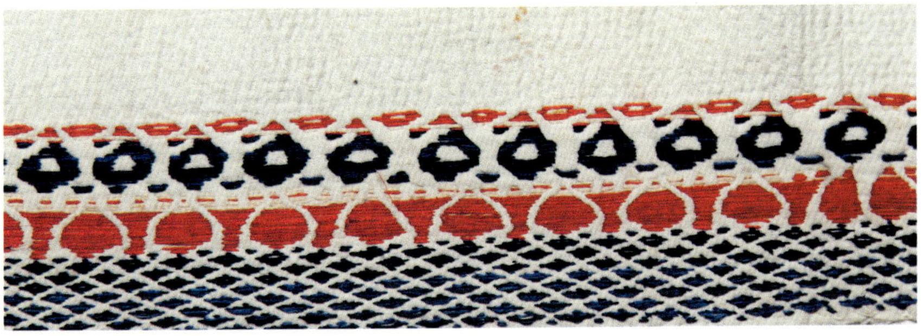

Bh-5

Rectangular *Kantha* having fine running stitches on the field and five petalled flowers with green leaves arranged in a creeper on all four sides. There are four plants at the four corners branching out of a pot in each corner. All the four pots are different in shape and size. The entire field is beautifully embroidered with birds and animals in very vibrant colours.

In the centre, a model of the Taj Mahal has been embroidered. The field has been embroidered with different designs like a stylized plant in a pot, two peacocks sitting on a branch, a butterfly, a brinjal, a mango with leaf, a stylized floral motif in a circle having a foliage border, a lotus with stem, a duck, a stylized cup, two parrots on the branches with floral and foliage motifs, a seven petalled flower with two leaves and a small elephant with a colourful trapping. On one side of the *Kantha* (length wise), there is a very richly embroidered dog and an elephant with colourful trapping, while on the other side there is a camel, a stag and a tiger. On the other two sides (width wise), one has a horse and the other a roaring tiger.

Most of the embroidery has been done with very rich chain stitches. The edges of the *Kantha* have a narrow *chatai* pattern.

Colours used are red, green, blue, yellow, brown, white, orange, rust, purple, mustard, grey and different shades of blue etc.

Material - Cotton

Condition - Stained, repaired and edges coming out.

Size - 197cmx139cm

Period - Late 20th Century

Place - West Bengal

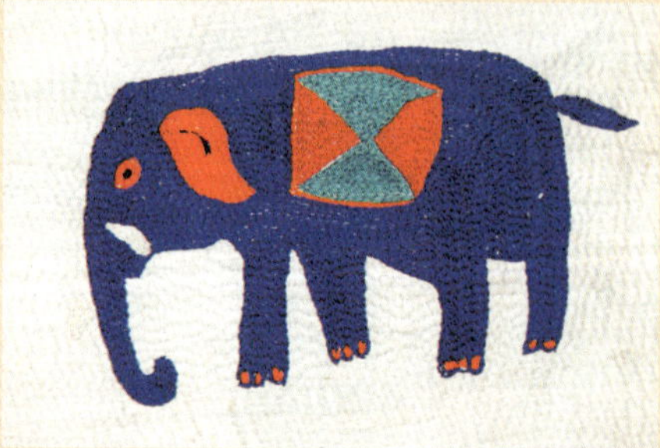

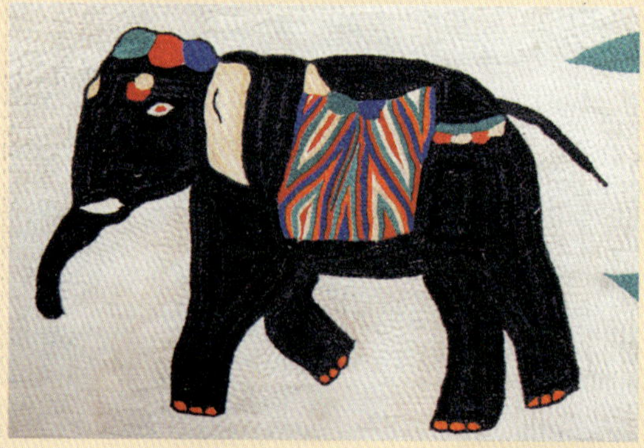

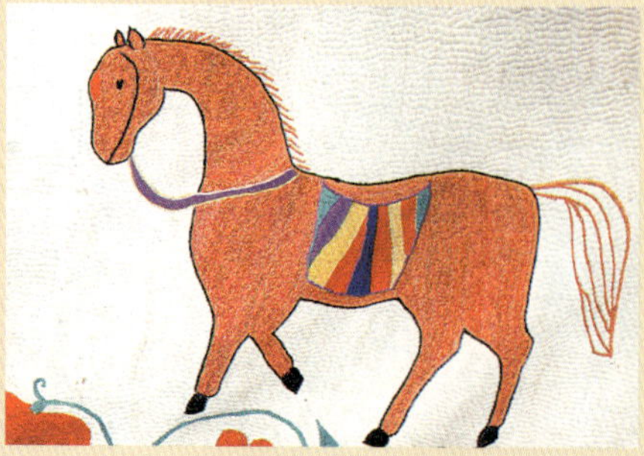

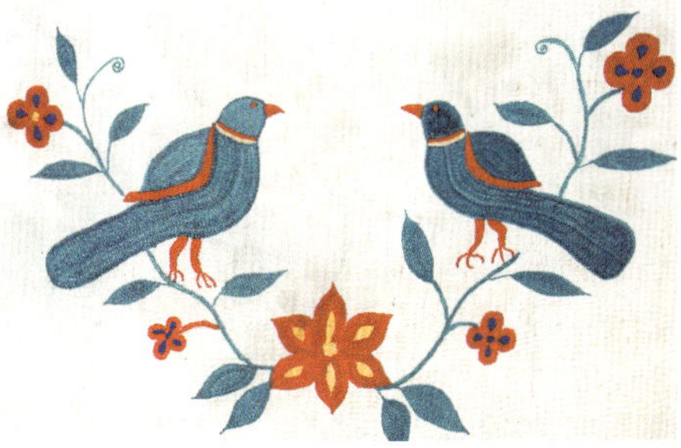

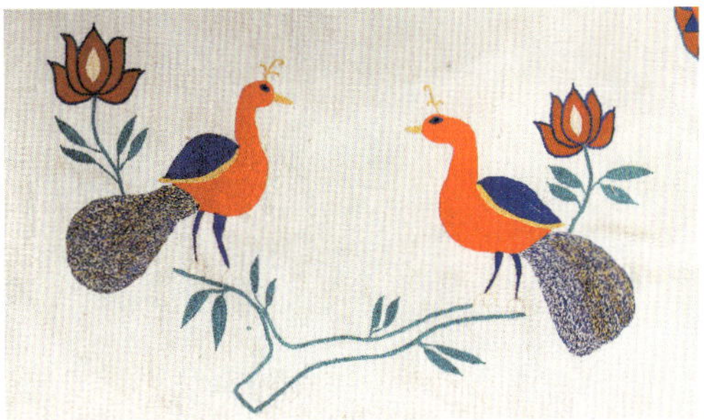

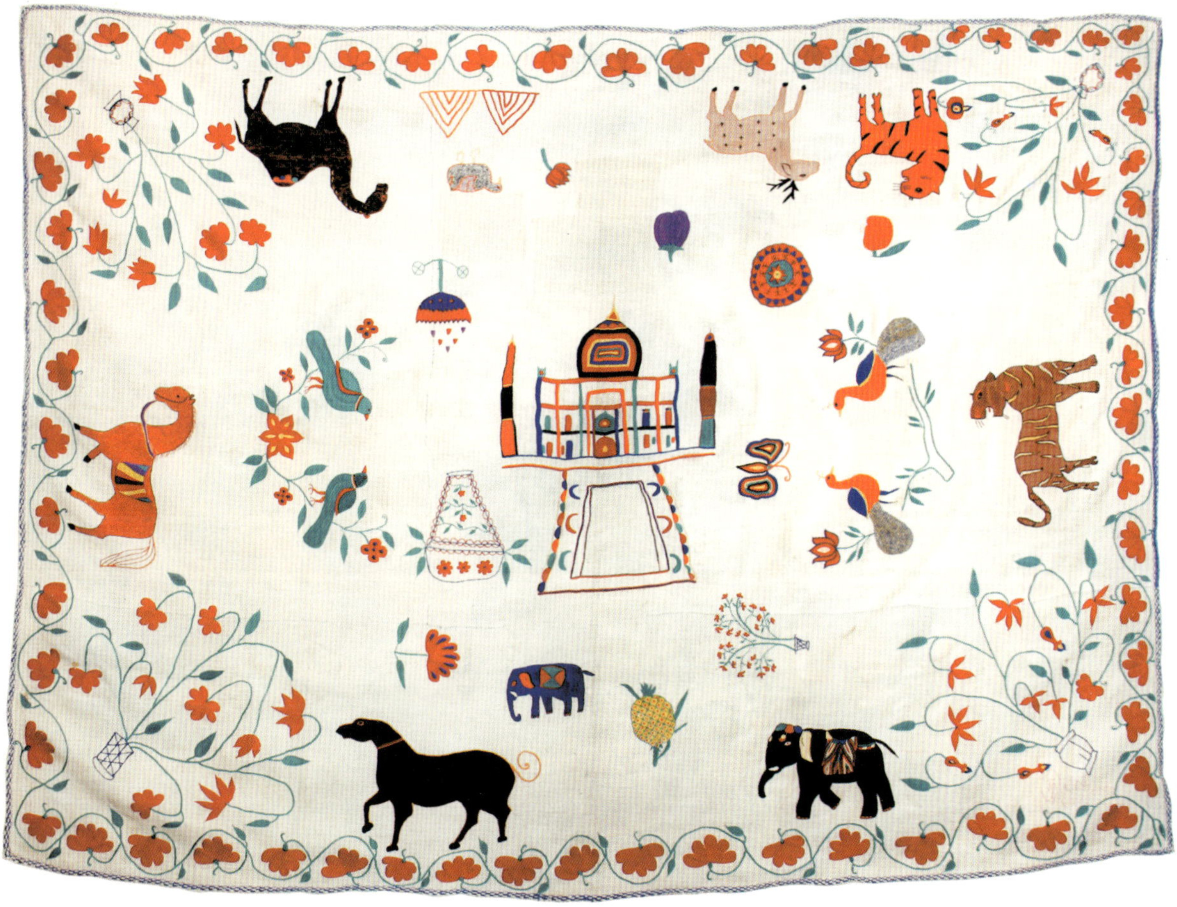

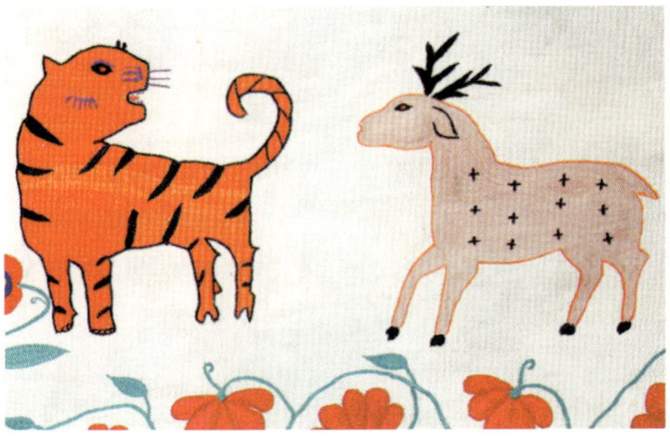

Bh-6

Rectangular *Kantha* with a circular lotus motif in the centre, which is surrounded by *shosti chinha* in circles. The entire inner side is richly embroidered in different layers with different types of foliage motifs. There are four stylized big *kalkas* (one in each corner), each of them resting on a single elongated leaf with curved off shoots. The border of the *kalka* is chequered, while its central space is filled with broad lines. The edges are serrated with curved ends. Inside the curved side of the *kalka*, there is a leaf pattern and a balloon shaped enclosure, while the Inner part of the *kalkas* has been embroidered in contrast colours with broad lines.

There are three sunlight motifs on the three sides of the *kalkas*, (one on top and two on the sides).

The border on four sides has rows of small *kalkas* on top, geometrical border (*chok par*) in the middle and multi-coloured lines in different stitches. The outer border has a dark pink colour cotton lining. Colours used in the four *kalkas in* the four corners are different from each other.

The colours used are very bright, which are red, mustard, black, blue, yellow, white, rust, pink and different shades of green.

Most of the embroidery has been done in satin and stem stitches.

Material - Cotton

Condition - Stained, repaired and stitches coming out.

Size - 195cmx110cm

Period - 19th Century

Place - West Bengal

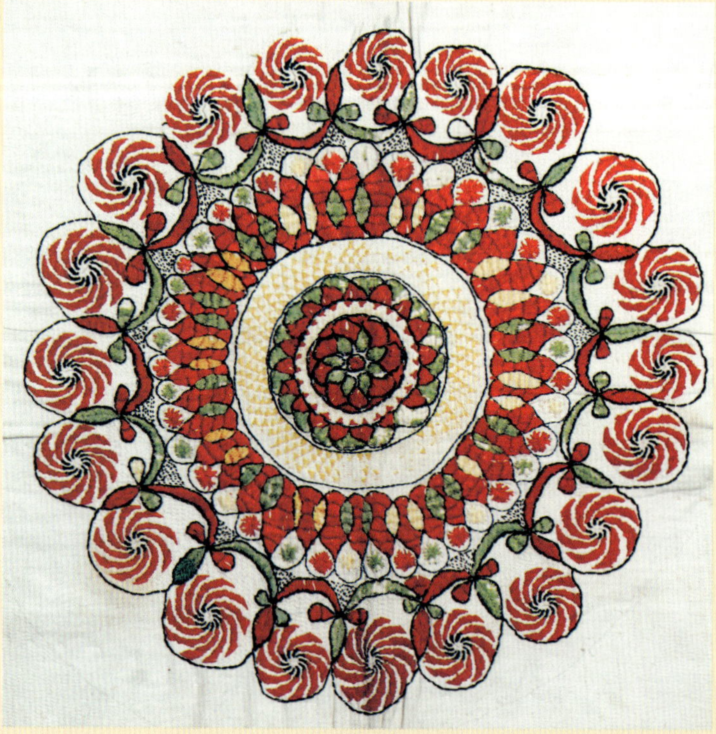

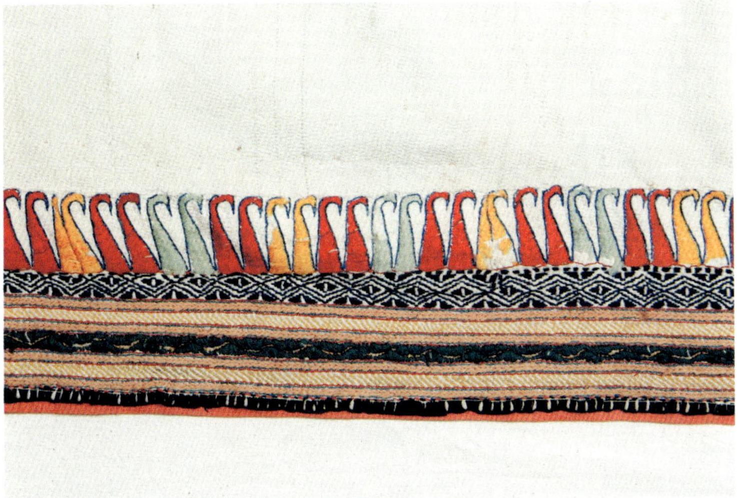

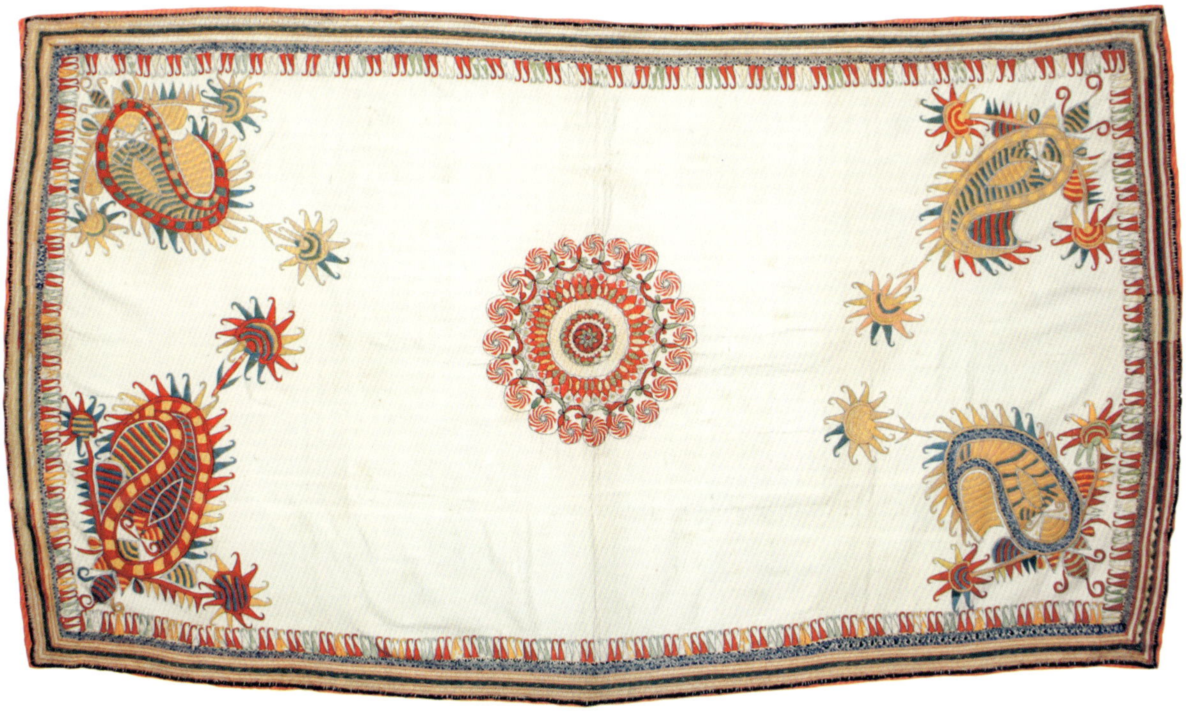

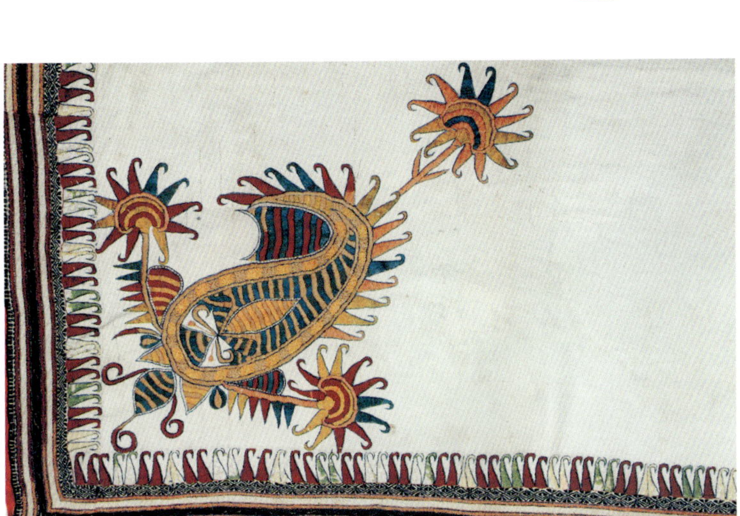

Bh-7

Rectangular *dorukha* or double sided *Kantha* having several layered lotus motifs in the centre in black and red colours, which is embroidered in chain stitch.

There are two *kalkas* joined together having trefoil patterns with a stem in each of the four corners.

Two rows of rams in walking posture are arranged lengthwise on either side.

Below the row of rams on one side, there is a creeper pattern in black colour. It is enclosed with double rows of chain stitches in red colour. They are standing on the *chattai* patterned border.

In one corner of one row there is one ram, fully embroidered with red thread ridden by a standing human figure.

The bodies of the other rams are filled with running stitches in red thread with a black outline. Width wise, there is a row of rams on both sides, embroidered with red thread, each having black eyes and black seats.

The rams are standing on a small border having a triangular pattern in red and black colours.

There is a broad border on all four sides having a *shosti chinha* pattern with a curved line in between.

The outermost border has a zigzag patterns enclosed with two red lines on two sides (lengthwise).

The field has close running stitches.

Material - Cotton

Conditions - Edges torn, repaired, and stained at places.

Size - 157cmx103cm

Period - 20th Century

Place - West Bengal

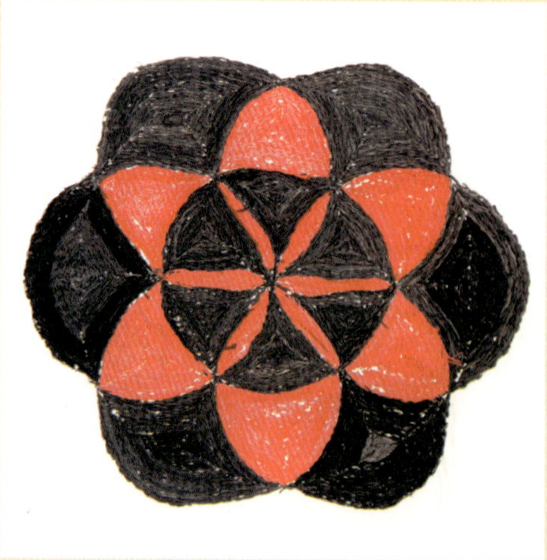

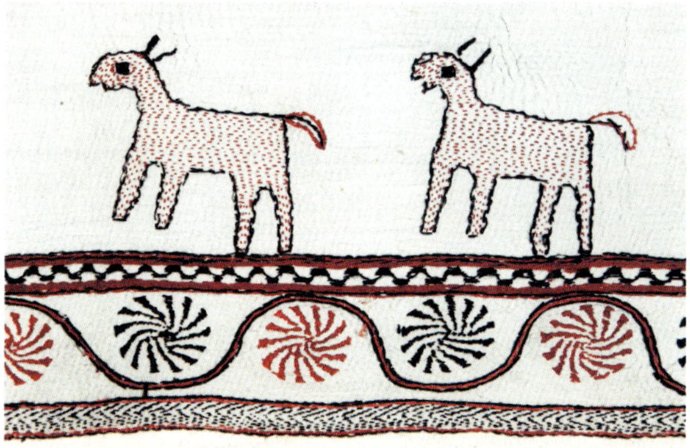

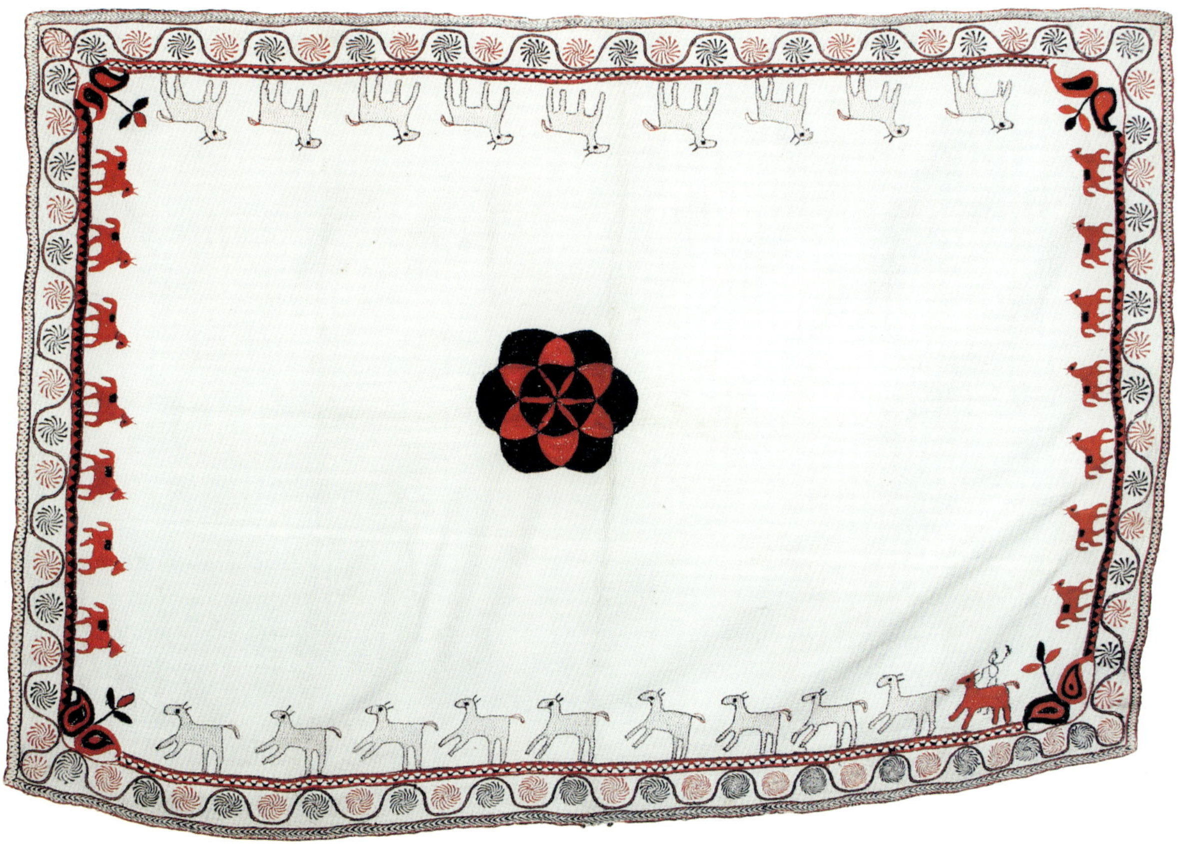

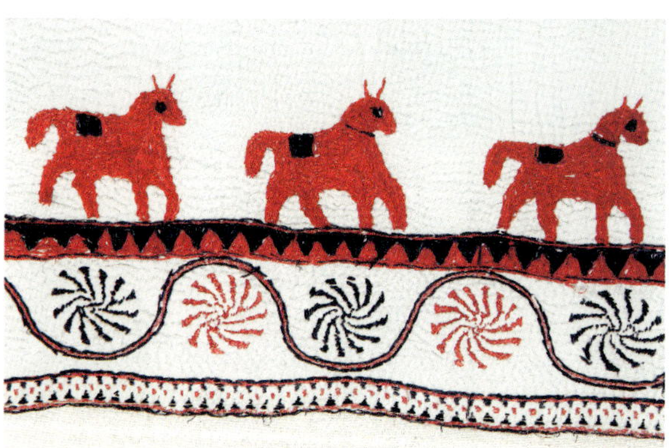

Bh-8

Rectangular *Kantha* in off-white colour, having old saree double borders of different designs and colours like green, blue, black, brown, orange, red etc on all four sides.

In the centre, there is a big lotus flower having eight petals. There are four female figures of different shapes and sizes, wearing different dresses, each having skipping ropes held in both hands and perhaps each having two wings on either side, which is symbolic of flying in happiness.

On the inner side of the border, there is a series of creepers and round petalled flowers on all four sides.

The rest of the field is covered with very colourful flowers of different shapes and sizes.

The central lotus and wings are embroidered in the *katiya* stitch while the other designs are mostly done in satin and stem stitches. The field does not have running stitches as in a typical *Kantha*.

Colours used are blue, black, green, yellow, orange, purple, brown etc.

Material - Cotton

Condition - Borders are torn, embroidery is coming out at places, repaired, tiny holes all over and the field is soiled and stained.

Size - 237cmx167cm

Period - 21st Century

Place - West Bengal

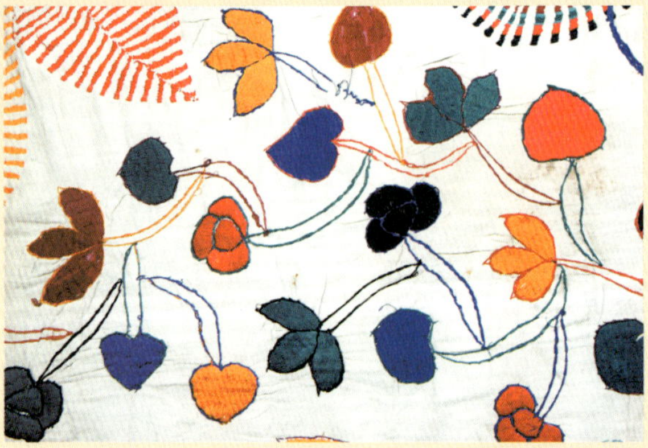

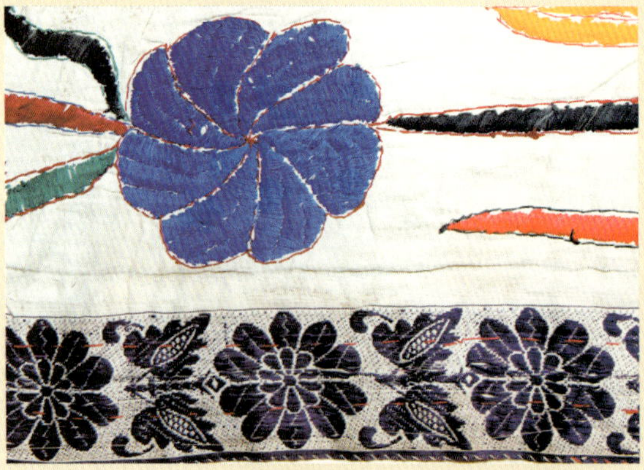

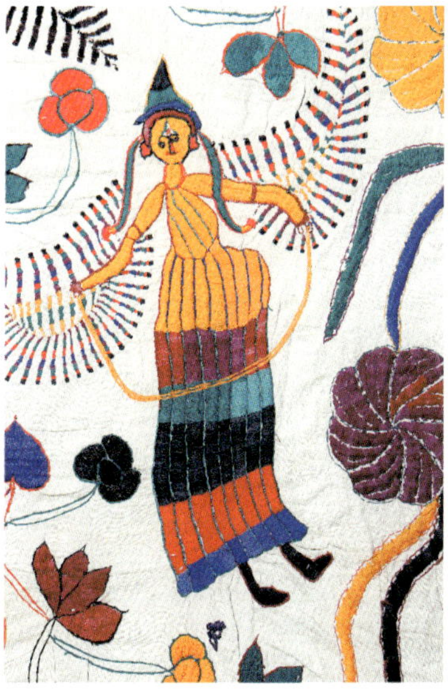

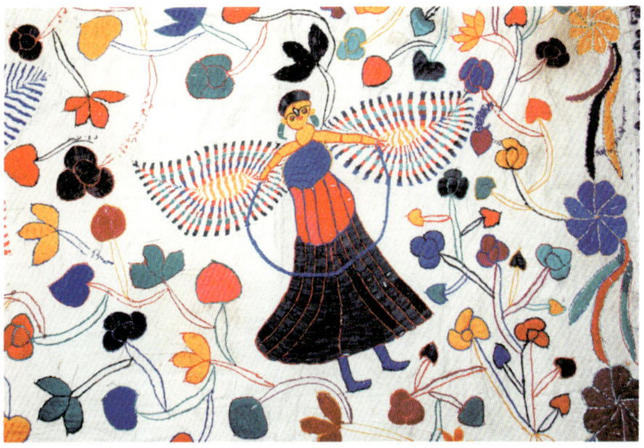

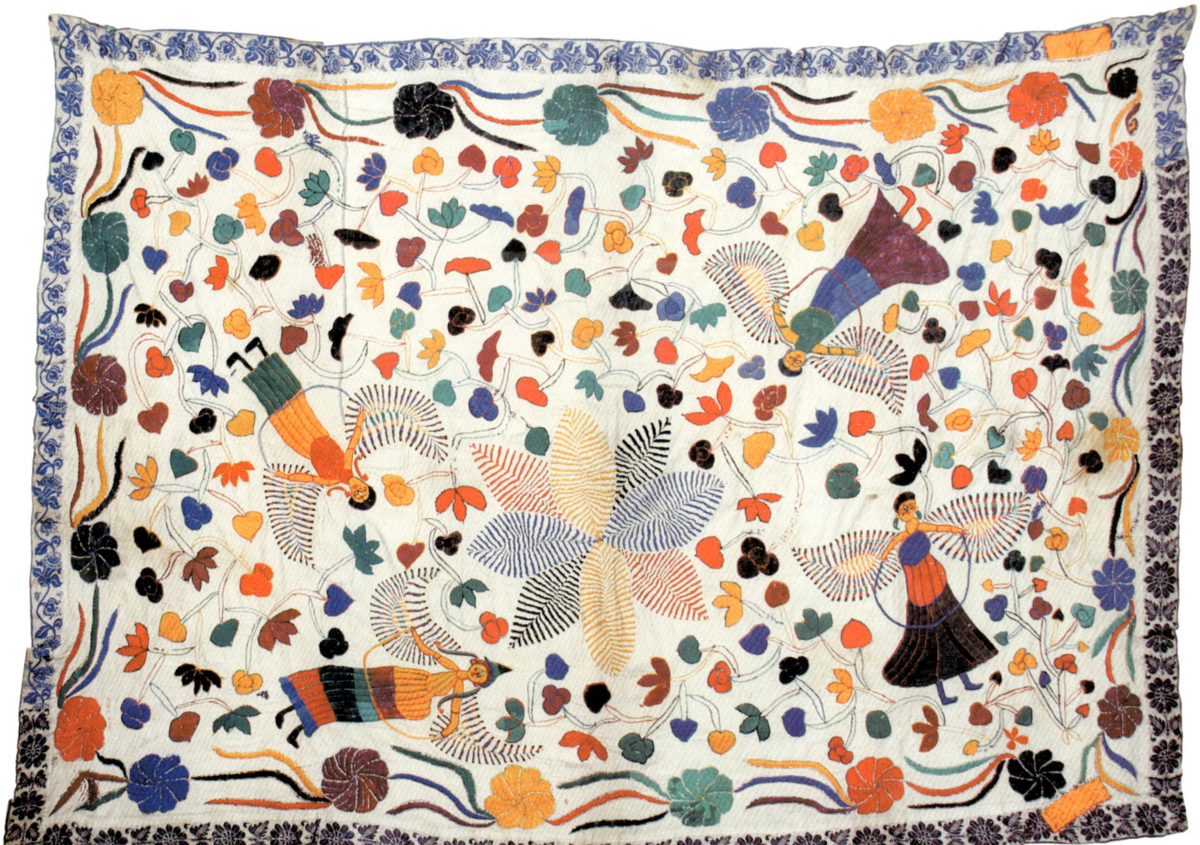

Bh-9

Rectangular *Kantha* divided into different enclosures and has a stylized lotus motif in the centre (in an enclosure).

There are six *shosti chinha* motifs around the lotus enclosed in a double circle. The circle has double betel leaves around it.

On the four corners, there is one stylized *buta* in a triangular pot in each corner.

There are six *shosti chinha* motifs in between the *butas*. In all the other enclosures there are different shapes and sizes of foliage motifs; different enclosures have different borders.

The outer border on two sides has *kalka* motifs arranged in a row enclosed by two small borders. The outer broader border of *kalka* motifs have geometrical designs, while the edges have button hole stitches.

On one side there is a geometrical border, while on the other side there are four rows of diamond patterns.

Most of the embroidery has been done in the *katiya* stitch with stem stitches in between.

Colours used are red, black, pink and grey.

Material - Cotton

Condition - Torn at places.

Size - 191cmx196cm

Period - Late 19th Century

Place - West Bengal

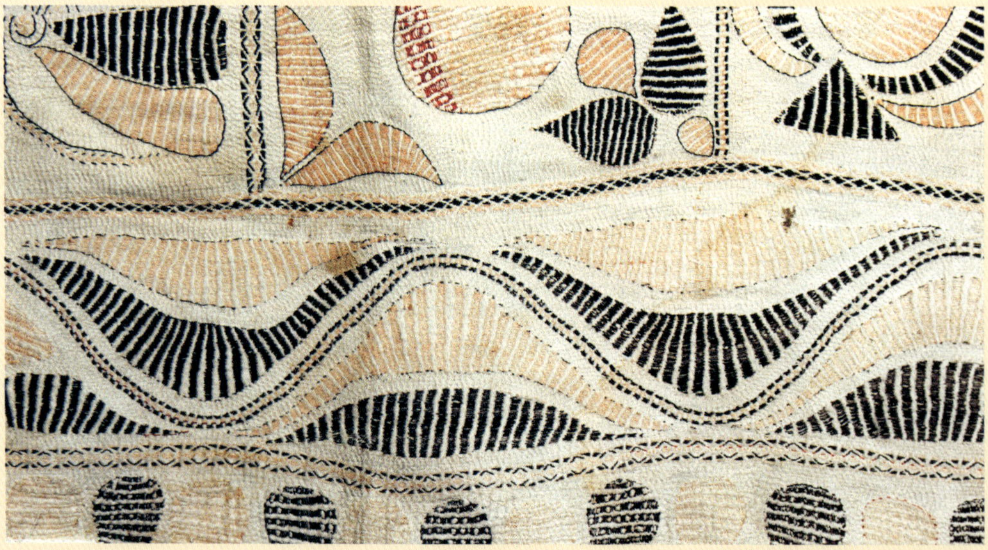

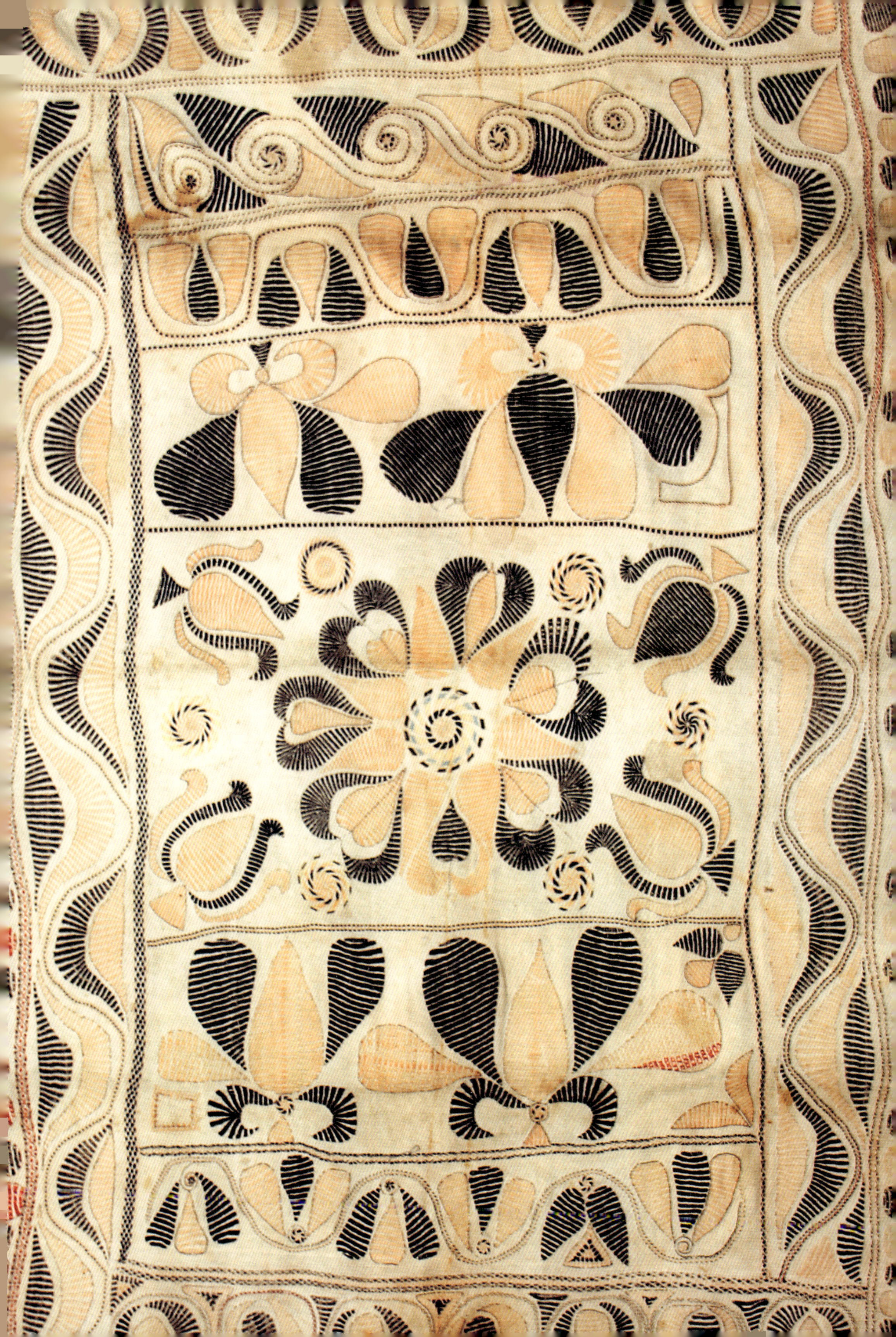

Bh-9 (CONTD)

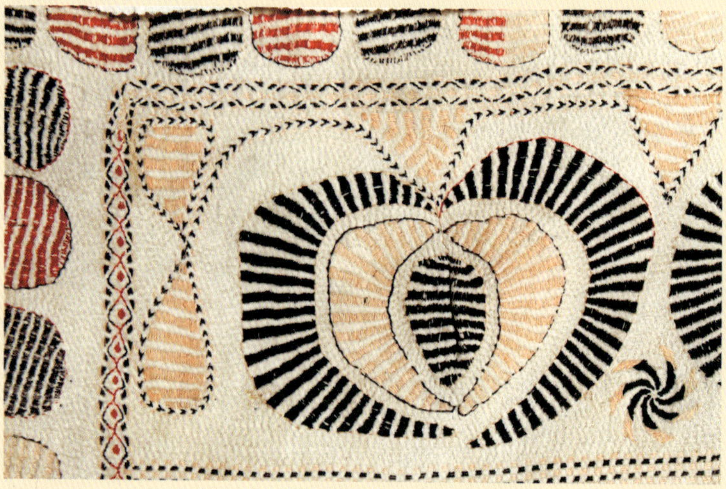

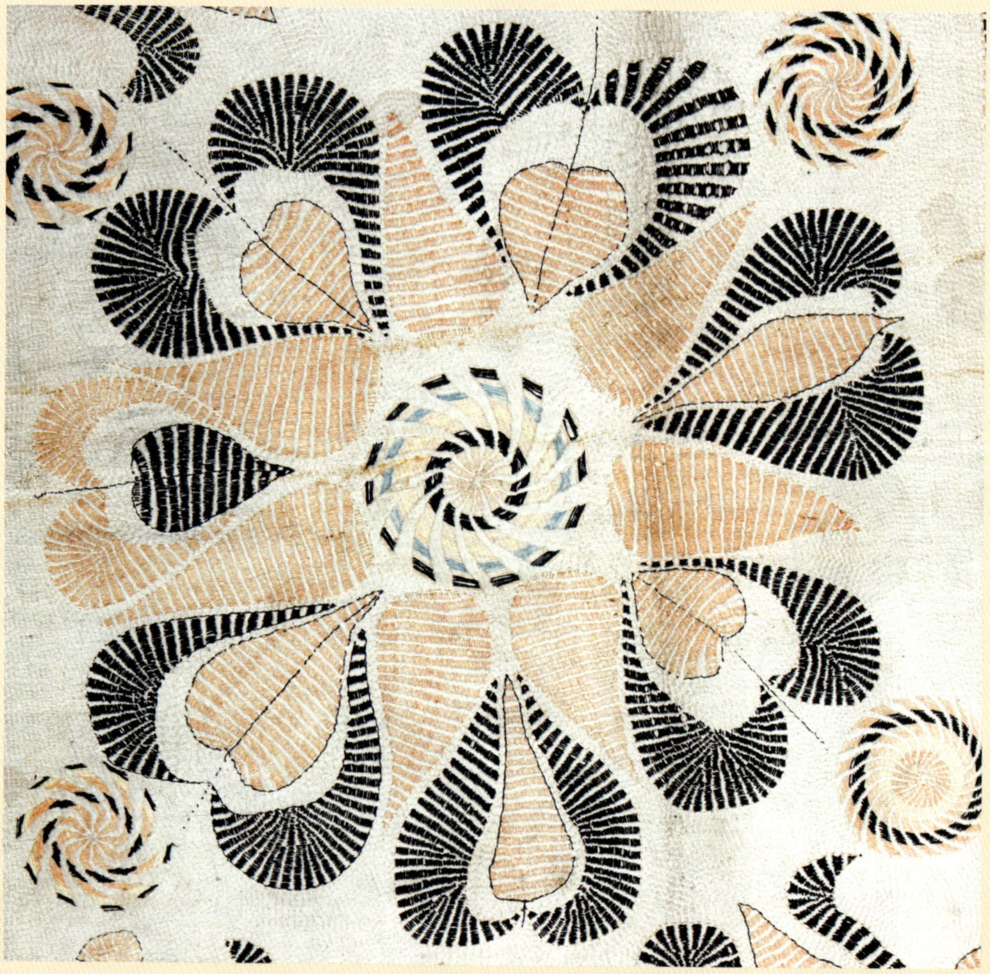

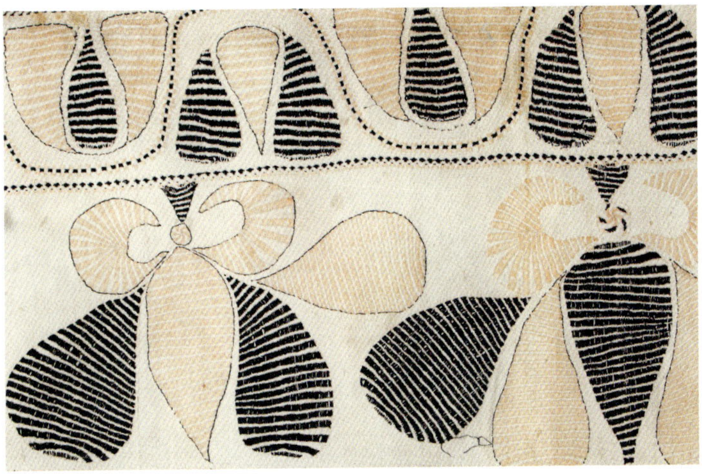

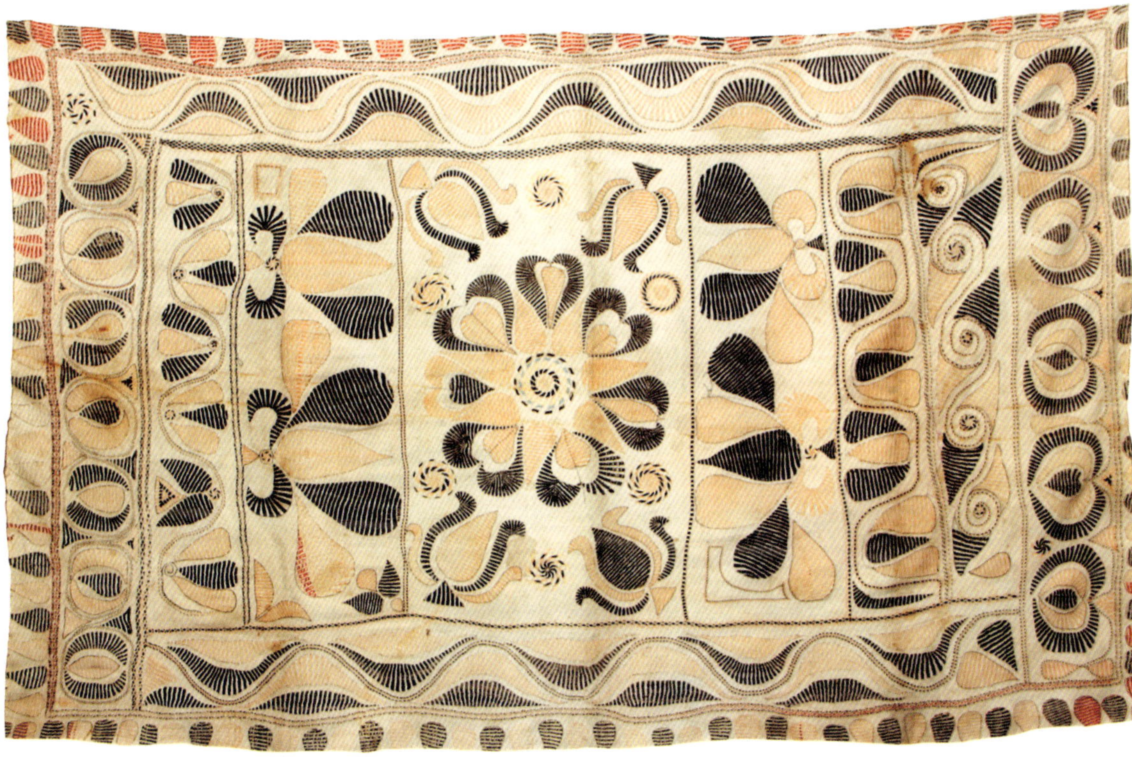

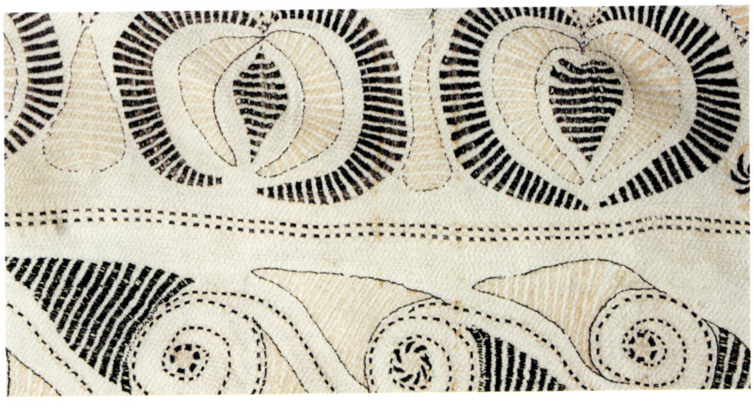

Bh-10

Small square *asana* embroidered with an eight petalled lotus in the centre, surrounded by creepers having leaf patterns. There are four ten petalled flowers, one in each corner, with Bangla inscriptions embroidered in between which is translated as below.

May *Shri Shri Durga Sahaya*(bless),

Shri Bijon Krishna Goswami

Please, please remember me (simple mortal)

Please do not forget

Hundred crore obeisance (Pranam) to your feet.

Shrimati Matangani Bala Dasi (Humbly)

There are two borders; the outermost is in a stylized uniform pattern sandwiched between double red lines. Above this border and red lines, there is a row of small *kalkas* and diamond motifs arranged alternately. The top of each *kalka* is curved.

Colours used are black, red and navy blue.

Material - Cotton

Condition - The edges are torn. The field is stained.

Size - 41cmx42cm

Period - Early 20th Century

Place - West Bengal

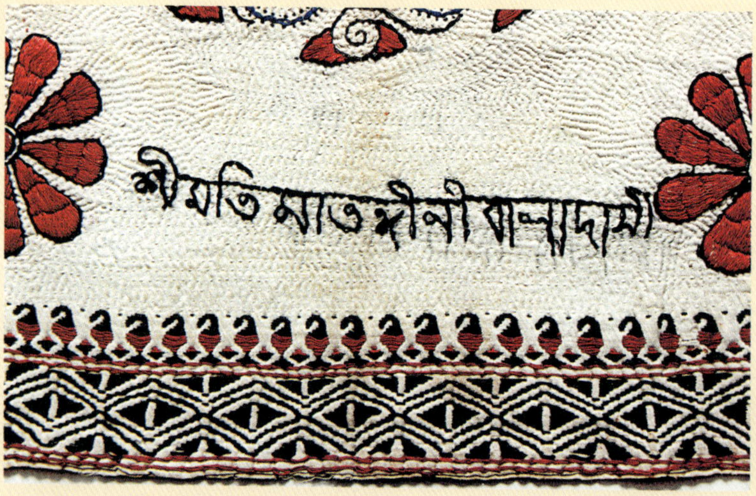

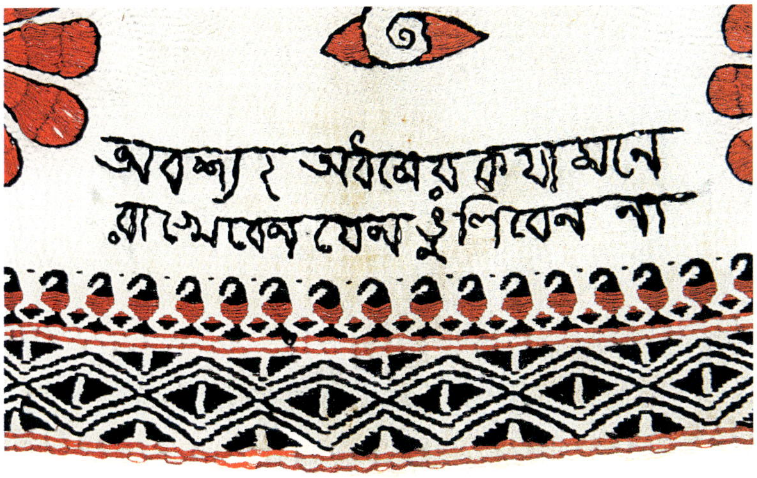
অবশ্য২ অধমের কথ্যা মনে
রাখিবেন যেন ভুলিবেন না

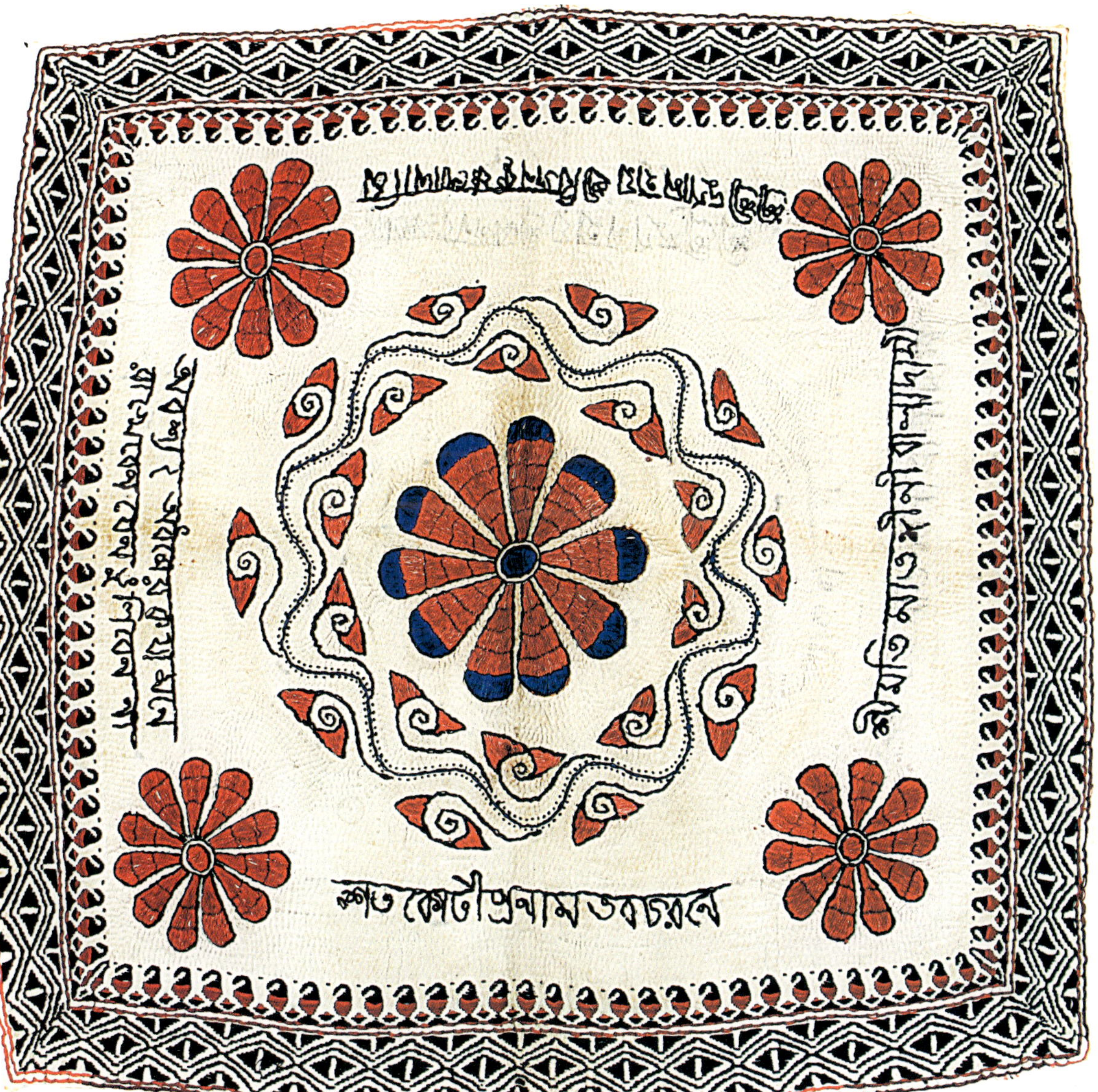

Bh-11

Rectangular piece of *Kantha with its field* rippled with vertical running stitches all over and decorated with a small border, having geometrical patterns.

There is a female figure standing in *Tribangha mudra*, who is wearing very beautiful clothes- a *choli*, and a *sari* with a beautiful sash in different designs. She is very well adorned and is also wearing a crown. Perhaps it is the figure of *Mohini*.

It seems the embroidery has been done at a later stage on the older cloth.

Colours used in embroidery are red, pink, black, yellow, green, white, and different shades of blue.

Material - Cotton

Condition - Badly damaged.

Size - 38cmx24cm

Period - 19th Century

Place - West Bengal

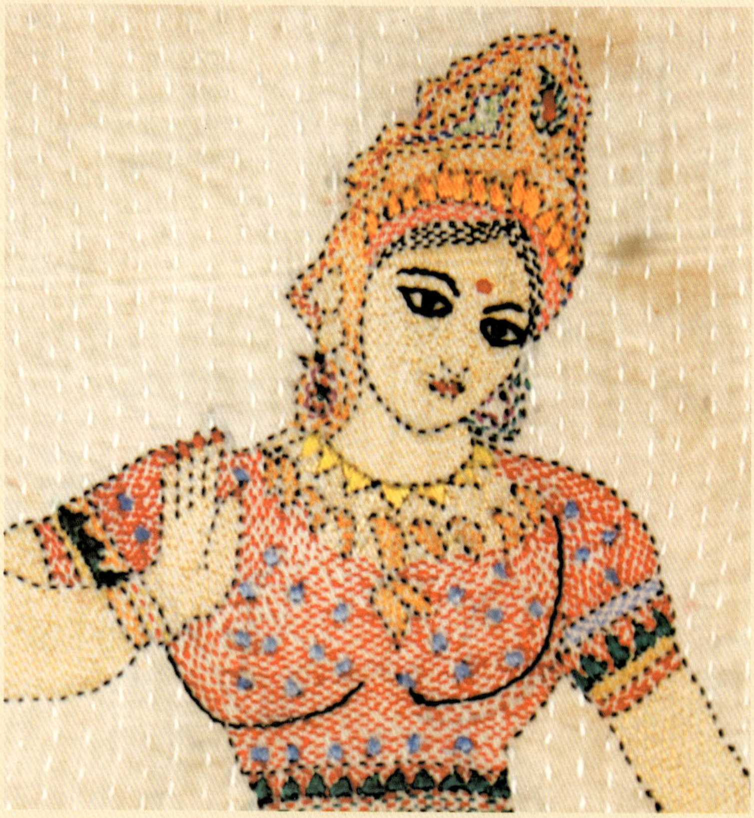

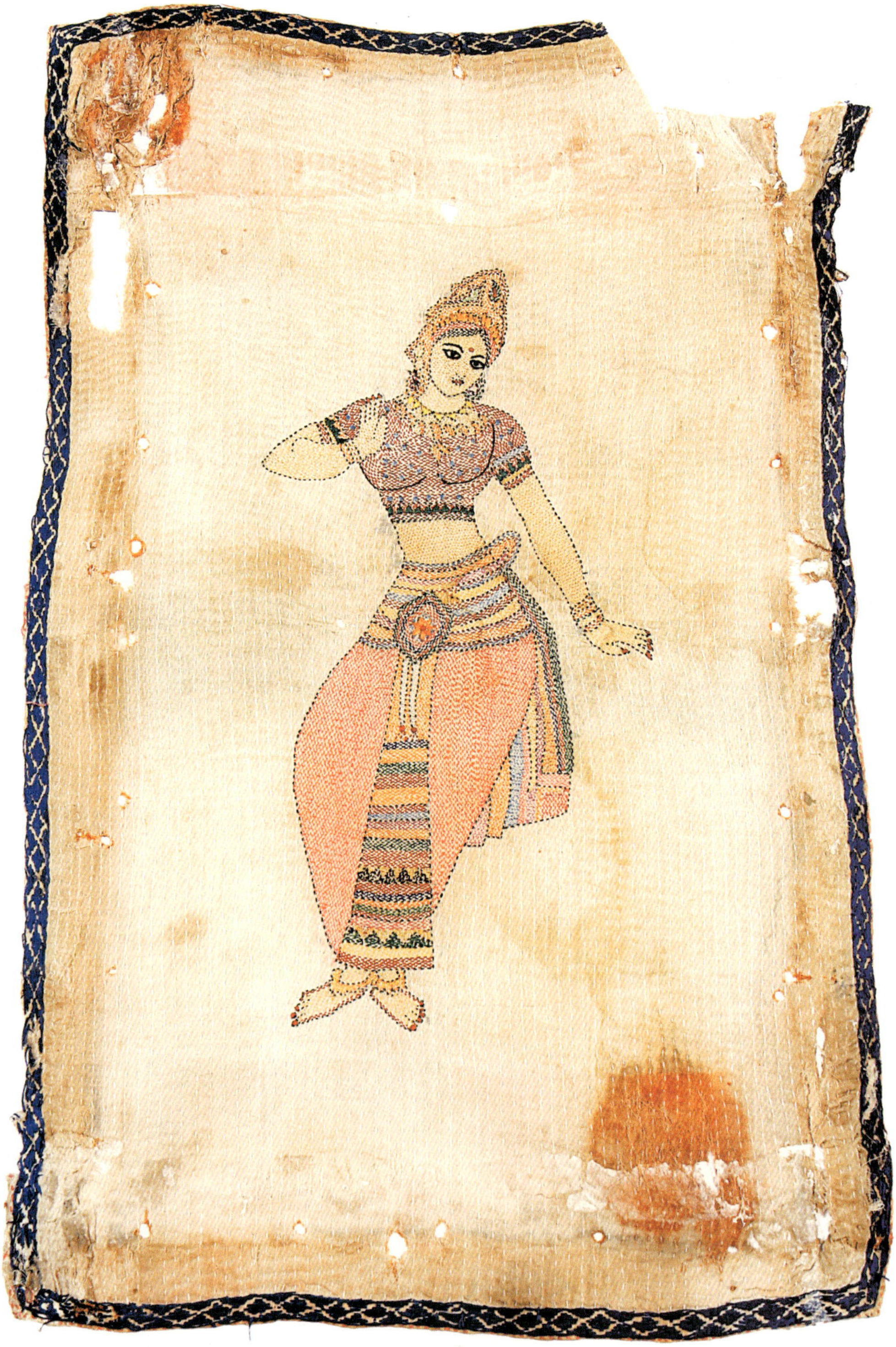

S.M.1

Rectangular small baby *Kantha* having blue, woven, floral designed sari border on four sides. The field is embroidered with stylized floral and foliage patterns in running stitches with blue and red colours.

Material - Cotton

Condition - Border damaged at places.

Size - 67cmx35cm

Period - 20th Century

Place - West Bengal

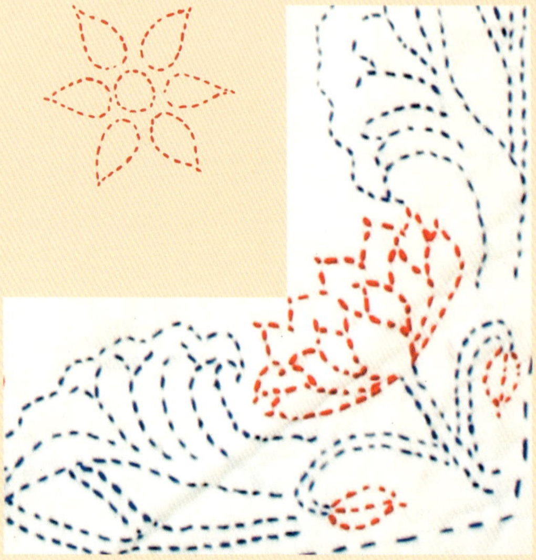

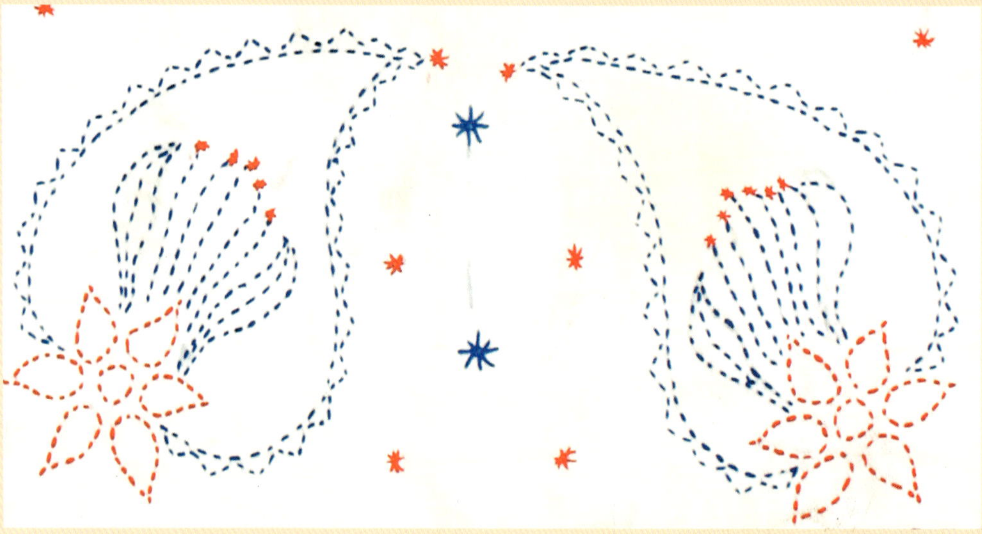

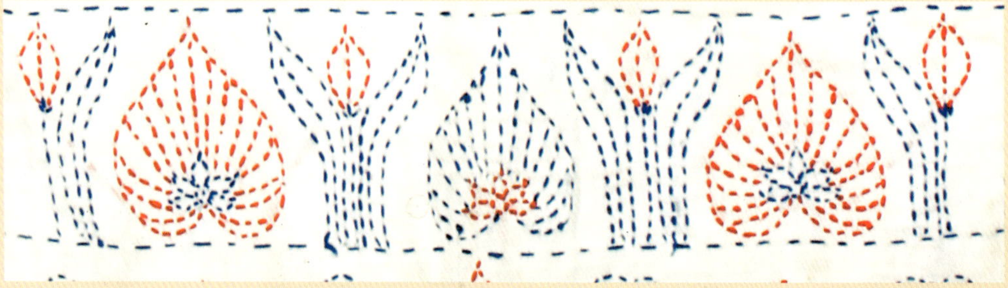

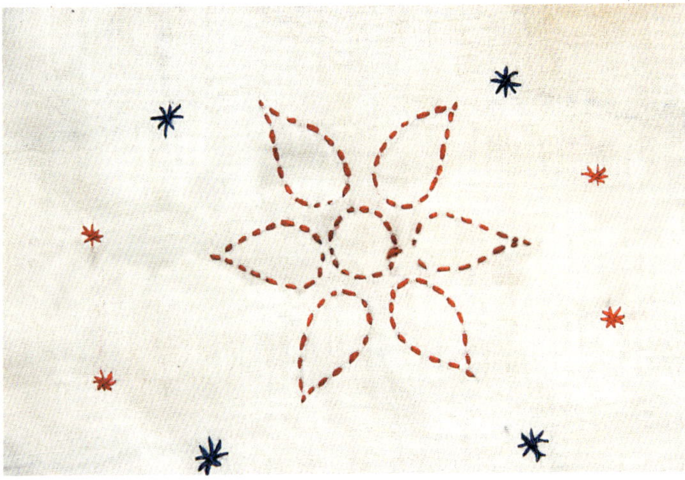

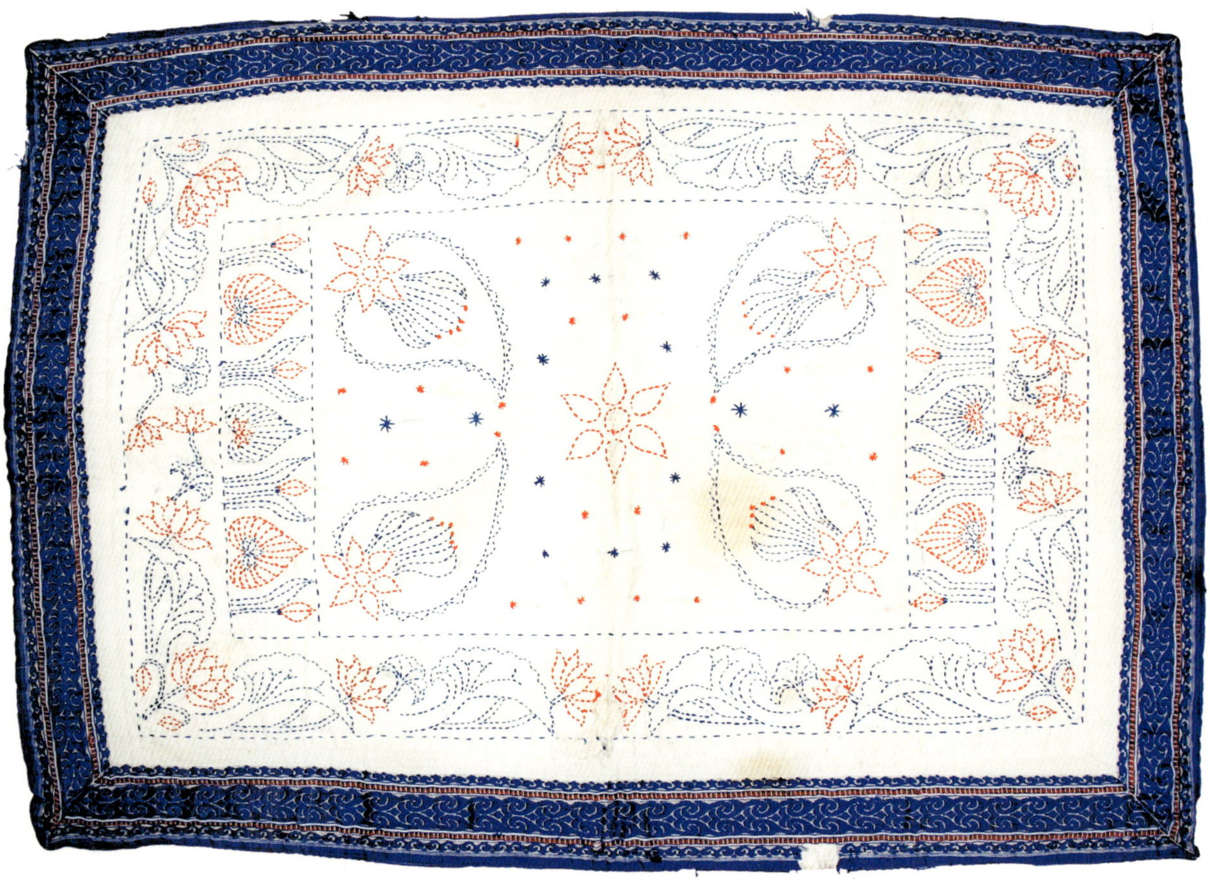

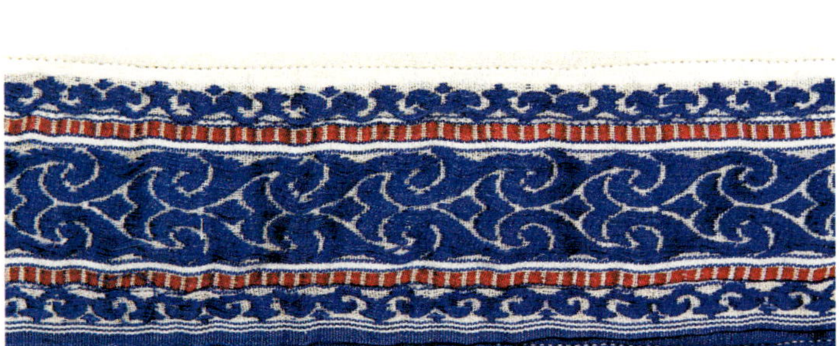

Glossary

Aatchala : With eight triangles or segments terms derived from *aatchala*, meaning eight- roofed. *Chala* refers to the sloping roofs of huts. Thus roofs can be *dochala*, with two segments, or *charchala* having four segments.

Addhi : Fine white cloth.

Almirah : Closet.

Alpana : Ritual drawings painted on the floor with a paste of ground rice flour.

Anajtaga : lit. A border pattern which is made of grain like design.

Anna : Food.

Apas : Peace.

Arshi : Mirror.

Arshilata : Wrap for mirror or mirror cover.

Asan : Seat.

Astadal Padma : Eight-petalled lotus.

Atharvaveda- : Ancient texts found in India.

Bakhiya : Back stitch.

Balish Kantha : Pillow cover.

Barochala : With twelve triangles.

Rumal : Plate cover.

Batua : Purse.

Beki : Curved, wavy and zigzag.

Beri : Pair of rounded tongs, which is meant for pots.

Bhoratphor : Filling stitch.

Bichhe par : Scorpion border

Bisataga : Waist garland border.

Bostani : Square cover for clothes and books.

Bothi : Fish cutter.

Buta : Floral motif with curling bud on top

Chakra : Wheel.

Charchala : With four triangles.

Chatai	:	Mat and woven matting; the name of a stitch resembling matting.
Chiktaga	:	Necklace border.
Chok par	:	Eye border.
Dastarkhan	:	Spread cloth for an eating place.
Devata	:	God or deity.
Dheki	:	Rice husker.
Dhoti	:	Lower garment which is worn by Hindu males and also as a sari by widows.
Dukkhu	:	Sadness, unfortunate and sorrow.
Dubba	:	Kind of grass.
Gachh	:	Tree.
Gadla	:	Roughly stitched quilt.
Gamla	:	Pot in which plants are grown
Ghat	:	Bank of river.
Gilaf	:	Pillow and blanket cover or cover.
Gopis	:	Village girls.
Grafitaga	:	Name of a border.
Guna	:	Ability or quality.
Gut	:	Name of a border.
Holud	:	Turmeric.
Jainainaz	:	Muslim prayer mat.
Jhoptaga	:	Brush border.
Kaitya	:	Name of a stitch which seems to bend or slope.
Kajal	:	Black soot or concoction made of herbs used as eye liner or doing eye make -up. It is also applied on a child's forehead to ward off the evil eye.
Kalam	:	Pen.
Kalka	:	Mango or Paisley design.
Kalpavrksa	:	Tree that fulfills wishes.
Kanghi	:	Comb
Kanha	:	The border which is the on the outer part of *Sujni*.

Kapa	:	Two separate piece of cloth where one is worn as a lungi and the other is used to cover the upper part of women. The size of the cloth is about 4' by 6'. Muslim women of Chapai Nawabgang used to wear this in olden times.
Kauter Khupi	:	Kind of motif which is called pigeon coop.
Khat Kantha	:	Used in a Palanquin.
Khejurchhori	:	Branch of a date tree.
Khol	:	Cover.
Kula	:	Winnowing fan.
Kurti	:	Stitched upper garment worn by both men and women.
Lagan	:	Also known as *holud*. One of the rituals is to tie the string around the wrist symbolizing marital union.
Lep Kantha	:	Thickly padded *Kantha* quilt used in winters.
Lik	:	Running stitch forming a pattern that resembles the Holbein stitch.
Likjhumka	:	*Lik* pattern in earring or jhumka design.
Liklohori	:	Wave like lik pattern.
LikPhor	:	Lik border.
Likphul	:	Lik pattern that resembles a flower.
Lik tan	:	Elongated version of *lik* pattern.
Lik tile	:	Lik that looks like roof tiles.
Lohira	:	Wavy.
Loria	:	Variation of Lohira.
Lohori	:	Wave motif but is also used for other *Kanthas* that has the same thick running stitch.
Lungi	:	Broad cloth wrapped and tucked around the waist, which hangs from the waist to the ankle.
Ma-taga	:	Kind if stitch.
Maachh par	:	Fish border.
Makara	:	Half fish and crocodile figure linked with Hindu religious art.
Mala taga	:	Garland border.
Matsyavatar	:	Fish consonant (Avatar) of Lord Vishnu.
Mohini	:	Female form that was taken by Vishnu according to Hindu mythology.

Moitaga	:	Ladder border.
Motor dana	:	Pea border.
Muchri	:	Same as golokdhanda and shostirchinho.
Mudra	:	Hand gestures used in dance.
NakshiPitha	:	Rice flour cake, on which elaborate designs are made.
Nolaktaga	:	Nose ring border.
Oar	:	Pillow cover.
Paan	:	Betel leaf
Palkirtopor	:	Palanquin cloth.
Pancha mala taga	:	Five garland border.
Panchtaga	:	Threaded running stitch border.
Pankha	:	Fan.
Par tola	:	Embroidered with Sari border patterns.
Patiphor	:	*Chatai* or mat stitch.
Phor	:	Border.
Par	:	Border.
Phulkari	:	Form of embroidery popular in Punjab. It has patterned running stitches.
Phul par	:	Flower border.
Pipre Sari	:	Border pattern which is based on kaitya.
Puranaghata	:	Full vase.
Rath	:	Carriage with wheels carrying icons of Vishnu.
Rumal	:	Handkerchief.
Sarir par	:	Sari border.
Salu	:	Red material used for cotton padded quilts.
Satadal	:	Hundred-petalled.
Satadal Padma	:	Hundred petalled lotus.
Sattva	:	Purity and truth.
Shaitphul	:	Also called likphul and anarasi.
Shamuktaga	:	Snail border.

Sheesha : Mirror.

Shostir Chinho : Swastika or muchri or golok.

Sijda : Touching the forehead to the ground in Muslim prayer.

Sujni : Embroidery similar to Bengal *Kanthas*. However, these quilts are made with red salu, worked with back stitch.

Ta'abiz par : Amulet border.

Taika : Spindle.

Tamas : Darkness.

Tejas : Heat; fire.

Tribhanga : A tri-bent posture or stance that is used in Indian sculpture, art and classical dance.

Bibliography

1. Ahmed, Perveen (1977) The Aesthetics and Vocabulary of Nakshi *Kantha*, Dhaka: Bangladesh National Museum.

2. Apte, V.S. (1966) Sanskrit-Hindi Kosh, New Delhi, First edition, Motilal Banarsidas Publishers.

3. Basak, Sila (2007) Nakshi *Kantha* of Bengal, New Delhi, Gyan Publication.

4. Brijbhushan, Jamila (1990) Indian Embroidery, New Delhi, Publications Division, Ministry of Information and Broadcasting, Government of India.

5. Chakrabarti, K.(2007) *Kantha*-The Traditional Art of the Women of Bengal.

6. Chattopadhyay, Kamladevi, (1977) *Kantha* Embroidery of Bengal, in Indian Embroidery, Wiley Eastern.

7. Dey. Bishan and John Irwin, (1947)The Folk Art of Bengal, in Marg, 1946-47,1(4): 45:54.

8. Dhamija, Jasleen (2004) Asian Embroidery, New Delhi, Abhinav Publications.

9. Dhamija, Jasleen (1964) The Survey of Embroidery Tradition, in Marg, XVII (2)

10. Dhamija, Jasleen (971)The *Kanthas* of Bengal, in The Times of India, Annual, pp-69-74.

11. Dhamija, Jasleen (1979) Living Tradition of Iran's Crafts, New Delhi, Vikas Publication.

12. Dutt, Gurusaday (1932)Catalogue of Folk Arts, In Indiana Society of Oriental Arts.

13. Dutt, Gurusaday (1995) *Kantha* ,Album of Art Treasures: Series 1, Bratacharigram, Bengal: Gurusaday Dutt Folk Art Society, Gurusaday Musuem.

14. Dutt, Gurusaday (2008) *Kantha*, Album of Art Treasures: Series 2, Bratacharigram, Bengal: Gurusaday Dutt Folk Art Society, Gurusaday Museum.

15. Ganguly, Kalyan Kumar (1958) *Kantha*: The Enchanted Wrap, in Indian Folklore Calcutta, 2(1):64.

16. Goswammy, B. N (2000) Piety and Splendour: Sikh Heritage in Art, New Delhi: National Museum.

17. Gode, P.K (1957) Sanskrit-English Dictionary, Prasad Prakashan, Poona, p-529.

18. Gupta, Charu Smita (2009) Sujani, The Fine Needlework of Bihar, in Sui Dhaga: Crossing Boundaries through Needle and Thread, New Delhi, Wisdom Tree, pp.52-55.

19. Irwin, John (1946) Indian Textile Trade in 17th Century Bengal, in Journal of Indian Textile History, II:59-74.

20. Kramrisch, Stella (1939) *Kantha* in Journal of Indian Society of Oriental Arts, VII, pp.141-67.

21. Mookerjee, Ajit (1939) *Kanthas* Embroidered Works in Folk Art of Bengal, Calcutta, University of Calcutta, pp-11-14.

22. Moreland, W (1925) Indian Exports of Cotton Goods in the 17th century in Indian Journal of Economics, 1924-25, V(3):225-45.

23. Morrell, Anne (1994) The Techniques of Indian Embroidery, London: B.T. Batford.

24. Morrell, Anne (1999) *Kantha* Quilting in Indian Embroidery Techniques at the Calico Museum of Textiles: A Working Guide, Ahmadabad: Sarabhai Foundation.

25. Padmaja, K (2005) The several layers of *Kantha*, in Sui Dhaga: Crossing Boundaries Through Needle and Thread, New Delhi. (A world embroidery conference organized by IIC and Craft Council of India at IIC).

26. Pathak, A (2012) in Embroidering Futures: Repurposing the *Kantha*, (ed) Sethi, Ritu, Indian Foundations for the Arts.

27. Varadrajan, Lotika (1981-92) Of Silks and Embroidery: Indo-Portuguese Textiles, in Marg, XXXV(3):89-96.

28. Sethi, Ritu (2012) Embroidering Futures, India Foundations for the Arts.

29 Vatsyayan, Kapila (2010) Embroidery in Asia, Sui Dhaga, Crossing Boundaries Through Needle and Thread, India International Centre, New Delhi.

30. Zaman, Niaz (2004) The Art of *Kantha* Embroidery, The University Press Limited, Bangladesh.

31. Zaman, Niaz (2006) The Nakshi *Kantha*: From the Ascetic to the Aesthetic in Textile Traditions of Bangladesh, Dhaka: National Crafts Council of Bangladesh.

Acknowledgements

Organizing Committee:

Chairperson & Chief Adviser
Mrs. Dipali Khanna, Member Secretary, IGNCA

Advisors
Mrs. Veena Joshi, Joint Secretary, IGNCA
Prof. Molly Kaushal, Janapada Sampada Division, IGNCA
Dr. Ramakar Pant, HoD (I/C) Janapada Sampada Division, IGNCA

Curator
Mrs. Krishna Lal

Exhibition Design
Sh. Neeraj Sahai

Catalouge Text
Mrs. Krishna Lal

Coordinators
Sh. Rajinder Singh Taragi
Dr. Sangeeta Dutta

Research & Exhibition Curatorial Support
Dr. Achal Pandya
Ms. Anaja Joshi
Sh. Shishank Pal
Sh. A. N. Khanna
Dr. Sanghamitra Basu
Dr. Manu Gupta

Print, Publicity & Catalogue/ Book Design
Sh. Neeraj Sahai, Pallavi Sahai
Picture Street

We deeply acknowledge:
Sh. Chhotelal Bharany and Dr. Sanghamitra Basu for lending kanthas for the Exhibition from their personal collection

Printing, Distribution and Book Display
D. K. Printworld

Technical & Administrative Support
Dr Jayanta Kr Ray, Director(A), IGNCA
Sh. S. C. Gahlaut, FA&CAO, IGNCA
Sh. Jayanta Chatterjee, DyFA&SrAO(JS)
Sh. Rajinder Singh Taragi
Sh. Narayan Hari
Sh. Davinder Bist

We are thankful to the following Divisions of IGNCA for their support
Conservation Unit
Sutradhara Division (Accounts Section, S&S, I&PR Unit)
Kala Darshana
Kala Nidhi
Cultural Informatics Lab
Media Centre
EMU

Important Telephone Numbers

Mrs. Dipali Khanna, Member Secretary, IGNCA
011 23383895

Mrs. Veena Joshi, Joint Secretary, IGNCA
01123389675

Dr Ramakar Pant, HoD (JS)(I/C)
01123388441

Mrs Krishna Lal
9810283743

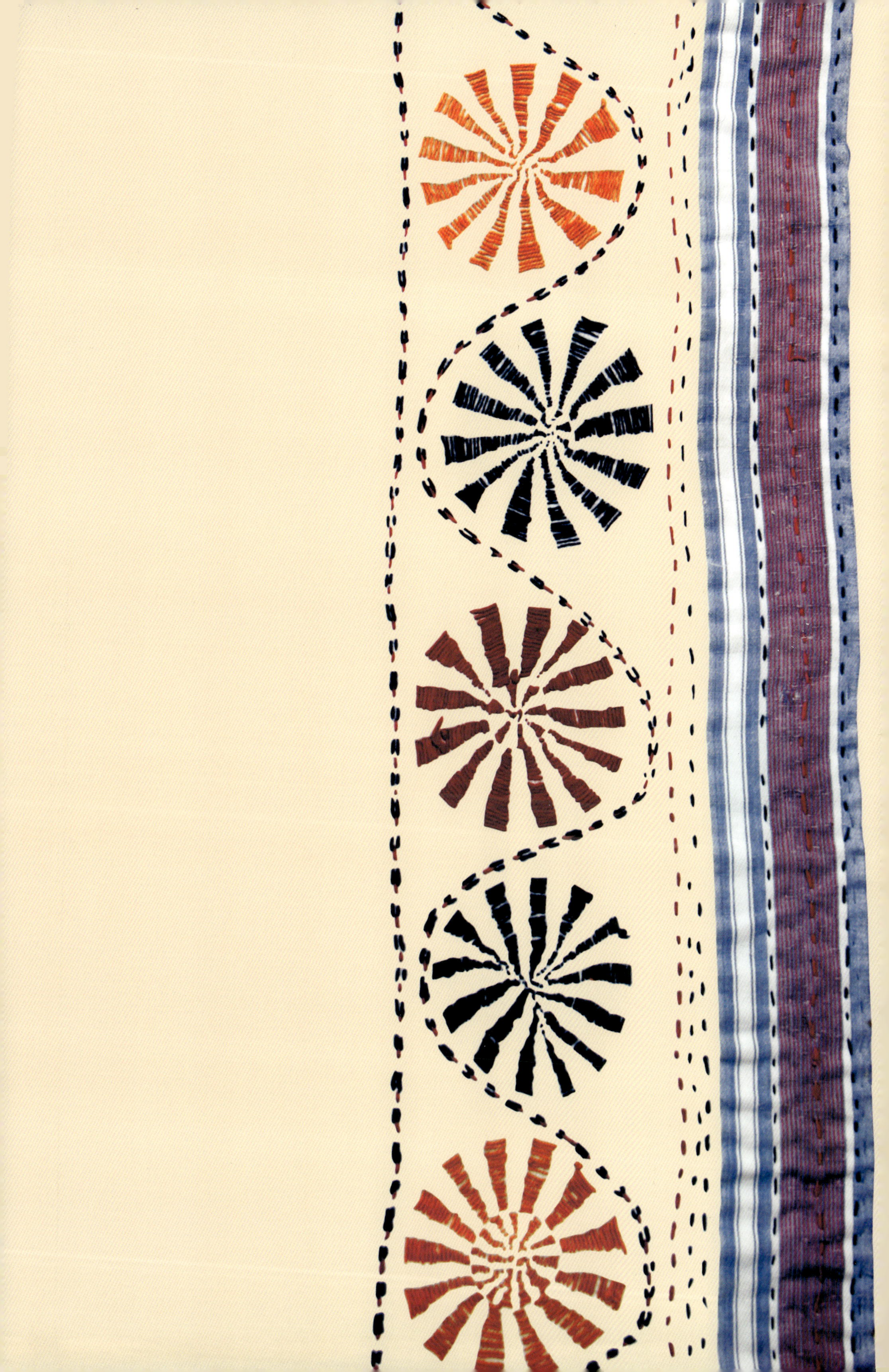